New York's Newsboys

New York's Newsboys

Charles Loring Brace and the Founding of the Children's Aid Society

KAREN M. STALLER

OXFORD
UNIVERSITY PRESS

OXFORD
UNIVERSITY PRESS

Oxford University Press is a department of the University of Oxford. It furthers
the University's objective of excellence in research, scholarship, and education
by publishing worldwide. Oxford is a registered trade mark of Oxford University
Press in the UK and certain other countries.

Published in the United States of America by Oxford University Press
198 Madison Avenue, New York, NY 10016, United States of America.

© Oxford University Press 2020

All rights reserved. No part of this publication may be reproduced, stored in
a retrieval system, or transmitted, in any form or by any means, without the
prior permission in writing of Oxford University Press, or as expressly permitted
by law, by license, or under terms agreed with the appropriate reproduction
rights organization. Inquiries concerning reproduction outside the scope of the
above should be sent to the Rights Department, Oxford University Press, at the
address above.

You must not circulate this work in any other form
and you must impose this same condition on any acquirer.

Library of Congress Cataloging-in-Publication Data
Names: Staller, Karen M., author.
Title: New York's Newsboys : Charles Loring Brace and the founding of the
Children's Aid Society / Karen M. Staller.
Description: New York, NY : Oxford University Press, [2020] |
Includes bibliographical references and index.
Identifiers: LCCN 2019048864 (print) | LCCN 2019048865 (ebook) |
ISBN 9780190886608 (hardback) | ISBN 9780190886622 (epub)
Subjects: LCSH: Brace, Charles Loring, 1826-1890. | Children's Aid Society
(New York, N.Y.) | Newsboys' Lodging House. | Street children—New York
(State)—New York—Social conditions—19th century. | Homeless
children—New York (State)—New York—Social conditions—19th century. |
Child welfare—New York (State)—New York—History—19th century.
Classification: LCC HV885.N5 S74 2020 (print) | LCC HV885.N5 (ebook) |
DDC 362.7/7569057632—dc23
LC record available at https://lccn.loc.gov/2019048864
LC ebook record available at https://lccn.loc.gov/2019048865

For
Dorothy Duley Staller,
granddaughter of Irish and German immigrants,
daughter of New-York social justice workers,
and mother of this very grateful author

Contents

Preface   xiii
    The Invisibility of Runaway, Homeless, and Disconnected
        Youth: Present and Past   xiii
    Modern Homeless Youth: What We Do and What We Know   xvi
    Intervention: Police Power versus Persuasion   xvi
    Nomenclature Debates: Unpacking the Complexity of the
        Problem   xix
    Extreme Pragmatism: Criminal Behavior and Survival Strategies   xx
    The Rhetoric of Morality: Juvenile Delinquent or Child Victim?   xxii
    Nineteenth Century Street Youth   xxiv
    Nineteenth Century Youth Vagrancy: An Emerging Public
        Problem   xxv
    Charles Loring Brace, Children's Aid Society, and a Newsboys' Lodging
        House   xxvii
    Historical Invisibility of Homeless Youth   xxix
    Nineteenth-Century Philanthropy: Humanitarian Aid or Social
        Control?   xxx
    Disciplinary Differences and Methodological Critiques   xxxi
    Newsboys, Their Lodging House, and Brace's CAS   xxxiv

Acknowledgments   xlv

Introduction
    New-York, a City of Layers and Philanthropic Woolen Strings   1
    Two Historical Threads: Juvenile Delinquency and Placing Out   7
    Juvenile Delinquency: Control or Prevention?   7
    Penal Character and Discipline within Child Asylums   10
    Reliance on Indenture and Contractual Rights   12

CAS Nexus: Juvenile Delinquency and Placing Out   13
Placing Out: Philanthropic Abduction or Normative Practice?   15
Charles Loring Brace's Innovations: Novel in Combination   21
The Newsboys' Lodging House: An "Asylum" of a Different Stripe   23
In This Book: An Outline of Chapters   24
Concluding Observations   27

1 **Mr. Brace's Arrival: Early Influences and New-York, 1848–1853**   35
Childhood Shapes a "Dangerous" Man of Reason   37
Mr. Brace's New-York, 1848–1850   43
"Want of Fear": Riots and Cholera, 1849   45
Charitable Discord and Discovering Inspiration   50
Tragedy and Trips   53
Unexpected Returns: Belfast, Slavery, and a Hungarian Prison   54
Mr. Brace's New-York Return   58

2 **Family Life Among the Poor in Mid-Nineteenth-Century New York**   71
Laying Down, Building Up, Crowding In   74
Tenant-House Living   78
Vermin, Sanitation, and Fever Nests   82
Special Nuisances: Livestock and Industry   83
Housing, Health, and Vagrant Children   84
Family Employment   85
Child Labor and Income   86
Newsboys and the Penny Press   88
Youthful Independence and Vagrancy   89
Matsell's Report Revisited   90
Mr. Brace's Invitation   92

3 **Creating the Children's Aid Society: Exploration and Experimentation**   101
Implementing an Idea: Daily Routine   102
The Press-Foreman and the Newsboys   103
Early Office Work: First Circular, an 1853 Blueprint   105
Bumpy Beginnings: Workshops for Boys   107
Gathering Speed: Industrial Schools for Girls   109
Visiting Agents   110

Board of Trustees   111
Exploration and Experimentation   112
Bold New Plan: A Lodging House for Homeless Newsboys   113
Belfast Revisited   114

4 **Opening the Newsboys' Lodging House: Proposal to Practice, 1854**   119
NBLH Facility   125
Basic Service Structure   127
The Bathing Requirement   130
Intake Dilemmas: Shaping Agency Policy   131
The Parent Problem   131
Coming Up Short   135
The Drama of the Theater   137
Intoxicated Youth   141
Lodging House as Experimental Model   143

5 **Eddying Point: Mr. Macy's Central Office**   151
A Place for Rich and Poor   153
Referrals to the Central Office and the NBLH   154
Difficult Cases   156
Central Office as Employment Agency   158
To the Country: Transfer Point and Temporary Lodging   159
One Hundred Miles, Due North   160
A Man of Good Humor   161
Endless Errands and Odds and Ends   163
Cash: In and Out   163
In-Kind, Comings and Goings   164
A Veritable Ringmaster   167

6 **The Earliest Lodgers: The Good and the Bad, 1855–1856**   173
The Nassau Coffee Saloon   179
The Professor Mentors Sunday (and Mr. Colopy)   183
An Incorrigible Rogue   186
Curbing the Drift to Delinquency   189
Pickpocketing   191
A Pocket Picked!   192
Pugilists and Politics   193
Mr. Tracy's Complicated Peace Work   197

7 Advancing the Lines: Building an Anti-Poverty Agenda, Newsboys' Lodging House, 1855–1861 — 205

An Educational Plan: Night School   207
One-Room Schoolhouse   208
Library and Reading Room   209
Common Education   211
Reading   212
Writing Class   213
Singing and Voice   214
Physical Activities   214
A Moral Educational Plan: Sunday Meetings   215
A Fiscal Educational Plan: Banking and Saving   216
An Employment Plan: Situations and Emigration Parties   220
Into the Country   222
Newsboys' Lodging House's Instability   225
Return Visit to NBLH   226
Metropolitan Police, Sabbath Selling, and Free NBLH Suppers   227
Untimely Deaths   230

8 Mr. Macy's Record Books: Newsboy Lodgers and the Emigration Branch, 1861–1866 and Beyond — 235

Critics: Asylum Advocates, 1859–1860   237
Mr. Macy's Update   241
Gone to War   243
Challenges and Changes, 1861: War, Leadership, and NBLH Growing Pains   245
Leadership   246
NBLH Growing Pains   247
Complications of 1863: Draft Riots, Catholic Critics, and a Board Resolution   248
Catholic Critics, 1863   251
A Board Resolution   253
From NBLH to Emigration Outcomes   255
Returning Home   255
Not Getting There   256
Spectacular Successes   257
Employment Opportunities   258

What to Make of Vagrancy? 259
Petty Theft and Worse 261
The Michigan Problem 263
Critics Again, The Prison Attack: Spreading the Seeds of Vice 264
Mr. Brace's Muscular Orphan Problem 265

9 **A Permanent Place: Building, Bridging, and Policy Advocacy in the Gilded Age** 275
Real Estate Investment 276
A Permanent Lodging House for Newsboys 279
The Charles and Mary O'Connor Years 280
New Directions: Inspirations from a Charity Fair 282
Policy Advocacy: Child Labor, Education, and Housing 283
Mr. Whitehead's CAS Factory Bill 284
Enforced Education, Truancy, and School Funding 286
Street Trades: An Education and Labor Problem 289
Housing Reform 289
Bridging the Class Divide in a Gilded Age 290
CAS Extended Family and Their Dependents 294

10 **The Society Mr. Brace Built: A Life's Work** 305
Neighborhood-Based Programing 306
Quantification and Amplification of CAS's Work 308
Outside New-York: The Emigration Branch 309
Financial Health, Real Estate Ownership, and Contributions 311
Prevention Claims: Juvenile Crime and Public Health 313
A Bittersweet Report: A Changing of the Guard 314
Devoted Workers and a Sound Foundation 315
Call to the Future 316
Mr. Brace's Death 317
Tributes: Words and Actions 318

Afterword
  Charles Loring Brace's Legacy and Implications: Bridging Support for Poor Families 325
Brace's Legacy: Challenging the Reductionist "Either–Or" Trope 327
Modern Implications: A Nod to the Future 335

Index 341

Preface

The Invisibility of Runaway, Homeless, and Disconnected Youth: Present and Past

IN 1849 GEORGE Matsell, New York City's first police chief, authored a lurid report raising alarms about what he saw as the increasing menace of vagrant and criminally inclined children populating the city streets.[1] I first learned of this report in the 1980s while sitting on a plastic chair in a dingy office tucked in the back corner of the Port Authority Bus Terminal (PABT) in New York City. I worked for a large shelter for runaway and homeless youth located down the street and was on one of my periodic visits to friends in the Youth Services Unit of the Port Authority Police Department. With my arrival the unit's commanding officer, Sargent Bernard "Bernie" Poggioli, had found a new audience for his theatrical rendition of Matsell's report. He read it aloud in his unique New-York brogue. Within minutes, I found myself joining his staff in a semi-competitive game of name-that-kid. Despite the intervening century, our youth were kindred spirits with the ones that Matsell described.

PABT is an enormous complex that occupies several city blocks and is one of the New-York's major transportation hubs. Hundreds of thousands of people pass through the terminal daily. In addition to the itinerant human traffic, PABT is home to more sedentary groups. They include homeless individuals who can find relative warmth and safety in its myriad tunnels as well as amenities like discarded food, public bathrooms, and electrical outlets. However, the homeless are not a monolithic group. Existing among them is a subcategory referred to as runaway teenagers, youth experiencing homelessness, unaccompanied minors, or disconnected youth.[2] Such children drift to urban settings like New-York in large numbers.[3] It was this group that occupied the full-time attention of Bernie's police officers and the scores of social workers at the homeless youth shelter where I worked.

In 2016, a *New York Times* journalist declared that "hundreds of homeless young people are in plain sight every day in New York City" but she pointed to their camouflage, "sitting on the floor at the Port Authority Bus Terminal and charging their phones as if they were college students awaiting a bus home" or staying with Uncle A.C.E,[4] referring to three subway lines connected with PABT. These trains run from the upper edges of the city's boroughs to their outer reaches and on them passengers "can spend hours unbothered and unnoticed."[5] The journalist concluded the "public seemed unaware of the young people."

If the general public seems unaware of the problem, there are dedicated groups of professionals who are not. In addition to social workers and police officers, social scientists have spent decades grappling with the size, scope, and characteristics of the population. Nonetheless, in the most comprehensive study to date, researchers drew the same final conclusion as the journalist: "Youth homelessness is a broad and hidden challenge."[6]

The significance of this broad and hidden problem is not restricted to the twenty-first century. Although modern recognition of homeless youth dates to the nineteen sixties and nineteen seventies—both Bernie's specialized police unit and my runway shelter were forged during this period—a confluence of factors associated with rapid urbanization produced a large crop of homeless young people in the mid-nineteenth century. In fact, Matsell's report can be read as evidence of this newly emerging social phenomenon.

In addition to Matsell and his police officers, charity workers and missionaries were concerned with New-York's vagrant youth. Among the most recognized of these was Charles Loring Brace. Brace was the first secretary of New-York's Children's Aid Society (CAS). It was an agency he built from scratch starting in 1853.

Today, Brace is best remembered for his contribution to what modern historians call the "orphan train movement," often cited as a precursor to our Child Protective Services (CPS) or foster care system. Through its emigration branch, CAS "placed out" children from the city, relocating them in families in the western United States. Less well recognized is the broad array of other services CAS offered poor children in the city. Among these were lodging houses. These facilities were remarkably similar to the modern shelters—like the one where I worked—in spirit and function.

A good deal of scholarship on nineteenth century urbanization is based on the premise that Matsell's writing or that of Brace and other charity workers—were partly designed to stoke the fears of upper-class citizens about the dangers of the poor. However, I argue this orientation has largely rendered the actual problem of youth homelessness historically invisible. There are dangers associated with minimizing the existence of unsettled young people in historical accounts. It can lead to overlooking their genuine needs, mischaracterizing the associated risk factors, tokenizing the interventions offered to help, and minimizing the significance of various different approaches to intervention.

Modern social science literature teaches us a good deal about the complex nature of the social phenomena of unaccompanied minors and its sequalae. These studies are useful in understanding the emerging problems in the nineteenth century as well. For example, vagrant children of mid-nineteen century New-York, just like those of today, had genuine need for basic amenities (such as food, clothing, and safe shelter). They faced real risks (to their health and safety). They were exposed to dangerous influences (such as gangs and street-based subcultures). Furthermore, there was reason to worry about the longer-term risks to their health, safety, future security and general well-being.

Today, the predominant historical accounts of nineteenth century charity workers, in general and Brace, in particular, start from a theoretical standpoint known generically as the social or moral control perspective. Bruce Belllingham summarizes its character:

> Brace and his colleagues [are portrayed] as presumptuous, arrogant meddlers practicing social control: they coerced children without guardians, and disrupted families where these existed intact. Child savers, the argument runs, were either blinded by their middle-class bias to the harm and suffering they caused the poor families who were subject to their assaultive ministrations, or they were indifferent to it. However benevolent their intentions may have been, and however selfless they were in their astonishing energy and devotion to social improvement, they "broke up" (their own phrase) and radically transformed the families which . . . would otherwise have remained, intact. Thus the revisionists judge the reformers mendacious.[7]

Bellingham and others offer critiques of the social control scholarship. Among them is that this scholarship often rests on assumptions that the poor were passive, agentless recipients of charity worker actions. This is particularly problematic when applied to studies of vagrant adolescents. For any modern practitioner who has worked with street-acculturated teenagers, the idea that that they are passive, rather than active agents, doesn't jib with reality. Nonetheless, embedded in social control narratives is an important implicit question about the use of coercion or force to induce compliance. How much legal authority, or police power, did charity workers wield over children and parents in the mid-nineteenth century?

While it is true that jural or carceral control was exercised by a variety of charities, particularly in light of increasingly supportive court decisions upholding this authority as constitutional, I argue that such accusations leveled at Brace and CAS are ill-founded. By not carefully attending to the ways in which the work of his society differed from that of other charitable organizations, we may be overlooking important developments in social work practice and service.

In particular, Brace's lodging houses operated exclusively based on the voluntary participation of vagrant children and rejected virtually all forms of contractual, jural, carceral control. He didn't accept children into the lodging house by court order; they came of their own accord and were free to leave. He often retrieved children from prison-like juvenile asylums, and he refused to indenture children by binding contract. While other charities relied on police officers, judges, penal institutions, and restrictive or punitive approaches, Brace rejected these practices. Anyone who has experience working with rebellious teenagers today will readily recognize the distinction between settings in which adults have the legal authority to detain youth against their will and settings requiring that they woo youths' involvement. The two situations require entirely different methods of interpersonal practice.

The question of how Brace built services around children's voluntary engagement in the nineteenth century remains unexplored. This book attempts to fill some of the research gaps through in-depth examination of Brace's flagship program in New-York, the Newsboys' Lodging House.

**

Modern Homeless Youth: What We Do and What We Know

**

Intervention: Police Power versus Persuasion

Arguably, the modern version of this problem of unsettled homeless youth first came to public attention in the 1960s and 1970s. Both Bernie's Youth

Services Unit (YSU) of the Port Authority Police Department and the runaway shelter where I worked have their roots in reforms from this era.

The YSU has been around in one form or another since 1972.[8] Sometimes called "the diaper squad," its specialized officers are tasked with patrolling the PABT and its environs and intercepting any unaccompanied minor drifting through the terminal.[9] To a large extent the primary goal of the YSU is prevention; it attempts to keep teenagers out of the juvenile justice or criminal justice systems.[10] Nonetheless it ultimately derives its authority from its police power. State law permits officers "the right to question youth regarding age and identity," so patrolling YSU teams can stop any person suspected of being a minor and detain them while they launch investigations, contact parents or child welfare agencies, and transport them to juvenile detention centers.[11]

A distinctly different approach is offered by the social workers at the runaway and homeless youth shelter located down the street. Rather than operating from threat of detainment or detention, this model of service is rooted in voluntary participation of street youth.

As a program model, runaway shelters were legitimized in 1974 with the passage of federal legislation entitled the Runaway and Homeless Youth Act (RHYA).[12] It enshrines three major types of service: *basic centers* (short-term crisis shelters often housing youth for less than a month at a time), *transitional living facilities* (congregate care facilities which offer residential housing and support services for young adults for 18 to 24 months, including maternity shelters for teenage mothers), and *street outreach and drop-in* programs. This final program group targets adolescents deemed at risk for exploitation and serves as a bridge between life on the street and sheltering programs.

This triumvirate of runaway and homeless youth services is an oddity in the overall landscape of child welfare programs. Forged in the midst of the youth rights movements of the 1960s when the baby boomers were coming of age, the system grew out of the hippie counterculture.[13] Three aspects of the radical roots of the service are still evident in spite of greater mainstream acceptance and professional maturity.

First, most runaway shelters compete for relatively small, time-limited public grants so service providers must cobble together revenue from other sources such as private donations, foundation grants, or philanthropically inclined businesses. This means programs for homeless youth are on less secure financial footing than the state's legally mandated CPS, juvenile justice, or public school systems.

Second, young people initiate service, so adolescent autonomy and personal agency are key. Youths' cooperation is essential.[14] Basing social services *exclusively* on the whims of adolescents is a highly unusual practice model. The significance of this feature cannot be underestimated. Not only must a child want to be in the program but he or she may also leave—essentially without consequence—at any time.[15] This youth-centered design presents unique challenges from the perspective of the service provider. The more alienated the youth, the more difficult the challenge. As a consequence, providers must be uniquely clued into adolescent subcultures and runaway shelters must be perceived by teenagers as youth-friendly, "cool," and "hip" or "rad" and "dope," depending on the generation.

Finally, a corollary to this is the lack of legal enforcement tools to compel participation, which contrasts with the police powers possessed by judges (in family, juvenile, or criminal courts), lawyers, police officers, school truancy officers, case workers, social workers, and teachers, in the CPS, juvenile justice, and public education systems. Children can be removed from families of origin and placed in foster or group homes based on allegations of abuse or neglect, and youth can be ordered into juvenile detention centers, jails, and prisons based on convictions for criminal behavior (juvenile delinquency or adult crimes), and status offenses.[16] For rebellious teenagers these adult-imposed interventions can be off-putting.

In short there is a fundamental distinction between interventions with street youth rooted in the police power of the state and those which are not. This distinction might be seen in the example of a YSU officer who picked up a runaway girl who claimed she was seventeen and produced forged documents to prove it. The officer wryly observed she possessed "an amazing capacity to color the truth."[17] The girl was detained until he was able to establish that she was only fourteen years old and then dealt with accordingly. Hallmark features of runaway and homeless youths' modus operandi include creatively "coloring the truth," carrying false identification cards, lying about parents, and being adept at deception. Lying is a survival strategy rooted in a well-founded suspicion of adults. However, in stark contrast to the officer's coercive approach, runaway shelter social workers are not likely to use threats to compel cooperation. Making sure a young person is safely sheltered, away from the influences of the street, is more important than the truthfulness of the initial account or the legitimacy of documentation. Correcting deceptions is part of a longer endgame that involves gaining the young person's trust.

***

Nomenclature Debates: Unpacking the Complexity of the Problem

Defining the homeless youth population's boundaries is a task that has flummoxed advocates, social scientists, and policy makers for decades. Colorful typologies are illustrative, but they can also be distracting. They are significant not at face value but rather because in the struggle to properly frame the issue, the underlying complexities of the social problem, and its dynamics, are revealed.

In the 1960s and 1970s a simple label, *runaways*, took hold.[18] The word carried with it assumptions that youth left home voluntarily and that their time away would be brief. Yet decades of research have consistently shown that children often come from messy, unstable family situations and that the road "home" is often complicated.

Poverty, family instability, family conflict, violence, and parental substance abuse significantly contribute to the problem.[19] Family violence is often fueled by parental use of alcohol or drugs.[20] Family conflict over a young person's gender identity, sexual orientation, or gender expression disproportionately contributes to the numbers of queer youth found among the runaway population.[21] In addition, friction with stepparents has been cited as a reason for leaving.[22]

Disturbing numbers of young people are ordered to leave, forced out, abandoned, or otherwise excluded from home by the actions of their parents, custodians, or caregivers.[23] So social scientists have experimented with other labels, attempting to capture the involuntary nature of the experience, such as *castaways, shoveouts, pushouts, kicked-out*, and *throwaways* or *thrownaways*.[24]

Youth seeking temporary refuge from conflict are sometimes described as *couch surfing*, the practice of moving from one temporary location to another without a secure place to be.[25] Young people with fragile social support networks can find themselves in far more dangerous situations than the couch surfers, particularly when trying to fend for themselves for longer periods of time.[26] Other labels emerged to capture the chronic nature of their problem: *youth experiencing homelessness, homeless youth*, and *street youth*. These unsheltered young people are inclined to substitute street networks (such as gangs, pimps, and sugar daddies) for failed family ones, acclimating to street subcultures that expose youth to a predictable set of risks.[27] Legislators and social scientists have repeatedly found that they are "vulnerable to violence, crime and sexual exploitation at the hands of other youth and adults."[28]

One might reasonably ask why, if families are so dysfunctional and unstable, the state does not intervene with its CPS system. The answer is that it does and, in some cases, that system does considerable damage in the process. A frightening number of homeless teenagers and young adults are dubbed "system involved." In general, this means they have been in and out of public systems of care including both CPS[29] and the juvenile justice system [30] or have been expelled from, or dropped out, of school.[31] Youth experiencing homelessness have typically been disproportionately involved with either or both the CPS and juvenile justice systems as well as prematurely dissociated (through their own volition or actions of the school) from public educational systems.

Taken together, these failures of both families and public systems of care contribute to a phenomenon described by an investigative journalist who spent a month interviewing New-York's "panhandlers on streets and subways": "A picture of a new beggar emerged: Young, apathetic, uneducated, the product of grinding poverty, he has left the economic system and has no thought of return."[32] The journalist was describing what social scientists now refer to as *disconnected youth*. By definition they are between the ages of 16 and 24 and are disconnected "from education, the workforce, and networks of social support"[33] They are "off-track to reach a future that includes self-sufficiency, economic stability, and overall well-being" and are alienated from traditional spheres of socialization and productivity.[34] All this haggling over defining and describing these overlapping phenomena suggests variations on the theme of the underlying condition of autonomous or semi-autonomous young people who are prematurely on their own, floating around, day and night, without adult supervision and without being engaged in traditional institutions of socialization.[35]

* * *

Extreme Pragmatism: Criminal Behavior and Survival Strategies

The longer youth are on their own, the higher the risk of arrest.[36] With "few legitimate means" for supporting themselves, they often cobble together what employment they can.[37] Dr. Richard Oberfield, a psychiatrist who specializes in child and adolescent psychiatry and works with homeless adolescents, characterizes these strategies as "extreme pragmatism." He argues under such conditions that work is "radically redefined to mean anything that brings in money. . . . Anything to get by."[38] Another way to think about this is that the lines between behavioral issues, minor annoyances, survival strategies, and criminal activity can blur pretty quickly.

Unfortunately, the experience of simply being homeless is often criminalized in the United States. For example, during the day vagrant youth who have no place to be can easily end up on the receiving end of a variety of public nuisance citations for behaviors such as loitering, disorderly conduct, or disturbing the peace. If they do have a place they want to be, they may lack the means of getting there. At the runaway shelter where I worked, scores of young people arrived with warrants for subway violations. Invariably, they had been temporarily detained by a transit authority cop who spotted them vaulting a subway turnstile, an act that results in a theft of services citation.

Vagrant youth may panhandle for cash. Public tolerance is inversely related to the aggressiveness of their tactics. Unsheltered youth looking for a safe place to sleep may end up squatting in abandoned buildings, sleeping in parks, or camping out under bridges or along railroad tracks. Whatever space choosen they inevitably exposes themselves to the possibility of being arrested, most often for trespassing.

In the 1980s, a small colony of homeless teenagers and young adults took up semi-permanent residence on New York Câity-owned property off Spring Street.[39] Deserted most of the time, the area was the storage site for tons of road salt used during snowy winter months. It was also the final resting place for broken Sanitation Department vehicles. The resourceful homeless tribe converted several vehicles into private residences. This lasted until the city beefed up security and fenced out the vagrants, effectively evicting them. The area, now trendy, is the site of a new municipal salt storage facility described as a "functional piece of architectural eye candy."[40] However, it is naïve to think evictions and neighborhood upgrades eradicate the underlying problem of homelessness. The colonies merely relocate.

In short, whether youth are charged with daytime public nuisance violations such as loitering or nighttime offenses such as trespassing, the mere condition of being homeless can be transformed into petty crimes at the discretion of irritated police officers or in response to the complaints of annoyed business owners, city officials, and private citizens.

More concerning than these low-level offences associated with homelessness is the slippery slope between minor public irritations and more intrusive criminal behavior, a problem well documented in the social science literature.[41] Bernie once told a reporter, "Begging is annoying until it becomes something else," adding that "crimes of opportunity are committed by the same people who are panhandling."[42] By definition, a crime of opportunity capitalizes on an unexpected moment, such as snatching an unattended bag. Yet successful snatches can embolden teenagers to engage in much more systematic and strategic patterns of preying on vulnerable tourists or inattentive commuters.

One pragmatic survival strategy is so historically constant it deserves special attention: selling sex or bartering sexual favors. Vulnerable young people who have limited legitimate employment options can always sell themselves. For teenagers this can include street walking, hustling (for boys), performing as strippers, posing for pornography, or exchanging sex for shelter (or drugs). Social scientists have repeatedly confirmed what is intuitively obvious: the more time young people spend on the street, the greater their risk for "sexual abuse, sexual exploitation, prostitution, or drug abuse."[43]

In the 1980s the prostitution areas were well known to anyone who worked with street youth. The girls were up in Hunt's Point in the South Bronx.[44] The boys worked off the West Side piers or on the Upper East Side in an area called The Loop because johns cruised the city blocks in cars, driving in a continuous loop. Cross-dressers sold sex in the meat packing district.[45] The physical location of these work areas may have changed since then, but like the floating homeless encampments, their existence somewhere in the city landscape is an immutable fact.

***

The Rhetoric of Morality: Juvenile Delinquent or Child Victim?

Dr. Oberfield has argued that for youth experiencing homelessness, who operate in an environment of extreme pragmatism, "values are transformed."[46] Arguably, this is not only true for the youth themselves, but to some extent may rub off on the professionals who work with them, who learn to suspend moral judgment or adapt to a different morality.

I can still vividly remember being on the receiving end of an extremely thoughtful lecture worthy of a university philosophy course delivered by a teenager. He had spent the better part of his life—from his early teens—fending for himself on the streets of New-York. As his oration unfolded it became clear that he found any form of robbery, particularly that involving female victims, abhorrent. However, he expressed no qualms about swiping food from a bodega when he was hungry. I had no reason to doubt the veracity of this young man's claim that he operated according to his own strict moral code. It had been tempered by life on the street and born out of practical necessity.

Undoubtedly small business owners would take a dim view of this shoplifting. Yet street-based social workers know that young people can get into far more serious trouble than stealing potato chips. To underscore the point, I add a sad footnote to the story of this likable young man: he was murdered during a prostitution tryst gone wrong. He was not the only young person to die during my stint working at the shelter. Another memorable death involved a teenager who succumbed to AIDS. By any measure, street life is dangerous, even fatal, for children and the health risks are many.

However, my point is that morality is a relatively slippery concept when applied to behavior placed in context. Evaluating "bad" behaviors requires an interpretative stance. For street youth who are engaged in "extreme pragmatism"—begging, panhandling, petty crimes, drug dealing, or prostituting—their behaviors invite a plethora of moral interpretations and representations. Are they juvenile delinquents and criminals or child-victims struggling to survive?

This fluidity of interpretation is consequential. First, the labels selected tend to influence public perception and often dictate public response. For example, in the 1990s some social scientists, politicians, and journalists chose to refer to the threat of juvenile delinquency with highly inflammatory rhetoric about "teenage super predators." A long, harsh public backlash ensued. Delinquency cases were increasingly removed from juvenile courts and transferred into adult criminal justice systems, accompanied by this political refrain: "Adult time for adult crime." In addition, public schools enacted zero tolerance policies. Decades later we have a well-documented school-to-prison pipeline partly attributable to these shifts in policy. Generations of children—disproportionately boys of color—paid the price. This leads to a second observation. Moral judgments are rarely equitably applied across racial, ethnic, gender, and other identity characteristics. In particular, boys with darker skin color are more likely to have their behavior characterized as criminal than their white counterparts.

One final observation about the malleability of these rhetorical choices is that they are often deployed purposively by actors seeking to sway public perception. For example, youth advocates have experimented with words for describing children's sex work. They have tried to highlight their vulnerability, using phrases such as *survival sex, sexual bartering, sexual exploitation,* and—most recently—*trafficking* (sexual or labor). Recasting prostitution as survival sex or sex trafficking is a good example of a purposive attempt to change the moral framing by highlighting the exploitive nature of the relationship. Embedded in the phrases are hints about who is victim and who is perpetrator, who has agency and who does not, and who should be punished or pitied. Yet in spite of the ever-changing labels, the underlying sexual conduct is basically the same. Whether teenagers and young adults engage in sex by choice, are driven to the act out of desperation, or are exploited by others tends to be a matter of interpretation. This leads to a final critical set of observations.

Advocates intentionally control messaging through their linguistic choices. Who among us has not been moved by charities advertising the plight of a sick child, an abandoned puppy, a desperate refugee, or a wounded veteran? This is not to suggest any malicious intent. Successful fund-raising for private charities or gaining support for social welfare causes is often entirely dependent on successful framing and marketing of missions. Runaway and homeless youth services are an excellent example. Given that they are less securely funded than public systems, the messaging used for garnering private donations must be carefully crafted.

***

Nineteenth Century Street Youth

This brings us back to Matsell's report of 1849 and the small group gathered in Bernie's office in the 1980s. Why did Matsell's descriptions of New York City's nineteenth-century children hold such sway with seasoned professionals more than a hundred years later? The answer is that while the language was different, the behaviors and circumstances Matsell described were eerily familiar.

Matsell complained about "vagrant, idle and vicious" children who "infest public thoroughfares, hotels, docks" and who "roam day and night wherever their inclination leads them," further describing the "juvenile vagrants" who congregated on the docks and piers and who were "in the daily practice of pilfering wherever opportunity offers." He noted they also begged and engaged in "small burglaries." It was possible for those of us gathered in Bernie's office to substitute a newer major port of entry, the PABT, for the busy nineteenth-century docks and to see survival strategies of "extreme pragmatism" in the begging, burglaries, and pilfering Matsell described.

Equally recognizable was the sexual bartering Matsell was referring to when he complained that girls "of tender years" submitted themselves "to the most loathsome and degrading familiarities" and fretted that the children were really just "embryo courtezans and felons" being schooled in "vice, prostitution and rowdyism." He observed that the children "consorted with the vilest of both sexes" and formed habits of vice. He also noted that they had "never seen the inside of a schoolroom." Moralistic framing aside, his complaints were not so unlike the alarms raised today of street acculturation, gang affiliation, criminality, prostitution, sex trafficking, and the practice of substituting street networks for failed family or public systems of care.

Matsell wrote that these children were found "sleeping in the markets, under sheds," and in "wagons and other places of shelter," in doing so foreshadowing current federal definitions of youth experiencing homelessness, which rest on their unorthodox sleeping arrangements.[47] It was not difficult for us to see the homeless colony that had staked out abandoned vehicles at the salt mines in the 1980s as akin to those children in the mid-nineteenth century who were found sleeping in coal bins. Substitute a pile of road salt for a bed of coal and the underlying nighttime conditions were more similar than different.

As for the causes of this youthful vagrancy, Matsell noted that some youth had "no homes whatever," and he pointed an accusatory finger at both parents and children. Of the former, he complained about their "mistaken leniency" and criminal carelessness. Of the later, he fretted about those who "absent themselves from the roof of their parents or guardians." He described the full spectrum of street youth: runaways, the homeless, and those facing family instability of some sort.

***

Nineteenth Century Youth Vagrancy: An Emerging Public Problem

Matsell described the emergence of a new public problem of disconnected and vagrant youth born out of conditions associated with mid-nineteenth-century urbanization and industrialization. A confluence of well-documented factors contributed to the problem. Among other things, New-York had been absorbing large numbers of poor immigrant families for decades but by mid-century, the strain was clearly being felt. Impoverished newcomers were settling in increasingly congested areas on the Lower East Side of Manhattan. They moved into overcrowded, unregulated tenement buildings constructed with little regard to the health and well-being of the residents. Housing, sanitation, and environmental conditions were so bad that air and waterborne diseases flourished. Cholera, yellow fever, small pox, and typhoid outbreaks were frequent.

As a result of these conditions, orphans were common but so, too, were "half-orphans," a term used to describe children of widows, widowers, or unwed mothers struggling on their own as single parents, often with many children. Family desertion (particularly by the breadwinner) and reconstituted families were not uncommon. In addition, neighborhood saloons and bars abounded. The abundant availability of alcohol added combustible fuel to family stress. In short, the ingredients associated with modern youth homelessness were present.

Adding to public health and family instability were economic pressures. Poor families relied on child earnings to supplement family income. By the mid-nineteenth century, apprentice-based child labor was in decline and was largely being replaced by tenement house sweatshops, manufacturing, and industrial employment in the city. Poor children were expected to work.

Significantly, however, human congestion wrought by urbanization also produced a brand-new market for child laborers. Each day, the bustling city streets were crowded with potential consumers. With a few pennies, children could purchase merchandise that could be peddled at a small profit. They sold an endless variety of things such as apples, pencils, matches, flowers, and newspapers. In addition to huckstering, children could sell services. They carried messages, shined shoes, held horses, and swept filth from crosswalks for the benefit of high society patrons in exchange for a few coins. Furthermore, there were plenty of opportunities for scavenging and recycling anything from rags to bones or wood scraps, all at a small profit. All told, these conditions gave rise to legitimate or semi-legitimate—if not particularly lucrative—employment opportunities for children, and by extension income to their parents, who were entitled to their earnings.

Yet the decline in apprenticeship training, coupled with new street markets for child labor, had secondary consequences. First, adult oversight of children was greatly diminished. The rise of street-based employment options left youth with neither parental nor employer supervision. Second, children's financial dependence on adults was greatly diminished. They could cobble together their own meager income through a combination of street vending, begging, scavenging, alms-seeking, and pilfering. So young children could be both physically and financially independent from adults. Taken together, the decreased supervision and increased financial independence meant that children were less beholden to adults than their rural counterparts or their historical predecessors. This also meant that children could grow up outside traditional systems of socialization.

It is also clear that, seen through a twenty-first-century lens, the longer-term prospects for these uneducated young people growing up on the streets—much like the prospects for today's "disconnected youth"—were less than rosy. It isn't impossible to envision for these young people the risk of life-long poverty, crime, violence, and poor health. However, street acculturation, gang membership, and criminal activity, if left unchecked, was arguably also a threat to the social order then, just as it is today.

***

Charles Loring Brace, Children's Aid Society, and a Newsboys' Lodging House

While Matsell documented this population and its attendant risks from the perspective of the police force, the children also caught the attention and sympathy of mid-century social reformers and charity workers. None would become more single-mindedly devoted to them than an ambitious young man named Charles Loring Brace.

In 1853, Brace accepted a position as secretary of the newly established Children's Aid Society (CAS). Starting with little more than personal ambition and exceptional vision, he became CAS's chief intellectual architect and over the next four decades built an internationally renowned child welfare agency. As tribute to the strength of the foundational roots, CAS continues to serve families in New York today over a century and a half later.

Brace is best remembered by historians for his contributions to the "placing out" system. Much less attention has been paid to Brace's work among the poor in New York City itself and the network of services established by CAS. Within a year, Brace opened the first of what would eventually become a half dozen lodging houses. The first and most highly touted of these residences was launched as the Newsboys' Lodging House (NBLH). It offered stable shelter, food, and clothing to New-York's homeless boys.

Like advocates today, Brace was strategic in his use of language. Brace used the term *newsboy* as a proxy for any poor vagrant boy. While some boys did sell papers, the NBLH residents engaged in the full range of street trades and labor available to poor children. Brace strategically selected the term *newsboys* from a variety of possible labels. The fabled newsboys were known, on one hand, for their cunning, industry, and entrepreneurial spirit. On the other hand, newsboys were often linked to pick-pocketing, thefts, and other crimes. For Brace, the fact the newsboy sat metaphorically between redemption and ruin was perfect for his campaign to build an institution for poor children. It was an image and message that Brace carefully curated, depending on his immediate audience. For church goers, he could remind them of their Christian duty of charity. For wealthy industrialists, he could appeal to their sense of making good investments in the entrepreneurial newsboys. For Nativists or those afraid of ethnic or religious difference brought by immigration, he could fan their fears by warning of the danger of leaving uneducated, unsocialized boys to drift into a life a crime or wield their political power at the polling place. No matter what his rhetoric, however, his intent was to build the financial security for a new mission devoted to children.

The NBLH quickly came to serve as an incubator for experimental ideas of how to work with street youth. Programing gradually expanded to include modest meals, evening classes, a reading room and library, a gymnasium, and a savings bank, among other amenities and educational tools. Given its success, the lodging house was replicated. Others were opened scattered throughout the city for both boys and girls.

These facilities filled a void and served an important role in stabilizing the otherwise chaotic lives of street children. Some were orphans, others had run away from home, and some had one or two parents who were unable to care for them for a variety of reasons often associated with ill health or extreme poverty. Some came from physically abusive homes. In short, they came from the same complex family situations we see reflected in modern social science literature on street youth.

Many youngsters resided at CAS's lodging houses for brief periods: a few days, weeks, or months. However, others stayed for years. So the lodging house served as both temporary respite during times of family or personal crisis as well as longer-term residences for young people experiencing homelessness. This is remarkably similar to the blend of basic centers and transitional living facilities in today's network of runaway and homeless youth services.

From a modern social work perspective, what is most notable about the entire operation is that Brace's program rested exclusively on the voluntary participation of its lodgers. Not only does this increase its kinship to our current runaway and homeless services network, but just as today's runaway services emerged as a radical alternative to mainstream institutions in the 1960s, Brace's lodging house reflected a completely different alternative to the other child institutions of his day.

Brace rejected coercive strategies that relied on courts and the prison-like child asylums and almshouses favored by other charity workers to constrain, isolate, and discipline poor children. His opposition to the asylum-based approaches is well documented in historical accounts. However, the corollary question that has received virtually no attention or even recognition is this: How did Brace build an agency based exclusively on the voluntary participation of vagrant children without resorting to policing?

***

Historical Invisibility of Homeless Youth

Remarkably few scholars of the nineteenth century have started from the premise that disconnected, abandoned children, street-acculturated teenagers, or homeless youth were, in fact, a serious social problem warranting attention and intervention. For example, Christine Stansell, a noted feminist scholar, built a gendered case for the changing role of domesticity during the nineteenth century in *City of Women: Sex and Class in New York, 1789–1860*. While she credits both Brace and Matsell with bringing "the problems of the street" to the "reform agenda" of the mid-nineteenth century, she nonetheless notes Matsell's report appears "weird and paranoid" and is critical of his assessment that "poor children were overrunning New-York's streets, spreading crime, disorder and disease into every thoroughfare, every cranny."[48] In addition, she finds fault with the police, who "often made scavenging synonomous with theft when defining crime and vagrancy."[49] She argues that Brace and reformers of the period derived some "imaginative zest" from "literary accounts" and that "literary convention as much as social reality created the urban horror" evident in their depictions.[50] She stated, "Throughout the 1850s, the CAS carried on the work Matsell had begun, documenting and publicizing the plight of street children in vivid prose."[51]

Vivid prose notwithstanding, it is difficult not to read into her scholarship an underlying suspicion about the content of the accounts. If the existence of street children is called into question, at least two sequelae may follow. First, there is a danger that the risks the children faced will be minimized. Second, actions taken by reformers to meet their needs can be tokenized or misconstrued.

For example, Stansell imposes a gendered interpretation on the NBLH, consistent with her theoretical orientation, while simultaneously diminishing the lodging house's value. She wrote that "Brace activated male sympathies to enliven the society's much-touted Newsboys' Lodging House, a boardinghouse where, for a few pennies, newsboys could sleep and eat." She went on to write, "The lodging house was, in fact, a kind of early boys' camp" that "knit poor boys and gentlemen into a high-spirited but respectable masculine camaraderie."[52] Similarly, Paul Boyer, another prominent historian of the period who studied the moral order imposed by charity workers, mentions CAS's New-York-based programs only briefly. He characterizes the NBLH as a place where "youthful news vendors and other street boys could repair for brief intervals while continuing this independent life."[53]

The scholarship of both Stansell and Boyer is undeniably important, but their decontextualized treatment of street children shows little insight into the realities of the new urban problem. While Stansell's characterizations of the NBLH are consistent with her gendered interpretation, the NBLH was arguably far more valuable as a service than a mere "boys' club." In fact, it provided a critical lifeline of support, meeting basic needs such as shelter, food, and clothing and served as a stabilizing influence on street children's otherwise piecemeal and pragmatic survival strategies. While not incorrect as far as it goes, Boyer's characterization of the NBLH as place where boys "could repair for brief intervals" doesn't acknowledge that some children stayed at the lodging houses for years at a time, according to internal documents from CAS, or that the facility offered a full array of support services. In accounts such as these, the population of homeless youth—as well as the needs and behaviors associated with it—are rendered historically invisible.

***

Nineteenth-Century Philanthropy: Humanitarian Aid or Social Control?

Historians of philanthropy have generally taken one of two basic views relative to the work of charity workers of the nineteenth century. One frames their efforts as primarily driven by reformers' humanitarian interests. The second takes the view that regardless of reformers' intensions, charity workers functioned as agents of moral and social control and in fact policed the poor.

In briefly summarizing the tension between the two lines of historical research, Friedman and McGarvie argue that the first wave of humanitarian scholarship "often resided in American schools of social work and represented narrowly focused remedial efforts for social improvement."[54] These scholars equated philanthropy with activities purported to be for the "'improvement in the quality of human life." The ultimate purpose of philanthropy was assumed "to promote the welfare, happiness, and culture of mankind."[55]

Critics found fault with humanitarian scholars' focus on "elite white male Protestants" at the expense of gendered, colonized, indigenous, racial, and ethnic perspectives.⁵⁶ Embedded in this critique were three distinct arguments, one concerning the interpretation of the reformers' motivations, the second having to do with the privileged perspective or positionality of the actors being studied, and the third about silencing, subjugating, or erasing other viewpoints.

In an attempt to correct these deficiencies, a second wave of historical scholarship displaced the humanitarian viewpoint. Friedman and McGarvie credit David Rothman's landmark work on asylums as one of the earliest in this new interpretation of nineteenth-century history.⁵⁷ This generation of scholars revisited the actions of mid-century reformers, arguing that charity workers imposed their class-based values on others and were intent on reproducing their own sensibilities and subjugating difference. This second wave of scholarship—promoting theories of social and moral control—has offered us valuable class, gender, racial, and ethnic critiques, such as those written by Stansell and Boyer.

Although Friedman and McGarvie suggest that a third wave of scholarship attempted to reconcile these two contradictory perspectives, one based on the idea of "sincere, benevolent intension" and the other on the idea of "social control in the interests of ruling class hegemony," they concluded that subsequent "waves of historiography were never able to provide an integrating focus."⁵⁸ The result is that historical accounts of nineteenth-century charity workers as humanitarians have lost favor to the more dominant narratives resting in the hands of social control theorists. Interpretations of Charles Loring Brace's life and his life's work establishing CAS are caught in the crosshairs of this debate.

***

Disciplinary Differences and Methodological Critiques

The social control epistemological frameworks now in favor are accompanied by disciplinary and methodological assumptions that have ignited challenges to historiographies by scholars trained in the social sciences and those from other disciplinary or professional vantage points.

Perhaps no student of Brace and CAS has confronted the epistemological and methodological limitations of historiography more succinctly than Bruce Bellingham, a sociologist.⁵⁹ Arguing against the social control theorists' interpretation as applied to Brace's "placing out" system, Bellingham noted that "welfare history cast in the idiom of social control hardly attempts to explain the most significant political question: how did charity accommodate working-class families to the economic or demographic miseries of early industrial society?"[60]

In answering his question, he calls into question the validity of a great swath of social control historiography that attributes particular motivations to individual actors and by extension their institutions without careful empirical, case-based, investigation.

Bellingham offers three important methodological critiques. First, he writes, "historical assumptions about the experience of institutional contact are theoretically given rather than investigated." At the heart of this concern is that by starting with a theoretical narrative, researchers use evidence that is selectively pieced together without sustained or systematic scrutiny. This results in dislodging actors and their efforts from the context of their work. Yet these theory-driven reports often offer sweeping generalized conclusions about reformers, their institutions, and their service recipients based on patchwork, and selectively censored, evidence.

Thomas Bender, a preeminent historian on social thought and the development of nineteenth-century social institutions, acknowledges as much about his own research methods. He writes that he "selected for close study" various actors and institutions that were "not linked by concrete associations in time and place" but rather around a "cluster of beliefs" and when connected resulted in "thematic links."[61] Bender specifically admits he used Brace's writing because Brace "provides an illustration" of the overall thesis.[62] Similar theory-driven narratives can be seen in Stansell's work on sex and class and Boyer's work on urbanization and moral order. For example, in establishing her gendered argument, Stansell concludes about the NBLH that Brace's "imagination was more caught up with boys than girls."[63] Yet this conclusion seems to ignore the factual evidence that CAS provided extensive analogous programming for girls, including lodging houses and industrial schools.

Secondly, Bellingham argues, to the extent that historians examine the development of a particular kind of social institution—such as those tracing the history of asylums or juvenile courts—they provide "macro-sociological explanations." Bellingham acknowledges, for example, that "deviance history does offer some explanations of the genesis and function of the institutional lineage it traces, but these are pitched at a middle level of analysis," such that scholars miss the opportunity to empirically examine the "motivations of reformers or the internal logic of organizational processes." The result is that rigorous, empirically-tested "structural explanations are absent, despite the fact that as a theoretically informed, non-empiricist field, deviance history prides itself on providing macro-level interpretations."[64]

In short, he is arguing that what is missing is any nuanced, contextual understanding of the developmental logic *within* a specific institution and any genuine attempt to holistically and contextually understand the motivations of the individuals associated with that organization. So social control-oriented scholarship, based on thematic ideas and selective evidence, tells us very little about the intentions of the actors or the internal logic of the institutions under investigation. Paradoxically, with this inattention to micro-level experience we also lose any nuanced understanding of the gendered, racial, and ethnic experiences of those clients interacting with the charitable institutions—the very groups about which historiographers are willing to make expansive theoretical claims.

Finally, Bellingham argues that the reasoning of social control historiographies fails because of a refusal "to concede that institutionalization is a relationship between active parties." Therefore, narrative accounts which assume moral reformers were colonizers of the poor necessarily rest on the assumption of complete lack of agency on the part of the recipients themselves. Of this lack of attention to interpersonal interaction and individual agency, Bellingham concludes the following: "For sociologists working in other fields of historical research, especially family and work studies, the deviance researchers' treatment of clients and their 'friends' and families as inert, malleable objects seems frankly incredible."[65]

Boyer's description of the atmosphere at the NBLH is an example of where paying heed to contextual evidence and interpersonal interaction might yield important findings. He wrote, "Contemporary visitors to CAS lodging houses invariably commented on the prevailing high spirits, the street slang, and the boisterous shouts of tough little gamins totally unintimidated by the surroundings of a benevolent institution." He goes on to say of Brace, "In his own lodging house talks, Brace favored a forceful, informal, and practical-minded approach, and he reveled in the discomfiture of guest speakers who were hooted down when they became excessively moralistic or sentimental."[66]

Yet arguably, Boyer misses the significance of this evidence of interpersonal interaction with street savvy teenage boys. The fact that the lodging house atmosphere was repeatedly described as "boisterous," that the boys were in "high spirits," and that "the little gamins were totally unintimidated by the surroundings" tells us a good deal about the social work practice environment being tolerated within the facility. In addition, the description of Brace as favoring an "informal approach" and disfavoring those who became "excessively moralistic or sentimental" serves as an additional, and significant, piece of evidence not only about Brace but also about the tone and philosophy of the agency as well as its sectarian and practical methods of engaging street youth, without legal coercion or overly moralistic sermons.

It is thus possible to generate evidence-informed hypotheses about the youth-friendly inner workings of CAS that can be further tested against other internal documents and external observations. In fact, CAS records are replete with evidence that good humor, extreme tolerance, and informality were central tenets of agency practice. There is ample evidence that the boys who resided at the NBLH lied, broke the law (sometimes repeatedly), pulled pranks on the agents, skipped curfew, drank (sometimes to excess), smoked, and gambled. Yet only in the truly exceptional case was a boy denied services. In fact, boys were repeatedly welcomed back to try again. Small failures were treated as learning opportunities and recognized as developmental necessities. Agents engaged children with good humor and rarely with moral judgment. Only by keeping this information in context does a more robust picture of the NBLH and the inner workings of CAS as an institution emerge. This evidence, and evidence offered throughout this book, is suggestive of an agency building its organizational practices around persuasion rather than coercion. However, seeing this requires not only evaluating the evidence in context but acknowledging the independent agency of the teenage clients of the NBLH.

Bellingham's three methodological critiques present a serious challenge to existing scholarship on nineteenth-century social institutions, which is theory-driven at the expense of empirical, case-based investigation. Building on Bellingham's work, I argue that by discarding the research questions most interesting to social work scholars, historical accounts may miss important developments and undervalue the significance of the very institutions being studied or the practice methods employed within them. I ask not only how CAS accommodated members of working-class families, but vagrant and homeless teenagers themselves. How did CAS engage children without resorting to policing or excessive preaching? What options did children have and why were they willing to choose CAS?

***

Newsboys, Their Lodging House, and Brace's CAS

This book focuses on the NBLH as well as its place and role in the network of CAS's other branches of service. The NBLH was opened in 1854 and operated under that name until 1890, when it was renamed the Brace Memorial Lodging House, immediately following Brace's death. It officially closed in 1942, when its residents—by then all older boys—were relocated and the building facility was handed over to the war effort.

With the closing of the NBLH, this model of service, which included providing crisis shelter and transitional living, literally vanished from the landscape of available options for children and young adults. It left a gaping hole in the service structure for young people who found themselves either temporarily or permanently homeless and living on the street. This void was not filled again until the rediscovery of youth experiencing homelessness in the 1960s and the enactment of the RHYA in 1974.

This book investigates the NBLH in the early years (1853–1890) when it was operating during Brace's lifetime. I start with a set of assumptions informed by social work practice, social science literature, and interpretative approaches to qualitative inquiry. First, youth experiencing homelessness in mid-nineteenth-century New-York was a serious social problem.[67] Furthermore, it was the product of a complex array of factors. No simple label—be it abandoned child, delinquent, dependent, vagrant, homeless child, orphan, or newsboy—fully captures the complexity of the social circumstances contributing to it. Second, given the complexity of the problem, social institutions needed to be flexible and responsive to diverse needs. Third, the dangers of ignoring vagrant children were real. These dangers could include street acculturation, criminal involvement, drug involvement, prostitution, substance abuse, lifelong poverty, poor health, and premature death. Fourth, children estranged from all other systems of socialization are the rightful recipients of moral, social, and civic guidance by adults concerned with their well-being. This has more to do with their developmental needs as youngsters than any desire by workers to exert control over the urban masses as promoted by the social control theorists. Fifth, engaging street youth requires unique practice skills and child-friendly models of intervention. I start with a deep-seated respect for the individual agency of adolescent actors, particularly street-wise teenage boys. Sixth, building an agency from scratch required creativity and flexibility. It required the good will and involvement of children and their parents as well donors, politicians, police officers, judges, and other charity workers. In short, CAS needed to develop its own niche in relation to the active agents and existing institutions around it.

This book is also a case-based investigation. As Bellingham has argued, close case study permits examination of the internal structure and overall integrity of a particular child welfare agency. The evidence comes from internal CAS documents, some of which were written for public consumption but many of which were not. I approach the investigation as a social scientist trained in qualitative inquiry and interpretative methods, and I seek to understand the internal logic of CAS practices and the integrity of the agency's overall design. Anchoring the study around the NBLH offers a number of advantages. First, as others have noted, the NBLH is less well described in the historical literature than other aspects of CAS programs. Second, examination of the lodging house permits exploring its connection to CAS's other branches and departments. Third, the nested examination of the NBLH creates a window through which to examine the development and evolution of CAS more generally. Fourth, taking a contextual approach permits a better understanding of the social work practice being utilized within CAS and the role it played in the landscape of existing options. Finally, grounding the investigation in the New-York facility brings some balance to existing scholarship, which has disproportionately emphasized CAS's emigration branch to the neglect of the extensive and comprehensive services it was offering in New York City.

There are three notable limitations. First, my primary focus is on boys. I start with them because that is where Brace started and because the NBLH was promoted as CAS's flagship program in New-York. The experiences of girls within CAS warrant independent investigation. Second, because the NBLH catered mostly to adolescents, I don't explore CAS practices with the youngest children taken in. Obviously, the needs of infants or toddlers are different than those of teenagers on the cusp of adulthood. Finally, while I attend to the educational programs offered through the NBLH's night school, thereby presenting a sample of CAS educational practices, I don't independently investigate the dozens of freestanding industrial schools associated with the agency.

In the end, this book is not an exercise in theoretical historical narration, although the empirical evidence paints a humanitarian, rather than social control, portrait of CAS practices. Instead, the book offers a pragmatic and hopefully inspiring look at the early development of social work practice and institution building, inductively constructed from existing documents. It seeks to understand how—when confronted by enormous, even paralyzingly complex, social problems—one person set about making life better for children, their families, and society as a whole. It was an approach designed not to destroy families or forcibly remove children but rather to support families and children in their normative practices (including delegating child care and assisting in labor transitions) under extraordinarily difficult and complex urban conditions. The evidence consistently shows that CAS was built around youth empowerment and voluntary participation. It resisted institutionalization and policing practices. It was unlike anything else on offer at the time. It was a project Charles Loring Brace tackled with enormous optimism, considerable zeal, and relentless determination.

Today's social services most differ from CAS's early offerings in two ways. First, unlike both our current CPS and our juvenile justice system, CAS rejected any form of state-enforced policing or coercion. Here, I would acknowledge the social control theorists' contentions that social work practice today, rooted in state police power, can be characterized as both controlling and reproducing of class-based sensibilities. Yet Brace operated before these mechanisms were in place. All indications are that he opposed the forces moving in that direction. Second, CAS attempted to provide an integrated, comprehensive, and seamless system of aid depending on the needs of children and their families. Today, our current practices are largely fractionated, siloed, uncoordinated, and piecemeal. Arguably, CAS's comprehensive system yoked together what today would be our runaway and homeless youth services network with CPS, public education, and help transitioning into the adult labor market with vocational training programs and employment referrals.

Brace took seriously the complexity of child and family poverty and stayed focused on long-term solutions. The continuum of care offered by CAS included reducing immediate suffering through crisis services. It also focused on the longer-term endgame of reducing illiteracy, delinquency, homelessness, and intergenerational poverty. Sadly, it is difficult to say the same of our current policies, where child poverty and family well-being receive relatively low priority and haphazard investment. This is particularly true for youth experiencing homelessness. Many such children are invisible to the general public, programs are underfunded, and homeless youth have fallen through the cracks in our public systems. As a society, we don't invest heavily in the future of these youngsters. Arguably Charles Loring Brace did.

Notes

1. George Washington Matsell, "Semi-Annual Report of the Chief of Police from May 1 to October 31, 1849" (unpublished report, New York, 1850).
2. Children, teenagers, and young adults who are living on their own and experiencing homelessness are generally recognized as a distinct category in the overall homelessness population. Other groups of study include homeless adults and families with children experiencing homelessness. What makes the adolescent population different is that the minors are often operating without any adult supervision or guidance.

3. Meghan Henry, Rian Watt, Lily Rosenthal, and Azim Shivji, *The 2017 Annual Homeless Assessment Report (AHAR) to Congress: Part 1: Point in Time Estimates of Homelessness* (Housing and Urban Development, December 2017), 48. The HUD study found that 64.4 percent of all unsheltered, unaccompanied youth experiencing homelessness were located in just five U.S. cities, one of them being New York. The others were Los Angeles, San Jose, Las Vegas, and Seattle. Similarly, in 2015, a New York State report on runaway and homeless youth found that 4,781 of the 7,953 youth using certified or licensed runaway and homeless residential programs in the state were located in the city. These numbers reflected "duplicate admissions" because 35 percent of the youth had more than one admission to the same program. This recidivism rate is troubling. Like the phenomenon of "couch surfing," the shelter recidivism rates suggest that a sizable number of youth are using shelters as part of a makeshift, piecemeal housing strategy. Recidivism hints at the instability associated with living on the margins.
4. Nikita Stewart, "Homeless Young People of New York, Overlooked and Underserved," *New York Times*, February 5, 2016, https://www.nytimes.com/2016/02/06/nyregion/young-and-homeless-in-new-york-overlooked-and-underserved.html.
5. Stewart, "Homeless Young People."
6. Matthew H. Morton, Amy Dworsky, and Gina M. Samuels, *Missed Opportunities: Youth Homelessness in America National Estimates* (Chicago: Chapin Hall at the University of Chicago, 2017), 6–8. They found that "one in 10 young adults, ages 18–25, and at least one in 30 adolescents, ages 13–17, experience some form of homelessness unaccompanied by a parent or guardian over the course of a year."
7. Bruce Bellingham, "Institution and Family: An Alternative View of Nineteenth Century Child Saving," *Social Problems* 33, no. 6 (December 1986): 542.
8. Jose A. Elique, "The Juvenile Runaway Phenomenon: A Law Enforcement Agency's Unique Approach," *FBI/Law Enforcement Bulletin* (February 1984): 1–6. YSU was originally started as an experimental response to the increasing numbers of runaway youth who found, at the time seedy, "Times Square area irresistible" and who used the bus terminal "as the gateway to New York City." The project was briefly funded through public grants and after proving successful, the operation was taken over by the Port Authority Police Department of New York and New Jersey. The original design was to pair social workers and police officers together to patrol the terminal, although there was never any doubt that the police officers were primarily in charge. Sergeant Poggioli headed the unit for several decades, finally retiring in 2003.
9. Howell Raines, "Catching Runaways Before the Street Gets Them," *New York Times*, April 13, 1978, https://www.nytimes.com/1978/04/13/archives/new-jersey-pages-catching-runaways-before-the-street-gets-them-the.html.
10. In New York City, YSU is not alone in its policing work. Both the New York Police Department and the city's FBI field office also have specialized units with officers

and agents dedicated exclusively to problems associated with unaccompanied young people. An example of this cooperative policing arrangement in New York City is the New York Child Exploitation and Human Trafficking Task Force, which combines the efforts of FBI agents and NYPD officers.

11. Elique, "The Juvenile Runaway Phenomenon," 3.
12. Karen M. Staller, *Runaways: How the Sixties Counterculture Influenced Today's Practices and Policies* (New York: Columbia University Press, 2006); Karen M. Staller, "Social Problem Construction and Its Impact on Program and Policy Responses," in *From Child Welfare to Child Well-Being: An International Perspective on Knowledge in the Service of Making Policy*, ed. S. B. Kamerman, S. Phipps, and A. Ben-Arieh (Dordrecht, The Netherlands: Springer, 2009, 155–173). The legislation was originally called the Runaway Youth Act but was quickly amended to include homeless youth as well and became known as the Runaway and Homeless Youth Act. It was later amended again to include youth at risk of exploitation.
13. Staller, *Runaways*.
14. For example, Covenant House, one of the largest homeless youth services providers in the country, identifies five guiding principles for its programs: immediacy, sanctuary, values communication, structure, and choice (see https://www.covenanthouse.org/homeless-charity).
15. Andrew M. Cuomo and Sheila J. Poole, *Annual Report 2015: Runaway and Homeless Youth* (New York: State Office of Children and Family Service, 2015), 12. In fact, youth disengage with services with distressing frequency. One study found nearly 30 percent of the children who left a runaway shelter in New York City did so voluntarily and without a future plan in place. Additionally, the study reported only 13 percent actually returned to their guardian's home.
16. Status offenses refer to behaviors that can be regulated only because of a youth's status as a minor. Most states have some version of the law with acronyms such as JINS, CHINS, PINS, and FINS. The "INS" part of these phrases generally means *in need of supervision* or *in need of services*. The initial letter reflects different conceptualizations and stands for *juveniles, children, persons,* and *families,* respectively. Status offense behaviors frequently include running away, truancy, failing to comply with curfews, and other acts of willful disobedience.
17. Elique, "The Juvenile Runaway Phenomenon," 5.
18. For example, under New York State law, a runaway youth is defined as "a person under the age of 18 years who is absent from his or her legal residence without the consent of his or her parent, legal guardian, or custodian." Under the same law a homeless youth is defined "a person under the age of 21 who is in need of services and is without a place of shelter where supervision and care are available."
19. Cuomo and Poole, *Annual Report 2015*, 9. For example, children flee home because they have been victims of physical, sexual, and emotional abuse or because they come from environments with high levels of domestic violence. See also Darla Bardine, "What Works to End Youth Homelessness? National Network

for Youth, 2015, https://www.nn4youth.org/wp-content/uploads/2015-What-Works-to-End-Youth-Homlessness.pdf; Yumiko Aratani, "Homeless Children and Youth: Causes and Consequences," http://www.nccp.org/publications/pdf/text_888.pdf (published September 2009); B. Sznajder-Murray, J. B. Jang, N. Slesnick, and A. Snyder, "Longitudinal Predictors of Homelessness: Findings from the National Longitudinal Survey of Youth—97," *Journal of Youth Studies* 18, no. 8 (2015): 1015–1034; Covenant House Annual Report, 2017, *Our Great Promise*. In a 1992 survey of runaway and homeless youth Deborah Bass found 26 percent had been victims of family violence and another 23 percent had been sexually abused. Deborah Bass, *Helping Vulnerable Youth: Runaway and Homeless Adolescents in the United States* (Washington, DC: NASW Press, 1992); Kevin Cwayna, *Knowing Where the Fountains Are: Stories and Stark Realities of Homeless Youth* (Minneapolis: Deaconess Press, 1993); Les Whitbeck, Melissa Welch Lazoritz, Davan Crawford, and Dane Hautala, "Administration for Children and Families, Family and Youth Services Bureau Street Outreach Program," Data Collection Study Final Report (April 2016); Morton, et al., *Missed Opportunities*.
20. Whitbeck, Lazoritz, Crawford, and Hautala, "Administration for Children and Families," 2. In 1992, Bass found in a street-based survey of homeless youth that over 20 percent cited the caregiver's drug or alcohol as a major contributing factor for leaving; nearly a quarter claimed to have been physically abused or beaten, 29 percent had parents who were alcoholic, and another 24 percent abused drugs.
21. Susanna R. Curry, Matthew Morton, Jennifer L. Matjasko, Amy Dworsky, Gina M. Samuels, and David Schlueter, "Youth Homelessness and Vulnerability: How Does Couch Surfing Fit?" *American Journal of Community Psychology* 60 (2017): 22. Chapin Hall researchers found that LGBT youth had a 120 percent higher risk of reporting explicit homelessness than non-LGBT youth.
22. Bardine, "What Works," 6. Bass's 1991 survey found that 45 percent of the runaway and homeless youth had an absent father.
23. Bardine, "What Works," 6. In a street-based study of homeless youth over half had been asked to leave by a parent or caretaker.
24. Sassafras Lowrey, ed., *Kicked Out* (Ann Arbor, MI: Homofactus Press, 2010); Staller, "Social Problem Construction," 155–173. Staller, *Runaways*.
25. Curry et al., "Youth Homelessness and Vulnerability," 23. How serious a problem this is depends on the circumstances, including the youth's age and stage of development as well as the number and duration of the homeless episodes.
26. Curry et al., "Youth Homelessness and Vulnerability," 27–34. Whitbeck et al. found that in its street-based sample of homeless youth just under one-third (29.5 percent) reported they had the option of returning home (Whitbeck et al., "Administration for Children and Families"). These youths reported first becoming homeless at the average age of 15 years and had a total lifetime rate of homelessness of just under two years (23.4 months).

27. Yumiko Aratani, *Homeless Children and Youth: Causes and Consequences* (National Center for Children in Poverty, September 2009), 6, http://www.nccp.org/publications/pdf/text_888.pdf; Kevin Cwayna, *Knowing Where the Fountains Are: Stories and Stark Realities of Homeless Youth* (Minneapolis: Deaconess Press, 1993).
28. Cuomo and Poole, *Annual Report 2015*, 2.
29. Covenant House, the largest runway and homeless youth shelter system in the United States, reports that more than one-third of its youth have formerly been in the foster care system. (CH Sleepout America). In a street-based sample of homeless youth aged 14 to 21, 50.6 percent reported having stayed in a foster home or group home. In 1991, Bass found that 38 percent of the runaway and homeless youth who were subjects of its investigation had been in foster care. In a 2015 report on youth homelessness in New York State, Darla Bardine reported "a disproportionate representation of foster youth among the homeless youth population," citing a study that found 51 percent of its homeless youth study population had stayed in a foster home or group home. Darla Bardine, "What Works to End Youth Homelessness? National Network for Youth, 2015, https://www.nn4youth.org/wp-content/uploads/2015-What-Works-to-End-Youth-Homlessness.pdf.
30. Bardine, "What Works," 7. Covenant House's 2017 annual report, which cites numbers from its programs in 31 U.S. cities and six foreign countries, claims that 37 percent of its youth has had a criminal justice history. Bardine reported of homeless young adults in four cities 20 to 30 percent had been arrested for activities that included panhandling, loitering, or sleeping in outdoors. Bass found that 27 percent of the runaway and homeless youth in its survey had been involved in the juvenile justice system. At particular risk are those who "age out" of foster care. This term refers to young people who have reached a threshold of adulthood (however that chronological age might be defined in a particular state) and are subsequently discharged with little preparation for living on their own. Many have spent years shuttling from one temporary foster home to the next or been placed in group homes or other congregate care residential facilities. Despite federal efforts to provide funding for some limited training in practical life skills such as financial management or job preparation, sizeable numbers of these newly minted "adults" are ill prepared for life on their own and end up homeless.
31. Aratani, *Homeless Children and Youth*, 7. Chapin Hall researchers reported in 2017 that "one of the strongest risk correlates for homelessness was a lack of high school diploma or GED." They found that "youth with less than a high school diploma or GED had a 346% higher risk of explicit homelessness than their peers who completed high school" (Morton, et al., Missed Opportunities, 12). In 1992, Deborah Bass found that 53 percent of the runaway and homeless youth in her study had trouble in school or educational problems (Bass, *Helping Vulnerable Youth*). Not surprisingly researchers have repeatedly found that youth who are truant, suspended, expelled, or who have dropped out of school are disproportionately

represented among youth experiencing homelessness (as well as in the criminal or juvenile justice systems). Social justice advocates refer to the school-to-prison pipeline. However, often an intermediary step in this pipeline is spending time on the street. In short, being out of school and on the street increases the likelihood of arrest.

32. Eric Pooley, "Beggars' Army," *New York Magazine*, August 29, 1988, 32.
33. Bardine, *What Works*, 9.
34. Bardine, *What Works*, 9. In 2016, the Social Science Research Council reported that 4.6 million fell into this category, which translates into "about one in nine teens and young adults (11.7 percent)."
35. Even when federal agencies weighed into the debate, they didn't do much to settle these definitional disputes. For example, there are at least three pieces of major federal legislation targeting this population: the RHYA, the McKinney-Vento Act, and the Missing and Exploited Children's Act. Yet even the federal departments overseeing these initiatives—the Department of Health and Human Services, the Department of Education, and Housing and Urban Renewal—don't see eye to eye. For example, under the McKinney–Vento Act, the child's evening living situation is the primary focus of attention. The law speaks of both "unsheltered" and temporarily "sheltered" (living in temporary accommodations like homeless shelters, group homes, or transitional living facilities). The act defines unsheltered youth as those "who have a primary nighttime residence that is a public or private place not designed for or ordinarily used as a regular sleeping accommodation for human beings," including those "who are living in cars, parks, public spaces, abandoned buildings, substandard housing, bus or train stations, or similar settings." On the other hand the RHYA is less concerned with evening sleeping arrangements and more concerned about the dangers faced by youth who are without proper adult supervision. Thus it focuses on "youth for whom it is not possible to live in a safe environment with a relative, and who has no other safe alternative living arrangement." Conversely, the Missing Children's Act takes a parental, rather than a youth, perspective, defining a missing child as "any individual less than 18 years of age whose whereabouts are unknown to such individual's legal custodian."
36. Aratani, *Homeless Children and Youth*, 7. Not surprisingly, the longer unaccompanied youth experiences homelessness "the higher the probability of committing a crime."
37. Aratani, *Homeless Children and Youth*, 7; Cwayna, *Knowing Where the Fountains Are*.
38. Pooley, "Beggars' Army," 34.
39. The plight of the homeless folks living in New York's abandoned sanitation vehicles in the late 1980s was documented in a 1990 independent film called *The Salt Mines*, by film makers Carlos Aparicio and Susana Aikin.

   The film explores the living situation, survival strategies, and eventual eviction of the colony by the city from Sanitation Department property.

40. Tanay Warerkar, "NYC's New Salt Shed Is a Functional Piece of Architectural Eye Candy," *Curbed New York*, January 22, 2016.
41. John Hagan and Bill McCarthy, *Mean Streets: Youth Crime and Homelessness* (Cambridge: Cambridge University Press, 1998). In a field study of more than four hundred youth who had left home and school and were living on the streets in Toronto and Vancouver, Hagan and McCarthy found high levels of both victimization and involvement in crime. Not surprisingly, studies have shown that the longer unaccompanied youth experience homelessness, the higher the probability of committing a crime" (see Aratani, *Homeless Children and Youth*, 7). In a systematic review of twenty-nine research studies conducted by Heerde, Hemphill, and Scholes-Balog in 2014, their findings showed homeless youth report engaging in physically violent behavior including assault, physically fights, and robbery, and commonly describe victimization experiences such as being physically assaulted, threatened with weapons, and robbed." Heerde, Jessica A., Hemphill, Sheryl A., and Scholes-Balog, " 'Fighting' for survival: A systematic review of physically violent behavior perpetrated and experienced by homeless young people." *Aggression and Violent Behavior*, 2014, 19: 50–66.
42. Pooley, "Beggars' Army," 33.
43. Greene, Sanchez, et al. 2003, section 2.1.4. For example, Covenant House's 2017 annual report from, which cited numbers from its programs in thirty-one U.S. cities and six countries, claims that 20 percent of its youth have been involved in human trafficking. Similarly Whitbeck et al. report in street-based study of homeless youth that almost one-quarter of the participants (24.1 percent) said that they had "agreed to be sexual" with someone in exchange for money, and 27.5 percent had agreed to be sexual with someone in exchange for a place to spend the night (Ryan, Kevin, *Our Great Promise: 2017 Annual Report of Covennat House*, https://www.covenanthouse.org/sites/default/files/inline-files/2017%20CH%20Corporate%20Annual%20Report.pdf).
44. For a raw documentary and rare inside look at life as a street hooker featuring girls and women working the stroll at Hunt's Point, see the 2002 independent film, *Hookers at the Point*, directed by Brent Owens.
45. In addition to an inside look at the colony of homeless individuals who lived in the salt mines, the 1990 documentary film, *The Salt Mines*, captures their work as transvestite prostitutes in the meat packing district. It primarily features three Latina transwomen but a minor identified as staying at Covenant House (a runaway youth shelter) and street outreach workers also make brief appearances. Of note, New York now has several runaway and homeless youth shelters specifically catering to the LGBTQI runaway and homeless youth populations such as Sylvia's Place.
46. Pooley, "Beggars' Army," 34.
47. One federal definition of youth homelessness rests fully on these unorthodox sleeping arrangements by referring to those "who have a primary nighttime

residence that is a public or private place not designed for or ordinarily used as a regular sleeping accommodation for human beings" making reference to those "who are living in cars, parks, public spaces, abandoned buildings, substandard housing, bus or train stations, or similar settings." In Whitbeck et al., study of street-based youth, more than half of the participants had slept or rested outside on a street, in a park, or on a bench (51.8 percent) and another 33.1 percent had "slept or rested in a bus station, airport, subway station, or train station" (Whitbeck et al., "Administration for Children and Families").

48. Christine Stansell, *City of Women: Sex and Class in New York, 1789–1860* (Urbana: University of Illinois Press, 1986), 194.
49. Stansell, *City of Women*, 205.
50. Stansell, *City of Women*, 196.
51. Stansell, *City of Women*, 197.
52. Stansell, *City of Women*, 212.
53. Paul Boyer, *Urban Masses and Moral Order in America, 1820–1920* (Cambridge, MA: Harvard University Press, 1978), 97–98.
54. Lawrence J. Friedman and Mark D. McGarvie, *Charity, Philanthropy, and Civility in American History* (Cambridge, UK: Cambridge University Press, 2003), 1.
55. Friedman and McGarvie, *Charity, Philanthropy, and Civility*, 4.
56. Friedman and McGarvie, *Charity, Philanthropy, and Civility*, 11.
57. David J. Rothman, *The Discovery of the Asylum*, rev. ed. (New York: Aldine de Gruyter, 2002).
58. Friedman and McGarvie, *Charity, Philanthropy, and Civility*, 5.
59. Bruce Bellingham, "Waifs and Strays: Child Abandonment, Foster Care, and Families in Mid-Nineteenth Century New York," in *The Uses of Charity: The Poor on Relief in the Nineteenth-Century Metropolis*, ed. Peter Mandler (Philadelphia: University of Pennsylvania Press, 1990); Bellingham, "Waifs and Strays"; 124.
60. Bellingham, "Waifs and Strays," 124.
61. Thomas Bender, *Community and Social Change in American* (Baltimore: Johns Hopkins University Press, 1975), x.
62. Bender, *Community and Social Change*, 132.
63. Stansell, *City of Women*, 212.
64. Bellingham, "Institution and Family," 536.
65. Bellingham, "Institution and Family," 540.
66. Boyer, *Urban Masses*, 98.
67. Similarly, Bellingham's investigation of CAS found that "child abandonment" was a genuine social problem in the mid-nineteenth century (Bellingham, "Waifs and Strays"; 125–128).

Acknowledgments

THIS BOOK HAS been a labor of love. Nearly twenty years ago, Barbara Levy Simon, a faculty member at the Columbia University School of Social Work where I was a doctoral student first mentioned that my study on runaway and homeless youth shelters reminded her of the Newsboys Lodging House. There is no telling how many research careers Barbara has launched with her esoteric knowledge of nearly everything, but I can say that this grateful former student let that seed germinate. This book is a direct result.

In 2010, I practically took up residence at the New-York Historical Society (N-YHS) as I ploughed through many of the 996 archival boxes and 490 bound volumes comprising *The Victor Remer Historical Archives of the Children's Aid Society*. I was extremely lucky to be able to consult with the collection's original archivist, Cherie Acierno, who did an extraordinary job cataloguing the thousands of miscellaneous documents in the collection and was so willing to share her knowledge of it. I owe a debt of gratitude to Maurita Baldock, N-YHS Curator of Manuscripts at the time. As do I Manuscript Department reference librarians, Ted O' Reilly and Tammy Kiter, of the Patricia D. Kingenstein Library, who cheerfully greeted me each morning and made allowances by designating an entire library cart for my personal use for months on end. Kindnesses were widespread including the museum's conservator who tried to pry apart documents fused together by water damage and the freight elevator operators who ferried visitors up to the library while the building was under construction. I owe all of them my grateful thanks for making me feel at home. It was an honor to be able to walk through those library doors each morning and to spend time in the beautiful space, with its treasure trove of documents, and in the company of such knowledgeable and kind staff.

I owe special thanks to Truda Jewett, Children's Aid Society Director of the Archives, who took me under her wing, becoming both friend and mentor. She shared her love of CAS with me often over dinners at her expense. Significantly, she graciously permitted me unrestricted access to otherwise restricted children's case records. I deeply regret that she died before I was able to share this final product with her but hope she would have approved.

More recently, others have offered me encouragement as I ambled toward a finish line. I'm particularly grateful to Lois Maharg who, among other things, attended to every tedious formatting detail of what she once dubbed my "novella of endnotes." Her enthusiasm and patience sustained me through the final drafts. Of course, any errors are mine alone. I am also grateful for the supportive team at Oxford University Press including Dana Bliss, Andrew Dominello, the anonymous reviewers who offered critical feedback on various draft chapters, Deepak Raj, and the behind-the-scene production crews who brought this book to life.

Then, of course, there were the stalwarts, friends and colleagues who served as counselors, consolers, and cheerleaders for the entire journey. They endured my tortoise-like progress without ever showing signs of lassitude. In the earliest days, Bill Meezan gave me intellectual permission to tell the story the way I wanted to tell it. I'm sorry he isn't here to see the final product but am grateful that his partner, Michael Brittenback, stepped in, offering love and support. Many were willing to read draft chapters with a critical eye, but supportive tone, including Dorothy Staller, Sandra Danziger, Sherrie Kossoudji, Lily Jarmon-Reisch, Michael Reisch, Berit Ingersoll-Dayton, Larry Root, and Zachary Shapiro. There are those who have listened to me talk about my "newsboys" for so long I'm sure they will be relieved this project has come to an end, including Denise Burnette, Mark Cameron, and Debbie Gioia. I owe you each enormous thanks, or as Mark would be quick claim, beer and barbeque.

On August 18, 1855, one of CAS's agents, Edward P. Smith, jotted down a note in his journal which read, "Our Saturday was a little enlivened by one of those incidents somewhat characteristic of us and which in the hands of a book maker would be of some value." Little could Mr. Smith have known how valuable each of those little jottings would be to someone 165 years later attempting to understand not only the children and the practices of CAS but, more important, the spirit and philosophy of the entire mission. Their notes reached across the centuries. Mr. Brace once said of his colleagues, "It is remarkable how little can be known in each generation of those before who have done the most to make the present better than the past. The best workers for human good seem to be silent." I hope I did justice to some of those silent workers and to the often overlooked street children with whom they worked from the scraps they left behind and in the process have given them all a voice.

Introduction
New-York, a City of Layers and Philanthropic Woolen Strings

> *In New York all that is best and all that is worst in America is represented.... Fling together ... Sodom and Gomorrah, a little of heaven, and more of hell and you have a faint picture....*
> *It is a city of colossal wealth and haggard poverty.*
> —DAVID MACRAE, *The Americans at Home*, 1870

TACKLING ANY PERIOD of history associated with New York City is to engage in an archeological quest of unknown proportions and porous parameters. One might start with a seemingly simple question about a child-oriented social service agency of the mid-nineteenth century only to be unexpectedly pulled into an exploration of gas lighting, estuaries, hackney cabs, oysters, bridge construction, the histories of paper clips, buttons, typewriters, sewage disposal, gang activity, and industry (particularly rail, shipping, and media) as well as little forays into theology and natural science. What once seemed a simple narrative task is suddenly littered with distraction. Simple historical background is a necessary part of providing contemporary readers unfamiliar with a period with enough of the basic contextual background to make sense of the primary narrative even while trying to drive novel scholarship forward. In the end, writing such a work is an exercise in humility, as one can only hope to capture a slice that will be satisfying on some counts while acknowledging it will be wholly unsatisfactory in other ways.

New-York is a city of layers, each seasoned with the flavors of the cultural and ethnic groups temporarily laying claim to its real estate before being displaced by the next new residents. Nonetheless, no layer stays buried permanently; all leave their imprint. Take something as simple as the city's name. In the mid-nineteenth century the hyphen remained between *New* and *York*.

After all, New-York had replaced New-Amsterdam, or, more accurately, Nieuw-Amsterdam, when the English displaced the Dutch. Yet before these colonial quests the same land had been inhabited by the indigenous Lenape people who called the place Manna Hata, or the island of many hills. Manna Hata morphed into the island of Manhattan, used synonymously with New-York. New-York remained interchangeable with Manhattan until 1898, when the island lassoed the Bronx, Queens, Brooklyn—previously Breuckelen—and Staten Island into its orbit, creating a constellation of five boroughs collectively known as Greater New York, or what we now call New York City. Or—at the risk of offending the entire rest of the state by the same name—just plain New York, without the hyphen.

Nonetheless, embodied in the Lenape name Manna Hata is a contextual clue, a reminder that Manhattan is an island. In the mid-nineteenth century its "island-ness" was a readily apparent fact of life. The slender 12-mile stretch of land was connected to the mainland—only in the wilderness of its northernmost end—by three bridges: the Harlem, Macomb, and King's.[1] It wouldn't be until 1883, with the opening of the Brooklyn Bridge, that the populous southern tip of the island would be conveniently tethered to Brooklyn, and New-Yorkers would begin to defeat Mother Nature's tendency to freeze the island into isolation during the winter months due to an u90ceremonious halt in the normally bustling ferry traffic.

However, in the early nineteenth century, being an island of a particular sort also offered the little city of New-York unique opportunities. Three rivers embraced it: the Hudson River, running along the north and west sides (sometimes called the North River) and separating it from New Jersey and the Harlem River, rounding off the northeast corner, slicing it off from Upstate New York, which spilled into the aptly dubbed East "River,"[2] splitting it from Long Island. These rivers converged at the southern tip of Manhattan and emptied into the protected New York Bay and Lower New York Bay. Beyond those relatively sheltered waters lay the great, rough expanse of the Atlantic Ocean.

The city's potential was enormous and New-Yorkers exploited it to its fullest. DeWitt Clinton, New-York's mayor-turned-state governor—who was heralded only in hindsight as a visionary—famously dug his "Big Ditch," a 362-mile passage slashed brazenly into the earth, across the entire width of the state. Opened in 1825, the Erie Canal created a continuous waterway between Albany and Buffalo. Buffalo, a city perched at the edge of Lake Erie, offered yet another gateway. Lake Erie was sandwiched between the Great Lakes of Ontario and Huron and beyond that—in watery, intestine-like connection—to lakes Michigan and Superior. Almost overnight the little port city of New-York distinguished itself from all the other port cities on the East Coast. By 1849, "3,000 ships from 150 foreign ports" had arrived in New-York's harbor, "carrying half of all America's imports and departing with nearly one-third of her exports."[3] No longer a mere "provincial port," New-York became a commercial powerhouse and crowning jewel of the East Coast. It alone offered continuous waterway passage from the Atlantic Ocean into the New York bays, up the Hudson River to Albany, across the state through the Erie Canal to Buffalo, and directly into the Great Lakes. The sprawling lakes permitted easy, efficient access to the far western states of Illinois, Michigan, Ohio, and Wisconsin, not to mention Canada. The Erie Canal moved products and people across great distances efficiently and inexpensively. It was so important that the number of days it was frozen closed during the winter months were anxiously watched, dutifully recorded, and annually reported.[4]

New-York, never a city to be defeated by setbacks no matter how catastrophic, has burned to the ground and risen from the ashes on countless occasions. The Great Fire of 1835 is a stellar example. Starting in a dry goods store on December 16 during "one of the coldest nights in memory,"[5] a fire raged out of control, racing west toward Broad Street, east toward South Street, and north toward Wall Street, leaping from one flammable site to the next. It consumed virtually everything in its path including 674 buildings covering thirteen acres in lower Manhattan.[6] The fire destroyed much of the existing city before it was finally wrestled under control in the late afternoon of December 17, 1835.[7] This, in spite of the fact that every fire company in the vicinity responded in full force, including seventy-five assorted "engines, hose-carts, and hook and ladder trucks."[8] The volunteer firefighters—it wouldn't be until 1865 that the rag-tag volunteers were organized into the more professional Metropolitan Fire Department—struggled.[9] The firemen faced nearly insurmountable odds; "gale force winds" carried the flames haphazardly from building to building. However, an even more devilish culprit was the freezing temperatures that left the men with precious little water with which to fight the flames.[10] Both the Hudson and East rivers were frozen nearly solid "except for a narrow channel," such that "only a tiny trickle flowed sluggishly in the ice-choked logs by which water was piped" and "the wells, cisterns, and reservoirs contained nothing but solid blocks of ice."[11] The volunteers were left no other option than trying to thaw "the cisterns and wells" and chop "the ice at the ends of piers and docks" in an attempt to liberate water for use against the raging flames.[12]

In the following days—as the ashes smoldered and the smoke cleared—two things were abundantly clear to New-Yorkers. First, even an island surrounded by water was vulnerable to complete destruction if there wasn't a reliable source of water. Second, if New-York didn't solve its water problem, the metropolis could not successfully continue to grow. The city's response was characteristic. Authorities began planning and constructing what would become one of the greatest civil engineering feats of its day, the Croton Water Works. When completed, the system would carry water more than forty miles from Upstate New York, all the way to within three miles of New-York's city hall in the southern tip of Manhattan.

The Croton project required building a 250-foot dam, a 33-mile aqueduct, a 1,450-foot "High Bridge" over the Harlem River into Manhattan—an engineering feat in its own right as the bridge had to soar high enough not to block the active river traffic below—a gigantic receiving reservoir, which collected 150 million gallons of water in the wilderness of Eighty-Sixth Street, and an equally impressive distributing reservoir at Fifth Avenue between Fortieth and Forty-Second streets, which covered four acres[13] and held 20 million gallons of water. It was a breath-taking feat of engineering. The Croton Water Works was opened with presidential pomp and ceremony on July 4, 1842.

Nonetheless, as stimulating as both the Erie Canal and the Croton Aqueduct were to New-York's economic well-being, they are also emblematic of another buried, or at least conveniently muted, recurring theme in New-York's history. It has always been a city of have and have-nots. On the one hand, each civil engineering project offered new ways for speculators, developers, industrialists, and merchants to make fortunes. On the other hand, the projects were built on the backs of exploited and exploitable labor. In these two cases, a good deal of that labor was supplied by poor Irish immigrants and black Americans. When Charles Dickens visited the U.S. (including Manhattan) in 1842, he wryly observed of its Irish immigrants, "It would be hard to keep your model republics going.... For who else would dig, and delve, and drudge, and do domestic work, and make canals and roads, and execute great lines of Internal Improvement!"[14] If these projects were built by the toil of society's lowest-rung laborers, they were also the ones least likely to benefit fully from the final product of their handiwork. Although the Croton water flowed freely from Westchester into the great holding tanks in New-York, it was not particularly democratically distributed after it got there. Croton water coursed through iron pipes "laid deep underground, to be secure from frost,"[15] supplying "1,400 fire hydrants" and "600 free hydrants."[16] While the wealthiest pumped the fresh Croton water directly into their homes and had plenty for use flushing out their sewer pipes, the Irish immigrants and other poor New-Yorkers who lived crowded into lower Manhattan had considerably less access. In poor neighborhoods landlords were not yet compelled to connect water (or sewer) lines to residential buildings. Hundreds of residents often shared a single outdoor hydrant.

By way of example, of the 600 free hydrants, two were located in the Eleventh Ward in an "exterior courtyard" among a group of five squat "tenant-houses," sheltering "almost 200 people (of all ages)" and comprising more than thirty families.[17] All these residents had to pump water from one of these hydrants, then lug it through the warren of narrow passageways between buildings. Most then had to hoist it up rotted wooden stairways or rickety ladders to the upper-floor apartments and attic garrets for daily use. The sewage situation was even worse for this complex. There were two outdoor public "privy vaults" in the courtyard which—at the time of one inspection in 1865—"were filled nearly to the surface."[18] To the extent the Croton Water Works had been built to reduce the risk of fire, it did little good in these neighborhoods. The tenant-houses were mostly "wooden structures, with passage ways barely passable under the best of situations" and "combustible materials routinely piled" up in areas intended for egress.[19] The net result, as Simon Brentano, an amateur fire historian and notable book merchant, testified to a tenement house commission "after meticulously compiling statistics on fire frequency in neighborhoods," was this: "If you want to know where the poor people live, just find out where the fires are."[20]

So New York was also a city with a long history of great and gaping disparities in income and the amenities associated with it. The nineteenth century was the first in U.S. history in which abject poverty and colossal wealth sat side by side, in close proximity and stunning contrast. Moneyed society was laying down one set of foundations for New-York's history, in banking, commerce, and industry. These foundations are reflected in the tales of families like the Astors, Carnegies, Rockefellers, Morgans, and Vanderbilts. Poor immigrants were laying down yet another set of scaffoldings. These are histories of the Italian, Irish, German, Chinese, Russian, English, Scottish, Austrian, and Dutch immigrants, and Catholics and Jews. By the mid-nineteenth century the tensions between and among groups based on class, ethnicity, race, income, education, and religion were simmering, and the disparities between them were acute and growing.

Nonetheless there was also a league of individuals who sought to bridge the gaps. They were practical humanitarians or agents of social control, depending on your interpretation. Either way, they acted as connective tissue for society during a period of rapid transformation. Many sought to shake the moral conscience of the wealthy at the same time as they sought to shape the moral character of the poor. Long before there was any talk of a welfare state or public social services, these individuals were discussing ways to alleviate suffering and help others in need. Among these do-gooders were preachers and missionaries, teachers and philanthropists, sanitary and health workers, and charity and social workers. These individuals were reformers and revolutionaries—radical and conservative—who attempted to bridge the increasingly wide social, economic, and cultural chasms. They were as much social buffers as they were class translators.

They were not, however, a monolithic group. They squabbled among themselves about the best means of approaching reforms. They argued about the underlying principles and philosophies that should guide their practices. They linked their work to religion or science or to a blend of both. They argued about the boundaries between missionary work and charity work. They directed their efforts at individual failings and social structures. In short, they were hammering out the foundational roots of social welfare, no less important than the foundational roots being laid in commerce, banking, and industry. In the nineteenth century, there was no bigger battleground or larger experimental playground for this work than the port city of New-York.

Among these pioneer workers was Charles Loring Brace. First arriving in New-York in 1848, he was among a small group of concerned Protestant gentlemen who gathered together on a winter evening in 1853 and passed a motion to form a "Children's Aid Society" (hereafter, CAS). The next morning, at precisely 9 o'clock, Brace entered a small office with a blank diary, intended for recording daily transactions, tucked under his arm. From there he began to build the society. As CAS's first secretary, a position he held for the rest of his life, he spent nearly four decades breathing life into his creation.

At the time of his death in 1890, CAS consisted of twenty-one industrial schools; five night schools; six lodging houses; one crippled boy brush shop; four summer charities; one dress-making, sewing machine, typewriting school and laundry; and two free reading rooms. The day and night schools alone employed over 100 teachers instructing 10,464 students, with an average daily attendance of 4,157 pupils.[21] CAS also claimed that over 100,000 boys had stayed at the Newsboys' Lodging House (NBLH)—one of several facilities of this type—during its 36-year history.[22] Additionally, CAS maintained a large "emigration" project that by 1890 had placed 75,000 children on farms in the West.[23]

***

Two Historical Threads: Juvenile Delinquency and Placing Out

Brace's various roles during this period have received considerable historical attention and been the subject of some debate. Scholars with diverse topical interests have pointed to his contributions to intellectual life of New-York;[24] his role in shaping institutions;[25] his contributions to an optimistic view of social Darwinism;[26] his place in family studies[27] and gender domesticity;[28] his participation in the moral and social control of the urban masses;[29] and his role in changing perceptions of community and urbanization,[30] as well as the changing attitudes toward children.[31] Brace's place in these histories is often tangential to the larger topic under investigation.

Two distinct threads of historical research are particularly relevant when considering Brace's contributions to social work practice, child welfare services and policy, and child welfare institutions. One line investigates the origins of the juvenile justice system, with its focus on crimes committed by minors and other kinds of unruly behavior collectively deemed juvenile delinquency.[32] The second line of scholarship examines the origins of our child protectives services or child welfare system, which focuses on child safety, targeting children at risk of abuse or neglect at the hands of their own parents, guardians, or care providers.[33] Scholars in this area write about the nineteenth-century emigration system, placing out, or the orphan train movements as a precursor to today's foster care system.

Although Brace and CAS are predominately associated with the latter, his work is invariably invoked in both historical threads. In addition, both lines of scholarship—that on juvenile delinquency and that on placing out—overwhelming rest in the hands of historiographers favoring social and moral control interpretations of nineteenth-century charity work. Interestingly, Brace tends to be portrayed as a minor hero in juvenile justice literature while he is more likely cast as a villain in the fostering movement, placing him in a somewhat paradoxical position on the whole when it comes to social control theories. His role at the nexus of the two warrants revisiting.

***

Juvenile Delinquency: Control or Prevention?

Perhaps no scholar is more associated with tracing the "invention of juvenile delinquency" than Anthony Platt. Platt cast reformers of the last quarter of the nineteenth century as working "hand in glove with capitalists to control the masses" while noting they portrayed themselves "as altruists and humanitarians dedicated to rescuing those who were less fortunate."[34] These self-proclaimed "child savers," he argued, "helped to create special judicial and correctional institutions for the labeling, processing, and management of 'troublesome' youth."[35] To some extent the nineteenth-century culmination of this movement occurred in 1899 with the establishment of the first separate court exclusively for children in Illinois. Platt argues this institution was ultimately responsible for diminishing "the civil liberties and privacy of youth."[36] Brace functions only as a very minor character in Platt's scholarship; nonetheless, it is important to understand how he is implicated as the juvenile delinquency narrative has developed.

Since Platt places the start of his historical investigation primarily in the 1870s, nearly twenty years after the foundation of CAS, the more immediate link with juvenile delinquency is that of the earlier juvenile asylum movement. David J. Rothman's landmark book, *The Discovery of the Asylum: Social Order and Disorder in the New Republic*, explores this larger terrain. Rothman uses the word *asylum* as an umbrella concept to cover a broad range of congregate care facilities designed to address a variety of social ills. This larger story is one of moving from mixed-use almshouses—which were catchall institutions for a variety of people—to those with more specialized functions. On the one hand were facilities for adults such as penitentiaries, nursing homes, or hospitals for the mentally ill (insane asylums). On the other hand were facilities for children such as orphanages, juvenile reformatories, houses of refuge, juvenile asylums, and group homes.

In New-York, the earliest roots of this lineage date to the opening of the first almshouse in 1700. Initially it was used only as place of last resort for those individuals who couldn't be readily absorbed by the community in family homes or work apprenticeships. Most often these were individuals with extreme health- or age-related infirmities or strangers without ties to the community. By the century's end, however, the nature and function of the municipal almshouse had changed dramatically. For example, city officials passed a law in 1736 that required placing the poor more generally into the almshouse. Increasingly this included single mothers, orphans, and abandoned or lost children.

New-York's reliance on mixed-population poorhouses only increased in the early nineteenth century. The influx of immigrants, urbanization, and the loss of New-York's sense of being a provincial village community put additional stress on the almshouse model.[37] In 1819, the city relocated its poverty operations from the increasingly congested lower Manhattan to the relative wilderness and exile of First Avenue and Twenty-Sixth Street, opening a facility known as Bellevue. In short order, Bellevue's "overcrowding was endemic" and the new facility was quickly bursting at the seams with fifteen hundred residents.[38] As the population within the public almshouse swelled and the facility infrastructure decayed, critics set their sights on reform.

For children, this reform resulted in the development of a flurry of new specialized institutions with a variety of overlapping missions and functions.[39] The earliest of these was the Orphan Asylum, opened in 1806. In 1825 New-York opened the House of Refuge for juvenile delinquents; in 1836, the city opened a colored orphan asylum, and by 1848, the city was operating the Randall's Island Nurseries. In 1851 the privately funded Juvenile Asylum for vagrant (but ostensibly nondelinquent) children was added to the mix.

Rothman notes that the use of institutions to care for children was new in the U.S., and it "fundamentally altered traditional practices" of caring for dependent children, which before had relied on turning to relatives or friends or binding children by indenture to apprenticeships as soon as they could work.[40] Advocates believed each new facility was an advancement as it removed children from mixed poorhouses and placed them with overseers exclusively charged with the supervision of youngsters.[41]

New-York's House of Refuge is frequently credited with being the first institution in the U.S. exclusively devoted to juvenile delinquents.[42] Initially founded by Quakers, the House of Refuge was developed following an earlier report issued by the Society for the Prevention of Pauperism in 1823, linking juvenile delinquency to pauperism. The report called attention to the fact that in a mere five years, "the number of youth under fourteen years of age charged with offenses against the law, has doubled" and that "the same boys are again and again brought up for examination."[43] Furthermore, it documented the appearance of several hundred children between the ages of seven and fourteen in criminal court, many of them homeless, poor, or abandoned.[44] The innovative proposal called for building a House of Refuge exclusively "for young convicts . . . where juvenile delinquents might be reformed" rather than mixed with adult prison populations only to be turned into hardened criminals.[45] Despite this supposed focus on juvenile delinquency, the House of Refuge, as its name suggests, "cast a wide net" and included "poor, idle, and 'vagabond' children" even though they "may not have been convicted of any specific crimes."[46] In essence, the House of Refuge functioned much like a general almshouse for young people. Its inmates consisted of a mixture of poor, homeless, and misbehaving children.

In a continuing effort to consolidate and isolate the poor, by the mid-nineteenth century, a spate of new congregate care institutions were erected on two islands in the East River. On Blackwell Island, four separate buildings for adults were introduced, including two almshouses—one for men and another for women—a penitentiary, and an insane asylum.[47] Children were relegated to the nearby Randall's Island. By 1848, ten brick buildings had been erected, which collectively became known as the Randall's Island Nurseries. Technically the children housed there were "still in the city almshouse, under the poor authorities of the city" despite their geographic isolation.[48] The nurseries quickly filled with over one thousand children, including infants, orphans, and dependent, vagrant, and homeless youth, in addition to those who had come to the attention of the police. In 1854, the privately run House of Refuge was relocated to Randall Island from Manhattan.[49] In short, by the mid-nineteenth century Randall Island was exclusively devoted to warehousing poor children.

***

Penal Character and Discipline within Child Asylums

Rothman has argued that asylum advocates for both adults and children "shared an intense faith in the rehabilitative powers of a carefully designed environment."[50] For children, the facilities were not only a place of shelter but also a place for training, discipline, and rehabilitation.[51] Despite the rhetoric of reform, evidence abounds that the institutions quickly took on characteristics associated with prisons. The managers of children's asylums shared a belief that "a daily routine of strict and steady discipline would transform inmates' character" and that the "asylum's primary task was to teach an absolute respect for authority."[52]

As Rothman has shown, this was done through "the establishment and enforcement of a rigorous and orderly routine."[53] Children's freedom was constrained. Days were carefully divided into predictable segments with bells signaling their beginning and end. Even minor transgressions were met with harsh disciplinary measures. House of Refuge records from the earliest years show that "few inmates in the course of their incarceration escaped the whip, the ball and chain, or solitary confinement."[54] Corporal punishment was routine, and restraints such as handcuffs or leg irons were not unusual. Lesser disciplinary measures included being sent to bed without supper or forced to drink "bitter herb tea," which caused the inmates "to sweat profusely."[55] In short, the methods of practice within asylums quickly assumed a punitive character.

Brace is well recognized for being an outspoken critic of child asylums as well as their methods of child discipline and control. Historians of all stripes have recorded Brace's vehement opposition. Paul Boyer wrote, "From the 1850s on, the asylum movement had no more outspoken and influential critic than Charles Loring Brace."[56] Rothman noted that "Brace claimed that the prison atmosphere of the reformatories—and for that matter of many of the orphan asylums—was a predictable phenomenon. This tone, he insisted, was endemic to a system of institutionalization, an inevitable result of rigid punishments, large dormitories, a precise schedule, and the rest."[57] Rothman concluded that Brace was "essentially correct in identifying the problem with the founding ideology."[58]

Among other criticisms, Brace claimed that the longer a child was in an asylum, "the less likely he is to do well in outside life."[59] Similarly, Boyer noted that Brace repudiated the asylum's "obsession with discipline, conformity, and hierarchal authority." Brace contended that the "drilled and machine-like institutional child" would only become "monastic, indolent, [and] unused to struggle," possessing little of the "independence and manly vigor" necessary for "practical life."[60] Christine Stansell has noted that Brace not only opposed practices associated with the asylum but that he also believed that "standards of desirable behavior could be internalized by children rather than beaten into them."[61] Thomas Bender characterized Brace's entire mission as one of discovering "a method for helping young people prune dangerous impulses" and not "plant mechanical virtues."[62]

Taken together, these reflections on Brace's position on asylums and the practices employed within them are significant for five reasons. First, Brace opposed institutional care that isolated children from the social environment where they would learn from experience. Second, he objected to the regimented life and discipline-driven practices employed within the facilities themselves. Third, he believed children could better internalize good behavior with general guidance offered by adults free from institutional constraints. Fourth, he believed the longer the child was in an institution the less likely the child's success in the long term. Fifth, he was more interested in preventing juvenile delinquency by pruning "dangerous impulses" than punishing youth for minor transgressions.

***

Reliance on Indenture and Contractual Rights

Another feature of these child asylums, less often discussed in the historical literature but worthy of note, is that many relied, in part, on indenturing or binding out their child inmates for periods of time. Catherine J. Ross has noted that "the master-apprentice relationship had long served as the legal substitute for adoption" or as a method of caring for poor children.[63] With the increase in child-oriented asylums the practice was adopted as a matter of institutional policy by asylum managers and trustees. Indenture served three related needs. First, it made "some person or family" responsible for both supporting and caring for the child. Second, it merely extended "a social procedure already commonly employed."[64] Third, it tutored children about labor skills and work ethic.

As this practice spread, questions were asked about the rights and responsibilities of various actors in the system as well as the legal authority for the custody and control of children. For example, in 1809, the New-York Legislature empowered the Board of Trustees of the Orphan Asylum with the ability to bind by indenture its children "without taking the parties before the police."[65] Girls could be bound out as house servants until the age of 18 and boys, as servants until aged 15, when they could be bound out again as "apprentices to virtuous mechanics in the hope of their becoming useful and happy members of the community."[66]

Yet as the use of contract labor and indenture expanded beyond the orphanage to other types of child asylums, the rights of living parents were also curtailed. Of particular importance was a legal decision in 1839, Ex parte *Crouse*, by the Pennsylvania Supreme Court in which a father challenged the constitutionality of the Philadelphia House of Refuge manager's detention of his daughter without jury trial. The court not only found that the facility was "not a prison, but a school" and therefore did not require a trial, but also the following:

> The object of the charity is reformation, by training its inmates to industry; by imbuing their minds with principles of morality and religion; by furnishing them with means to earn a living; and, above all, by separating them from the corrupting influence of improper associates. To this end may not the natural parents, when unequal to the task of education, or unworthy of it, be superseded by the *parens patriae*, or common guardian of the community?[67]

The court went on to hold that "the right of parental control" was "a natural, but not an unalienable one." This legal doctrine, known as *parens patriae*, provided the legal justification for charity worker intrusion on parental rights. It was based on the presumption of parental unfitness and neglect.

In New-York, Rothman reported, "Parents lost all prerogatives upon the child's commitment" and "officials had sole discretion over delinquents until their age of majority" for any child placed in the House of Refuge.[68] Furthermore, children were "hired out by contract to businessmen who submitted closed bids for the labor of the boys."[69] In 1875, New-York passed a law which officially extended the authority to indenture children to private and public "associations and societies" but also placed legal custody in the hands of the "asylum instead of the parents until the indenture ended" and required a judge "to approve the signing of the contract."[70] In short, as the practice of indenturing children was increasingly utilized by public and private institutions, the rights of parents were diminished; the role of the courts was formalized; and the police power of the municipality was expanded to include trustees and managers of the child asylums through the doctrine of *parens patriae*.

Charles Loring Brace was as adamantly opposed to indenturing children as he was to committing them to asylums in the first place. Interestingly, historians often register his opposition to indenture exclusively in the scholarship on emigration rather than within the context of juvenile delinquency discussions. Nonetheless, his opposition to jural intervention was part of a larger and more comprehensive theory of practice.

***

CAS Nexus: Juvenile Delinquency and Placing Out

Importantly, all of the scholarship on CAS at the nexus of the juvenile delinquency and the placing out system rests on a simplistic and reductionist narrative trope. It goes like this: Brace opposed the asylum system but was an avid and enthusiastic supporter of placing out. For example, in a single sentence Rothman credits Brace as being a "leading exponent and publicist for this critique" on asylums "as well as one of the first reformers to organize a placing-out program."[71] Bender argued that "what remains most vital in Brace's thoughts and work is his articulation of an alternative to institutional care for deviant and dependent children" in his placing out work.[72] Steven Mintz reminded readers that "however repugnant the orphan train idea may seem to us today, many reformers shared Brace's view that it offered a positive substitute for institutional placement."[73] In short, Brace is repeatedly characterized by this relatively easy and formulaic narrative that pits one type of institutional intervention directly against another. One reason for this is that Brace himself tended to use his rejection of the asylum model as a direct defense of—or justification for—his emigration branch. However, much is lost in this framing.

Formulation as an either–or proposition deflects attention from the fact that CAS was operating a half dozen congregate care facilities for sheltering children in New-York in addition to its emigration work. Brace called these facilities *lodging houses*, not asylums, and referred to those residing within them as *lodgers*, not inmates. In doing so, he intentionally and strategically kept them conceptually distinct from the almshouses and asylums associated with the poor. Nonetheless, like the child asylums, his lodging houses sheltered hundreds of children every night. The children's situations were akin to the situations of those children committed to city asylums. In fact, the records indicate that Brace's workers located prospective child lodgers by intervening with police officers, visiting courts, and retrieving children from Randall's Island, as well as municipal prisons and jails, whenever possible.

A reasonable set of questions arises: Why have Brace's lodging houses completely escaped historical comparison with child asylums? Why haven't the lodging houses been discussed in the context of juvenile delinquency literature? Arguably, the answer lies in the fact that they were so dramatically different in nature, and operated from such a different set of principles, that such comparisons seem misplaced.

Prime among these differences was that children at CAS lodging houses could come and go freely. No legal authority or charity workers required them to be there. Engagement practices were rooted in persuasion, not coercion. The lodging houses rejected rigid schedules (although they maintained evening curfews) and harsh discipline. Children's minor transgressions were deemed learning opportunities. The practices were built around Brace's deep-seated belief that children better internalized good behavior in a natural environment with guidance from adults.

The lodging houses provided safe, clean dormitories but staff also distributed clothing and eventually offered simple meals. Evening classes and Sunday meetings were conducted, but attendance was not required, although incentives were sometimes built into the program (such as offering a free dinner to those who attended the Sunday meeting). Children were charged a small entrance fee (although no truly needy child was turned away) and encouraged to participate in a "savings bank" designed to teach responsibility and independent living skills. The youth worked during the day—not through indenture—by choosing their own occupations, sometimes with the help of CAS staff, who made employment referrals.

In short, although the lodging houses offered shelter care to hundreds of children a night, the operating principles, organizational structure, and practice methods employed were radically different than those associated with child asylums. In fact, the entire design was built around Brace's objections to the asylums. The lodging houses enacted Brace's program of "pruning dangerous impulses" and rejecting rigid structures. They were his response to both juvenile delinquency and poverty. His focus was on prevention rather than control and punishment. In fact, the lodging house design reflected the practical application of Brace's entire critique of asylums.

Nonetheless, existing historical scholarship virtually skips over these lodging house facilities in preference to examining CAS's emigration branch. This area dominates our existing understanding of Brace's contributions.

***

Placing Out: Philanthropic Abduction or Normative Practice?

Overall, Brace is credited with playing a leading role in what historians have called—I would argue very misleadingly—the "orphan train movement." Those who study this movement broadly often combine the efforts of dozens of different charity organizations engaged in similar practices (many with different internal policies) and consign and replace nearly a century's worth of developments into a single monolithic movement. Nonetheless, Brace's contributions to the early roots of the movement are universally acknowledged.

Most of these historiographies are constructed from theoretical perspectives that cast charity workers, or "child savers," as self-appointed agents of moral control. Bruce Bellingham—who is a critic of this general interpretation—characterizes these narratives as often hostile to charity workers. Specifically in regard to CAS's emigration department, he writes, "Yes, this argument runs, Brace sympathized with mourning mothers and sick parents but his solution was to raise the family tragedy of filial deprivation to a deliberate policy of philanthropic abduction."[74]

An illustration of this philanthropic abduction narrative can be found in Boyer's classic work on the urban masses and moral control. Part of his thesis rests on the argument that Brace "welcomed the social upheaval wrought by urbanization" as a destructive force on family cohesion which then freed children to break free.[75] In line with his theoretical orientation, Boyer argued that "one can better understand Brace's attitude toward the children who roamed the streets of New-York" not as "pathetic victims of a cruel and unheeding metropolis but exceptional individuals who . . . had managed to shake off a debased and stultifying family environment." Given this, "the duty of the reformers was not to try to reconstitute that shattered family . . . but to complete the break to freedom the child had already begun."[76] Boyer wrote that Brace failed to understand "well-founded fears" of parents about "an urban order in which the frayed bonds of family, community, and church could be severed with a single stroke by a charitable organization determined to release slum children from the few social strands still holding them, thus granting them the ambiguous gift of total freedom."[77] Boyer concluded that "Brace plunged with enormous zest into his campaign to release the slum family's grip upon its ablest members."[78]

Boyer's thesis carries with it a plethora of untested hypotheses not only about Brace and his agency but also about the families and children with which he worked. In so doing, philanthropic abduction narratives such as this one do considerable damage to the reputation of Brace and his agency.

Bellingham leads the way in challenging this kind of abduction narrative in his sustained and meticulous investigation of CAS's internal emigration documents.[79] Importantly, after careful scrutiny, he found that CAS's placing out system was not an unwelcome or hostile intrusion on happily functioning families but, in fact, reproduced normative family practices of delegating custodial care during times of economic or personal hardship. In the end, Bellingham concluded "that policy ambitions to police families, transform character, socialize reproduction, colonize private life, inculcate labor discipline, and so forth" which have been used to structure the social control narratives "had little to do with the actual practice of child saving" by CAS.[80] In short, his investigation starkly contradicts the very essence of the philanthropic abduction narratives.

Building on Bellingham's study, I tease out six problematic assumptions which tend to be embedded in the philanthropic abduction narratives, based on evidence from CAS records. It is important to remember that dozens of different charitable societies were engaged in similar practices and it is possible that some of them may have been guilty of the offenses claimed in the abduction narratives. However, careful investigation of CAS emigration records not only challenges these narratives, but also substantially contradicts them.

First is the proposition that charity workers took a hostile view of poor parents. The argument is that they perceived poor parents as universally unfit, neglectful, inadequate, subhuman, or criminal and that this unfitness provided them a justification for their aggressive child removal tactics. This assumption doesn't withstand empirical scrutiny when applied to CAS. In Platt's work on delinquency he noted that Brace's attitudes to parents, unlike the attitudes of other reformers who believed poor children often came from criminal stock, were the exception to the rule.[81] Bellingham concluded, "Others have noted the CAS's hostile description of children's parents, but I found that the problem of neglectful, abandoning parenting was substantially made up."[82]

In fact, most evidence points to Brace being well versed in the complicated factors contributing to family stress. He was often sympathetic to parents. Brace wrote the following about them:

> The majority are not ... criminals, but of honest people made suddenly unfortunate.... Parents die suddenly and leave their offspring adrift on the streets; persons in good circumstances are brought to poverty and their families fall into vagrancy; husbands separate from wives, and the boys go forth to cut their own way; step-mothers or step-fathers neglect the children of the former marriage.... The honest poor cannot earn bread for their little ones.... It often happens too that a widow is left with sons who are not vicious, but with strong, pleasure-loving temperaments, whom she cannot control.... Or differences occur between father and mother on religious subjects, and the daughters rush forth to find a more peaceful home elsewhere. Intoxicating liquor breaks up innumerable homes.[83]

With the possible exception of Brace's allusions to stepparent neglect of nonbiological offspring and parental use of liquor, the family problems he identified have little to do with the child neglect, poor parenting, and criminality that permeate philanthropic abduction historiographies.

A second untested assumption embedded in philanthropic abduction narratives is that the primary interest of poor families was in the continuity of child custody. Thus, in these narratives, placing out children reflected a radical intervention that forcibly broke up families, substantially disrupting the lives of all involved. Bellingham writes, "These accounts of domination assume parents had an interest in filial continuity that lost out to the hegemonic interest (variously constructed) of power holders (variously identified) in promoting family permeability to 'tutelary' or control strategies."

Upon investigation, Bellingham found exactly the opposite.[84] He demonstrated that placing out was merely an extension of normative coping strategies used by poor families in an era when discontinuity of custodial care was common. In fact, charity workers functioned as "surrogates for kin on whom parents normally relied in searching for foster care during hard times."[85] In this regard CAS supplemented and aided family practices rather than interfered with family functioning and well-being. Bellingham found, rather than an abrupt and radical departure from the norm, that there was "much mutual accommodation of helper to helped and few dramatic changes in the trajectory of the children's careers."[86] In fact, he argued that "judged against the standard of what the families would have done anyway," placing out "was not much of an intervention" at all.[87]

Bellingham concluded that placing out was an extension of normative family practices and "that custody surrenders were voluntary and that they jibed with parent interests."[88] Further, he hypothesized that "given the survivorship problems attending high death rates and other structural conditions of working-class misery in the nineteenth century city" parents "might . . . even have welcomed the placing-out of their children as a benefit to the child, helping him or her negotiate some life course transition."[89]

In fact, internal evidence in CAS records points to parents and kin having actively sought out the help of CAS. In addition, the agency's written policy—which appears to have been substantially enforced—required parental or guardian consent before CAS agents could place children out. In short, the documented relationship with poor parents coupled with Brace's understanding of their struggles undermine basic assumptions commonly asserted in philanthropic abduction narratives.

The third assumption in the narratives is that children's lives were changed for the worse because of their removal. Bellingham noted that "the hostile formulation that parents who delegated care of their children exposed them to 'greater risks' begs the question: greater than what?" He concluded that "the only sensible yardstick is whether the hazards were greater than those that would have followed from not delegating."[90] Yet historiographers have rarely grappled with the very reasonable question of what might have happened to these children had they been left to fend for themselves in New-York, or had poor families been left to cope with the hardship of too many children—often far from their homelands and communities of support and among strangers—by themselves. While it is impossible to definitively answer these hypothetical what-if questions, an equally valid hypothesis might be that leaving children and families to struggle on their own would have led to worse outcomes and greater suffering.

Fourth, champions of the philanthropic abduction narratives tend to be unduly swayed, and even distracted, by rhetorical choices used by charity workers rather than investigating actual practices. For example, Brace himself admitted he used the words *farmers* or *farm families* as a proxy for a variety of employment situations unrelated to farming. He used *newsboy* to distract the public from more derogatory delinquency framings. Furthermore, although Brace sometimes referred to *orphans*, Bellingham argued that he was attempting to "promote sentimental adoptions as a child saving intervention" grafted onto "the normal temporary fosterage transactions that poor families pursued independently."[91] In other words, Brace deployed rhetorical strategies in service of his advocacy and institution-building efforts. His use of *orphans* and *adoption* relative to the emigration branch were nearly exclusively used for building public support rather than because they accurately reflected the nature of the children's family structure.

While some charity organizations may have worked exclusively with orphans, CAS certainly did not. So merely referring to the placing out system as the "orphan train movement" propagates a myth. In addition, the fallacy facilitates straw man arguments. For example, Joseph M. Hawes wrote that CAS agents "combed the city for suitable candidates" but when they couldn't find enough, "they placed out children whose parents were still living."[92] The portrait suggests that CAS needed to raid poor families to produce a fresh supply of children to fuel its endeavors. Mintz wrote, "Brace was convinced" that the "children he sent westward were neglected" when "most were neither orphaned nor abandoned."[93] He went on to report dismissively that "roughly half had at least one parent alive."[94] In a variation on this theme, Stansell reported that CAS agents "acknowledged that their 'orphans' were sometimes runaways with fictitious histories."[95]

This superficial and selective examination of the evidence is troubling. Once a narrow focus on orphans is assumed, any deviation can be portrayed as an intrusion, a transgression, a hostile and unwelcome act by charity workers. Having made an a priori decision about the type of child agencies should be placing out, philanthropic abduction theorists are permitted to claim that any child falling outside those conditions supports their conclusion that placing out was in reality a euphemism for child-snatching. Doing so negates the complexity of the problems confronting poor families, ignores the strategies they would have used anyway, and minimizes the significance of the flexible support being offered by CAS in light of a variety of family hardships.

Fifth, in addition to the fictional assumption that the orphan train movement was created exclusively to deal with parentless children is an equally erroneous contention. that placing out was used exclusively for the purposes of adoption or fostering. Vivian A. Zelizer wrote, "Recent evidence suggests that poor urban families used the CAS as a quasi-employment agency for their children." Pointing to Bellingham's analysis, she noted he "shows that the most common single motive for surrendering custody of children to organizations was the children's need for a job."[96]

Not only did CAS place children out for the purpose of providing them employment "in the country" but the agency also found many children employment situations in New-York and the immediate vicinity. In short, work placements in the West were merely part of a continuum of help CAS offered poor children and families in locating suitable employment. In fact, narrowly drawn philanthropic abduction accounts have underestimated the significance of this larger practice. Much like Bellingham's conclusion that placing out merely replicated normative child custody delegation strategies, so, too, CAS's labor placements replicated, and facilitated, normative child labor practices.

Sixth, given this hybrid nature of work-and-family fostering, scholars who have examined the placing out movement tend to underappreciate the distinction between institutions that relied on formal indenture contracting as part of their programmatic practices and those that did not. Brace staunchly and unambiguously opposed indenturing children. In fact, he forcefully asserted his opposition time and again.

Some historians, such as Henry W. Thurston, have argued that this distinction is superficial. He claimed that whether the indenture contract existed or not, the net effect was essentially the same. I argue this misses the more significant point that indenture necessarily involved legal contracting, which altered the rights and responsibilities of all the actors involved. It often required participation by judges and impacted the relative rights of parents, children, and foster parents.

Brace's wholesale rejection of indenturing must be seen as only a small part of a much larger and more important pattern. He rejected all forms of legal or authoritarian intrusion. This was true not only in regard to placing out but also throughout the entire CAS operation. He universally rejected coercive and controlling tactics and respected the individual agency and decision-making of the actors with whom he worked. Taken together, historical accounts of CAS that are anchored in narratives of social and moral control are not consistent with the evidence. CAS was far more supportive of poor children and their families than either the philanthropic abduction narratives, in particular, or the social and moral control theorists, more generically, would suggest.

***

Charles Loring Brace's Innovations: Novel in Combination

Given the disproportionate attention given to CAS's emigration branch, it isn't surprising that Brace's overall innovations are underappreciated. Bender has offered one insight into this shortcoming. While criticizing those who insist Brace's enthusiasm for placing out rested in his attitudes toward urbanization, Bender argued that "by assuming that Brace's advocacy of country homes reflected his anti-urbanism, historians have failed to notice that an increasing percentage of CAS's budget and energies were directed toward helping children who would reside permanently in the city."[97] In fact, CAS operations started in New-York and this work only expanded exponentially over time.

Other scholars who have briefly taken up CAS's New-York–based operations have downplayed Brace's innovations. For example, Thurston argued, Brace was neither the inventor nor originator of "each of the different kinds of work" which were "adopted and used by coordination upon a scale city-wide."[98] He argued that all such strategies had been used previously, were used by other societies, or had been patterned after European counterparts and therefore showed little originality. Similarly, Hawes noted that "in many respects" CAS's industrial schools were "remarkably similar to the ragged and industrial schools of England." However, he went on to note that "what made them different" was "their relationship with the placing-out system."[99]

These observations deserve further scrutiny. First, CAS operations in New-York were arguably even more substantial than operations in the agency's placing out branch. In terms of sheer numbers, CAS worked with far more children in New-York than those it placed in the country. Yet these services have received relatively little historical attention. Second, CAS engaged in a variety of "different kinds of work." This work included operating industrial schools, night schools, lodging houses, and a central office and engaging in neighborhood outreach and food and clothing distribution, among other activities. In fact, the emigration branch—so disproportionately represented in the scholarship—was only one department in a much larger CAS child welfare agency. Third, these other services were offered "city-wide." In fact, CAS was not a centralized organization but rather operated its facilities—in particular the lodging houses, night schools, and industrial schools—in dozens of poor neighborhoods scattered throughout the growing city. Unlike efforts to consolidate and isolate the poor on Blackwell and Randall islands, CAS relied on neighborhood-based services and often responded to the unique ethnic needs of the community, such as CAS's long-running Italian and German schools. Fourth, while duly noting that CAS branches were "remarkably similar" to other organizations, scholars have failed to ask a more significant question: how were they different? This is important for two reasons: (i) with each modification the CAS model became uniquely its own, and (ii) the minor adaptations brought each operating branch of service under a consistent agency philosophy. In short, the similarity of practices between individual branches of CAS and other organizations isn't half as interesting or important as the composite picture created by examining the agency as a whole. It is only then that Brace's unique vision of social work philanthropy clearly emerges. Finally, these various services were being "used by coordination" or in relationship to all the other branches. Brace himself took note of this final feature and acknowledged its importance. Speaking of the industrial schools, he wrote, "These measures, though imitated in some respects from England, were novel in their combination."[100]

Brace's true innovation lies in the last two factors. Although the individual components of his program may have been analogous to what other charities were doing, each was altered in keeping with his overall philosophy of service. Also, the totality of alterations, coupled with the fact that each was brought together under a single unified umbrella, made them "novel in combination." Altogether, Brace was offering a radically different program based entirely on voluntary participation of the poor and he built an extremely comprehensive child welfare agency.

In fact, CAS offered a stunning array of integrated services, which ameliorated immediate suffering, aided children and families in normative practice under difficult circumstances, and focused on prevention, targeting poverty, illiteracy, and crime. He tackled health disparities as well as income, food, housing, and employment instability. Perhaps even more striking was the fact that CAS sustained this comprehensive set of interventions decade after decade, arguably having a profound impact in reducing child poverty in New-York in the nineteenth century.

***

The Newsboys' Lodging House: An "Asylum" of a Different Stripe

There may be no better way to remedy the limitations and omissions in the existing scholarship on CAS than by focusing attention on the NBLH. It was here that Brace first experimented with an alternative program for street youth that sought to put into practice his unique philosophy on juvenile delinquency and poverty prevention. In the public mind, there was no single population at greater risk for delinquency, a fear Brace happily fanned to garner support for his project.

Examining the NBLH offers an excellent opportunity to see how workers engaged with the boys, adapted practices and policies in response to both successes and failures, and dealt with complex family life. By using the NBLH as anchor, it is possible to investigate CAS's novelty "in combination" and the continuum of care the agency provided. The NBLH was linked to CAS's educational programs, outreach efforts, Sunday meetings, employment referrals, food and clothing distribution, and the emigration branch. It is also possible to see how each modification of these programs bent the design toward Brace's guiding principle of working from persuasion rather than coercion. Practices within the NBLH demonstrate Brace's complete rejection of methods and measures associated with other child asylums. He also disavowed the value of restrictive industrial training in favor of more common educational training. Pedagogy employed at the night school rejected the rigid methods associated with the Free School movement. While the NBLH supplemented the normative practice of helping children find employment, this was done without the legal constraints of indenture. The boys referred to the emigration branch from the NBLH help reveal the nature of its hybrid work-and-fostering function. These boys often stayed in touch with their families and returned to New-York, demonstrating the fluid nature of the system. Similarly, it is possible to trace the range of outcomes associated with boys who were placed out (although it is impossible to make definitive claims about the overall success or failure of the emigration program as a whole).

In short, the NBLH sat squarely within the philosophic mission of the agency. It illustrates how services were delivered, developed, modified, adapted, evaluated, and publicized. In particular, it shows how front-line, day-to-day decisions helped give shape to the agency's overall form and function.

***

In This Book: An Outline of Chapters

In the following chapters, I trace this history and link the development and evolution of the NBLH to CAS's overall design and Brace's overall vision. The chapters are as follows.

Chapter 1, "Mr. Brace's Arrival: Early Influences and New-York, 1848–1853" examines factors shaping the character, intellect, and politics of Charles Loring Brace. Born into a Connecticut family of educators, scientists, clerics, jurists, and abolitionist activists, Brace abhorred dogma, fearlessly challenged convention, and earned a reputation as a "dangerous" thinker. In 1848, the 22-year-old moved to New-York to study at Union Seminary. He volunteered among the poor but was disillusioned with missionary work. More practical solutions were needed. After an eventful European walking tour, Brace's returned to New-York with a heightened sense of urgency in finding a meaningful career.

Chapter 2, "Family Life in Mid-Nineteenth-Century New-York" describes the living and working conditions of poor families, with a focus on children. As desperate immigrants—particularly Irish Catholics fleeing famine—poured into the little island of Manhattan, wealthy landlords were profiting from new experimental housing structures called tenant houses. Tenement conditions in and around these unregulated, multifamily dwellings were horrific. Poor families eked out a living. and child labor was essential. Child street traders, particularly newsboys, were ubiquitous. With the death or desertion of parents, child vagrancy and youth homelessness were common, as was juvenile delinquency. In this context, Charles Loring Brace received a handwritten invitation to head a new mission for poor children.

Chapter 3, "Creating the Children's Aid Society: Exploration and Experimentation" describes the establishment of CAS, Charles Loring Brace's earliest activities, and the trustees' role in shaping agency policy. Brace was appointed CAS's first secretary in 1853. He immediately set to work systematically collecting evidence about child poverty and experimenting with programs such as a shoe pegging workshop, boys' meetings, and industrial schools for girls. As funding trickled in, Brace hired visiting agents to scour poor neighborhoods and establish relationships with poor families and homeless children. During a nighttime excursion, Brace was particularly intrigued by the newsboys he saw. They were entrepreneurial and hardworking but also prone to drinking, gambling, and sleeping out. In them Brace saw the perfect poster child for CAS. He set his sights on establishing an experimental lodging house for newsboys to enact his alternative to the House of Refuge and his own ideas about preventing juvenile delinquency.

Chapter 4, "Opening the Newsboys' Lodging House: Proposal to Practice, 1854" describes its first formative year under the guidance of Superintendent Charles Tracy. Situated on the top floor, the NBLH had windows providing light and ventilation, gas lighting, and an indoor washroom, amenities that were not available in tenements housing the poor. Program participation was voluntary, unlike that of juvenile asylums. The rules were minimal: orphans only, curfew, no intoxication, and a fee of six cents a night designed to foster responsibility. Tracy quickly established a reputation for fair dealing. Adaptations were required. Boys arrived claiming abusive parents, came in "short" their six-cent fee, and arrived after curfew or drunk. Tracy's daily decisions gave shape to NBLH policies and practices but demonstrate flexibility, often tailoring decisions to the unique developmental needs of each child. The NBLH served as a model and CAS soon launched a half dozen more lodging houses for boys and girls.

Chapter 5, "Eddying Point: Mr. Macy's Central Office" illustrates the eclectic responsibilities of Jared Macy, assistant secretary of CAS, as he coordinated the society's ever-expanding efforts from the CAS central office. The office was an eddying point between rich and poor. Macy entertained wealthy volunteers, philanthropists, and employers as well as poor children and needy families. This chapter examines the central office's link to the NBLH and illustrates how it facilitated intra-agency referrals. Macy sent boys needing shelter to the NBLH. In turn, the NBLH staff referred boys with disabilities, those seeking employment, and boys being screened for placement in the country through the emigration branch to Macy. His duties included distributing food and clothing to poor children. He accounted for cash and in-kind donations (e.g., books, bed sheets, and bathtubs) and oversaw their distribution among CAS's lodging houses, industrial schools, and evening schools. Like an experienced ringmaster, Macy managed the entire flow for the rapidly growing agency.

Chapter 6, "The Earliest Newsboys' Lodging House Residents: The Good and the Bad, 1855–1856" portrays the lodgers' backgrounds and daily lives as street traders. This colorful group included Fatty, a rotund boy who folded newspapers; Little Booch, a "fancy" match seller; the Professor, a beloved good Samaritan and perpetual wanderer; and Johnnie, an aspiring seminary student. Most were honest and hardworking. A few such as Cogan, an "incorrigible scapegrace," and Patterson, banished from New-York by court order, seemed on a dangerous path toward juvenile delinquency and illustrates CAS's prevention efforts. Despite the predominance of Irish Catholics, lodgers included Protestants and a few Jews, white and occasionally black, both U.S. and foreign born. With the rise of nativist and anti-immigrant movements and the approaching Civil War, NBLH staff had to keep the peace among lodgers as well as maintain public support in a country and city increasingly divided.

Chapter 7, "Advancing the Lines: Building an Anti-Poverty Agenda, Newsboys' Lodging House, 1855–1861" examines lodging house Superintendent Charles Tracy's techniques for initiating evening activities designed to foster wary vagrant boys' independence. He creatively introduced the idea of a debate club, a savings bank, common education classes, and Sunday meetings. Evening classes were held in spelling, reading, composition, orthography, history, and singing. Classes were a source of laughter as well as learning. The monthly opening of the Newsboys' Savings Bank was a celebrated affair. Occasionally the lecture room was converted into a gymnasium or dance hall. The talented Tracy was quickly promoted by CAS to help develop an experimental western emigration program. Briefly destabilized by its lack of leadership, the NBLH was soon back on course with the hiring of Charles O'Connor and his wife, Mary O'Connor, as the new superintendent and matron.

Chapter 8, "Mr. Macy's Record Books: Newsboy Lodgers and the Emigration Branch, 1861–1866" explores the link between the NBLH and CAS's placing out program during the tumultuous Civil War years. Brace believed country life was healthier than urban life and offered unique opportunities because of labor scarcity in the West. Some were immediately swept up in the Civil War. Others were integrated into family life or found employment. Some ran away. Others stole cash or property. Nonetheless, Brace defended the emigration branch against both Catholics, who accused him of proselytizing, and the "asylum interest," which favored placing children in reformatories or indenturing them. Nonetheless, Brace worried about "muscular orphans," older boys ill prepared for country life.

Chapter 9, "Permanent Place: Building, Bridging, and Policy Advocacy in the Gilded Age" recounts how, after the Civil War, the firmly established CAS began investing in real estate, engaging in policy advocacy, and calling on wealthy New-Yorkers to attend to the poor. The NBLH was overflowing with orphaned and half-orphaned children. CAS trustees commissioned an architect to design a new facility exclusively tailored to its needs. Opened in 1874, the seven-floor building had a schoolroom, gymnasium, dining hall, laundry facilities, servant hall, and quarters for the superintendent's family. While sharing physical characteristics with asylums, the program continued to operate exclusively on the voluntary participation of the lodgers. The trustees also turned to policy reform, drafting a progressive child labor bill in 1871 and advocating for compulsory education, school funding, and boarding house regulations. At the same time, wealthy New-Yorkers were urged to donate funds and actively volunteer among the children in the belief that exposure would help combat the growing class schism during the Gilded Age.

Chapter 10, "The Society Mr. Brace Built: A Life's Work" summarizes Charles Loring Brace's work, examines the breadth and impact of the Children's Aid Society. At Brace's death in 1890, CAS was a massive, multiprogrammed child welfare agency that had served poor children for nearly forty years. Arguably, CAS's impact on child poverty in New-York during the latter half of the nineteenth century was enormous. In the aftermath of Brace's death, the NBLH was renamed the Brace Memorial Lodging House. Thus, starting a new chapter for the lodging house as well as for CAS, with Brace's son, C. Loring Brace at its helm.

The "Afterword" identifies limitations in historical characterizes of Brace's work using an "either–or" narrative trope, pitting his opposition to child asylums, associated with development of the modern juvenile justice system, against his embrace of placing out, associated with the development of child protective services. His legacy suffers by undervaluing contributions in five areas: CAS operated an extensive network of urban programs, bridging urban-rural divides; lodging houses were a radical new modality contrasting directly with asylums; CAS's connected branches of service were novel, resulting in intra-agency referral and a continuum of care; the entirety rested on voluntary participation, soundly rejecting common policing practices; and Brace actively attempted to bridge class divides. Today, CAS would encompass our runaway and homeless services networks, child welfare, public education, labor interventions, and social safety net programs, while opposing juvenile or criminal justice involvement. Brace's focus was on prevention and sustained comprehensive aid. Herein lie lessons for modern practitioners.

***

Concluding Observations

Many social work and social welfare histories place the beginning of the profession at the turn of the twentieth century, during the Progressive Era. There are good reasons for doing so. It was at this point when the lines between juvenile delinquency and child fostering began crystalizing into separate formalized legal institutions.

Nonetheless, I would argue there is good reason to revisit the work done nearly a half century earlier. Brace worked at the crucible of myriad social ills before they became compartmentalized and packaged into separately recognized public problems. He was an early resister of what would develop into jural institutions associated with the social control accounts of charity work and the police power of the state, including today's juvenile justice and child protective service systems. The existence of both of these institutions was ultimately justified, in large part, by the legal doctrine of *parens patriae*. However, Brace was opposed, in principle, to these tactics and the underlying assumptions about parents and children upon which they were based.

Viewed in its entirety, Brace's plan offered a holistic and comprehensive agenda for intervention. It was as ambitious in size as it was in scope. The various CAS programs and branches worked separately but always with a common philosophical mission and set of core principles as envisioned by Brace. It was a plan built on supporting poor children (and, by extension, their families) by alleviating their immediate suffering but also offering pathways out of poverty with an eye on cultivating their longer-term success. At the same time as Brace aided poor children, he also sought to goad, cajole, bully, and threaten rich New-Yorkers and other Christian families into caring about the less fortunate. He continually reminded the rich that these poor children were no different than their very own but for the accident of their birth.

Although it may be dangerous to conflate the views of an entire sprawling agency with the views of one man, there are certain reasons for directly linking the two. Brace was the undisputed intellectual architect of the overall design. He put the basic policies in place, even if others interpreted and implemented the details. He oversaw the society's operations and was its public spokesperson. Additionally, Brace family members, including his brother, wife, and sons, worked for the agency, expanding the family influence. On Brace's death in 1890, his son, C. Loring Brace, would be appointed the society's second secretary. The result was that a Brace family member would be at the helm of CAS for its first eighty-six years of existence. One CAS report elegantly summed up this relationship: "The Brace family and the CAS have been all bound round with a woolen string. No one has known where the Braces ended and where the CAS began, and no one could know for they have been parts of each other."

After Charles Loring Brace's death in 1890, his wife of thirty-six years wrote a letter to an old friend. She asked him if he had any remembrances of her late husband that predated the day she had met the two of them for the first time in Belfast in 1850. The man, Frederick Law Olmsted, had counted

Brace among his best friends since boyhood. Olmsted wrote back at length. Among other reflections, he remembered that Brace's "interest in humane undertaking" was so notable that "shortly after he left college, and before he took a leading part in any organized movement," Olmsted had jokingly dubbed him "My Dear Philanthropist."[101] Of course, Olmsted—known as a father of landscape architecture—left his own mark on New-York. Among his greatest legacies is Central Park. Olmsted permanently altered the terrain of the city and made enormous contributions to his chosen profession. His close friend, the "dear philanthropist," did so as well. Arguably, Brace's impact on the city and on his profession of applied philanthropy, or social work, was no less significant in scope or historic influence. Brace's handiwork is merely less visible to the public eye. Uncovering his contribution requires some archeological excavation of New-York's layers.

Notes

1. *The Great Metropolis; or Guide to New-York for 1847* (New York: H. Wilson, 1847), 53.
2. Technically the East River is not a river but rather a tidal tributary. This is significant if you have to navigate its waters or in times of extreme weather events, like hurricanes. However, for the purposes of day-to-day life, most New Yorkers merely talk about it as the East River.
3. James Trager, *The New York Chronology: The Ultimate Compendium of Events, People and Anecdotes from the Dutch to the Present* (New York: Harper Resource, 2003), 94.
4. For example, during the winter of 1845–1846, the Hudson River was closed at Albany for 107 days, from December 3, 1845, through March 20, 1846. *The Great Metropolis*, 66.
5. Herbert Asbury, *All Around the Town: Murder, Scandal, Riot and Mayhem in Old New York* (Repr., New York: Thunder's Mouth Press, 1934), 141.
6. Glen P. Corbett and Donald J. Cannon, *Historic Fires of New York City* (Chicago: Arcadia, 2005), 18–21; Donald Mackay, *The Building of Manhattan* (New York: Dover, 1987), 23.
7. Corbett and Cannon, *Historic Fires*, 18–21; Mackay, *The Building of Manhattan*, 23.
8. Asbury, *All Around the Town*, 143.
9. Corbett and Cannon, *Historic Fires*, 36.
10. Corbett and Cannon, *Historic Fires*, 19.
11. Asbury, *All Around the Town*, 141–142.
12. Asbury, *All Around the Town*, 143.
13. The distributing reservoir of the Croton Water Works was located on the land where the Midtown branch of the New York Public Library now stands. Remnants of the base of the original holding tank can still be seen in the library's foundation.

14. Charles Dickens, *American Notes, New York* (New York: John W. Lowell, 1883), 70.
15. *The Great Metropolis*, 55.
16. *The Great Metropolis*, 56.
17. *Report of the Council of Hygiene and Public Health of the Citizens' Association of New York upon the Sanitary Conditions of the City* (New York: D. Appleton, 1866), 175, 177.
18. *Report of the Council of Hygiene and Public Health*, 175, 177.
19. Andrew S. Dolkart, *Biography of a Tenement House in New York*, 2nd ed. (Chicago: Center for American Places at Columbia College Chicago, 2012), 28.
20. Corbett and Cannon *Historic Fires*, 47.
21. *Thirty-Eighth Annual Report of the Children's Aid Society* (New York: Wynkoop, Hallenbeck, 1890), 3.
22. *Thirty-Eighth Annual Report*, 11.
23. *Thirty-Eighth Annual Report*, 1–2.
24. Thomas Bender, *New York Intellect: A History of Intellectual Life in New York City from 1750 to the Beginning of Our Own Time* (Baltimore: Johns Hopkins University Press, 1987).
25. Thomas Bender, *Community and Social Change in America* (Baltimore: Johns Hopkins University Press, 1978).
26. Richard Hofstadter, *Social Darwinism in American Thought* (1944; repr., Boston: Beacon Press, 1992).
27. Bruce Bellingham, "Institution and Family: An Alternative View of Nineteenth Century Child Saving," *Social Problems* 33, no. 6 (December 1986); Bruce Bellingham, "Waifs and Strays: Child Abandonment, Foster Care, and Families in Mid-Nineteenth Century New York," in *The Uses of Charity: The Poor on Relief in the Nineteenth-Century Metropolis*, ed. Peter Mandler (Philadelphia: University of Pennsylvania Press, 1990); Bruce Bellingham, "Little Wanderers: A Socio-Historical Study of the Nineteenth Century Origins of Child Fostering and Adoption Reform, Based on Early Records of the New York Children's Aid Society." PhD diss., University of Pennsylvania, 1984.
28. Christine Stansell, *City of Women: Sex and Class in New York, 1789–1860* (New York: Alfred A. Knopf, 1986).
29. Paul Boyer, *Urban Masses and Moral Order in America, 1820–1920* (Cambridge, MA: Harvard University Press, 1978).
30. Thomas Bender, *Toward an Urban Vision: Ideas and Institutions in Nineteenth Century America* (Baltimore: Johns Hopkins University Press, 1975).
31. Vivian A. Zelizer, *Pricing the Priceless Child: The Changing Value of Children* (New York: Basic Books, 1985).
32. David J. Rothman, *The Discovery of the Asylum*, rev. ed. (New York: Aldine de Gruyter, 2002; Anthony M. Platt, *The Child Savers: The Invention of Delinquency*, 40th ed. (New Brunswick, NJ: Rutgers University Press, 2009); Joseph M. Hawes, *Children in Urban Society: Juvenile Delinquency in Nineteenth-Century America*

(New York: Oxford University Press, 1971); Henry W. Thurston, *The Dependent Child: A Story of Changing Aims and Methods in the Care of Dependent Children* (New York: Columbia University Press, 1930); Alexander W. Pisciotta, "Treatment on Trial: The Rhetoric and Reality of the New York House of Refuge, 1857–1935," *The American Journal of Legal History*, 29, no. 2 (April 1985), 151–181; Bender, *Toward an Urban Vision*, 134–136.

33. Catherine J. Ross, "Society's Children: The Care of Indigent Youngsters in New York City, 1875–1903" in *Families by Law: An Adoption Reader*, ed. Naomi R. Cahn (New York: New York University Press, 2004), 11–18; Miriam Z. Langsam, *Children West: A History of the Placing-Out System of the New York Children's Aid Society, 1853–1890* (Madison: State Historical Society of Wisconsin for Department of History, University of Wisconsin, 1964); Boyer, *Urban Masses and Moral Order*, 132–157.
34. Platt, *The Child Savers*, 4.
35. Platt, *The Child Savers*, 3.
36. Platt *The Child Savers*, 4.
37. Hawes, *Children in Urban Society*, 33.
38. Rothman, *Discovery of the Asylum*, 197.
39. Horn, Stacy *Damnation Island: Poor, Sick, Mad & Criminal in 19th-Century New York* (Chapel Hill, NC: Algonquin Books of Chapel Hill, 2019).
40. Rothman, *Discovery of the Asylum*, 206.
41. Thurston, *The Dependent Child*, 39; Miller, June *Abandoned: Foundlings in Nineteenth-Century New York City* (New York: New York University Press, 2008), 69; Horn, *Damnation Island*, 150–151.
42. Robert S. Pickett, *House of Refuge: Origins of Juvenile Reform in New York State, 1815–1857* (Syracuse, NY: Syracuse University Press, 1969), 26; Pisciotta, "Treatment on Trial," 151–181.
43. Hawes, *Children in Urban Society*, 28.
44. Hawes, *Children in Urban Society*, 28.
45. Hawes, *Children in Urban Society*, 28.
46. Boyer, *Urban Masses and Moral Order*, 95.
47. Miller, *Abandoned Children*, 51.
48. Thurston, *The Dependent Child*, 88.
49. Miller, *Abandoned Children*, 74.
50. Rothman, *Discovery of the Asylum*, 206.
51. Rothman, *Discovery of the Asylum*, 210.
52. Rothman, *Discovery of the Asylum*, 213–214.
53. Rothman, *Discovery of the Asylum*, 213–214.
54. Rothman, *Discovery of the Asylum*, 231.
55. Hawes, *Children in Urban Society*, 47.
56. Boyer, *Urban Masses and Moral Order*, 96.
57. Rothman, *Discovery of the Asylum*, 258–259.

58. Rothman, *Discovery of the Asylum*, 260.
59. Rothman, *Discovery of the Asylum*, 258–259.
60. Boyer, *Urban Masses and Moral Order*, 96.
61. Stansell, *City of Women*, 211.
62. Bender, *Toward an Urban Vision*, 143.
63. Ross, "Society's Children," 16.
64. Thurston, *The Dependent Child*, 12.
65. Thurston, *The Dependent Child*, 46.
66. Thurston, *The Dependent Child*, 46.
67. Ex parte Crouse, 4 Wharton 9 (PA, 1839).
68. Rothman, *Discovery of the Asylum*, 223; Pisciotta, "Treatment on Trial," 151–181.
69. Pisciotta, "Treatment on Trial," 155.
70. Ross, "Society's Children," 12.
71. Rothman, *Discovery of the Asylum*, 258–259.
72. Bender, *New York Intellect*, 198.
73. Mintz, Steven, *Moralists & Modernizers: America's pre-Civil War reformers* (Baltimore: Johns Hopkins Press, 1995), 116.
74. Bellingham, "Institution and Family," 542.
75. Boyer, *Urban Masses and Moral Order*, 101.
76. Boyer, *Urban Masses and Moral Order*, 101.
77. Boyer, *Urban Masses and Moral Order*, 102.
78. Boyer, *Urban Masses and Moral Order*, 101.
79. Bellingham, "Little Wanderers," 343–349.
80. Bellingham, "Waifs and Strays," 129.
81. Platt, *The Child Savers*, 36.
82. Bellingham, "Waifs and Strays," 125.
83. Charles Loring Brace, "The 'Placing Out' Plan for Homeless and Vagrant Children" (Lecture presented at the Conference of Boards of Public Charity, New York, September 7, 1876), 135.
84. I substantially replicate Bellingham's finding using an entirely different sample of CAS emigration records. Bellingham examined the earliest records and did not discriminate between girls and boys. I looked exclusively at the records of boys during the Civil War years. All the boys had stayed at the NBLH prior to placing out. (See Chapter 8 of this volume.) In short, although our sampling strategies differed, our findings were concordant.
85. Bellingham, "Institution and Family," 550.
86. Bellingham, "Waifs and Strays," 125.
87. Bellingham, "Waifs and Strays," 125.
88. Bellingham, "Institution and Family," 550.
89. Bellingham, "Institution and Family," 548.
90. Bellingham, "Waifs and Strays," 126.
91. Bellingham, "Waifs and Strays," 129.

92. Hawes, *Children in Urban Society*, 19.
93. Mintz, *Moralists & Modernizers*, 116.
94. Mintz, *Moralists & Modernizers*, 116.
95. Stansell, *City of Women*, 210.
96. Zelizer, *Pricing the Priceless Child*, 172; Bellingham, Bruce, "Little Wanderers," 119.
97. Bender, *Toward an Urban Vision*, 147.
98. Thurston, *The Dependent Child*, 113.
99. Hawes, *Children in Urban Society*, 89.
100. Thurston, *The Dependent Child*, 113.
101. David Schuyler and Gregory Kaliss, eds., *The Papers of Frederick Law Olmsted: Volume IX: The Last Great Projects, 1890-1895* (Baltimore: Johns Hopkins University Press, 2015), 467.

I

Mr. Brace's Arrival

EARLY INFLUENCES AND NEW-YORK, 1848–1853

> *[The] four young literary thieves . . . all boys between the ages of 9 and 12 years, who were arrested by Officer Stowell of the 4th Ward, having been detected in the act of stealing . . . 500 copies of the Illustrated Magazine, the property of N.H.B. Smith, whose premises the young rascals had broken open. The books were recovered in a basement on the south-west corner of Fulton and Nassau streets where they had been deposited by these thieving newsboys. Justice Osborne committed them all to prison, prior to their being sent to the House of Refuge.*
> —Herald Police Intelligence, 1848

IN SEPTEMBER 1848, when Charles Loring Brace initially set foot in the Great Metropolis—the "London of America" as one travel guide from the era claimed—New-York's first police chief, George Washington Matsell, was still trying to convince the resistant officers of his three-year-old municipal police force to wear uniforms.[1] The best he had been able to muster—and even that, only under threat of immediate dismissal—was getting them to don an "eight-point, star-shaped copper badge."[2] Nonetheless, when it came time for Matsell to write a semi-annual report to Mayor Woodhull in October 1849, Matsell dedicated the entire document not to his efforts to wrangle his "coppers" to order but rather to flag the most serious danger he saw facing the city. It was the "deplorable and growing evil" of "the constantly increasing number of vagrants, idle and vicious children . . . who infest our public thoroughfares, hotels, docks, &c."[3] In the eyes of the brand new police chief, these children were a persuasive and potentially explosive problem. Many established New-Yorkers agreed: the offspring of poor immigrants flooding into the city appeared to be a public menace of enormous, and growing, proportions. At the time, Mr. Brace had no inkling that these very street urchins, so threatening to Chief Matsell, would become his life's work nor that they would provide solutions to his own intellectual curiosity and personal quandaries.[4]

Mr. Brace probably arrived in New-York by taking one of the daily steamship ferries from New Haven. It was the same journey Charles Dickens had documented seven years earlier, although Dickens had little respect for the American version of this vessel, which he described as "a sullen, cumbrous, ungraceful, unshiplike leviathan."[5] The steamship carrying Mr. Brace would have skirted Randall's Island with its municipal nurseries for poor children, then passed through the turbulent "Hell Gate"—a narrow and treacherous tidal strait in the East River where the currents from the Long Island Sound collided unpredictably with currents from the New-York Bay amidst "huge granite boulders" that protruded from "the swirling water"[6]—and next skirted Blackwell's Island, which contained an assortment of asylums, jails, and poor houses for warehousing some of New-York's least desirable adult residents. A little further south and along the east side of the island, he would have passed Bellevue Hospital. Eventually the steamship would have rounded the bulge of southern Manhattan and entered the relatively narrow passageway between Manhattan and Brooklyn as it headed into Peck Slip, just east of City Hall.

Mr. Brace's first view of New-York was likely similar to that of Dickens. Dickens's wrote, "There lay stretched out before us, to the right, a confused heap of buildings, with here and there a spire or steeple . . . and in the foreground a forest of ships' masts, cheery with flapping sails and waving flags."[7] The busy little bay would have been congested with river traffic as Mr. Brace's steamboat tried to make its way safely among the "ferry-boats laden with people, coaches, horses, waggons, baskets, boxes: crossed and re-crossed by other ferry-boats: all travelling to and fro: and never idle."[8] Indeed, no fewer than forty-eight different steamboat lines would have been dodging each other during the day.[9] Also among the small ferry boats and river steamers, there would have been a stately, "two or three large ships, moving with slow majestic pace . . . making for the broad sea" and Atlantic transit.[10] Within a year of Mr. Brace's arrival, the busy little port city of New-York would boast "sixty docks, piers, slips and wharfs" along its East River below Fourteenth Street with another fifty dotting the Hudson River on the west side of the island.[11] Like Dickens, he would have heard "the city's hum and buzz, the clinking of capstans, the ringing of bells, the barking of dogs, the clattering of wheels."[12]

Once on land, Mr. Brace would have had to dodge the helter-skelter movements of vehicles, horses, and pushcarts as well as contend with the congestion of pedestrians, peddlers, and free-ranging livestock, including pigs and chickens. Mr. Brace might have been met by his good friends, the Olmsted brothers, in a private carriage. Or he might have hired a hackney cab or taken one of the eighteen horse-drawn omnibus lines that shuttled people up and down or back or forth across the island.[13] In short, there were a colorful collection of conveyances: hackney cabs, coaches, "gigs, phaetons, large-wheeled tilburies,"[14] and many of these were "built for the heavy roads beyond the city pavement."[15] This was because New-York's paved streets of circular cobblestone could abruptly turn into packed dirt or knee-deep mud, depending on the weather. Despite all of these transportation options, it is probable that the young, athletic Mr. Brace chose instead to hire a "baggage smasher"—most often a vagrant teenage boy—to cart his luggage uptown, while he hiked the distance up Broadway to around Eighth Street on foot.

Mr. Brace arrived in New-York with a sketchy, short-term plan although, truth be told, he also had harbored some very grand ambitions. His immediate strategy was to continue his study of theology at Union Seminary and moonlight as a teacher to pay for his education. He had absolutely no intention of staying in New-York very long. In fact, he confided in friends and relatives that he could probably endure New-York for about a year "but not much more" because certainly, "the novelty must wear away then."[16]

Childhood Shapes a "Dangerous" Man of Reason

Although Mr. Brace arrived with limited means and a skeletal plan for the future, the seeds of the man he would become were already deeply planted. The Brace family could trace its New England ancestry back to the 1660s, and his family lineage included an interconnected web of prominent New England families.[17] On his father's side "were leaders in religious and political life of Connecticut" who had served "the State on the bench, in the pulpit, and in the legislature."[18] On his mother's side, relatives included Lyman Beecher, who sired—among his thirteen children—abolitionist writers, preachers, and the activists Harriett Beecher Stowe, Charles Beecher, and Henry Ward Beecher.

Charles Loring Brace's impressive family connections spun ever outward to include other intellectual and social luminaries. For example, his cousin, Jane Lathrop Loring, married Asa Gray, a preeminent American botanist and Harvard faculty member. Gray would eventually introduce Mr. Brace, as a young man, to the work of his friend and colleague, Charles Darwin. Brace would not only read an advance copy of *Origin of the Species* but would reread the book cover to cover no fewer than thirteen times during his life, returning to it like a scientific Bible.[19] Gray's own work linking theology and evolutionary science would infiltrate Brace's thinking as well. The impact of both Darwin and Gray on Mr. Brace would be enormous. It will help inform Mr. Brace's own benevolent view of social Darwinism reassured by the fact that evolution must work on the moral history of mankind as well as physical thus guaranteeing "the final fruition of human virtue and the perfectibility of man," that aid for the poor was not incompatible with this evolution, and that it was possible to reconcile any apparent tension between theism and science.[20]

Charles Loring Brace—Charley to his family and friends—was born in Litchfield, Connecticut, on June 19, 1826. He was the second of four children, with an older sister, Mary, and two younger siblings, James and Emma. Little is known about his mother, Lucy Porter, who died when Charles was fourteen.[21] However, his father was a major influence in his son Charley's life. John Pierce Brace was a teacher by profession, but he also had an established reputation as a scholar in the natural sciences—particularly in botany and mineralogy.[22] Initially, he supported his family by taking a headmaster job in Litchfield, Connecticut. Later, in 1833, when his son turned seven, the elder Brace moved his family to Hartford, Connecticut, to take a teaching position at the Hartford Female Seminary, a school founded by the eldest of Lyman Beecher's children, Catharine Beecher. Consistent with the general family leanings toward progressive views, the Hartford Female Seminary insisted on using the same unmodified curriculum normally reserved for boys. It was a practice his son would eventually employ as well. Among John Brace's most talented and adoring students would be his own relative through marriage, little Harriet Beecher. She would call the elder Brace "one of the most stimulating and inspiring instructors I ever knew"[23] and grew up to honor her favorite teacher by using him as the character of Mr. Rossiter in her book *Old Town Folks*.

There is no doubt that John Pierce Brace was a gifted teacher and dedicated instructor to all of his female pupils. However, it is unlikely that he had a more eager or hard-working student than his very own son, Charley. The devoted father purportedly read aloud to his son two hours a day for years. The pair spent endless hours in conversation, discussion, and debate over subjects ranging from history to theology, politics, or science. The son would proudly brag to his friends that his Dad was a "Cyclopedia."[24]

Given the elder Brace's love of the natural sciences—and the fact that the Brace family home was within "easy reach of streams and country walks"[25]— it is not surprising that the outdoor environment served as a natural extension of the classroom. Together, father and son spent days at a time exploring the environs, looking for plants, prowling for bugs, examining rocks, and fishing for trout or pickerel. When Charley wasn't exploring with his father, he was likely doing so with his best friend and classmate, John Hull Olmsted, and John's older brother, Frederick Law Olmsted. The trio "did a great deal of rowing and some shooting and angling" together.[26] Later in life, Frederick would recall one afternoon when the three boys made "a fine run of fourteen miles on skates" but it was brought to an abrupt end "in a cold bath" when the ice broke under their collective weight.[27]

These experiences would be imprinted on Charles Loring Brace's character and instill a deep-seated belief in the power of the outdoors. On a personal level, he would find nothing more soothing, inspiring, or healing than an afternoon of fishing or an all-day hike in the country. In 1847 he wrote to a friend that on a recent evening he had looked at the stars and "really saw them" for the first time in months.[28] "There came over me then," he wrote, "partly from will and partly unconsciously, a most awing sense of Infinite Power, and I comprehended my perfect helplessness, as I should go out into that Eternity. The idea would have been overwhelming almost, if it had not been for the remembrance of Christ."[29] Brace believed in the transformative power of nature, but, more significantly, in nature he would also find answers to practical questions. With the abundant and nearly limitless resources of the western frontier, he would see the potential solution for social ills as large as unemployment, poverty, and crime.

Perhaps as a result of these forays into the country with his father, the younger Brace was an avid walker. He thought nothing of tackling the distances between Connecticut cities such as New Milford, Leitchfield, and Sharon on foot, walking twenty miles a day. He once started out at 5:45 in the morning and walked the nearly eighteen miles between Litchfield and Sharon, marshaling on through a steady downpour before arriving in the evening "completely chilled through" but clearly proud of the fact that trip had cost him a grand total of fifty-three-and-a-half cents (thirty-one-and-a-half to have his trunk sent and additional twenty-two cents for "eatables").[30] The return trip turned out to be challenging for a different reason. "How those hills do accumulate just before Litchfield! It seems as if one would never reach the top of that range," he complained in a letter to his father. But he also proudly reported, "my first nine miles I accomplished in two hours . . . pretty good walking that!"[31] The Olmsted brothers sometimes joined Brace on these walking tours. Later in life, Frederick fondly recalled, "I remember once being with him for a week or two on a walk which took us through Litchfield, Stockbridge, and Lenox."[32]

Owing to both training and temperament, Brace was a precocious student. Tutored under the watchful eye of his father, he was well prepared for college by his sixteenth birthday. He easily passed his entry examination at Yale, writing in his private journal, "It was perfectly simple."[31] He and his friend John Olmsted entered Yale together in 1842 and were roommates for four years.[33] Brace graduated in 1846, and he began seminary in New Haven a year later.

As a student and young man, Brace often wrote home seeking guidance from either his father, whom he worshiped, or his younger sister Emma, whom he adored. One of his early struggles was with an attempt to balance the seemingly competing forces of ambition and religious obligation. It was a topic on which he sought advice. In 1843, Brace wrote to his father, "I want to know whether a person can be ambitious and still attend to his Christian duties."[34] Posing a similar question to his younger sister Emma, she responded reassuringly, "I do not see why you cannot be ambitious and at the same time have this feeling in subservience to God's will; why cannot you perform your duties to God at the same time, and ask his blessing upon your efforts."[35]

This struggle is visible in the young college student's decision to enter an essay competition in 1843. Although several topics were available, the ambitious Brace selected the subject of moral philosophy because he deemed it "more difficult and more beneficial for me to write upon."[36] However, he admitted to his father that he did not want to write on it "theoretically" but rather "to view it practically."[37] The younger Brace sketched out his ideas, predicting his essay would have something to do with the relationship "of man to society, to himself and his God."[38] Still further he explained he planned to look at the link between moral philosophy and the way it "cooperate[s] with Christianity," its link to "continued improvement," and, perhaps most significantly of all in historic hindsight, "its influences on the evils now threatening our country."[39] This triumvirate of self, society, and God, and negotiating the appropriate balance among them, showed seeds of a personal project that would occupy him for the rest of his life. In these nascent expressions, Mr. Brace began to shape a life philosophy, a principled blueprint for living a moral life through practical service.

Not surprisingly, the various personal and educational threads that twined to create Charley Brace produced a free and independent thinker. He composed his arguments thoughtfully but then subjected them to critique. He often wrote long letters to family or friends laying out complicated theological or political positions but invariably concluded his letter with a sentence such as, "I should like your opinion on all these points."[40] Brace actively sought out those whose ideas were different than his own as a method of testing his logic and forging his beliefs. Opposition helped him sharpen his reasoning and hone his logic.

There was nothing he enjoyed more than dragging others into a heated debate. Among his frequent sparring partners were the Olmsted brothers. Their verbal jousting could last for hours. Brace once reported spending six or seven hours with Frederick Olmsted in "a torrent of fierce argument, mixed with divers oaths on Fred's part."[41] In turn, Fred recalled that Brace would engage in political, scientific, philosophical, or ethical discussions with equal vigor, never showing "fatigue, lassitude, or ennui" and "always disposed to pursue a debate through the night."[42] Brace's sister Emma was all too familiar with her brother's habits and took all this verbal dueling in stride but she was not above needling him, as younger sisters are wont to do. She once invited her brother and his friends for a fishing outing but couldn't resist playfully adding, "If you young gentlemen (ahem!) are afraid I shall talk too much, and disturb your deep mediations or logical reasoning, I will promise to be the best little girl that ever was, and hold up my hand every time I want to speak."[43]

In the mid-nineteenth century, as the country inched its way toward a civil war, there was no more contentious topic than slavery. In keeping with Brace's eagerness to be exposed to new ideas, he attended a lecture by radical abolitionist Wendell Phillips. He was enthralled with Phillips' oratory skills and admired "his ability to bring along the audience."[44] Mr. Brace confessed he had been moved to tears at this event. It was a combination of passion and logic that most impressed the thoughtful Brace. He wrote a friend, "They present one aspect of the human mind we cannot dwell on too much. . . . It does show for the time real '*devotion* (worship) to principle.'"[45] Devotion to principle would be yet another hallmark of all of Brace's life work.

Mr. Brace's willingness to question everything made him a bit of an intellectual maverick and not infrequently brought him into conflict with those around him. In college he didn't hesitate to challenge cherished views held by classmates. Of them, he once confided in a close friend, "I find myself . . . with somewhat different views of things from many here."[46] On more than a few occasions over the course of Brace's life, his ideas would be labeled "dangerous." It was an accusation levied at him by even some of his closest friends. On one such occasion Brace began a letter, "It is not pleasant to have an old friend declare one's opinions 'dangerous,' so perhaps you will forgive me the intrusion, if I give you my reasons for holding them, at some length, and possibly I may show you they are not so very 'dangerous,' even if they are false."[47]

He then went on for pages, writing a lengthy treatise on religious doctrine that had taken days to compose.

For a deeply spiritual man who had a sprawling family tree heavy laden with clergymen and preachers, this willingness to rethink religious doctrine and church practices in the mid-nineteenth century seemed particularly threatening to some. Later in life his views on Christianity would sometimes earn him the reputation of "unitarianism" and "semi-infidelity."[48] Brace ultimately would be unwilling to adhere to any religious denomination that espoused a dogmatic approach to Christian practice. Additionally, he was willing to demand evidence and insist on sound reasoning on religious topics that others were willing to accept on blind faith. He once told a friend, "I believe that God answers prayer, for the Bible tells us that. But I want some other reason, some satisfying evidence in my own experience."[49] In general, Brace would be willing to collect his evidence from scripture but also to gather it from scientific text, practical experience, and personal experimentation. His positions were melded from all the best information he had at hand.

For Brace the only thing that was truly dangerous—even more dangerous than being wrong in one's opinion or one's reasoning—was holding any idea or belief as too sacred or too cherished to be investigated. "We may reason wrong; we may be prejudiced or foolish or weak," he noted, "but that there can be anything wrong in searching for truth freely, or in uprooting the dearest opinion to see what lies under it, or in applying our individual judgment to any truth (be it even God's existence), I do not see."[50] Among Brace's most persistent characteristics was his catholic approach to truth-seeking. He wrote to his good friend Fred Kingsbury in 1849, "I am more and more determined to be true to myself. It's a most complicated chain around you, this of custom and 'what-we-always-have-been-educated-to-believe.'"[51]

For Brace, failing to ask questions was an impediment to progress and there was no greater threat than dogma. He abhorred it. Early in life he resolved "never for a moment to refuse hearing a truth because it is new, and never to be afraid to dig under a belief because it is old and dearly loved."[52] Not only was Brace willing to question the seemingly unquestionable, but finding the truth demanded it. For him being proven wrong by others was merely part of the development of idea. Much later his old friend Kingsbury would recall that Brace was "utterly devoid of dogmatism: and his mind always seemed in an attitude of inquiry, ready to receive with hospitality any suggested thought."[53]

All of these elemental factors came into play in Charles Loring Brace's adult life, including his lifelong curiosity, his love of nature and learning, his eagerness to debate, and his willingness to either modify his position or hold firm in the face of criticism, depending on his own independent assessment. Values and morals were not abstract, theoretical, concepts to him but rather required practical application. Brace would spend his life driven by ambition tempered by his obligations to God.

To be sure, Brace came from privileged stock. But it was one deeply committed to social causes and public service. His circle of family and friends included reformers, abolitionists, scientists, naturalists, theologians and ministers, public servants and statesman, and educators and scholars. To appreciate the fusion of these interests, talents, and sensibilities is to begin to understand the factors that influenced him and would animate his life's work.

Mr. Brace's New-York, 1848–1850

Upon arriving in New-York, the twenty-two-year-old Mr. Brace quickly put his sketchy plan into action. He settled into a boarding house near Union Seminary, which was then located at University Place near Washington Square Park. He rented a cheap room, which, he confessed to a friend, "isn't just the best, being a basement," describing it as "a somewhat fashionable resort for up-town mosquitoes."[54] His room was located just to the west of the Bowery, a curving thoroughfare that eventually straightened up at Fourteenth Street, turning into Fourth Avenue as it ran northward toward the wilderness.[55] Nonetheless, the Bowery itself served as a territorial divide between the more affluent neighborhoods on the west and the poorer immigrant ones to its east. Mr. Brace's basement room, in a boardinghouse just to the west of the Bowery, put him at the fulcrum of a city that was beginning to divide along class lines.

Mr. Brace quickly and easily secured an instructor's position at the Rutgers Female Institute on the Lower East Side, teaching Latin for four and a half hours a week at a salary of six dollars a week. This position was well-suited to his overall plan, as it was "little interruption [to his studies] and good pay."[56]

He was quickly swept up in the intellectual life of the city. Along with Fredrick Olmsted, Mr. Brace attended "Saturday evening literary gatherings at the home of Anne Charlotte Lynch, a young teacher and poet." She lived nearby, just off Washington Square, and her salon had become the heart of "the city's literary life." It was "the first intellectual circle in the city's history that included both men and women on what seemed to have been equal terms."[57]

Not surprisingly, given his love of hiking, Mr. Brace quickly learned that the "greatest possible relief" from studying was to take a stroll down Broadway and look at the "perfect *flood* of humanity as it sweeps along."[58] He wrote of this urban landscape, "It's rather overpowering to think of that rush and whirl being their regular every-day life."[59] For a boy who had grown up in the quaint countryside, everything about life in New-York stood in sharp contrast. Among other things, he wrote that he was "thoroughly stunned by the unceasing din."[60]

Of course, the "flood of humanity" that swept alongside Mr. Brace included throngs of newly arrived immigrants, including the latest wave of Irish immigrants. Although Irish potato crops had failed sporadically since the 1830s, the crisis reached dire extremes in the mid-1840s. Starting in 1845 and then continuously for another seven sequential years, ending only around 1852, the potato blight destroyed the annual potato crop in a country almost entirely dependent on them. During those devastating years, "a million people died of starvation or starvation-related diseases and epidemics."[61]

Mr. Brace was sympathetic to the plight of these desperate, starving, and impoverished people. Writing a friend, he asked, "Don't you think poor Ireland is a-catching it? It seems to me the hardest problem going on just now in this world is how that country is to be saved. . . . A human soul shoved into eternity, all for want of a mouthful of grain, when there's many a waving field of it open to all."[62] In the Irish crisis, Mr. Brace saw a practical problem of gigantic proportion that required both sympathy and solution as a moral imperative. Starving to death from "want of a mouthful of grain" was senseless, particularly when resources were more broadly available. In the "waving fields" in the U.S. that were "open to all," Mr. Brace saw both salvation and a solution.

Of course, Irish immigrants of the mid-1840s were not alone in making the port city of New-York their home. Waves of immigrants had come before and even greater numbers would follow. In the 1830s there was a steady flow of German immigrants. Much more "massive emigration" occurred between 1846 and 1854, when the number of German immigrants quadrupled from fifty thousand to two hundred thousand.[63] Following the influx of Irish and Germans were other waves of European immigrants. In the 1850s and 1860s Northern Italians came, followed by massive migration of southern Italians in the 1880s. The Chinese trickled in and then came in increasing numbers in the 1870s and 1880s. Eastern Europeans Jews followed them in 1880s.[64]

Although large numbers of immigrants, particularly European immigrants, were driven from homelands by identifiable events—crop failures, wars, political unrest, and persecutions—the neat summary of arrivals by nationality tells too simplified a tale. It defies the ever-present diversity of people at any point in time. For example, in 1851, the ship manifest of a single vessel sailing from Liverpool to New-York listed its passengers' countries of origin as the U.S., Great Brittan, France, Germany, Santo Domingo, Prussia, Canada, Spain, and Belgium.[65] Taken together, the population of New-York grew dramatically in both number and diversity. The little island of Manhattan struggled to absorb them all.

"Want of Fear": Riots and Cholera, 1849

The influx of foreigners, combined with native-born "Americans" and free African Americans (New York State abolished slavery in 1827), contributed to growing tensions, which were compounded by emerging problems associated with income inequality. Political tensions were also fermenting between nativists and immigrants. In 1821, an amendment to the New York State Constitution had abolished the property requirement for voting. The legacy of this change was that huge numbers of male immigrants who were flooding into Manhattan, Irish and otherwise, represented an untapped political force. To some native-born Americans this was no small threat. Increasingly there was a general sense of foreboding, a roiling below the surface, the ever-present threat of chaos that might erupt along any combination of these fault lines. Chief Matsell's fledgling police force was charged with keeping order, but it was also illustrative of the simmering tensions.

Organized street gangs had existed since the 1830s, but they appeared to be growing increasingly dangerous and menacing by the 1840s. One example had been the emergence of the Bowery B'hoys,[66] a gang of nativists highly agitated by the arrival of immigrants—Irish-Catholics, in particular. However, by mid-century, the Bowery B'hoys had become "an inclusive, flexible term" which was "often used interchangeably with 'rowdies,' 'roughs,' or 'shirt-sleeves,' to describe average workers through-out the nation."[67]

In part, this general criminality, and rowdiness of boys and young adults had resulted in the passage of the Municipal Police Act of 1844, a piece of state legislation that authorized the creation of the municipal police for New-York. The act was immediately met with political resistance, resulting in delays in its implementation for a year. The state legislation called for the appointment of police officers by city ward aldermen. This locus of political power at the alderman level spurred immediate resistance from the Know-Nothing political party. The Know-Nothings, comprising nativists, balked at the idea that political power would rest so directly in the hands of ward leaders in areas densely packed with foreigners.[68] They favored centralized authority that would give the power (and patronage) to appoint police officers to the city's mayor. The issue was settled in May 1845, when Democrats wrestled municipal control away from the Know-Nothings and "the city council passed an ordinance adopting the 1844 state law." This city ordinance finally gave birth to Chief Matsell's police force, with officers appointed by ward aldermen. This temporarily quelled, but hardly permanently eradicated, the assorted hostilities.

Matsell's force had managed to maintain a lid on the social cauldron, which had been constantly simmering for four years. However, in 1849 it finally boiled over in a full-blown and deadly riot. For many New-Yorkers, the event served as a wake-up call and left its mark for years to come. As it happened, not only did this eruption occur a mere eight months after Mr. Brace's arrival in New-York and just a few blocks from his boarding house, but Mr. Brace himself felt compelled to wander intentionally into its midst.

At first blush, the cast of characters at the center of the riot seem an unlikely source for unleashing violence. The events orbited around two thespians, a British Shakespearean actor, William Charles Macready, and his American counterpart, Edwin Forrest. Macready, a highbrow British actor, was a favorite among aristocrats and stood in sharp contrast to the American-bred Forrest, who had honed his acting skills in the melodramas favored by New-York's lower classes.

Similarly, the playhouse at the center of the dispute—the Astor Theater, sometimes known as the Astor Opera House, depending on the evening's fare—was associated with class. It was owned by William Blackhouse Astor, son of the wealthy merchant, fur trader, and real-estate speculator, John Jacob Astor. The senior Astor had died the previous year, making William—who was a property tycoon in his own right—among the richest men in New-York. William Blackhouse Astor's property portfolio ran the gamut, including tenant-house slums in the lower wards as well as valuable properties and establishments designed for the wealthiest New-Yorkers elsewhere. Among the latter was the Astor Theater, which catered to the well-heeled. To underscore its elitist practices, the theater maintained an evening dress code, requiring kid gloves and waistcoats, accoutrements well beyond the means of poorer New-Yorkers.

The theater's location, on Lafayette Street between Astor Place and East Eighth Street, was also symbolic. To its east was the Bowery, where immigrant inhabitants of the Lower East Side resided. To its west were the decidedly more affluent areas of Washington Square Park, Union Seminary, and the homes of middle- and upper-class New-Yorkers.

In short, taken together, the actors, the playhouse, and its location were markers of class and nativity. So the pump was primed on the evening of May 7, 1849, when William Macready took the stage at the Astor Theater in the role of Macbeth. Disgruntled Forrest fans had managed to infiltrate the upper balconies. Midway through the performance, they commenced with loud hisses, punctuated by cries of "Down with the codfish aristocracy." Subsequently the cries gave way to showering the stage with an impressive array of rotten produce.[69] Although theater riots "were commonplace in New York"[70] this event was a mere precursor for the organized efforts that would follow.

It took a great deal of coaxing to get Macready back to the theater for his scheduled performance on May 10, and this was only accomplished after dozens of prominent New-Yorkers signed a petition begging him to return. In the meantime, on the other side of the class divide, grassroots organizers, ostensibly Forrest supporters, were rallying their forces. They posted flyers reading, "Shall Americans or English Rule in this City?" and called on "all workingmen to express their opinions this night at the English Aristocratic Opera House." The broadsides were signed by the "American Committee."[71] As tensions built, Police Chief Matsell sensed that his officers were not remotely up to the task of suppressing the agitated locals. It is possible that Matsell was also concerned about the loyalties of his mostly Irish officers, who had been appointed by their local aldermen. In any case, Matsell "informed Mayor Woodhull that he lacked the force to quell a serious riot."[72] The mayor summoned the National Guard, a much more formidable military presence than Matsell's still un-uniformed coppers.

On May 10, the evening of the performance, 250 of Chief Matsell's cops were stationed inside and outside the theater. More significantly, an additional 350 militia men assembled in Washington Square Park several blocks from the theater.[73] The performance began peacefully enough. However, as the evening wore on, the crowd outside the theater began to grow. It included many curious bystanders, among them Charles Loring Brace and George Templeton Strong, a prominent local attorney. It would have been impossible for any New-York resident, and certainly not young men like Mr. Brace or Mr. Strong, to be unaware of the brewing crisis and its potential for becoming explosive.

When the crowd reached an estimated "ten thousand," some of its rowdier members "began hurling paving stones, which smashed through the windows and sailed into the audience" of the theater.[74] Mayhem ensued. His coppers demonstrably outmatched, Matsell called for the military backup. He then "warned the crowd that force would be used, a notification drowned out by enraged voices crying, 'Burn the damned den of the aristocracy!'"[75] When the additional forces arrived the soldiers fired into the crowd. Describing the event, Mr. Strong scrawled into his diary, "Row last night at the Opera House, whereof I was a spectator. Mob fired upon, some twelve or fifteen killed and four times as many wounded, a real battle, for the b'hoys fought well and charged up to the line of infantry after they had been fired upon."[76] Although the actual casualty rate is a detail lost to history, it seems safe to say that around two dozen people were killed and hundreds more, wounded.

Tensions lingered. The next day, Mr. Strong noted that "prospects of a repetition of the performances tonight on a larger scale" were a real possibility "for the blackguards swear they'll have vengeance."[77] Among other things, "the houses of the gentlemen who signed the invitation to Macready to perform last night" had been "threatened."[78] Apparently that included the wealthy Strongs, because Mr. Strong reported next, "going up now to clean my pistols, and if possible to get my poor wife's portrait out of harm's way" and that his father-in-law was "making every arrangement and is a good deal alarmed."[79]

That evening, Mr. Strong reported that on one side, "the police and troops" looked much in earnest, "guns loaded and matches lighted—everything ready to sweep the streets with grape at a minute's notice."[80] On the other side of the divide, "the mob were in a bitter bad humor but a good deal frightened."[81] In the end, Strong reported that the "overt acts that were committed, on the Bowery side, were met by prompt measures and with instant success" from the militia. The B'hoys did manage to volley off some rounds of their own and "some of the cavalry were badly hit with paving stones."[82] Nonetheless, according to Strong, when ordered to either disperse or be the subject of "a little artillery practice ... they scampered."[83]

For New-Yorkers, the deadly disturbance was a warning. It was not the first riot in New-York's history nor would it be its last. However, it did seem to signal a new *kind* of urban tension, based on class and cultural differences between the "exclusives," or "upper ten," on the one hand, and the "great popular masses," on the other.[84] Reportedly, the riot left "behind it a feeling to which this community has hitherto been a stranger—an opposition of classes—the rich and the poor ... a feeling that there is now in our country, in New York City, what every good patriot has hitherto considered it his duty to deny—a *high* and *low* class."[85] In addition to revealing the class fault line, the riot was also a reminder of how loosely controlled the passions of the city were and how easily they might be unleashed. The poor immigrants were—in the words of many commentators of the day—the "dangerous class."

Although Matsell did not specifically mention the Astor Place Riots in his report on vagrant street children to Mayor Woodhull seven months later, it could not have been far from either man's mind. Matsell wrote of "the large number of vagrant children ages six to sixteen in the lower wards of the city who survived by stealing, begging, and prostitution, or who simply made nuisances of themselves by hanging around street corners."[86] Both men were aware that this population of alleged vagrant boys and wayward girls were the very ones growing up to form the "dangerous class." However, at the heart of the problem were boys. In particular they were threatening both for the physical power they wielded as well as their potential political power. In short, there were threats to upper-class society on a number of fronts, including disruptions to the political and social order. It was possible to envision a city that might erupt in sudden violence and in which future political control might be wrested away from the more genteel.

For Mr. Brace, venturing into the heart of the riot required an explanation to his father. In a letter attempting to deflect criticism that his actions had been foolhardy, the son wrote, "I am not naturally susceptible to fear" and "this same insensitivity stands by me when I can be of real service to others by exposing myself."[87] Significantly, he yoked his explanation about drifting toward the riot to the same instinct that had caused him to watch "over the death-struggles of a man in the cholera."[88] Brace had tended to the dying man without consideration of his own health.

That year, a cholera epidemic had yet again stricken the city. The outbreak in 1849 was sufficiently severe that George Templeton Strong kept track of it in his diary over a number of months. "Twenty-five cases reported yesterday and twenty-three today," he wrote on June 4.[89] "Thirty-eight cases of cholera reported, and nineteen deaths," he scrawled on June 7.[90] By July, he wrote, "Cholera the all-pervading subject and has been so for the past fortnight. Increase considerable, especially as shown by the Inspector's Weekly Report, the only reliable authority. The report shows a hundred deaths and upwards daily for the week ending Saturday last."[91] Indeed, in one "fever nest"—an area designated for the exceedingly high rates of contagious diseases— located on the Lower East Side where a Dr. Guernsey practiced, he found that in a cluster of just five tenant-house buildings, during a three-week period, "forty-two individuals died . . . and not one recovered that was taken sick."[92] While cholera could decimate entire families, it also wreaked havoc on family structure leaving children orphans or half-orphans. It wasn't until September of that year that the number of deaths had fallen off sufficiently that the Board of Health decreed it would issue "no more reports" on weekly cholera deaths.[93] However, by that time, five thousand people had died in the outbreak.[94]

Given the fatalities associated with cholera, Mr. Brace's affirmative decision to tend to the sick was either courageous or foolish, depending on your point of view. Either way, his decision to embrace the bodily risks associated with both riot and disease had required a confession to his father. In return, the young man clearly expected a stern lecture of condemnation. Instead, he received only validation. His father wrote, "Very early I exposed you to danger, urged you to climb, to swim, to do many things that many parents thought wrong and dangerous, for the very purpose of so familiarizing you to danger that you should be superior to fear."[95] He believed by thus exposing his son, it had "produced a physical effect upon your stomach, which has again operated on your character."[96] In his son's willingness to approach the physical dangers of riot and disease, the proud father saw only his son's strength of character.

Charitable Discord and Discovering Inspiration

The twin fears of disease and disorder were not unrelated in the view of many New-Yorkers, particularly those of the upper classes. For them, both plagues could be traced to the poor wards of Manhattan, where native-born Americans, African Americans, and destitute immigrants shared increasingly cramped quarters. However, for Mr. Brace, exposure to New-York's immigrants, their poverty, and their living conditions engaged the practical side of his brain and the Christian character of his soul. He began volunteering, getting involved with missionaries, charity workers, and other concerned individuals who were looking for ways to be of service.

In the 1840s, existing opportunities for helping the poor were segregated by age, gender, race, religion, and physical ability. In New-York, they included two facilities for the elderly (the Aged and Indigent, and Old Ladies Home); asylums for people with disabilities (the Bloomingdale Lunatic Asylum, Deaf and Dumb Asylum, and Institution for the Blind); services for pregnant women (Lying-In Facility for Destitute Females, and Magdalen Female Benevolent Facility); and the "Colored" Home.[97] In addition, there were six different institutions for orphans or half-orphans. Some of these were segregated by race (Colored Orphan Asylum) or religion (Protestant

Half-Orphan Asylum, Roman Catholic Orphan Asylum, and Roman Catholic Half-Orphan Asylum).[98]

The net result was that a battle was beginning to take shape, not only for the soul of New-York's poor but also over the best method of saving or serving them. Just before Mr. Brace arrived, *The Great Metropolis* carried a full-page advertisement announcing an "appeal for aid" for a new "House of Industry and Home for the Friendless."[99] It reported that one thousand dollars had thus far been collected for a project that had been "contemplated for months." The aid being sought was for single, unemployed girls and women who were "orphans, fatherless, and friendless." The advertisement fretted that these women were often "subjected to fraud, imposition, wrong treatment, ignominy, and destined for an early grave." It argued that their only crimes were "poverty and want of employment." The organizers behind the advertisement lamented the fact that the only "available shelters" were "the Tombs, Alms-House or Watch-house." They promised that the proposed charity would offer not only shelter but employment and job training, claiming this was a better method for helping these "virtuous, *helpless*, poor."[100]

This notion of serving the poor through the practical intervention of offering shelter, employment, and job training was not without controversy. An alternative approach was rooted in addressing their spiritual, rather than their physical, state of being. An example of this method is evident in the work of The New York Ladies Home Missionary Society, which was first organized in 1844 and designed as a "'Missionary Society,' according to the common acceptation of the term among Christian Churches."[101] For these ladies, missionary work involved proselytizing, saving souls though preaching, and distributing Bibles. As a method of intervention, it stood in direct contrast to the proposed House of Industry. The battle lines between *missionary* work and *charity* work were being drawn.

Related to the Ladies' work, other Christians were tending to the spiritual needs of children, offering Sabbath services, or boys' meetings. One of the first of these was started in 1848 by "members of the Carmine Street Presbyterian Church" in a "Hall at the corner of Christopher and Hudson Streets."[102] These missionaries proceeded undeterred even though they occasionally found it necessary to summon Matsell's police officers to keep the unruly gamins in order.

Despite all these options available to Mr. Brace, on Sunday, October 29, 1849, he spent an afternoon in service that would prove to be pivotal. Mr. Brace had taken a ferry over to Blackwell's Island, an outpost where New-York deposited a variety of adult denizens presumed undesirable, including the poor, the insane, criminals, prostitutes, and assorted others.[103] They were housed in several facilities, including the Lunatic's Asylum, two almshouses (one for men and the other for women), and a penitentiary and penitentiary hospital for patients with venereal diseases. (Soon to be added would be the Charity Hospital for Incurables and a workhouse designed as a minimum security prison.)[104] For Mr. Brace, what started out as a day of practical service turned into a source of inspiration.

He penned an enthusiastic letter to his father. "I have one of the most exciting and interesting days I ever spent, last Sunday, on Blackwell's Island,"[105] he started. He went on to claim, "I never had my whole nature so stirred up within me." Mr. Brace reported to his father that he had "preached without notes" in the morning to paupers at the Almshouse Chapel and spent the afternoon visiting prisoners, hospital patients, and the insane. Mr. Brace was particularly stirred by the hospital inmates who were "diseased prostitutes, brought there mostly to die."[106] He expressed a mixture of pity and hopelessness for these women: "You felt you were standing among the wrecks of the Soul; creatures cast out from everything but God's mercy. Oh! 'twas the saddest, most hopeless sight."[107] Despite his despair, the situation seemed not unlike the Irish potato famine. It posed a practical problem which required a solution.

Characteristically, his letter had started with a long critique of the current state of affairs in the Christian church. Mr. Brace wrote, "What I realize constantly of our New England religion" is that it is "affecting so sadly little any of our practical business relations."[108] He went on to complain that it didn't make the merchant honest, and it didn't inspire men with "genial kindness and charity towards one another."[109] It didn't affect "a politician's duties" or influence "his operations."[110] Brace was beginning to affirmatively articulate views that had long been percolating. Christianity as practiced had not only grown inefficient, but it had also lost its bearings in the real world. "There's so much of the dogma—Calvin piety," Brace complained, "and so little which makes men better men."[111] He went on to lament, "I am almost hopeless sometimes, and I fully believe that New England piety, if it doesn't change very considerably soon, will, in course of two or three generations, run out. This may sound extravagant. But do think of it."[112]

Mr. Brace continued, "We have such a formal idea of Christianity—that missionary-giving and prayer-meeting and Bible-reading and revivals are religion." However, he asserted, "I certainly can see very little in which piety affects social relations in New England or here, except in keeping from the worst crimes; which isn't much."[113] Brace's college essay about balancing society, self, and God in a practical theology were then in full play. Just five months after the Astor Place Riot, Mr. Brace was particularly concerned that "piety" have some practical impact on the "social relations" between New-York's increasingly separated classes.

Tragedy and Trips

Despite this budding interest in a "new piety" and work among the poor, personal tragedy struck Mr. Brace, delivering a serious blow and diverting him from his immediate path. On February 17, 1850, his beloved younger sister Emma died. The death not only saddened Brace but also sent him spiraling into depression. John and Frederick Law Olmsted sought a solution to their friend's melancholy and suggested that together they head off on a walking tour of Ireland, England, and the Rhine Valley. Certainly, reasoned the Olmsted brothers, rambling the countryside would cheer up their old friend Charley.

The trio sailed off for Europe on May 3, 1850, traveling on a packet ship to London in a cramped cabin shared with a stranger and packed with freight.[114] They passed the time reading aloud when the sea was not too rough, playing chess—with pieces they cut "out of card-board" with "cork pedestals" attached to a "pin-point . . . so they would not slip off" the board or "blow away"—and, of course, engaging in heated debate.[115]

The older Olmsted found his debates with Brace as vexing as ever, including one Olmsted had inadvertently started when he casually observed, "a reasoning mind" must have "constructed" the universe for "purposes of his own." This had set Brace off, who demanded, "You must back up farther" and asked, "What is God's God?"

After chewing on that for a while, Brace finally conceded—only for the purpose of argument—"an imaginary something that put the world together." But he pushed the argument further, asking, "What's the good of saying that" he created the universe "if you don't know any thing more. What did he create us for?" This eventually caused the increasingly exasperated Olmsted to mumble something about taking things on faith, saying that although he "never saw this being . . . which we will call God, I can tell you something more about him, not that I actually know, only I have heard."

"Heard! Heard! How?" Mr. Brace shot back. Olmstead's response, "Why, people tell me and I've read," did not satisfy his sparring partner. Which led the pair into an argument on the relative fallibility of the New Testament.

Olmsted argued, "We have a reliable account of the way he lived, we can infer what at least is the general character and tendency of his motives and purposes, and judge pretty well what he wants of us." Mr. Brace was unwilling to budge: "But is it not together more likely a man making such pretentions, was an impostor?" Olmsted engaged with this line of argument for a while only to have Brace retort, "A very nice model of a man, no doubt, *if* one must believe the story; but you see I don't." At which point, in Olmsted's words, Mr. Brace "went off into a long and labored attack upon the Bible as being called an infallible guide." Olmsted conceded a "few of his points being fair and reasonable." However, others were "utterly absurd . . . mere narrow-minded caviling and play upon words." Mr. Brace had admitted that he would worship "divine qualities" but "not the human," retorting that "Christ said he was God, which is nonsense, and I don't swallow it." At that point, Olmsted was determined not to encourage his opponent any further, so he "attempted very little reply" because "it was evident" Mr. Brace "would sail tack for tack with me all night."

Unexpected Returns: Belfast, Slavery, and a Hungarian Prison

Once in Liverpool, the trio immediately started trekking. Donning "well-seasoned, India-rubber *army* knapsacks" crammed with essentials and picking up "a strong hooked hickory-stick," they traveled two hundred miles over six days, sometimes hiking as many as thirty to forty miles in a single day.[116] The young men covered England, including London, Henley, Oxford, Stratford-on-Avon, Warwick, Kenilworth, Birmingham, Chatsworth, the Derbyshire moors, York, Fountain's Abbey, Lancashire, Westmoreland, and Liverpool.[117] Eventually they sailed from Liverpool to Ireland to begin the next leg of their journey. However, Belfast turned out to be a very significant stop for the young Mr. Brace.

Among other things, the three young men had been "supplied with letters of introduction" to the family of "Mr. Robert Neill of Belfast," who "had always welcomed Americans with peculiar friendliness."[118] Mr. Neill "was a strong anti-slavery man, and numbered amongst his American friends William Lloyd Garrison, Henry C. Wright, and Frederick Douglass, who had all been his guests."[119] For Mr. Brace this was a comfortable political fit. Brace himself was friends with Garrison and also Theodore Parker, another vocal abolitionist. The Olmsted brothers were more moderate in their views on slavery. In fact, Frederick had once written a mutual friend saying as much: "I am not a red-hot Abolitionist like Charley, but am a moderate Free Soiler."[120] Back in New-York Mr. Brace had brought Garrison and Parker to Olmsted's home on Staten Island in the hopes that an evening of heated debate might woo him away from his moderate stance. Fred confessed on these occasions they had had "stirring discussions" but the abolitionists hadn't been able to dissuade Olmsted from his basic position.[121]

Mr. Neill turned out to be a generous and accommodating host. In addition to his shared sensibilities about slavery, Mr. Neill and his home offered a second attraction. He was the father of a charming and intelligent daughter, Letitia. Privately, Mr. Brace was smitten by the earnest Miss Neill, who worked among the "ragged children" in Belfast.

From the Neills, the traveling men continued their walking journey for another six months. Eventually, however, on October 24, 1850, the Olmsted brothers returned to New-York, leaving Brace behind.[122] The still-restless Mr. Brace decided to travel on alone to Austria and Hungary. This would be a fateful decision for several reasons.

Among other things, the Olmsteds' return to New-York roughly coincided with the enactment, in the U.S., of the Fugitive Slave Act of 1850. The Olmsteds and Brace differed in their positions on this particular piece of legislation. Their debates continued in their written correspondence. Their frustrations and dismay with each other's positions were clearly evident and would temporarily strain—but not permanently destroy—their friendships.

Mr. Brace himself was unwavering in his basic condemnation of slavery both in the U.S. and in its larger historical context. "I do not wish to rant," he wrote his father in 1849. "But it is the deepest feeling of my heart, that no darker stain rests on this country than this slavery. Men *must* see it sometime."[118] Mr. Brace viewed the African slave trade as "the most dreadful curse which has perhaps ever afflicted humanity."[123] Much later in life, he would return to the topic, authoring an ambitious book covering the "history of humane progress under Christianity."[124] With regard to slavery, Mr. Brace pointed an accusatory finger at the Church for its moral failure, writing, "worse still the guilt of this great crime rests on the Christian Church as an organized body."[125] Neither Catholics nor Protestants escaped his condemnation.[126] Slavery, in Brace's view, was the "great crime of history before which all others pale in enormity and wickedness."[127]

The Fugitive Slave Act of 1850 was a temporary compromise between northern Free-Soilers and southern slave-holders. Free-Soilers, like Olmsted, while opposing the extension of slavery to new western territories, felt comfortable avoiding the larger questions about the morality of the institution of slavery itself.[128] For Brace, the Fugitive Slave Act of 1850 brought the issue of slavery more directly to the doorstep of the free North, a situation that he felt no moral or ethical man could deny.[129] Among other things, the act required affirmative compliance with fugitive slave laws and prohibited assistance to runaway slaves.

Mr. Brace's position was absolute and resolute, like those of his relatives, the Beechers. For example, Charles Beecher delivered a sermon on the legislation entitled "The Duty of Disobedience to Wicked Laws"[130] while his sister wrote her influential novel, *Uncle Tom's Cabin*. Brace himself called the law "one of the most abominable instruments ever framed" and asserted that "I would rather be sent to Sing-Sing for life than in any way help to execute it."[131] Mr. Brace, like his Beecher relatives, believed the law required civil disobedience and noncompliance because it transferred personal responsibility for slavery onto individuals. Wrote Brace, "I should fear to die with such a sin on my soul as sending a free, innocent fugitive into slavery. And all the Congress laws of a century could not make me innocent."[132]

Brace was unwilling to recognize US federal law when it conflicted with his own sense of moral culpability. He wrote, "I would never obey it [the law] while God preserves my reason. I consider it as one of the most unjust, wrong laws ever passed in the history of nations."[133] He defended this position on civil disobedience by saying, "Of course, I consider conscience above all human laws."[134] John Olmsted volleyed back with a familiar accusation, that Brace's views were dangerous. He wrote that it was "a dangerous doctrine that every man's conscience can decide on the law."[135] Brace had no problem standing his moral high ground but also found additional support in the country's history: "The principle I state is one on which our nation was founded, and our Revolution entered on. I cannot understand how there can be a doubt about it," Mr. Brace responded.[136]

Mr. Brace's badgering occasionally provoked the Olmsteds to the point of taking offense. Arguing with Brace about the extent of individual moral culpability and responsibility for the federal law, John Olmsted noted, "I don't quite like your remarks about the Fugitive Slave Law. You seem to assume that I am less abhorrent, less willing to lay down anything, more blinded by contiguity, than you. That I should totally deny. You say it makes us at last personally responsible before God for slavery. How? . . . The responsibility rests entirely on those who made the law, and those who voted for those who made the law."[137] Brace wrote back in dismay, "After reading your letter . . . I don't understand it. I can't understand it. Does Fred think so? Do all good men there think so? Is America going to the devil?"[138]

If Mr. Brace understood the idea of slavery theoretically and intellectually, he would soon get a small taste of oppression first hand. He continued his solo walking tour, eventually arriving in Hungary. Here Brace "fell under suspicion of the Austrian Government, still nervous from the affairs of 1848."[139] Official allegations included that Mr. Brace was "serving as a conduit between Hungarian exiles in England and republican revolutionaries still in the country."[140] The net result was that Mr. Brace found himself imprisoned along with others alleged to be "dangerous persons." Writing from prison, he denounced the accusation as absurd and vowed, "when once I am out, I will never let the matter rest while I can push it. . . . Such an outrageous act of oppression shall not be left unnoticed, if I can do anything."[141] He was furious: "I cannot speak or write one-tenth of what I feel. People would think me crazy. But I do, I must, till I die, feel for the oppressed, like one who has shared their dungeons with them."[142] This taste of injustice left a lifelong impression on the young, thoughtful Mr. Brace and he would act on his passions as soon as he was able.

He was ultimately freed, in 1851, after spending five weeks in the prison fortress of Gros-Wardein. The police ordered him to leave the country immediately. Mr. Brace did so readily. However, in his banishment he found himself temporarily penniless and stranded. Word of his predicament drifted back to Belfast where, according to Brace, Robert Neill "heard of my stress" and "like a trump sent me a ten-pound note which gave me a new coat . . . and vest."[143] The monetary bailout was also accompanied by an invitation to stay with the Neills until Mr. Brace could get his bearings and wait for additional funds from home. It was an invitation he eagerly accepted, out of need but perhaps for other motivations as well. He set off to Belfast to "live in the family, write, etc."[144]

While staying with the Neills, he took his meals at "a delightful coffeehouse," and he reported to John Olmsted, "All the while with Miss Letitia (no danger), delightful sisterly friendship, and walks and talks." Despite Mr. Brace's assurances about his "sisterly friendship" with Letitia, it is likely that this characterization confirmed, rather than quashed, his friend John's suspicions. At first opportunity Mr. Brace returned to New-York. Nonetheless his thoughts of Letitia lingered. Certainly an intelligent woman who worked among the "ragged children" and who liked nothing better than "walks and talks" possessed the kind of characteristics that the twenty-four-year-old Mr. Brace found undeniably appealing.

Mr. Brace's New-York Return

Making good on his personal promise, when Mr. Brace returned to New-York, he resolved to give testimony to his experiences in Europe. He entered a period of what he called his "Kossuth fever," fueled by his moral outrage and the indignity of being subjected to overt oppression. He lectured on Hungary and wrote daily in the hopes that he might "arouse public sympathy with the oppressed."[145] In doing so, he began to test his skills as public advocate for a social cause. During this period he became what he called "a patent writing machine," working from 8:00 a.m. until 12:00 p.m.—with occasional "interludes" for "lager beer and theological discussions"—until a book on these experiences was completed.[146] This was the first of dozens of books he would write during his life.[147]

Mr. Brace also reengaged with charity work. Among other things, he spent time mulling over the public controversy that had engulfed his friend and compatriot in service to the poor, the Reverend Lewis Morris Pease. Reverend Pease had been appointed as missionary at the Five Points in the spring of 1850 under the "direction and patronage of the Ladies Home Missionary Society." This turned out to be a very ill-suited match and didn't last long. Almost immediately Pease realized that the needs of his charges went well beyond those solved by handing out Bibles and preaching the Gospel. Pease came to believe that poor women of the Five Points drifted to prostitution and vice out of desperation and want of legitimate employment. Reverend Pease, being a "practical man," had set out "to obtain work for them to do," eventually locating a "shirt manufacturer" willing to employ the untrained women.[148] The women's participation in this employment experiment was voluntary, but there were a few rules, such as avoiding intoxication, pledging abstinence, and regularly attending "at some place of worship." Undeterred by the rules, thirty-five women eagerly showed up on the first day.

The Ladies of the Missionary Society were unhappy with Pease's initiative. Among other things they argued that theirs was "a religious, not a charitable association."[149] They accused him of failing to deliver the requisite sermons to the poor. Pease chafed at their approach. He was adamant that not only were concrete services necessary, but they were also "a pre-requisite" or, at very least, must be "co-existent with religious services and teaching."[150] Furthermore, he believed that "vice and crime could not be combated successfully" without removing the root causes of "ignorance and poverty."[151] The two positions reflected a deeply held "philosophical difference of opinion as to how to meet the more pressing needs of the residents."[152]

Initially, the disagreement was resolved through an amicable split. The Ladies hired a new, more compliant minister to attend to the community's "spiritual and pastoral" needs. In the meantime, Pease and his wife took up the "physical" aspects of charity work under the auspices of the Temperance Society.[153] However, tension finally boiled over when the Ladies accused Reverend Pease of siphoning off funds for his version of charity while still employed under the auspices of their missionary work.

Reverend Pease and his wife would eventually stabilize their work in a program known as the Five Points House of Industry. But their experiment of providing employment had revealed a second problem. Poor working women found "their miserable lodgings" were increasingly distasteful to them.[154] With the help of supporters, the couple opened a boarding house, charging the women "$1.25 a week for board" and "paying them all their earnings above this sum."[155] It was "a non-denominational new institution with an altogether different approach to delivering services."[156] This kind of work muddied the idea of missionary work still further by offering a hybrid model of charity, housing, and employment.

Taken together, the arguments exposed several distinct questions about the practice of charity work. Among them were how best to serve the poor, what the boundaries were between different kinds of missions, how distinct missionary work was from charity work, and, finally, how competition over limited philanthropic funds should be managed.

Mr. Brace watched all this with interest. He considered the Peases friends and mentors. He had worked side by side with them since his first arrival in New-York. Like them, Mr. Brace found that drawing a sharp distinction between the poor's "spiritual" needs and "physical" needs made little sense. Reminiscent of his college essay on moral philosophy, Brace was coming to believe that new religious work must have a practical component. He aligned himself with Reverend Pease's thinking about religion, service, and poverty. Although Mr. Brace had participated in missionary work, he was increasingly skeptical that sermons alone were the answer to enormous and complex social problems.

Personally, the young Mr. Brace was also still struggling with what to do in life. Writing his book on Hungary had served as a short-term goal but it begged the larger question of his life's vocation. Nonetheless Brace was coming to some tentative conclusions. In the spring of 1852 he wrote his father, "I don't care a straw for a city pastor's place," saying instead that he wanted to be the kind of city missionary who "go[es] down among those who have no friend or helper," offering true Christian inspiration. In characteristic fashion he also pledged, "I want to be true—true always. Not orthodox, or according to any one school or sect, but to follow my own convictions of truth."[157] Brace began to develop his ideas about a "new piety," which he was quick to admit wasn't new at all. "It is," he would later write, "old as Christ."[158] Nonetheless, if this form of piety could be resurrected and "manifested through the whole Christian community, as it has been in a few in all ages, many of the old 'stumbling-blocks' of religion would be taken away."[159]

Mr. Brace actually found an unlikely ally in Police Chief Matsell, at least in part. In issuing his dire warning about juvenile vagrancy, crime, and delinquency to Mayor Woodhull, Matsell had concluded his report with recommendations of his own. Among them were that "these children could be compelled to attend our schools regularly or be apprenticed to some suitable occupation." He argued that over time this kind of intervention would do "more to improve the morals of the community, prevent crime, and relieve the city from its onerous burthen of expenses for the Alms House and Penitentiary than any other conservative or philanthropic movement with which I am presently acquainted."[160]

Taken together, concerned citizens like Brace, Pease, and even Matsell were in basic agreement that neither preaching at the poor nor locking them up in prisons, poor houses or asylums was a very effective strategy. Absent some sort of investment in education, provision of job training, opportunities for employment, or other structural approaches to the problems of poverty, vice, and crime, social conditions were just going to continue to get worse. If anyone needed proof of the consequences of letting things ferment, all they needed to do was recall the deadly Astor Place riot.

Notes

1. *The Great Metropolis; Or, Guide to New-York for 1847* (New York: H. Wilson, 1847), 53; Raymond Kelly, "The History of the New York Police Department" (n.d.), 5; James Lardner and Thomas Reppetto, *NYPD: A City and Its Police* (New York: Henry Holt, 2000), 31. The objection may have been partly ideological. As Lardner and Reppetto explain, "A more disciplined and centralized force might have come across as a 'standing army'—something that many early Americans, not just New Yorkers, had hoped to do without. Uniforms, besides the military connotations, were servant's 'livery'—a symbol of the Old World class distinction that Americans had fought a revolution against."
2. Kelly, *History of the NYPD*, 5; Lardner and Reppetto, *NYPD: A City*, 7.
3. Thomas L. Harris, "Juvenile Depravity and Crime in our City: A Sermon by Thomas L. Harris" (New York: Charles B. Norton, January 13, 1850), 14–15.

4. I use "Mr." in reference to the major CAS employees in the remainder of the book to emulate the practices of the day as well as to humanize the characters and focus on their decision-making. In doing so my goal is to help give the reader a better understanding of the complexity of the problems charity workers faced and the reasoning behind their decisions to examine early social work practice. One helpful reviewer of this manuscript asked why I didn't use Rev. Brace instead of Mr. Brace. The answer lies in the fact that although there are occasionally references to Rev. Brace in the documents, the vast weight of the evidence suggests he was commonly referred to as Mr. Brace. This includes the handwritten trustee minutes, an internal diary, business correspondence, staff references to him, and the "in memoriam" published at the time of his death in the CAS Annual Report (although a resolution passed by the Board of Trustees at the same time calls him Rev. Brace). In itself, I think this is further evidence that CAS was moving in the direction of becoming a secular—or at least not overly religious—agency. Brace didn't fancy himself a religious missionary. He was also warned by the trustees to keep his radical religious and political views disassociated with those of the agency for fear they would jeopardize CAS's reputation. CAS actively sought out participation of trustees, staff, and volunteers, from a variety of faiths, although predominately from Christian dominations.
5. Charles Dickens, *American Notes for General Circulation* (London: Chapman & Hall, 1842), 66–67, reprinted as "Charles Dickens' 'New York' in *American Notes*" in *Lovell's Library: A Daily Publication of the Best Current & Standard Literature* 5, no. 210 (1883): 659–75.
6. Judith Berdy and the Roosevelt Island Historical Society, *Images of America: Roosevelt Island* (New York: Arcadia, 2003), 43.
7. Dickens, *American Notes*, 68.
8. Dickens, *American Notes*, 68.
9. *The Great Metropolis*, 111.
10. Dickens, *American Notes*, 68.
11. James Trager, *The New York Chronology: The Ultimate Compendium of Events, People, and Anecdotes from the Dutch to the Present* (New York: Harper Resource, 2003), 95.
12. *The Great Metropolis*, 111; Dickens, *American Notes*, 68.
13. *The Great Metropolis*, 101.
14. Dickens, *American Notes*, 69.
15. Dickens, *American Notes*, 69.
16. Charles Loring Brace to Fredrick J. Kingsbury, September 30, 1848, in *The Life of Charles Loring Brace*, ed. Emma Brace (New York: Charles Scribner's Sons, 1894), 58.
17. Ferrie, Helke, "An interview with C. Loring Brace," *Current Anthropology*, 38, no. 5 (Dec 1977): 851–869, 851.
18. Emma Brace, *Life of C. L. Brace*, 2.
19. Emma Brace, *Life of C. L. Brace*, 300.

20. Richard Hofstadter, *Social Darwinism in American Thought* (Boston: Beacon Press, 1944; reprinted 1992), 16. Asa Gray was an early and important intellectual defender of Charles Darwin in the U.S. According to Hofstadter, "after painstaking study ... and admirable foresight" of an advance copy of Darwin's book Gray wrote "a series of articles to defend evolution from the forthcoming charges of atheism" (p. 13). Among other things Gray argued science "should be looked upon not as the foe of religion, but rather as a complementary study of the ways in which the First Cause operated in the natural world" (p. 29). Influenced by Gray, Mr. Brace would eventually argue that an infinite Creator should "be able to arrange forces on a general plan," such that "the great object of Progress and Completeness is being steadily worked out." Charles L. Brace, "Review of Worlesungen uber den Menschen, etc. By Carle Vogt: Naturliche Schopfungsgeschiecte by Ernest Haeckel: Sechs Vorlesungen uber die Darwin'sche Theorie by L. Buchner: Fur und Wider Darwin by Fritz Muller," *The North American Review* 110, no. 227 (April 1870): 284–99. Mr. Brace wrote in summary:

> The Divine Architect does not apparently plan from the beginning (as we might have expected) the size and shape and fitness of each stone in his wonderful edifice. He appears, on the contrary, to arrange forces which are continually shaping and reshaping the countless blocks; some come forth imperfect, some crumble and become material for other uses, some have no apparent connection with his plan; many seem tentative, others even obscure, and injure the harmony; still at length, through all the confusion, and destruction, stone is laid upon stone, here one for lintel, there another for arch, here for strength, there for beauty; columns, arches, and pinnacles appear, and at length a structure of matchless symmetry, harmony, beauty, and grandeur rises from the ruin below; one never to our view completed, but always rising imperceptibly to greater perfection. (p. 298)

For Brace, the universe was the result of "almost infinite intertwining of causes" which resulted in "the astonishing and incredible complication and interdependence of the kingdoms of life," He argued that every thread—pointing by way of example to "each little violet ... which gladdens our eye on a country walk"—was dependent "for its existence on a balancing and interworking of innumerable forms of life. However, "that there is at the centre ONE holding the tangled threads of his vast network of causes, or rather that the power which is continually weaving on this immense 'loom of life' is One,—to us such a scientific conception has in it something corresponding to our highest moral intuition of HIM the 'All-controlling.'"

Specifically, Mr. Brace believed that in human evolution, evil must ultimately die out while good would triumph. According to Richard Hofstadter and Thomas Bender unlike the harsh application of social Darwinism associated with thinkers like Herbert Spencer—who opposed any form of public support for the poor including "state-supported education, sanitary supervision . . . [or] regulation of housing conditions," Mr. Brace believed that the poor deserved aid through the use of, "public and private financial resources and voluntary work of middle-class men and women." Joseph M. Hawes has pointed to the implicit importance of the environment in Darwin's theory, not because it determined "the patterns of evolution" but rather it provided "the challenge against which the natural variations struggled." For Brace, the urban environment produced just such a challenge for poor children, however, he saw the solution as in providing them the material support they needed, bringing them under proper influences necessary in the struggle and, when possible, changing their environment.

21. The Brace family historian, John Sherman Brace, documented another sibling, Urial, born after Emma and before James. However, Urial is not mentioned in Emma Brace's book on her father's life. See Brace, J. Sherman *Brace Lineage* (Bloomsburg, Pa: G.E. Elwell and Son, 1914), 40, and Emma Brace, *Life of C. L. Brace*, 3.
22. F. J. Kingsbury, "Charles Loring Brace," *Journal of Social Science* 27 (October 1, 1890): 50–52.
23. David Schuyler and Gregory Kaliss, eds., *The Papers of Frederick Law Olmsted*. Vol. 9, *The Last Great Projects, 1890–1895* (Baltimore: Johns Hopkins University Press, 2015), 468.
24. Emma Brace, *Life of C. L. Brace*, 5.
25. Schuyler and Kaliss, *Papers of F. L. Olmsted*, 467.
26. Schuyler and Kaliss, *Papers of F. L. Olmsted*, 467.
27. Charles Loring Brace to Fredrick J. Kingsbury, February 11, 1847, in Emma Brace, *Life of C. L. Brace*, 33.
28. Emma Brace, *Life of C. L. Brace*, 33.
29. Charles Loring Brace to John Pierce Brace, September 3, 1844, in Emma Brace, *Life of C. L. Brace*, 20.
30. Emma Brace, *Life of C. L. Brace*, 20.
31. Schuyler and Kaliss, *Papers of F. L. Olmsted*, 467.
32. Charles Loring Brace, private journal, October 1842, in Emma Brace, *Life of C. L. Brace*, 8.
33. Schuyler and Kaliss, *Papers of F. L. Olmsted*, 467.
34. Charles Loring Brace to John Pierce Brace, January, 1843, in Emma Brace, *Life of C. L. Brace*, 16.
35. Charles Loring Brace to Emma Brace, undated (*ca.* 1842), in Emma Brace, *Life of C. L. Brace*, 12.
36. Charles Loring Brace to John Pierce Brace, December, 1843, in Emma Brace, *Life of C. L. Brace*, 21.
37. Emma Brace, *Life of C. L. Brace*, 21.
38. Emma Brace, *Life of C. L. Brace*, 21.
39. Charles Loring Brace to John Pierce Brace, December, 1843, in Emma Brace, *Life of C. L. Brace*, 22.

40. Charles Loring Brace to Frederick J. Kingsbury, undated, in Emma Brace, *Life of C. L. Brace*, 39.
41. Charles Loring Brace to Frederick J. Kingsbury, undated, in Emma Brace, *Life of C. L. Brace*, 61.
42. Schuyler and Kaliss, *Papers of F. L. Olmsted*, 467.
43. Emma Brace to Charles Loring Brace, undated (*ca.* 1842), in Emma Brace, *Life of C. L. Brace*, 13.
44. Charles Loring Brace to Frederick J. Kingsbury, May 25, 1849, in Emma Brace, *Life of C. L. Brace*, 67.
45. Emma Brace, *Life of C. L. Brace*, 67.
46. Charles Loring Brace to Frederick J. Kingsbury, November 2, 1847, in Emma Brace, *Life of C. L. Brace*, 35.
47. Charles Loring Brace to Miss Blake, undated, in Emma Brace, *Life of C. L. Brace*, 43.
48. Charles Loring Brace to a Trustee, August 7, 1864, in Emma Brace, *Life of C. L. Brace*, 264.
49. Charles Loring Brace to Frederick J. Kingsbury, undated, in Emma Brace, *Life of C. L. Brace*, 41.
50. Emma Brace, *Life of C. L. Brace*, 38.
51. Charles Loring Brace to Frederick J. Kingsbury, November 1849, in Emma Brace, *Life of C. L. Brace*, 78.
52. Emma Brace, *Life of C. L. Brace*, 39.
53. Kingsbury, "*Charles Loring Brace*," 50–52.
54. Charles Loring Brace to Fred Kingsbury in Emma Brace, *Life of C. L. Brace*, 61.
55. George Templeton Strong, *Diary*, November 20, 1848, in Allan Nevins and Milton Halsey Thomas, eds. *George Templeton Strong Diary* (New York: MacMillan, 1952), 335. Strong noted in his diary that "all the cross streets have rows of houses starting up on them, and ten years more of this growth will carry the city beyond the Lower Reservoir." This would be the Croton Reservoir at Fifth Avenue between Fortieth and Forty-Second Streets.
56. Charles Loring Brace to Frederick J. Kingsbury, undated, in Emma Brace, *Life of C. L. Brace*, 61.
57. Thomas Bender, *New York Intellect: A History of Intellectual Life in New York City from 1750 to the Beginning of Our Own Time* (Baltimore: Johns Hopkins University Press, 1987), 195. While Mr. Brace could be patronizing and paternalistic toward women at times, he nonetheless held relatively progressive views. His commitment to girls and women's education, as well as his participation in gender diverse intellectual circles is testimony to that. In addition, his personal correspondence to female friends and relatives, demonstrates genuine respect and high regard.
58. Charles Loring Brace to Frederick J. Kingsbury, undated, in Emma Brace, *Life of C. L. Brace*, 58–59.
59. Emma Brace, *Life of C. L. Brace*, 58–59.
60. Emma Brace, *Life of C. L. Brace*, 59.

61. Thomas Sowell, *Ethnic America: A History* (New York: Basic Books, 1981), 21.
62. Charles Loring Brace to Frederick J. Kingsbury, 1848, in Emma Brace, *Life of C. L. Brace*, 55.
63. Sowell, *Ethnic America*, 55.
64. Sowell, *Ethnic America*, 80. According to the *Manual for the Use of the Legislature of the State of New York for the Year 1857* (New York: Weed, Parsons), 201, and *Report of the Council of Hygiene and Public Health of the Citizens' Association of New York upon the Sanitary Conditions of the City* (New York: D. Appleton, 1866), 121, the population of New-York, inclusive of all the wards leaped from 197,112 in 1830 to 805,358 in 1860. It was tremendous increase in just three decades. Adapted from *Manual for the Use of the Legislature*, 201, and *Report of the Council of Hygiene*, 121.
65. Manifest of passengers aboard the S. S. Africa, sailing from Liverpool and arriving in New York on February 17, 1851. http://www.immigrantships.net/v7/1800v7/africa18510217.html
66. David S. Reynolds, *Mightier Than the Sword: Uncle Tom's Cabin and the Battle for America* (New York: W. W. Norton, 2011). Reynolds writes that "by the 1850s, 'the b'hoys' had become an inclusive, flexible term, often used interchangeably with 'rowdies,' 'roughs,' or 'shirt-sleeves,' to describe average workers through-out the nation" (p. 146).
67. Reynolds, *Mightier Than the Sword*, 146.
68. Lardner and Reppetto, *NYPD: A City*, 23.
69. Edwin G. Burrows and Mike Wallace, *Gotham: A History of New York City to 1898* (New York: Oxford University Press, 1999), 761.
70. Burrows and Wallace, *Gotham*, 761.
71. Burrows and Wallace, *Gotham*, 763.
72. Burrows and Wallace, *Gotham*, 763.
73. Burrows and Wallace, *Gotham*, 763.
74. Burrows and Wallace, *Gotham*, 763.
75. Burrows and Wallace, *Gotham*, 763.
76. Strong, *Diary*, 351.
77. Strong, *Diary*, 351.
78. Strong, *Diary*, 351.
79. Strong, *Diary*, 352.
80. Strong, *Diary*, 352–53.
81. Strong, *Diary*, 352–53.
82. Strong, *Diary*, 352–53.
83. Strong, *Diary*, 352–53.
84. Burrows and Wallace, *Gotham*, 765.
85. Burrows and Wallace, *Gotham*, 765.
86. E. P. Smith and L. A. Merkel-Holguin, eds., *A History of Child Welfare* (New York: The Child Welfare League of America, 1996), 329.

87. Charles Loring Brace to John Pierce Brace, undated, in Emma Brace, *Life of C. L. Brace*, 73–74.
88. Emma Brace, *Life of C. L. Brace*, 74.
89. Strong, *Diary*, 353.
90. Strong, *Diary*, 354.
91. Strong, *Diary*, 358.
92. *Report of the Council of Hygiene*, 175, 177.
93. Strong, *Diary*, 362.
94. Christine Stansell, *City of Women: Sex and Class in New York, 1789–1860* (New York: Alfred A. Knopf, 1986), 199.
95. John Pierce Brace to Charles Loring Brace, undated, in Emma Brace, *Life of C. L. Brace*, 75.
96. Emma Brace, *Life of C. L. Brace*, 75.
97. *The Great Metropolis*, 71–72. Just over a decade later, Mr. Brace himself will do a thorough investigation of the charitable organizations in the city for *Putnam's Monthly* and publish an article on *The Benevolent Institutions of New-York*. Brace will count among them twenty-three asylums, ninety societies, seventy-five secret and benefit societies, eight hospitals and seven dispensaries. The specialized organizations catered to the "deaf and dumb," blind, "lunatics," poor widows with small children, old ladies home, and at least nine different organizations for sailors and their dependents (including a sailors' home, colored sailors' home, marine society, marine hospital and a home for sailors children) among others.
98. *The Great Metropolis*, 71–72.
99. *The Great Metropolis*, 4.
100. *The Great Metropolis*, 4.
101. Trustees of the House of Industry, "Facts Rebutting Assaults upon the Five Points House of Industry: Through the Character of Rev. L. M. Pease" (New York, 1854), 4.
102. First Annual Report of the Children's Aid Society (1854), 7.
103. Blackwell's Island will be renamed Welfare Island in an attempt to spruce up its reputation in 1921. In 1971 it was renamed Roosevelt's Island. At the time of Mr. Brace's visit, the island included two almshouses (one for men and one for women), a penitentiary and a hospital for the mentally ill. By 1885, this same island will include from north to south the Female Lunatic Aslyum, Work House, Male Almshouse, Female Almshouse, Maternity Hospital, Work Shops, and Penitentiary and Charity Hospital. See also Horn, Stacy *Damnation Island: Poor, Sick, Mad & Criminal in 19th-Century New York* (Chapel Hill, NC: Algonquin Books of Chapel Hill, 2019).
104. Berdy, *Images of America*, 43–58.
105. Emma Brace, *Life of C. L. Brace*, 75–76.
106. Charles Loring Brace to John Pierce Brace, October 31, 1849, in Emma Brace, *Life of C. L. Brace*, 76.

107. Emma Brace, *Life of C. L. Brace*, 76.
108. Emma Brace, *Life of C. L. Brace*, 76.
109. Emma Brace, *Life of C. L. Brace*, 76.
110. Emma Brace, *Life of C. L. Brace*, 76.
111. Emma Brace, *Life of C. L. Brace*, 76.
112. Emma Brace, *Life of C. L. Brace*, 76–77.
113. Emma Brace, *Life of C. L. Brace*, 77.
114. Both Charles Loring Brace and Frederick Law Olmsted published books based on their experiences on their walking tours. These kind of "literary tourist" books were popular and Mr. Olmsted confessed that he spent "a great many long winter evenings in reading the books so frequently written by our literary tourists." F. L. Olmsted, *Walks and Talks of an American Farmer in England* (New York: Putnam, 1852), 1. In the case of Mr. Olmsted, the first volume of *Walks and Talks of an American Farmer in England* was so successful that he published a second volume, *Walks and Talks of an American Farmer in England in the Years 1850–51, Part II* (New York: George P. Putnam & Co., 1852) the same year, 1852. The bulk of these volumes report interesting stories and anecdotes from the travels. However, Part 2 also includes an appendix: "Information and Advise for Those Wishing to Make a Pedestrian Tour in England, at the Least Practicable Expense." The appendix reads like a 1850s version of the popular travel guide published a century later called *Europe on $5.00 a Day*, although Mr. Olmsted's book could have been entitled *England on 75 Cents a Day*. Mr. Olmsted's advice covers passage and transport, giving information on the benefits and discomforts of packet-ships, freights, screw steamers or mail steamers (which were "not so comfortable" but faster), short conveyances (rail, coach, boat), expenses for board and bed, equipment, knapsacks, clothing, rain gear, and drinking flasks (don't bother), as well as routes and distances. I've drawn information from these accounts for this chapter.
115. Olmstead, *Walks and Talks, Part II*, 20. Olmsted wrote, "Charley has had some capital games" with a "cabin passenger" who promised to introduce him "at a London chess club."
116. Olmsted, *Walks and Talks, Part II*, 185–87.
117. Olmsted, *Walks and Talks, Part II*, 187.
118. Emma Brace, *Life of C. L. Brace*, 90.
119. Emma Brace, *Life of C. L. Brace*, 90; emphasis in original.
120. Schuyler and Kaliss, *Papers of F. L. Olmsted*, 470.
121. Schuyler and Kaliss, *Papers of F. L. Olmsted*, 467–68.
122. Schuyler and Kaliss, *Papers of F. L. Olmsted*, 470.
123. Charles Loring Brace, *Gesta Christi: or A History of Humane Progress under Christianity*, 4th ed. (New York: A. C. Armstrong, 1882), 364.
124. Brace, *Gesta Christi*, 365.
125. Brace, *Gesta Christi*, 365.

126. Brace, *Gesta Christi*, 365, 367. In Brace's view the Catholic Church committed the "fatal error" in arguing that conversion "would outweigh the sin of man-stealing or slavery." Not to be so easily swayed, Brace concluded that "the dark stain of African slave trade and of human bondage on a new continent is forever on the garments of the Roman Catholic Church." Similarly, in exploring the role of the Protestant Church he wrote, "Nor does the Protestant Church escape" because "for a century and a half, a Protestant power—Great Britain—led in that most shameless traffic,—the plundering [of] one continent of human beings to sell them as slaves in another." Brace concluded that Protestants "knew they were sinning against both God and man in their horrible trade." Only the Quakers escape Brace's wrath.
127. Brace, *Gesta Christi*, 365.
128. Perhaps in an effort to further influence Olmsted, in 1852, Mr. Brace would recommend Fredrick to the editor of the *New-York Daily Times* for an assignment traveling in the south and reporting on slavery and the economy. Olmsted's dispatches were published along the way and were ultimately compiled in book, *The Cotton Kingdom: A Traveller's Observations on Cotton and Slavery in the American Slave States, 1853–1861*. As Eric Foner and Thomas Bender have both noted, the letters were important to the development of the free labor ideology of the emerging Republican party. Thomas Bender, *New York Intellect: A History of Intellectual Life in New York City from 1750 to the Beginning of Our Own Time* (Baltimore: Johns Hopkins University Press, 1987), 196. See also Tony Horwitz, *Spying on the South: An odyssey across the American divide* (NY: Penguin Press, 2019).
129. Charles Loring Brace to Mrs. Asa Gray, February 6, 1851, in Emma Brace, *Life of C. L. Brace*, 117.
130. Charles Beecher, *The Duty of Disobedience to Wicked Laws: A Sermon on the Fugitive Slave Law* (New York: John A. Gray Printer, 1851). Charles Beecher delivered this sermon in 1851 to the congregation of the Free Presbyterian Church in Newark, New Jersey. It was later published and reprinted at the request of the congregation. Beecher justified his position in scripture and reason but concluded with a rousing, clear, and direct articulation of the Christian and citizen's duty. After pleading for "no warlike measure of resistance" and "no deeds of blood," he advised the following:

> If a fugitive claim your help ... break the law, and help him on his way, *directly* if you can, *indirectly* if you must. Feed him, clothe him, harbor him, by day and by night, conceal him from his pursuers and from the officers of the law. If you are summoned to aid in his capture, refuse to obey. If you are commanded by the officer to lay hands on the fugitive, decline to comply; rather, if possible, detain the officer, if you conveniently can, without injury to his person, until the victim is clean gone.

Beecher's strongly held views also proved controversial. The Free Presbyterian Church was expelled from the Presbyterian Synod in 1853. The parishioners reorganized as a Congregationalist church. In 1863, Beecher was convicted of heresy by an Ecclesiastical Council and forced to leave his congregation. The charges against Rev. Beecher were that he "does not preach according to the creed of the Church and of the Orthodox Churches generally in New-England." See "The Trail of Rev. Charles Beecher," *The New York Times*, July 26, 1863.

131. Charles Loring Brace to John Pierce Brace, 1850, in Emma Brace, *Life of C. L. Brace*, 102.
132. Charles Loring Brace to Mrs. Asa Gray, February 6, 1851, in Emma Brace, *Life of C. L. Brace*, 117.
133. Emma Brace, *Life of C. L. Brace*, 117.
134. Emma Brace, *Life of C. L. Brace*, 117.
135. Emma Brace, *Life of C. L. Brace*, 117.
136. Emma Brace, *Life of C. L. Brace*, 117.
137. John Olmsted to Charles Loring Brace, December 1850, in Emma Brace, *Life of C. L. Brace*, 109–110.
138. Charles Loring Brace to John Olmsted, undated, in Emma Brace, *Life of C. L. Brace*, 112.
139. Kingsbury, "Charles Loring Brace," 50–52.
140. Schuyler and Kaliss, *Papers of F. L. Olmsted*, 470.
141. Charles Loring Brace to John Pierce Brace, June 11, 1851, in Emma Brace, *Life of C. L. Brace*, 138.
142. Charles Loring Brace to Miss Baldwin, October 5, 1851, in Emma Brace, *Life of C. L. Brace*, 147.
143. Charles Loring Brace to John Olmsted, October 17, 1851 in Emma Brace, *Life of C. L. Brace*, 146.
144. Emma Brace, *Life of C. L. Brace*, 146.
145. Emma Brace, *Life of C. L. Brace*, 148.
146. Charles Loring Brace to Frederick Kingsbury, undated, in Emma Brace, *Life of C. L. Brace*, 148.
147. Kingsbury, "Charles Loring Brace," 50–52. Charles Loring Brace claimed he wrote for "recreation" but he was a prolific author. His books included *Hungary in 1851* (1852), *Home Life in Germany* (1856), *Norse Folk* (1859), *Races of the Old World* (1871), *Sermons to Newsboys* (1866), *The New West* (1869), *The Dangerous Classes of New York and Twenty Years' Work among Them* (1880), *Christianity and the Relations of Nations* (1880), *Gesta Christi* (1882), and *The Unknown God* (1890). Among other things Thomas Bender argues that both Brace and Fredrick Olmsted

> responded to the needs of the new city and its opportunities by creating a new kind of intellectual career. They made careers out of the theory and practice of

reform. They expressed their ideas not only in books and articles but in institutions and, in Olmsted's case, in the physical transformation of the city itself. Finding the traditional learned professions inadequate to both the times and their own ambitions, they created new ones.

Ultimately Mr. Brace would do so with his focus on CAS.

148. "Our City Charities—No. III: The Five Points House of Industry," *The New York Times*, February 22, 1860.
149. "Our City Charities."
150. Trustees, "Facts Rebutting Assaults," 5.
151. Herbert Asbury, *All Around the Town: Murder, Scandal, Riot and Mayhem in Old New York* (1929; reprint, New York: Thunder's Mouth Press, 1934), 17.
152. Trustees, "Facts Rebutting Assaults," 6.
153. Trustees, "Facts Rebutting Assaults," 6.
154. "Our City Charities."
155. "Our City Charities."
156. Asbury, *All Around the Town*, 18–19; CAS Trustees, "Facts Rebutting Assaults."
157. Charles Loring Brace to John Pierce Brace, 1852, in Emma Brace, *Life of C. L. Brace*, 154.
158. Emma Brace, *Life of C. L. Brace*, 151.
159. Emma Brace, *Life of C. L. Brace*, 151.
160. George W. Matsell, *Semi-Annual Report of the Chief of Police from May 1 to October 31, 1849* (New York, 1850), 58–61, 62–66. Documents of the Board of Aldermen of the City of New York. 5.17—Part 1. Document No. 3. Board of Aldermen: January 7, 1850 (New York: McSpedon & Baker, 1850).

2

Family Life Among the Poor in Mid-Nineteenth-Century New York

> *What are the fifty newspapers, which those precocious urchins are bawling down the street . . . what are they but amusements? Not vapid waterish amusements, but good strong stuff . . . pimping and pandering for all degrees of vicious taste, and gorging with coined lies the most voracious maw.*
>
> —CHARLES DICKENS, New York, 1842

THE PORT DOCKS were all atwitter. "I can hardly hear myself think," complained a journalist in 1851, "for the noise of the news-boys, who are crying the arrival of the Africa, from Liverpool."[1] Indeed, the arrival of any passenger ship, packet, or steamer from Europe was a cash cow for the little hawkers of the daily penny presses. The sinking of a vessel—which happened with unfortunate frequency—would have bolstered sales still further. No matter, really. With an eye toward profits, the boys could move their wares with a creative cry that might only loosely correspond to the actual content of the paper. So rapid was the distribution of "extras"—or "oixtrays!"—as the boys would bellow with breaking news and so close were the major printing offices on Printers Row that by the time passengers of the Africa disembarked, the fleet-footed newsboys might well be greeting them with news of their own arrival. "Ere's the Africa! Just arrived, thirteenth edition, e-e-e-er it is!"[2] Nonetheless, with each new ship arrival came both new customers but also new competition for the newsboys.

The Africa shuttled back and forth from Liverpool—the biggest emigration port in Europe at the time—with regular frequency, each time bringing new families and more children. In 1851 the steamship's master, Alexander Ryrie,[3] attested to the fact that he had deposited 118 passengers in the port city of New-York on February 17, and he brought another eighty-two on September 24. Master Ryrie's vessel was relatively small compared with the Malabar, which Master Hugh Leeds piloted into the harbor on May 6 that same year, leaving 263 passengers before heading back to its home port of Dublin.[4]

Travelers had a variety of vessel options such as packet-ships, freights, screw steamers, or mail steamers, which were "not so comfortable" but faster.[5] Large numbers of immigrants "came in the hold of cargo ships—ships built with little or no regard for the needs of passengers."[6] Among the lack of amenities were food, water, and proper waste disposal to accommodate a ship's human cargo. The water for such journeys might have been "ordinary river water," which "was often brackish or muddy."[7] Most cargo ships had no toilet facilities, so "filth, odor, and disease were common."[8] Passengers were expected to bring their own food for the trip, but this must have been a grim irony for those fleeing famine in Ireland.

Passage across the ocean varied, much like life in the city immigrants were about to enter. For those with money, cabins offered comparative comfort and privacy but were a luxury beyond the reach of many impoverished and desperate emigrants. Of Africa's 118 passengers only 46 traveled in cabin class. The remaining seventy-two were crammed into the cheaper steerage compartments.

Steerage passengers descended a steep ladder to the small uncomfortable spaces "between-decks," where they were likely to discover their quarters consisted of a berth to be shared by five adults. Or worse, rows of bunks in which each emigrant had a three-by-six-foot shelf that was "still reeking from the ineradicable stench left by the emigrants of the last voyage—and these shelves were stacked up with just over two feet of space between them."[9] Girls and women faced additional challenges in that "most ships made no effort to segregate the sexes," leaving them "so vulnerable to molestation at night that many slept sitting up on their bundles of belongings rather than lie down on the shelves."[10] Noted Frederick Law Olmsted of traveling in steerage, "You will probably have a very miserable time, but it will be over after a while, and you will have seen a peculiar and memorable exhibition of human nature, and will go ashore with a pleasure not imagined."[11]

On May 6, 1851, Master Leeds of the Malabar appeared before the collector of the customs for the district of New-York and swore that the ship's manifest was "a full and perfect list of all the passengers taken on board."[12] Among other things he was willing to swear to the accuracy of the name, age, and gender of each of his 263 passengers. However, Leeds was also supposed to attest to the "part of the vessel occupied by each during passage" as well as his passengers' occupations.[13] He did not bother to fill out these sections of the vessel's manifest and apparently the information wasn't important enough to be demanded by customs officers. Perhaps it was too self-evident to warrant anyone's extra time. The country of origin was simply listed as Great Britain for everyone on board. More specifically, the ship had sailed from Dublin and the names on the manifest—Farley, McSimmon, Byrne, Maloney, Sullivan, McNally, Kelly, and Kennedy—had a decidedly Irish flavor. It seemed obvious enough that this was another ship in the endless fleet of those ferrying Irish potato farmers to their new destiny.

Emigrants with the luxury of time to plan their departures often sent the family breadwinner ahead before summoning dependents. This pattern allowed for an organized settlement of families in a new land. However, when the Malabar sailed from Dublin she was brimming with entire families, suggesting urgency and immediacy associated with their departure. Among those on board were the following: the Farrells and their thirteen-year-old son; the Mulrany's with three children under five; and the Dillions arriving by the dozen, with seven children under the age of thirteen (including one-year-old twins). The Reads and the Walshes both came with four children; the Read family flock was under thirteen while the Walshes were under nine. Both the Byrne and the Sheridan families brought three children under the age of thirteen, and the Berrys had three children under age three.[14] But it wasn't at all clear that an adult had accompanied six-year-old James McNally and his one-year-old sister. All told, nearly twenty-one percent of those on board the Malabar—fifty-five passengers in total—were under the age of fifteen. The Malabar's manifest captured a census of children arriving aboard one ship on one day. Of course, the port of New-York had received, was receiving, and would continue to receive many transatlantic vessels day in and day out, brimming with children, for decades.

Thankfully, according to Master Leeds's attestation, none of his passengers had died in transit. Safe passage wasn't a given. For the Irish, although they fled famine and almost certain starvation in Ireland, the journey could be dangerous as well. Disease was common. In 1847, "the most disastrous year of all," estimates were that twenty percent of the famine victims "died en route to America or upon landing."[15] If a parent or guardian died along the way, children arrived in the city port of a foreign country on their own.

The secondary consequence of all these fatalities was the additional hardship it imposed on a single remaining parent or on the orphaned children themselves. If six-year-old James McNally and his one-year-old sister had indeed arrived alone, it is hard to say what would have happened to them in 1851. Perhaps a family member would have met them. Or they might have been taken in by a kindly acquaintance. Care-giving arrangements were fluid, and in the absence of kin, care was often provided by kindly neighbors or complete strangers. Alternatively, the municipal almshouses, such as the Randall Island Nurseries or other child asylums or orphanages awaited them.

For example, two years later, fourteen-year-old Mary C. arrived as a true orphan. Both of her parents had already died before she set sail for the U.S. with her Aunt Mary and, according to the records, "Aunt Mary paid passage to N.Y. and died on the way, buried in the water."[16] With the death of her aunt and guardian, Mary was on her own when she stepped off the ship in New-York. By the time she found her way to charity offices, she told an agent she was willing to "go anywhere and do anything."[17] Her desperation is apparent even in this briefest of sketches.

As the exhausted passengers of the Africa and the Malabar disembarked, they might have been partially revived by the vibrant energy that ricocheted off the docks. Stepping on U.S. soil for the first time they would have been swarmed by street children offering to cart their trunks, sweep the streets in front of them, polish their boots, and sell them apples, flowers, candy, or newspapers.

It wouldn't have been difficult to predict the short-term future for many of the children descending the gangplanks of the Malabar and the Africa. The sons and daughters of the Reads, Berrys, and Byrnes would soon be joining the ranks of the little dock laborers. They would blend into the collective swarm of children who were trying to supplement meager family incomes or survive on their own.

***

Laying Down, Building Up, Crowding In

Disembarking families would soon be absorbed into the chaos and congestion of lower Manhattan. This was true despite the grand plan laid out for the orderly growth and development of the great metropolis several decades before.

By the early nineteenth century, New-York had been growing "organically" for centuries.[18] In January 1804, the city's common council took its first step at imposing some constraints on the haphazard nature of the city's expansion.[19] Three years later, the state legislature passed "an Act relative to improvements touching the laying out of streets and roads in the city of New-York, and for other purposes." Three men—Gouverneur Morris, Simeon DeWitt, and John Rutherford—were charged with the task of developing a blueprint for orderly growth. Specifically they were given "exclusive power to lay out streets, roads, and public squares, of such width and direction, as to them shall seem most conducive to public good, and to shut up, or direct to be shut up, any streets or parts thereof which have been heretofore laid out." After considering other intricate arrangements, the trio settled on a right-angled grid. As tedious as this simple grid was to some—chief among its critics would be Frederick Law Olmsted—it was ultimately a "visionary act of city planning."[20] Yet the democratic appearance of the design masked the inequities it would eventually foster.

When the men issued their final commissioner's report of 1811, it proclaimed that the long slender island of Manhattan—only twelve and a half miles from south to north and two and a half miles at its widest point east to west—would be laid out pursuant to a plan of streets and avenues. They recommended sixteen wide avenues, running south to north. Twelve of the avenues were to be numbered First Avenue through Twelfth Avenue, with the latter falling closest to the Hudson River. Four additional truncated avenues designated by the first four letters of the alphabet would be located to the east of First Avenue.[21] These broader avenues were then to be crosshatched—at right angles—by numerically ordered streets running from First Street all the way up the island and culminating in the envisioned northernmost 155th Street. As unimaginative as this naming system was, in 1811, the imaginary gridlines suddenly gave the wild, swampy, hilly island of Manhattan a future order. Henceforth it would be a city governed by coordinates. Each intersection—Fifth Avenue and Forty-Second Street or Twelfth Avenue and Forty-Eight Street—would have its place in the system. Soon to vanish from New-Yorkers' vocabulary would be the cardinal directions—north, south, east, and west. They would be replaced by references to uptown, downtown, and crosstown.

Although it would take decades to transfer "the straight lines . . . from paper to terrain"[22] the commissioners' plan of 1811 was "a vision of brazen ambition."[23] The grid "reconceptualized the island in one fell swoop." It also "rationalized the real estate market" and laid out a pathway for profit.[24]

The grid was a gift to be utilized by those with the vision—and the disposable capital—to do so. John Jacob Astor was just such a man. Astor had prospered by fur trading in the early nineteenth century but with the commissioners' plan imminent, he smelled more lucrative opportunities. His "wealth permitted him to speculate almost at will."[25] Astor began investing in Manhattan real estate, demonstrating his farsightedness through his willingness to buy any farmland or swampland he thought might become valuable. For Astor, that was just about any piece of property above Canal Street.

As one story goes, in 1810 Astor sold a piece of prime Wall Street real estate for eight thousand dollars to a buyer who bragged that the lot would be worth twelve thousand in short order. While Astor agreed that this was very true, he advised the gloating buyer to watch carefully as Astor invested *his* eight thousand dollars in the purchase of eighty lots above Canal Street.[26] Astor smugly retorted, "By the time your lot is worth $12,000, my lots will be worth $80,000."[27] This prophecy proved true enough. Astor "reaped huge profits as new neighborhoods developed" predictably along the imaginary gridlines.[28]

The same year the commission issued its 1811 report, Astor also purchased "four twenty-five-foot wide lots" on Orchard Street on the Lower East Side of Manhattan.[29] These investments were of a decidedly different nature than his speculative purchases to the north of Canal Street. These plots were earmarked for rental.

By 1842, Astor's real estate portfolio was weighted toward "rentals and leases."[30] In a little over twenty years, Astor increased the number of tenants on his rent rolls from 174 to 450 and increased his rental income from $19,194 to $194,000.[31] Among Astor's tenants were some of New-York's poorest residents. At the time of his death in 1848, he was New-York's "richest man" and "its biggest land owner."[32]

The original commission had been empowered to shut down streets as well as plan new ones. However, the men made no pretense of trying to untangle the existing mess below Canal Street. A tour guide from 1847 noted that "the compact part of the city is situated on the south end of New-York or Manhattan Island."[33] That was an understatement. This "compact" area comprised a dense warren of narrow streets. Each road, path, and alleyway had been laid down centuries before and answered to its own historic ancestry.

For a novice pedestrian trapped within its maze, the chaotic arrangement of streets may have been confusing. The logic is more apparent from a bird's-eye view. The streets were laid out roughly parallel to the jagged contours of the coastline of lower Manhattan. Like the ripples of currents starting from opposing extremes, these roadways merged in the center of the island in an awkward hodgepodge of intersections.

New York's political wards were mapped according to a similar historic pattern. Manhattan was originally settled from the southeast corner, moving north and west. Its First Ward covered the entire southern tip. As the island widened, one set of wards—the Second, Fourth, and Seventh—ran along its east coast, while a second set—the Third, Fifth, and Eighth Wards—ran along the Hudson River to the west, like teeth of an open zipper. The ward missing from this litany—the Sixth Ward—was the first landlocked wedge, stuffed in the center. It was mostly hemmed in to the north by Canal Street.

Putting these evolutions of urban development together, the landlocked Sixth Ward was also home to one of the most awkward—and ultimately most notorious— intersections in New-York's history. In sharp contrast to the neat, clean angles of the regimented uptown grid, the heart of the Sixth Ward consisted of an ungraceful collision of three streets: Orange, Cross, and Anthony. While Orange and Cross Streets intersected at right angles, Anthony Street barreled straight into the intersection, where it came to an abrupt dead end.[34] The resulting ganglion created by five inward vectors gave rise to an misshapen pentagon. The spot was called the Five Points. It would earn a reputation as one of the world's poorest and most dangerous slums, a symbol of degradation, and a focal point of human misery.

Making matters still worse for Five Points' residents in the mid-nineteenth century, the Sixth Ward was a particularly unpleasant plot of land. Although it had once been the location of Collect Pond, a bucolic body of fresh water, by the turn of the nineteenth century it was so thoroughly polluted from years of dumping human and industrial waste that it was a public nuisance. Among other things, "dead animals, together with every species of rubbish and offal, were thrown into it."[35] The common council decided the best way to rid the city of the nuisance was to fill it in. So in the first years of the nineteenth century, Collect Pond was buried in landfill and any other materials readily available. Within ten years—just as city's grid was being announced—it became clear that the soggy landfill needed to be better drained, so city engineers began funneling water to an open canal running alongside Canal Street and empting into the Hudson River. The solution was only temporary, as the open canal began to fill with raw sewage. It needed to be paved over within a decade.

Meanwhile, the old Collect Pond area—although still soggy and badly irrigated—was a construction site on which the city built a prison, or "house of detention."[36] The large building was officially called the Halls of Justice, described by city promoters as a "unique and beautiful specimen of the Egyptian style of architecture."[37] However, virtually all the locals called the place The Tombs and Charles Dickens—never short of opinion—described it as a "dismal-fronted pile of bastard Egyptian."[38] The place was as gloomy as its nickname suggested, and damp, to boot. The addition of The Tombs to the Sixth Ward only enhanced the dreary ambiance of the Five Points area and contributed to its sordid reputation. Yet thousands of poor and newly arriving immigrants would call the Five Points home.

***

Tenant-House Living

John Jacob Astor's investments in real estate and his rapidly aggregated family wealth were a bellwether of things to come. Great wealth was being concentrated in the hands of a few New-Yorkers while a countervailing force of impoverished immigrants was flooding the city. Among other things, New-York residential housing options were increasingly diverse.

The richest New-Yorkers built mansions that flaunted their wealth. For those taking flight from the congested lower wards, the great grid of 1811 offered them the equivalent of runway lights for landing uptown. Single men of more moderate means could lease hotel rooms for extended periods of time. The Astor Hotel—yet another property owned by its namesake—was of this ilk. Often run by widows, boarding houses ranging in price and quality provided another option. It wouldn't be until the 1860s that the first recognizable "apartment" building—based on French flats—was introduced on the menu of housing options. However, for those at the bottom end of the income spectrum, New-York began experimenting with an entirely new kind of building. These buildings were unique in character and designed almost exclusively for the purpose of warehousing poor people.

Eventually New-York engineers and architects would figure out how to better diffuse human density. With the opening of the Brooklyn Bridge in 1883, bridges and later tunnels would help disperse people laterally off the island. With the introduction of new building materials such as cast iron and the invention of the elevator, architects begin to envision a city that could disperse density vertically in buildings with higher elevations. However, beginning in 1830, the only way New-York could absorb waves of poor immigrants was inward. They were increasingly packed into squat, compact three- or four-story buildings in the lower wards, folded into the bowels of the city, where work, play, and indoor, outdoor, private, and public life all merged into one.

The new genre of housing fell under the generic label of *tenant house*, a term that would eventually morph into tenement or tenement building. A tenant house was created in one of two ways. As wealthy families vacated single family residences in lower Manhattan to move to bucolic Fifth Avenue and other uptown locations, their homes were carved up into smaller units that could be rented to unrelated families. For obvious reasons they were dubbed *reconstructed* tenant houses. This distinguished them from *new or modern* tenant houses, which were built from scratch for the exclusive purpose of sheltering unrelated families.

Legislative reforms were slow in coming. It took at least two major reports on the conditions within these buildings and neighborhoods, one issued in 1857[39] and the second in 1866, before the state began taking affirmative action.[40] The first baby steps in policing the conditions came in 1867. Prior to this—for nearly forty years—tenant houses were allowed to develop their particular character unfettered and unregulated. By the 1850s they had matured into a full-blown industry of squalor.

The first serious concerns were raised in 1856 when the New York State Assembly—worried about rumors of housing conditions in these buildings—appointed a select committee to give an accounting and to make recommendations. When the inspectors finally ventured into these neighborhoods to collect evidence and formulate recommendations, they were appalled. They reported finding conditions "far exceeding the limits of previously conceived ideas of human degradation and suffering."[41] In ward after ward, they reported, the tenant house "rises in squalid deformity, to mock civilization with its foul malaria, its poison-breeding influences, its death-dealing associations."[42] The inspectors faulted city planners and blamed conditions on municipal neglect and the lack of any form of regulation.

Ultimately, the committee's findings were as simple as they were overwhelming. These tenant houses—whether reconstructed or modern—suffered from "want of air," "want of water," "want of room," "want of light," and "want of cleanliness." However, this list of "wants" doesn't do justice to the creative ways that too many people were packed into too small a space with too few basic amenities like light, water, and waste disposal. If tenant houses shared a single common characteristic, it was that they were built to hold as many people as possible, experimenting with new ways of increasing human density in smaller patches of cubic feet. It is worth considering the densities separately—density by block, density by building, density by floor, and density by room—to fully appreciate the magnitude of this overcrowding.

Each block was overcrowded with tenant house buildings. In some wards this was accomplished by a practice that would seem alien a century later. One square block contained a line of "front" and "back" building structures. The front buildings were narrow four- or five-story buildings nested tightly against each other and facing the street. Directly behind this line of buildings was a second row of structures known as *back buildings*. They were usually located at a distance of twenty or twenty-five-feet behind the front structure.[43] These back buildings could themselves be three- or four-floor buildings or a mere "collection of sheds built of rough boards, each containing four dark rooms," which were "cramped, miserable apartments, scarce fit for dog kennels."[44] These back buildings faced a third row of buildings "at a distance varying from a few inches to two feet . . . the corresponding rear houses of the next street."[45] Finally there was a forth row of buildings, about "twenty or twenty-five feet in front of these last mentioned." They were "the corresponding row of front houses" from the next street over.[46] In short, one square city block could be filled with four rows of buildings, two sets fronting the streets and two sets crammed in the interior. Given this construction scenario, it isn't difficult to imagine how quickly fresh air and light become precious commodities.

Getting from the street to an apartment in one of the back buildings could be a dangerous and tricky business. To conserve as much space as possible, the back structures were often reached through exceedingly narrow passageways or alleys. The committee described reaching one three-story back building through "an alley, the widest portion of which was but two feet, the narrowest nineteen inches."[47] The passageways to the back structures were thus dark, narrow, and often either littered with trash or knee-deep in mud.

Each tenant-house building was carved into as many rentable spaces as could be justified, including cellars and attic garrets. The inspectors noted the particularly poor conditions at the buildings' extremes, describing "the miserable hordes that crowded beneath mouldering, water-rotted roofs, or burrowed among the rats of clammy cellars."[48] In between cellar and attic, each floor of the new tenant houses was carved into four apartments, two toward the front of the building and two facing the back. Each apartment comprised two rooms, with a windowless interior room at its core. So the front room of the front apartments might be afforded some light from the street, but the back apartments were often abutted by other back structures. The net result was dark space with virtually no ventilation.

Upper stories were reached via internal staircases located in the center of the building or by steep external ladders. To conserve space, the width of these interior passages, much like the alleyways between buildings, was of "such dimensions that two can barely pass." Given their interior location, "all methods of admitting air or light to them" were "dispensed with."[49] The committee found in many buildings that "not only were the stairways crooked and inordinately steep, but they were so dark that faces could not be distinguished."[50] Charles Dickens entered a tenant house, taking his readers on a journey inward and upward, "ascent these pitch-dark stairs, heedful of a false footing on the trembling boards, and grope your way with me into this wolfish den, where neither ray of light nor breadth of air, appears to come."[51] While the residents might have carried gas lamps or candles, more often than not their hands were probably filled with a sloshing bucket of water or baskets of produce. In the end, the passageways were damp, dark, grimy, slippery, littered, and airless.

In addition to the crowding of buildings, apartments, and floors, each room *within* each apartment was likely to be overcrowded; in some cases a single room accommodating dozens of individuals. For the more fortunate ones, a one- or two-room apartment might contain a single family of varying size. One young immigrant described how his family of eight managed in a one-room residence. Five children—two boys and three girls—shared a single mattress stuffed with "chaff" by sleeping three "at the head and two at the foot" of the bed.[52] At the same time, his parents shared a separate bed with a newborn infant.

Less fortunate families often shared one- or two-room apartments with other unrelated tenants. The inspectors described finding five families of twenty people in "one room, twelve feet by twelve . . . with only two beds."[53] They reached another, by ladder, where they found an eighteen-by-thirty-foot room where three families lived "under the broken and leaky roof."[54] At 39 Baxter Street—in the heart of the Five Points—in a rear building, the committee found "fifteen persons living in one room, the height of which, from floor to ceiling, was seven feet, and the floor fifteen feet by fourteen."[55]

Some tenants sublet their space to additional boarders to help defray the cost. Apartments were priced according to location, most renting from two dollars to eight dollars per month.[56] Invariably, the rooms that were "situated in the back of the building" were both "cheaper and darker" than those in the front.[57] In one "miserable garret," inspectors found a mother who was paying "three dollars per month for a portion" of the space. She had "been obliged to sell her bedstead to meet rent, and slept with her baby on the floor."[58]

At the other end of the income spectrum, building owners were making huge profits in rent collected for deplorable, substandard housing. The more people landlords could cram between the dank basements and leaking roofs, the more lucrative the property. In one building alone, inspectors calculated rents amounting to ninety dollars per month were extracted from poor tenants.

***

Vermin, Sanitation, and Fever Nests

Mold, fungi, insects, roaches, and rodents could be counted among the residents in tenement houses. In some apartments, vermin "overran the walls, floors and ceiling" and some "tortured occupants complained that they had not slept for several nights."[59] Inspectors described walls as "black and mildewed."[60] One apartment occupant complained that the wood ceiling "was soaked with water that entered through the broken roof whenever it rained" and other residents "were obligated to move their drenched beds from spot to spot as the dropping became too troublesome to permit sleep."[61] In another apartment, inspectors noted "smoke-discolored lathing, through which thick moisture was constantly oozing."[62] The damp conditions favored the growth of mold, mildew, and mushrooms.

Water, sewage, and garbage conditions could be dire as well. Landlords were not required by city or state law to connect tenant houses to either water or sewer lines. Water for the residents was often drawn from "a hydrant connected to the Croton water pump in a common yard."[63] The sewer situation was even worse. Most residents used external outhouses, privy vaults, "middle sinks" or "school sinks," or other public facilities located in the interior courtyards. In some cases these privy vaults were ostensibly connected to sewer lines by drains, although it wasn't uncommon for drains to become clogged by rubbish or garbage thrown into the vaults by residents.

In other cases, there were no drains, and privies or vaults needed to be shoveled out by human caretakers or night-soil men. In one district, inspectors reported that "one-half of the tenant-houses have no sewers connected with them; consequently, the stench from all of the water-closets, during the summer, is absolutely unbearable and perilous."[64] Inspectors found that the vaults "sometimes become filled to overflowing," causing the outdoor yards to become "covered with their contents."[65] This flooding was most likely to occur "after a hard rain, where the spout from the house is so arranged as to conduct the rain-water from the roof into the privy vault, which overflows, spreading the contents not only over the yard, but in some instances in the cellar, the bottom of which becomes covered with this semi-liquid filth."[66]

The public health issues that resulted from these conditions were many. They included air- and water-borne diseases and the associated fevers and intestinal maladies they produced. Among them were malaria, typhus, typhoid, and scarlet fever as well as small pox, diarrheal maladies, cholera, and dysentery. One later hygiene report linked diarrheal diseases to a combinations of "stagnant water, obstructed drainage, putrefying garbage, decomposing animal matters, putrid exhalations from various sources, deteriorated food articles, and the use of water from wells into which the putrid soakage of filth had percolated."[69]

***

Special Nuisances: Livestock and Industry

As if the human congestion wasn't problematic enough, these districts were often shared with livestock and industries. A hygiene report of 1866 succinctly summarized the ways in which these mixed use neighborhoods created "special nuisances" for public health (see Figure 2.1).

Residential neighborhoods were shared with chickens, geese, hogs, cows, goats, and horses. So too were the industries associated with them. Among

Table 2.1. Enumeration of Special Nuisances

1. Filthy streets
2. Neglected garbage and domestic refuse
3. Obstructed and faulty sewers and drains
4. Neglected privies and stables
5. Cattle pens and large stables in the more populous districts
6. Neglected and filthy markets
7. Slaughter-houses and hide and fat depots in close proximity to populous streets
8. Droves of cattle and swine in crowded streets
9. Swill-milk stables and their products
10. Bone-boiling, fat-melting, and their accompaniments within the city limits
11. The sulphuretted, ammoniacal (sic), and carburetted gases and offensive exhalations that are needlessly liberated and widely diffused in gas manufacture and purification
12. The accumulations of dumping-grounds and manure-yards in vicinity of populous streets
13. The present management of refuse and junk materials in the city
14. The unreasonable overcrowding of the city railway cars, and the absence of all sanitary authority, permitting the unguarded transit and public exposure of persons with small-pox and other loathsome maladies in the public conveyances and otherwise in the streets
15. The neglect of dead animals in the streets and gutters of the city

Source: Report of the Council of Hygiene and Public Health of the Citizens, 1865, xciii.

other things, work horses were plentiful, as were stables to house them and blacksmiths to shoe them. In the Sixth Ward alone, there were forty-three stables, some "situated between the front and rear of tenant-houses" and others located "in the basement of tenant-houses."[67] Geese were kept for down, chicken for eggs, and cows for milk. In addition, all were used for food and slaughterhouses were located next to tenant houses, schoolyards, and churches. It wasn't until 1867 that owners of swine were "prohibited by ordinance from letting them run at large in the built-up portions of the city."[68] So added to the list of human congestion and waste was that produced by livestock of all kinds, some of it wandering freely about.

Other industries and businesses also flourished in residential neighborhoods. Stores, breweries, and ale houses operated on the ground floor of tenant buildings. For example, in addition to The Tombs, the notorious Sixth Ward had 182 dwellings, 43 stables, 406 liquor stores, 29 brothels, 117 manufacturers, and 528 stores.[69]

In sum, the tenant houses served as homesteads, workhouses, brothels, stables, stores, pig pens, and chicken coops, together forming a tightly packed, unregulated conglomeration. Undoubtedly residents did what they could to keep their own dwellings clean and neat and safe, but they received no help in the form of municipal services or regulatory controls. Outside critics were quick to attribute the wretched living conditions to the character of the residents who inhabited them. The 1857 hygiene report noted that "here, in the tenant-house, exist the pauper and criminal population, from whose ranks are recruited the '*dangerous classes*' that become thieves, bullies, murders, and law-breakers of every kind,"[70]

***

Housing, Health, and Vagrant Children

Given the state of residential housing and the general health and sanitation conditions during this period, it is not so difficult to see why children were at risk. Diseases flourished and illness were common. Parents died, leaving orphans. Accidents, whether by carriage collision on overcrowded streets or due to unregulated sweatshop conditions increased the likelihood of disability or physical incapacity, putting children at risk. Parental hospitalization or ill health left children temporarily or permanently on their own. Single parents, particularly women, struggled. Children fled apartments to spend the night sleeping in the relative fresh air of the streets or docks. Others were put out by struggling parents, and child abandonment was a genuine problem.[71] In short, health and housing conditions were such that homeless and vagrant children, readily apparent on the city streets, was a natural result.

***

Family Employment

Employment opportunities for people living in the lower wards were varied. Some worked in saloons, ale houses, grocery stores, or junk shops. Women might work in needle trades, provide domestic help, or do laundry. Men were likely to become watchmen, shoemakers, drivers, and cartsmen. Unskilled, semi-skilled, and skilled jobs were available, from ditch digging to watchmaking. A variety of manufacturing jobs existed. Sometimes these were located in small factories or workhouses scattered throughout the neighborhood. Sometimes sweat shops operated out of tenant-house apartments. Street peddlers were plentiful and sold everything imaginable.

The jobs available to impoverished and unskilled immigrants were decidedly unglamorous. There was widespread consensus that the very lowest rung of all belonged to the rag and bone pickers.[72] Perhaps no single family occupation better illustrates the abject poverty and desperate living and working conditions for families in areas like the Five Points than rag and bone picking. Hordes of workers would "sally out at daybreak with their baskets and pokers" in search of refuse to recycle.[73] They combed "gutters, sinks, hospital yards, and every vile locality imaginable."[74] They returned to empty their "baskets, bags and carts . . . into a common heap"[75] or place them on small wooden platforms "choking up the narrow entries" with "bags and baskets of calves' heads, offensive putrid portions of the jowls and bones in every stage of decomposition."[76] They would pick through the pile, rescuing scraps of meat "to prepare soups and ragouts" and separating bones from rags. Bones were boiled and rags, washed and dried and then sold "to adjacent shop-keepers who live by the traffic."[77]

All this—the sorting, bone boiling, rag washing, and drying—was conducted "in the single apartment used for cooking, eating, sleeping, and general living purposes, by the tenants."[78] As one inspector noted, to "these horrible practices are superadded the personal filth, stagnant water, fixed air, and confined, dark and damp holes, all characteristic of the tenant-house system. . . . It is no wonder that these unfortunate people are yearly decimated" by a variety of epidemics that have "made frightful havoc among them in past years."[79] In addition to the diseases, the noxious stench of these combined activities, including "fermenting organic matter" and "putrefying carcasses" was nearly beyond human comprehension.[80] From blocks away one could smell "the effluvia of putrefying flesh, from numberless bone-boiling places and bales of filthy rags stored in cellars and sheds."[81]

Life was particularly difficult for these human scavengers in the winter months, when snow covered the rags and bones. "In such seasons, the children are sent out to sweep crossings or beg," reported the inspectors in 1857. They were also adept "in vice at the tenderest ages."[82]

***

Child Labor and Income

In poor families, children were essential contributors to the family income. Their labor helped parents pay the rent and put food on the table. Parents were legally entitled to whatever children earned. As children aged, some parents essentially charged their children for room and board. Much later, Mr. Brace would reflect on a young boy who was expected "to earn the eighty cents by his boot-blacking" for his father or he was not to return home.[83] The father "did not care in the least how long his son would remain out sleeping under market stands . . . but he insisted on the boy paying over to him, when he would return, at the rate of eighty cents per day for all the time of his absence."[84]

Well before child labor laws, poor children worked in a stunning variety of industries and occupations. They were hired in factories manufacturing hoop skirts, and they rolled cigars, braided ropes, made tassels, colored maps, and folded newspapers. They served as canal boys or stevedores. In tenement-house apartments they stitched shirts, stuffed pillows with goose down, and made hats.

The most visible child laborers were engaged in street-based trades. These children often generated income from a hybrid mix of selling, begging, and petty theft. Their ragged appearance made them objects of charity from passersby as well as enhanced sales of their merchandise. They carried mail, messages, and bags. They bundled scraps of wood and strapped tobacco. They fetched and hoisted ropes on sailing vessels. They shined shoes and swept the filth from cross walks. They peddled everything from apples, corn, buttons, pencils, and pins to matches. They swiped and pilfered things too, such as loose coal, coffee, oranges, cotton, and tin.

Sixteen-year-old Johnnie Morrow wrote an autobiography in 1860, illustrative of the variety of ways that children contributed to family support.[85] His family barely eked out a living in New-York, and Johnnie was an essential contributor. For a while he sold matches. Starting with a small stock purchased in the wholesale market, he could repackage the loose matches and sell them at a small profit. He also peddled a variety of books and magazines.

Sometimes his father sent him out with "three or four cents to slip into the hands of some stevedore as he was shoveling coal into the bunker of a vessel." In return, Johnnie reported, "The stevedore would pitch a shovelful of coal into my basket."[86] The transaction worked to the benefit of the stevedore and the boy but clearly to the disadvantage of the person paying to fuel a ship.

Other days, Johnnie's father dispatched his son to collect "firewood from wood-piles on the steamer-docks" or "find stray pieces lying neglected on a wharf where there had stood a few days before a huge pile." The father was not particular about his son's methods of procurement and cared little, Johnnie reported, about "how dishonestly I might come by my daily load."[87] So Johnnie was left with no other option than to make "a cautious prowl around some large pile" which "would generally afford an opportunity to make way with a good-sized stick."

The docks—in a constant state of flux with cargo coming and going—were particularly vulnerable to this sort of pilfering. The practice of snatching items from a pile, bag, or bale or siphoning from a keg, cask, or barrel was fairly common. The job was best accomplished by children working together. Of this practice Mr. Brace noted, "I have sometimes stopped, admiringly, to watch the skill and cunning with which the little rascals some not more than ten years old, would diminish a load of wood left on the docks; the sticks were passed from one to another, and the lad nearest the pile was apparently engaged eagerly in playing marbles. If the woodman's attention was called to his loss, they were off like a swarm of cockroaches."[88] While not necessarily approving of their thieving, Brace nonetheless admired their street savvy and cooperative efforts of the boys. Less approving was Police Chief Matsell, who reported he had dealt with "one instance" in which an "entire bale of cotton was stolen piecemeal" from the docks, and the boys were only "caught when they returned for the purposes of filching the bag itself."[89] Matsell complained that he simply didn't have the manpower to post police officers on every dock, pier, and wharf to stand guard.

***

Newsboys and the Penny Press

On September 3, 1833, Benjamin H. Day launched New-York's first "penny press," *The Sun*.[90] Introducing a daily newspaper that sold for a single cent was a radical, revolutionary, and—many believed—foolhardy move. "What! At this cent? It is too small a business," was a common refrain.[91] Mr. Day knew he would have to make up for the diminutive price by selling enormous quantities of the *Sun* if his experiment was to be a success. This would require "much labor and the strictest economy."[92]

Mr. Day eyed the poor, semi-vagrant street boys. Initially, he "rounded up six or eight boys and gave each 125 sheets" and assigned them a selling district. He paid the boys "$2 a week for selling these," and he admonished the boys "not to desert their district during the day unless [they] had sold out [their] allotment."[93] The first day of this new arrangement he discovered that there were "several active boys in the squad," and they had sold out their entire stock in a mere two or three hours.[94] So the publisher added an incentive. If the boys rid themselves of their 125 papers, they could come back and get more papers "at $.09 a dozen," thus increasing the boys' profit margin.[95]

Mr. Day began to see the potential in using these boys as a critical arm of the penny press's distribution apparatus. The boys worked hard and hustled. They were competitive and motivated to move stock. They were cunning enough to figure out how to do this successfully, and even small incentives kept the boys coming back for more.

Given his success, "within short order other publishers were chasing his tail, including James Gordon Bennett, a Scottish immigrant who introduced his own penny paper, *The Herald*, in 1835."[96] Mr. Day's disciplined, regimented, district-based approach to distribution gave way to a more chaotic, laissez-faire system favored by Mr. Bennett. He "insisted on up-front cash payment for copies."[97] With this change, the newsboy role shifted from that of salaried employee to working on commission as independent contractor. Significantly, the upfront purchase of merchandise meant the boys incurred financial risk. If they failed to get rid of their entire stock of newspapers before the next edition—or the latest extra—rendered their wares obsolete, they got *stuck short* and had to absorb the financial loss. As hard as this was on the boys, it also helped fortify their public image. The boys had to learn to gauge market conditions daily. Inclement weather or dull headlines diminished sales. The newsboys adjusted accordingly. This earned them the reputation of being among the brightest, shrewdest, and hardest working children in the street-based occupations.

By 1847, no fewer than eighty different papers were being published in New-York.[98] Among them were general rags (such as *The Sun*, the *Tribune*, and *The Herald*), specialty papers (such as *National Anti-Slavery Standard* and *Youth's Temperance Advocate*), papers by language or nationality (such as *German Staats Zeitung, Die Zeit, Deutsche Schnellpost*, and *Irish Volunteer*), and assorted religion-based papers. Not all were distributed by newsboys, but they were responsible for disposing of an enormous quantity and a great diversity of newspapers.

By the 1850s newsboys had become an ubiquitous presence. "No city," a tourist guide would later gloat, "possesses so large or alert an army of newsboys"[99] as New-York. Twenty years earlier newsboys hadn't existed, but by the mid-nineteenth century publishers could barely survive without them. The penny press had grown into a gigantic and competitive business and the newsboys were an indispensable part of its success.[100] Publishers relied on the energy and leg- and lung-power of hordes of poor boys to build their fortunes.

***

Youthful Independence and Vagrancy

All this selling and scavenging took time. In fact, it often required a full-time commitment. Poor children's need to work long hours meant that few attended school regularly. At best their attendance was sporadic; at worst, they did not attend at all.

However, the fact that children could earn a living in such a variety of different occupations also placed them in an interesting social position in the mid-nineteenth century. Their financial independence afforded them a level of freedom and loosened their dependence on adults. Mr. Brace wrote of New-York's street children with some admiration: "They could dodge an 'M.P.' as a fox dodges a hound; they disliked anything so civilized as a bed-chamber, but preferred old boxes and empty barns, and when they were caught it required a very wide-awake policeman, and such an Asylum-yard as hardly exists in New York, to keep them."[101] Many poor children—particularly teenagers but even younger children as well—lived a vagrant or semi-vagrant lifestyle free of adults either by choice or necessity.

A fair number of these children had "no assignable home" and often flitted from "attic to attic, and cellar to cellar," Mr. Brace would later write.[102] Vagrant and homeless children could be found sleeping in market houses, open stairways, ash barrels, coal-boxes, empty railway cars, and wagons. He reported finding "two little newsboys" who spent one winter sleeping "in the iron tube of the bridge at Harlem" while "two others made their bed in a burned-out safe in Wall Street." In addition they "ensconced themselves in the cabin of a ferry-boat . . . [and in] old boilers, barges, steps, and above all, steam-gratings."[103]

As a secondary consequence of children's financial independence and flexible living arrangements, concepts like vagrancy, homelessness, criminality, immorality, prostitution, begging, and peddling melded in the public mind. Many New-Yorkers looked at this uneducated, semi-homeless multitude of poor children surviving on a combination of work and petty crime and begging with fear and despair. For them, the path from poverty to vice or crime seemed inevitable. The growing class of uneducated, unsupervised or poorly supervised, restless teenage boys and girls appeared to be particularly threatening to the social order.

***

Matsell's Report Revisited

These children were the subject of Police Chief George Washington Matsell's semi-annual report to New-York's mayor in 1849. Matsell carefully divided the children into five distinct groups.

The first consisted of those who "congregate around the piers, &c., where merchandize is chiefly landed."[104] While he credited these children with being "cunning and adroit," he also recognized that they "daily pilfer immense quantities of cotton, sugar, spirits, coffee, teas, &c, from the bales, hogsheads, casks, bags, [and] chests" that littered the piers.[105] The children were able to pierce a bag "in a manner so sly" that one was "forced to believe the bag burst by accident" and carry off its contents. It was possible for children to make off with twenty pounds of coffee or from fifty to one hundred pounds of sugar "through these undetectable depredations."[106] This same system of "petty abstraction" put "all exposed articles of movable nature" at risk. Dock children didn't limit their pilfering to cargo coming and going from the port. Matsell noted that in the "absence of other articles of plunder," the children were willing to "wrench the knobs from doors, steal building hardware from unfinished buildings, lead and copper pipes and even tin roofing."[107] In short, even if things were nailed down, they might not escape the nimble little fingers of the hungry "dock rats" and "street arabs."

Matsell's second "class of youthful vagrants" were the "crossing sweepers."[108] Matsell's scorn for these "small girls" was palpable. They are "filthy in extreme, both in person and language."[109] He opined that "one looks in vain for a single attribute of innocent childhood in their impertinent and preserving demands" and "shameless advances."[110] He condemned citizens who bestowed pennies on these children thinking they were performing acts of "charity and mercy" because the girls spent them at night "visiting the galleries of the minor theatres, or in the lowest dens of drunkenness and disease which abound in the Five Points and its vicinity."[111]

Matsell's third class of children were also "mostly girls of tender years" who were "frequently neatly dressed and modest looking."[112] While these children sold "fruits, socks, toothpicks," Matsell argued that this was merely a ruse to gain access to offices and other places where "in the secrecy and seclusion of a turned key, they submit their persons for the miserable bribe of a few shillings, to the most loathsome and degrading familiarities."[113] Of these child prostitutes, one of Matsell's captains reported, "I have known several instances where these children have grown up, and are now living in a state of prostitution, while others are already in the hospital, and some have been sent to the prison or Blackwell's Island."[114]

Matsell's fourth class were boys whom he generically lumped in the category of "baggage smashers." These gamins congregated around steamboat landings and railroad depots apparently for the purpose of carrying parcels for persons arriving in the city. According to Matsell, "A large portion of them have no homes whatever; they will not hesitate to steal when opportunity offers, and lead idle and dissolute lives, generally sleeping in the markets, under sheds and occasionally in cheap lodgings." He concluded that they had "evil propensities" and "not unfrequently . . . small burglaries" were "traced home to them."[115]

Matsell's final group consisted of boys not unlike the baggage smashers except that they were "the children of respectable parents" who, "through a mistaken leniency, or a criminal carelessness," allowed the boys "to spend their evenings and Sabbaths in small gatherings on the corners of the streets."[116] Matsell found that these boys would "often steal, and many of them absent themselves from the roof of their parents or guardians, for weeks together, sleeping in markets, wagons and other places of shelter, consorting with the vilest of both sexes, and forming habits of vice and dissipation which cling to them through all their after years."[117] In short, these boys took to the street by choice while the baggage smashers were more likely to be without stable homes or families. Nonetheless, in Matsell's eyes, the boys ended up in the same place as the others—as vagrant rogues and petty criminals.

Like Chief Matsell, Mr. Brace and others were troubled by "the immense number of boys and girls floating and drifting about our streets, with hardly any assignable home or occupation, who continually swelled the multitude of criminals, prostitutes, and vagrants."[118] Shortly before his sister Emma's death in 1850, he wrote her expressing his dismay and astonishment. "New-York is whirling on as usual. You can have no idea, Emma, what an immense vat of misery and crime and filth much of this great city is! I realize it more and more. Think of ten thousand children growing up almost sure to be prostitutes and rogues!"[119] Brace shared the view that these children might go astray given the dire conditions in the city. However, he did not see these outcomes as inevitable or preordained. They were a natural result of the environment in which the children lived.

Mr. Brace's work with Reverend Lewis Pease, his trips to Blackwell Island, and his work among the boys at Sabbath meetings had led him to some firm conclusions of his own. For one, children held greater promise than adults. Mr. Brace described ministering to adults as "Sisyphus-like work" that "soon discouraged all engaged in it."[120] His work with children at the Sabbath meetings led him to a different conclusion. In Mr. Brace's view, these meetings "cleared the way" by showing "the character of the material" at hand. He was coming to believe that new intervention strategies were necessary and that permanent reform could only be "brought about by and under changed conditions."[121] His interest was on preventing the outcomes he witnessed among the adults, not just diminishing the existing suffering.

**

Mr. Brace's Invitation

On the evening of January 5, 1853, a group of Protestant men gathered to talk among themselves "on the subject of a mission to the children." These men "had all been working separately in different districts of the city" but had come to similar conclusions.[122] The January meeting was an effort to pool their collective thoughts on the matter.

A few days after that, Mr. Brace received a letter from them containing a proposition. The handwritten note was scratched out on small sheet of lined, light blue paper. It was dated January 9 and began warmly, "My Dear Sir."[123] It was followed by a simple paragraph containing a big idea:

Messrs. King, Howland, Leonard, Elliott, Eaton and self had a talk last Wednesday evening on the subject of a mission to the children. We concluded that the best thing for their interest in our power was to try to secure your services for them. We are able to offer you a salary of $1000 and to bear the expenses of the office, and we hope that you will feel called to accept the proposition. I can tell you a great deal more if I can see you and hope that you will give me the opp'y very soon. At all events do meet us on Wednesday evg at 8 p.m.

The letter was signed by William C. Russell.

Mr. Brace was surprised by the invitation.[124] He was flattered but he fretted. Taking such a position would distract him from his current path as student and scholar. Although he was increasingly disillusioned with the idea of doing "pastor's work" and had expressed these concerns to family and friends, he had not settled on a course of action.[125] He was leaning toward missionary work that was "not orthodox, or according to any one school or sect" but work that would more closely "follow [his] own convictions of truth."[126] Quite simply, Brace saw the life of Jesus Christ as a model for his vision of missionary work. He wanted to travel among the poor embodying Christian values and inspiring others through deeds rather than words.

Mr. Brace struggled with the offer. Ten days after receiving it, he still hadn't decided. He was, however, beginning to lean toward accepting it. As was his customary practice, he solicited his father's advice. The son wrote:

> I have just about decided . . . on an important step for me; that is, to be city missionary for vagrant boys during the year, with office and salary ($1000). I have hesitated a good deal, as it interrupts my regular study and training, but this is a new and very important enterprise. The duties are to organize a system of boys' meetings, vagrant schools, etc. which shall reach the whole city; to communicate with press and clergy; to draw in boys, find them places in country, get them to schools, help them to help themselves; to write and preach, etc., etc. A new and rather expanded thing at present, but to become clearer as we go on. Mornings in office, afternoons in visiting. It suits my sympathies, as variety, and is or can be of infinite use. Still it will keep me here, even in hottest weather, and it binds me down for a year. What do you say? Is it the best field for my talents? Can I do more elsewhere for humanity?[127]

In the end, Mr. Brace accepted the offer. He penned another letter to his father two weeks after starting work. He wrote, "The enterprise is a great one, and for a year I can stand it. Then onto some wider and more intellectual field!"[128]

Notes

1. "From New York," *Daily Ohio Statesman*, September 24, 1851.
2. "The Cry of the Newsboy," *Frank Leslie's Illustrated Newspaper*. October 18, 1856.
3. In the transcriptions of the manifests from the Africa in 1851, the ship's master is listed as A. Ryrie in one and A. Ryne in another. I am assuming that one is an error made in transcribing the handwritten documents and that they refer to the same individual. I have chosen to use the spelling Ryrie here, with its Gaelic origins, over Ryne, which is more likely Dutch, Swiss, or German.
4. Manifest of passengers aboard the ship Malabar, sailing from Dublin, Ireland, and arriving in New York on May 6, 1851, http://www.immigrantships.net/v7/1800v7/malabar18510506.html.
5. Frederick Law Olmsted, *Walks and Talks of an American Farmer in England in the Years 1850-51, Part II* (New York: George P. Putnam, 1852). 182.
6. Thomas Sowell, *Ethnic America: A History* (New York: Basic Books, 1981), 21–22.
7. Sowell, *Ethnic America*, 21–22.
8. Sowell, *Ethnic America*, 21–22.
9. Sowell, *Ethnic America*, 21–22.
10. Sowell, *Ethnic America*, 21–22.
11. Olmsted, *Walks and Talks, Part II*, 182.
12. Manifest of passengers aboard the ship Malabar.
13. Manifest of passengers aboard the ship Malabar.
14. Manifest of passengers aboard the ship Malabar.
15. Sowell, *Ethnic America*, 22.
16. "Day Book" by Unknown CAS Agent 1854 February 4-September 9 (March 15, 1854) in Series V-Diaries, Memoirs, and Historical Sketches by CAS Employees, circa 1853–circa 1980; Subseries V.1 Diaries and Journals of Agents of the CAS, circa 1853–circa 1865; vol. 45. The Victor Remer Historical Archives of the Children's Aid Society (1836–2006). New-York Historical Society Archives.
17. "Day Book" vol. 45, March 15, 1854.
18. Hilary Ballon, ed., *The Greatest Grid: The Master Plan of Manhattan, 1811–2011* (New York: Columbia University Press, 2012), 17.
19. Ballon, *The Greatest Grid*, 27.
20. Ballon, *The Greatest Grid*, 9.
21. Ballon, *The Greatest Grid*, 41.

22. Ballon, *The Greatest Grid*, 57. Breathing life into the grid was a feat unto itself. It would take the legendary surveyor John Randel Jr. fourteen years—from 1807 to 1820—to complete "a detailed atlas of the island." His farm maps and other records are still vital real estate documents as well as works of art. Bringing the grid to life would also take ongoing commitment from a changing cast of characters in city and state government.
23. Ballon, *The Greatest Grid*, 13.
24. Ballon, *The Greatest Grid*, 87.
25. Arthur D. Smith, *John Jacob Astor* (Philadelphia: J. B. Lippincott, 1929), 256.
26. Smith, *John Jacob Astor*, 256.
27. Smith, *John Jacob Astor*, 256.
28. Andrew S. Dolkart, *Biography of a Tenement House in New York City*, 2nd ed. (Chicago: The Center for American Places at Columbia College Chicago, 2012), 6.
29. Dolkart, *Biography of a Tenement House*, 6.
30. Ballon, *The Greatest Grid*, 91.
31. Ballon, *The Greatest Grid*, 92.
32. Ballon, *The Greatest Grid*, 87.
33. *The Great Metropolis; or Guide to New-York for 1847* (New York: H. Wilson, 1847), 53.
34. Although the Five Points no longer exists, you can still get a sense of the place by venturing into lower Manhattan—either in person or via Google Maps—and standing in front of the side entrance (on Worth Street) of the U.S. District Court of the Southern District of New York (500 Pearl Street) directly across the street from Columbus Park. Baxter Street is to the west of Columbus Park and intersects Worth Street. The Five Points was originally created by the intersection of Orange, Cross, and Anthony Streets. Baxter Street was once named Orange and Worth Street was once called Anthony. Cross Street no longer exists but was located where the New York Supreme Court Building now sits (60 Centre Street). For the best description of the evolution of this location see Tyler Anbinder, *Five Points: The 19th-Century New York City Neighborhood That Invented Tap Dance, Stole Elections, and Became the World's Most Notorious Slum* (New York: A Plume Book, 2001), ix–xi.
35. *Report of the Council of Hygiene and Public Health of the Citizens' Association of New York upon the Sanitary Conditions of the City* (New York: D. Appleton, 1866), 76.
36. *The Great Metropolis*, 60.
37. *The Great Metropolis*, 60.
38. Charles Dickens, *American Notes for General Circulation* (London: Chapman & Hall, 1842), 71.
39. In response to a resolution passed in the New York State Assembly on March 3, 1856, a special committee consisting of John M. Reed, A. J. H. Duganne, William Shea, Eli Curtis, and Sam Brevoort was appointed to investigate complaints about the

condition of tenant houses in New York's poorest wards. Among the complaints, they were called upon to investigate were that tenant houses "often carried to a great height, without proper regard to the strength of the foundation walls; that said buildings are cut up into small apartments, which have very little ventilation; that the halls or passage-ways through said buildings are unproportionately narrow, and not constructed with proper care to the safety and lives of tenants; that these houses are mostly filled with the poorer class of persons, hundreds of whom are often crowded into a single building, without any means of egress in case of fire or sudden alarm, except through a single narrow passage." The committee collected evidence through observation and testimony. It reported, in detail, on the conditions found as well as made policy recommendations. The committee's final report was transmitted to the legislature on March 9, 1857 (John M. Reed, A. J. H. Duganne, William Shea, Eli Curtis, and Sam Brevoort, *Report of the Select Committee Appointed to Examine the Conditions of Tenant Houses in New-York and Brooklyn* [Albany, New York: C. Van Benthuysen, Printer to the Legislature, March 9, 1857], 3).

40. The first tentative steps taken to police some of the most dangerous and dehumanizing aspects of life in these buildings occurred in 1867. At that time, tenement buildings were defined as follows: "Every house, building, or portion thereof which is rented, leased, let or hired out to be occupied or is occupied as the home or residence of more than three families living independently of another, and doing their cooking upon the premises, or by more than two families upon a floor, so living and cooking, but having a common right in the halls, stairways, yards, water-closets or privies, or some of them" (Dolkart, *Biography of a Tenement House*, 13).

41. John M. Reed et al., "Conditions of Tenant Houses," in *Report of the Select Committee Appointed to Examine the Conditions of Tenant Houses in New-York and Brooklyn* (Albany, NY: C. Van Benthuysen, Printer to the Legislature, March 9, 1857), 3.

42. Reed et al., "Conditions of Tenant Houses," 10.

43. *Report of the Council of Hygiene*, 239–240.

44. Reed et al., "Conditions of Tenant Houses," 17–18.

45. *Report of the Council of Hygiene*, 239–240.

46. *Report of the Council of Hygiene*, 239–240.

47. Reed et al., "Conditions of Tenant Houses," 18.

48. Reed et al., "Conditions of Tenant Houses," 13

49. Reed et al., "Conditions of Tenant Houses," 23.

50. Reed et al., "Conditions of Tenant Houses," 23.

51. Dickens, *American Notes*, 77

52. John Morrow, *A Voice from the Newsboys*" (San Diego: University of California Press, 1860), 39–40, Digital Archive, www.hathitrust.org.

53. Reed et al., "Conditions of Tenant Houses," 13–14.

54. Reed et al., "Conditions of Tenant Houses," 16.

55. Reed et al., "Conditions of Tenant Houses," 18.
56. Reed et al., "Conditions of Tenant Houses," 16.
57. Reed et al., "Conditions of Tenant Houses," 24.
58. Reed et al., "Conditions of Tenant Houses," 16.
59. Reed et al., "Conditions of Tenant Houses," 27.
60. Reed et al., "Conditions of Tenant Houses," 15.
61. Reed et al., "Conditions of Tenant Houses," 15.
62. Reed et al., "Conditions of Tenant Houses," 15.
63. Dolkart, *Biography of a Tenement House*, 40.
64. *Report of the Council of Hygiene*, 80.
65. *Report of the Council of Hygiene*, 239–240.
66. *Report of the Council of Hygiene*, 239–240.
67. *Report of the Council of Hygiene*, 81.
68. Jacob Riis, *How the Other Half Lives* (New York: Dover, 1971), 6.
69. *Report of the Council of Hygiene*, 73.
70. Reed et al., "Conditions of Tenant Houses," 51; emphasis added. Modern historiographies employing a social control lens tend to argue that the charity workers and reformers of the period equated the housing conditions to the people living within them. For example, Stansell argued that, "with the invention of tenement classes . . . the distinction between people and their surroundings began to blur, and humanitarian sentiment faded away." Christine Stansell, *City of Women: Sex and Class in New York, 1789–1860* (New York: Alfred A. Knopf, 1986 p. 200).
71. Bruce, Bellingham, *Waifs and Strays: Child Abandonment, Foster Care, and Family in Mid-Nineteenth Century New York*, In Peter Mandler, *The Uses of Charity: The Poor on Relief in the Nineteenth Century Metropolis* (Philadelphia: University of Pennsylvania Press, 1990).
72. Writing of London of 1854, Steven Johnson says, "It is August 1854, and London is a city of scavengers. Just the names alone now read like some kind of exotic zoological catalogue: bone-pickers, rag-gatherers, pure-finders, dredgermen, mudlarks, sever hunters, dustmen, night-soil men, bunters, toshers, shoremen"; Steven Johnson, *The Ghost Map* (New York: Riverhead Books, 2006), 1. This was certainly true of New York as well. While these jobs were unpleasant, before an organized sanitation department existed, many of them were absolutely vital in keeping the city running. As Johnson reported of London, "Mayhew discovered these people were actually performing an essential function for their community. 'The removal of the refuse of a large town,' he wrote, 'is perhaps, one of the most important of social operations.' And the scavengers of Victorian London weren't just getting rid of that refuse—they were recycling it"; Johnson, *The Ghost Map*, 15.
73. Reed et al., "Conditions of Tenant Houses," 21.
74. Reed et al., "Conditions of Tenant Houses," 22.
75. Reed et al., "Conditions of Tenant Houses," 21.

76. Reed et al., "Conditions of Tenant Houses," 21.
77. Reed et al., "Conditions of Tenant Houses," 21.
78. Reed et al., "Conditions of Tenant Houses," 22.
79. Reed et al., "Conditions of Tenant Houses," 22.
80. Reed et al., "Conditions of Tenant Houses," 22, cited in footnote.
81. Reed et al., "Conditions of Tenant Houses," 20.
82. Reed et al., "Conditions of Tenant Houses," 21.
83. Charles Loring Brace, *The Dangerous Classes of New York and Twenty Years' Work Among Them*, 3rd ed. (New York: Wynkoop & Hallenbeck, 1880), 205.
84. Brace, *The Dangerous Classes*, 205.
85. The book's title, *A Voice from the Newsboys*, was strategic. Although Johnnie Morrow occasionally peddled books and magazines, he never considered himself a newsboy per se. Johnnie's friend and mentor explained: "The class to which he belongs is most generally recognized under the term 'Newsboy,' but properly embraces all those of either sex, in great cities, who at a tender age are compelled to rely on their own wits and exertions for support." The newsboys were among the most recognizable and plentiful of the street vendors, and they held special sway in the public mind for good reason. The significance of Morrow's description of the various activities he engaged in is an excellent example of how children (and poor families) employed pragmatic survival strategies by piecing together income where they could. It is akin to the variety of pragmatic strategies employed by street youth described in today's social science literature.
86. Morrow, *Voice from the Newsboys*, 28.
87. Morrow, *Voice from the Newsboys*, 27–28.
88. Brace, *The Dangerous Classes*, 176.
89. George Washington Matsell, "Semi-Annual Report of the Chief of Police from May 1 to October 31, 1849" (unpublished report, New York, 1850).
90. The penny press revolutionized the newspaper industry in at least three ways. First, the primary consumers of newspapers shifted from wealthy businessmen, merchants, and politicians, to the common man (and, a bit later, to women). As Bennett noted in his first issue of the *Herald*, "it is equally intended for the great masses of the community—the merchant, mechanic, working people—the private family as well as the public hotel—the journeyman and his employer—the clerk and his principal" (Seitz, pp. 38–39). Publishers capitalized on the rapidly increasing size of the city and its diverse population. Second, given the new audiences, the content of the papers radically altered the nature of reporting. Newspaper content shifted from coverage of stodgy political and shipping news to include gruesome crime reports, colorful human interest accounts, fashion stories, and sport scores. In particular, crime, violence, and titillating sexual topics turned out to be lucrative subject material. Third, the financial model for supporting the industry shifted in two ways: (a) revenue was derived from direct sales but also increasingly from selling space for advertisements and classifieds,

and (b) as noted, the distribution of the penny press required rapid distribution so street sales began to outpace home delivery. In short, a basic change in the market required fundamental shifts in thinking about newspaper publishing from reporting to dissemination. Don C. Seitz *The James Gordon Bennetts: Father and Son, Proprietors of the New York Herald* (1928; Indianapolis: Bobbs-Merrill).

91. Isaac C. Pray, *Memoirs of James Gordon Bennett and His Times* (1855; repr., New York: Arno Press, 1970), 181.
92. Pray, *Memoirs of J. G. Bennett*, 180.
93. Pray, *Memoirs of J. G. Bennett*, 181.
94. Pray, *Memoirs of J. G. Bennett*, 181.
95. Alfred McClung Lee, *The Daily Newspaper in America: The Evolution of a Social Instrument* (New York: Octagon Books, 1975), 261.
96. Lee, *The Daily Newspaper*, 261.
97. Lee, *The Daily Newspaper*, 261.
98. *The Great Metropolis*, 115.
99. *The Sun's Guide to New York: Replies to Questions Asked Every Day by the Guests and Citizens of the American Metropolis* (New York: R. Wayne Wilson, 1892), 241.
100. Historians of the newspaper industry argue about the extent to which street distribution impacted the overall field. It was certainly a factor. However, revenue was increasingly driven by advertisements and classified ads as well. In addition, major technological advances were being made in printing presses and newsprint production. Both cheaper paper and faster, more agile printing presses increased the viability of the penny press and contributed to its success.
101. Brace, *The Dangerous Classes*, 176.
102. Brace, *The Dangerous Classes*, 29.
103. Brace, *The Dangerous Classes*, 100.
104. Matsell, "Semi-Annual Report."
105. Matsell, "Semi-Annual Report."
106. Matsell, "Semi-Annual Report."
107. Matsell, "Semi-Annual Report."
108. Matsell, "Semi-Annual Report."
109. Matsell, "Semi-Annual Report."
110. Matsell, "Semi-Annual Report."
111. Matsell, "Semi-Annual Report."
112. Matsell, "Semi-Annual Report."
113. Matsell, "Semi-Annual Report."
114. Matsell, "Semi-Annual Report."
115. Matsell, "Semi-Annual Report."
116. Matsell, "Semi-Annual Report."
117. Matsell, "Semi-Annual Report."
118. Emma Brace, ed., *The Life of Charles Loring Brace* (New York: Charles Scribner's Sons, 1894), 155.

119. Charles Loring Brace to Emma Brace, February 15, 1850 in Emma Brace, *Life of C. L. Brace*, 82–83.
120. Emma Brace, *Life of C. L. Brace*, 155.
121. Emma Brace, *Life of C. L. Brace*, 155.
122. Emma Brace, *Life of C. L. Brace*, 156.
123. Children's Aid Society, "William C. Russell to Charles Loring Brace. Original Letter of Founders Asking C.L.B. to Be Secretary, and Typescript of the Same" (January 9, 1853), in The Victor Remer Historical Archives of the Children's Aid Society (1836–2006). New-York Historical Society Archives. Guide to the Records of the Children's Aid Society, Series IV, box 19, folder 1, New-York Historical Society; also see box 23, folder 10.
124. Emma Brace, *Life of C. L. Brace*, 156.
125. Emma Brace, *Life of C. L. Brace*, 154.
126. Charles Loring Brace to John Pierce Brace, undated in Emma Brace, *Life of C. L. Brace*, 154.
127. Charles Loring Brace to John Pierce Brace, 1853 in Emma Brace, *Life of C. L. Brace*, 156–157.
128. Charles Loring Brace to John Pierce Brace, 1853 in Emma Brace, *Life of C. L. Brace*, 160.

3
Creating the Children's Aid Society

EXPLORATION AND EXPERIMENTATION

Minister-craft is passing away. Our papers are the pulpits
—CHARLES LORING BRACE, letter to Theodore Parker, 1853

HAVING AGREED TO accept their invitation regarding a "mission to the children," Mr. Brace joined five men—Messrs. Charles W. Elliot, William C. Gilman, Benjamin J. Howland, Moses G. Leonard, and William C. Russell[1]—on the winter evening of February 8, 1853 ready to take formal action. Three other members of the group were absent: Messrs. Augustine Eaton, William L. King, and A. D. F. Randolph.[2] All were "men of influence in the community," from a number of professional backgrounds including businessmen, lawyers, judges, and bankers, and they were "representatives of every shade of religious opinion" (within the Protestant spectrum).[3] While they were men of faith, none were ministers or priests.[4] All had been "actively engaged in the Boys' Meetings . . . or in other charities."[5] They shared a common view that working with adults—as Mr. Brace had once opined—was "like pouring water through a sieve."[6] Instead, they wanted to focus their charity work primarily on children because that was where "the seed of future good character and order and virtue" could "be widely sown."[7] It was there that their prevention efforts might be most effective. The men quickly set to work. Mr. Howland, serving as chair, made a motion, seconded by Mr. Leonard, to "form ourselves into a Society to be called Children's Aid Society."[8]

As the evening wore on, they took additional actions to propel the initiative forward. Mr. Gilman was charged with preparing "a form of incorporation for this Society."[9] Mr. Brace and Mr. Russell were appointed to a subcommittee to "wait upon" a number of other gentlemen, including Hon. John L. Mason, J. Earl Williams, and George Bird to gauge their interest and "invite them to join this committee as working members."[10]

That evening, they took two additional actions. First, they "resolved, that Mr. Brace be authorized to procure a book for Memoranda of Daily Transactions" in which he was to make note "of whatever shall be done by him, as Agent, and whatever of interest may occur in the office."[11] Second, they resolved "that the office hours be from nine o'clock to noon."[12] With these two simple, formal resolutions, the cadence of Mr. Brace's workday was established, as was his responsibility for documenting all CAS activities. It would be his job to bring the idea of a society to life.

***

Implementing an Idea: Daily Routine

Two days later, sitting in his new office, Mr. Brace picked up the oversized ledger book he had purchased and thumbed past the marbleized face pages until he reached a clean, light blue sheet. Carefully centering his words at the top of the page, he wrote "Daily Record" and, directly below that, "Thursday Feb. 10th 1853." Then he recorded his activities:

> Engaged in the morning in the business relating to the office—preparation of a tract to be entitled "Boys' Meetings"—and an Appeal to the citizens of New York for the Children's Aid Society. Visited in the afternoon the Eleventh Ward.

What followed was a detailed narrative of his investigation of the Eleventh Ward. He recorded facts, figures, and observations, demonstrating his early commitment to building his work only after systematically collecting evidence of community needs. Of the twelve thousand children in the ward aged five to sixteen, he estimated that five thousand were not attending school. Furthermore, he noted that many of these were "on the streets . . . at all times, without any restraint."[13] His accounting didn't stop there. Two hundred children were engaged gathering wood chips on the docks, "100–150 boys were known by the police to live exclusively by thieving," and "over 100 young girls . . . race the streets day & night."

Mr. Brace investigated the ward, interviewing experts, visiting clergymen, observing conditions, and counting children. He began to collect the facts and formulate the arguments upon which he would build the society.

***

The Press-Foreman and the Newsboys

The next day, Mr. Brace not only attended to office duties in the morning and explored the Eighth Ward in the afternoon, but he also added a "night excursion" to his workday. He roused himself at midnight and headed over to Printers Row. Once there, he "went down to the *Tribune* Office and in company with the press-foreman, who knows this class . . . visited the coffee and cake cellars where the *News boys* congregate about this hour" and were "taking their supper."

The foreman told Mr. Brace that the boys "sleep often on the stairs and steps of the printing offices and in summer in the Park, and are up at early light for their papers." As a matter of fact, the newsboys worked a very long day. The boys had to be up at the crack of dawn to purchase their stock of morning papers. They had to hustle to sell them before the afternoon papers were issued and the cycle began again. It was demanding work. At midnight they could gather, at leisure, in the warmth of saloons and cellar eateries—like the subterranean Nassau coffee shop—before finding a place to sleep atop a steam grate, in an abandoned hay cart or on the docks.

Mr. Brace recorded his observations of the newsboys. He guessed they were "not more than ten or twelve years of age" but they "had all the manners of old *roués*—drinking coffee, smoking and talking of gambling." He also noted, "They are very keen and sharp, and live perfectly independently of anyone, sometimes making a great deal of money and spending it as freely."

Mr. Brace was so intrigued that he deliberately returned to visit the newsboys again on March 7. He wanted to see them in action. He scrawled the following in his diary:

> Slept in a friend's room in the *Tribune* office last night and went into the press room early in the morning to see the Newsboys gathered. There were some hundreds—crowding and swearing, not averaging 13 years of age. They most sleep on the floors of the alleys and in the boxes for charcoal and wood. They will earn sometimes even $5 or $6 a week. They go to Theatre every night and gamble and drink, very many of them. There were several women and girls among these, but I could not get at them.[14]

The foreman of the *Tribune* had offered an opinion that would resonate with Mr. Brace. He believed that "a course of interesting lectures on some scientific subject might draw them in, in the evenings, and pave the way for good religious influence." More importantly, the foreman suggested, "A cheap lodging house would be an excellent mode" of reaching them. The man may have shrugged in conclusion, adding, "Now they grow up the keenest and most ungovernable set of lads in the City." Mr. Brace noted that "it would require a very peculiar and patient influence to reach them" and added a personal promise: "I shall take steps to become more acquainted with them." He recognized work among these street acculturated children would required both specialized knowledge as well specialized interpersonal skills. Additionally, it seemed clear from the start he would have easier access initially to boys than girls.

Mr. Brace gave all this some thought. He had already planned to establish lodging houses for homeless children—both boys and girls—as soon as CAS had the money to do so. In his opinion, there was no point offering moral instruction if the children's bodily needs weren't being met. First and foremost, they needed shelter, food, and clothing. He was already set in his belief that missionary work, "the old technical methods—such as distributing tracts, and holding prayer-meetings, and scattering Bibles," were dangerously outdated.[15] He recognized that the children "are in no way affected directly by such influences as these."[16] Instead, Mr. Brace declared, "New methods must be invented for them."[17] What the press foreman was proposing was exactly in keeping with Mr. Brace's thoughts about such new approaches.

More important, Mr. Brace intuitively sensed there was something unique and important about the newsboys as a gaggle. He was intrigued for several reasons. First, they were "keen and sharp," so they reflected a positive set of American values. Second, they were entrepreneurial. In fact, they functioned like shrewd little capitalists (albeit on a small scale) and embodied the Protestant work ethic at its best. Third, because they lived "independently of anyone," they were exactly the kind of vagrant and homeless street youth CAS hoped to engage. Fourth and relatedly, given the fact that the newsboys worked nearly full time and lived independently, they had little time for formal education or religious training. Fifth, although they earned good money, they spent it freely at saloons, at low theaters, and on smoking, drinking, and gambling. In Mr. Brace's view, they were constantly exposed to, and tempted by, these questionable influences. Finally, despite their good traits, the population could also be seen as a potential threat. These boys were the very ones who might eventually join street gangs and engage in criminal behavior. In time, this uneducated class of vagrant boys would be eligible to vote and potentially hold enormous political clout.

Taking all these factors into account, Mr. Brace must have instinctively realized he had found his perfect poster child for the fledging society.

Although CAS was interested in helping all children—boys and girls, young and old, housed and homeless—the newsboys were a perfect symbol. In a single image and a single occupation, it might be possible to create an allegory for the mission. These boys stood at the crossroads of salvation and ruin.

Furthermore, Mr. Brace liked the idea of a lodging house. He saw no reason to constrain these energetic newsboys to a house of refuge, almshouse, jail, or asylum where their finest traits would be dampened. These boys were exposed to exactly the kind of social environmental influences and temptation that would help forge character, all the boys needed was the security of a roof over their heads and little guidance and encouragement.

***

Early Office Work: First Circular, an 1853 Blueprint

One of Mr. Brace's most important early office tasks was drafting a "circular" announcing CAS to the public. No doubt his plan of intervention would be met with vocal resistance by missionaries and asylum advocates, so it needed to be carefully crafted. He had to make a case for his grand vision.

Mr. Brace presented a first draft to the trustees on February 21. The group tinkered with it and appointed a subcommittee to make alterations. It wasn't until March that a final version was ready for broad dissemination, both in New York and—perhaps even more significantly—across the country. The circular was undersigned by the secretary and all twelve CAS trustees.[18]

It contained at least five noteworthy features. First, it framed the problem of vagrant children as a *potential* social and political threat. Mr. Brace needed an argument to gain the attention of the increasingly tone-deaf upper class. These boys and girls, he warned, "will soon form the great lower class of our city. They will influence elections; they may shape the policy of the city; they will assuredly, if unreclaimed, poison society all around them. They will help to form the great multitude of robbers, thieves and vagrants who are now such a burden upon the law-respecting community."[19] There was nothing new about linking poverty and crime in public discourse. Almshouse and juvenile asylum advocates had been doing that for decades. What was new was drawing specific attention to the future impact of neglect. The CAS plan proposed taking more than stopgap measures to curtail crime; at its core it focused on *prevention*.

Second, and significantly, Mr. Brace equated rich and poor children. Of the poor he said, "We remember that they have the same capacities, the same need of kind and good influences, and the same immortality, as the little ones in our own homes." In doing so, he sought to minimize class-based morality distinctions and highlight the similarity in developmental needs of all children. What differentiated rich and poor children was that the earnings of poor children were a crucial component of family income and necessary for survival. Children from poor families mixed honest labor (by peddling goods or sweeping crosswalks) with begging, petty pilfering, bold robbery, and prostitution. Mr. Brace saw these choices as driven by dire environmental conditions. "The great temptation" leading to deviant behavior, he argued, arose "from *want of work*." Third, Mr. Brace was critical of existing practices. "Thus far, almshouses and prisons have done little to affect the evil."[20] Nonetheless, recognizing that the newly launched CAS was inviting criticism on this front, Mr. Brace pledged that he would render these institutions "a hearty co-operation, and, at the same time . . . fill a gap, which, of necessity, they all have left."[21] From the start, Mr. Brace recognized he needed to tread lightly when it came to the powerful asylum advocates while establishing and distinguishing his own work.

Fourth, and most important, Mr. Brace laid out his grand plan and pledged that it would be acted upon "as means shall be furnished." The vision was stunning in its size, scope, and complexity. It consisted of a seamlessly connected set of interventions that included community-based programing like Sunday meetings, reading rooms, and industrial schools for children from nearby tenement houses that offered food, common education, and vocational training. In addition, CAS would assign visiting agents to each neighborhood to offer help, do outreach, and make referrals. The plan called for lodging houses for homeless children. It promised to build employment connections with New-York–based manufacturers and with families who might take vagrant and orphan children into their homes. Beyond that, it pledged to make connections with farmers, manufacturers, or families in the country that might have employment or offer homes to poor children in need.

Finally, having laid out CAS's purpose and methods, Mr. Brace asked the public for its support: "We earnestly ask the contributions of those able to give, to help us in carrying forward the work." He politely acknowledged that not every concerned adult had the freedom to volunteer their time but argued CAS "shall be a medium through which all can, in their measure, practically help the poor children of the city."[22] It was a gentle reminder to every New-Yorker that this was their civic and Christian responsibility. Mr. Brace understood that the competition for funding among charities was fierce.

At the time, he had counted no fewer than twenty-three different asylums and ninety other societies in New-York, virtually all of them hungering after donations from the wealthy. At least as important in building his agency would be the public's sympathy and good will.

Embedded in the circular were several important principles that undergirded CAS's mission and challenged then-existing interventions. First, home life was superior to institutionalization. Second, meeting basic needs (shelter, food, and clothing) was a prerequisite to achieving any other aims. Educational efforts were pointless if not accompanied "in union with the supply of bodily wants." Third, education would eradicate bigger social problems. Mr. Brace wrote, "Self-help we believe to be the only cure for a large part of the vice, crime, poverty and disease which exists in our city."[23] In short, cultivating children's individual skills and talents and encouraging their industry were more beneficial than confining children to asylums or jails. Finally, children were better off in the country than in congested, unhealthy urban environments with overcrowded housing and poor sanitation. Mr. Brace believed they were best served by "an entire change of circumstances."[24]

Mr. Brace's plan was both local and national in reach. It addressed immediate basic needs (food, clothing, and shelter) but was built on prevention measures with an eye on long-term solutions. The circular was the cornerstone upon which CAS would be built. Virtually all the component parts of the plan and its fundamental principles were laid out in this visionary blueprint. Systematically, brick by brick, Mr. Brace would put each element of the design into place, test it, and expand, modify, or abandon it until the cumulative result became a massive agency with an elegantly interconnected design for waging a comprehensive and longitudinal antipoverty campaign on behalf of poor children in New-York.

***

Bumpy Beginnings: Workshops for Boys

Mr. Brace began his pragmatic trial-and-error approach immediately. Among his earliest experiments was establishing a shoe pegging workshop for boys. He built an alliance with Mr. Bigelow, owner of a "shoe manufactory in Centre Street," who promised he could employ as many as five hundred boys. Hopeful, Mr. Brace advertised for a skilled foreman to teach the boys the trade and rented a loft space on Wooster Street in which to do it.[25]

Although twenty boys promptly appeared, Mr. Brace quickly discovered a number of flaws in the idea. First, there was the "irregularity" of the workforce. Second, there was a good bit of "work spoiled" in the process, and, third, it was difficult to compete "with skilled labor and often with machinery."[26] Mr. Brace complained that no sooner had he "got employment for numbers of street-boys" than "the machine was suddenly invented for pegging shoes, which drove us out of the field."

Abandoning shoe pegging, Mr. Brace moved on to several other occupations, "paper box and bag-making, carpentering, and other branches" but quickly admitted to "an axiom" that "benevolence cannot compete with Selfishness in business."[27] "Moreover," grumbled Mr. Brace, "these artificial workshops excite the jealousy of the trades."[28] After several months of futile attempts, he declared the entire workshop endeavor an unmitigated disaster. Undeterred, he simply moved on to other ideas.

However, he had learned a good deal in the process and made adjustments accordingly. Among other things, while adults could be counted on to be punctual and reliable, street-accultured teenage boys—who were in the practice of roaming freely—offered an additional hurdle. The child asylums benefited from the fact managers and overseers carefully regulated children's time and restricted the child's movements, Mr. Brace was determined to cultivate these habits in the children themselves without artificial constraints. The experiment solidified Mr. Brace's belief that teaching the trades "are not so necessary in this country as in Europe, because the demand is so great here for children's labor."[29] He reported, "We soon discovered that if we could train the children of the streets to habits of industry and self-control and neatness, and give them the rudiments of moral and mental education, we need not trouble ourselves about anything more. A child in any degree educated and disciplined can easily make an honest living in this country."[30] There was no need to train children for a specific industry or trade. In fact, Mr. Brace had learned during his shoe pegging experimentation that too narrow a work focus might be a liability.

The net result is Mr. Brace would make adjustments. Mr. Peace's House of Industry workhouse wasn't so effective with children. European industrial schools would not serve as the best model for CAS's schools. Nor would he follow the patterns of discipline and restraint associated with almshouses, industrial boarding schools, or asylums. With each modification, the service model would be uniquely CAS's own.

***

Gathering Speed: Industrial Schools for Girls

In addition to the boys' workshops were the girls' industrial schools. Mr. Brace opened two within CAS's first year, one in the Fourth Ward in the basement of the Mariners' Chapel on Roosevelt Street and the second, devoted exclusively to German children, at 202 Houston Street. Mr. Brace hired a "salaried Matron" at three hundred dollars per year for each school. However, the actual instruction was largely delivered by a group of dedicated ladies who volunteered their time.

The object of the first industrial schools was to "reach a class of girls, not now reached by the Public Schools." Poor girls were too dirty and ragged for public schools. Even if the cleanliness hurdle could be met, their attendance was irregular given their need to work. Mr. Brace, recognizing that the girls' incomes were necessary for survival in poor families, had to offer "business inducements" at the industrial schools. The children would "learn something, with which to support themselves," but they would also "get a dinner and receive clothes as they make them" in exchange for attendance. This was a common refrain for all CAS programs, Mr Brace was quick to point out relative to "our public schools" that "before children can be taught, they must be fed and clothed."[31]

In doing so, Mr. Brace understood the needs of poor working families. His goal was not to disrupt them but rather offer complimentary support by allowing flexible school attendance, creating positive incentives, and supplementing their basic needs. His industrial school model was not residential. Girls would come and go from home. Schools were located in the neighborhood and geared toward the dominant ethnic group in the vicinity. Morning sessions at the industrial schools included education in "common English branches." At noon, a free "plain cheap dinner" was supplied by CAS. In the afternoon, the girls learned "something, with which to support themselves."[32] Initially, this was sewing or some "industrial occupation," which included straw-braiding and crocheting, although the offerings would become more diverse and advanced in time. However, they also learned practical skills to promote independence such as "plain cooking as a tenement house family would need" rather than training them to be servant girls for the wealthy. Neighborhood-based industrial schools were designed for girls (and eventually boys) with families living in nearby tenements. However, CAS would happily secure better employment for the girls in New-York or "in the country," if they so desired.

The industrial schools served two important purposes. Educating girls and introducing them to useful skills was one. In the first year alone, two hundred girls attended classes. Equally important, in Mr. Brace's view, was the fact that by volunteering in the schools *upper class* women (and men) interacted directly with poor children. Mr. Brace insisted that it was "the great evil of our city life that classes become so separated. Union Square or the Avenues know as little of Water Street or Cherry Street, as if they were two different cities. The poor and the rich are forming almost castes toward one another."[33] In his view, "these Schools make one link between them."[34] He believed that once exposed to poor children, "no lady" could "afterwards pass one of them in rags and dust in the street, as indifferently as before."[35] So in addition to instructing poor children, Mr. Brace was attempting to tutor the wealthy in tolerance.

***

Visiting Agents

Within two months of CAS's founding, Mr. Brace and the trustees decided to divide the city into "ten or more districts" with the idea of employing "at least one permanent paid agent of the C.A. Society" in each district.[36] Each visiting agent was charged with the duty to visit families, seek out vagrant street children, and become "known as a 'friend' in the ward—not technically, as a Missionary or Minister, but as a helper."[37]

These agents would be neighborhood based. Each visitor was directly connected to one of the industrial schools and they would make referrals to the central office.[38] In addition, Mr. Brace corresponded "with officers of every church in the city—for the purposes of engaging their active cooperation in supporting these paid agents."[39] The agents systematically visited prisons and juvenile asylums. During the first year, CAS removed twenty boys from prison, "where they had been placed for being homeless." CAS agents assured authorities they would find better placements for the children.

Mr. Brace hired visiting agents as soon as funds were available. Mr. Edward P. Smith from Union Theological Seminary was hired at a salary of four hundred dollars per year (notably, one hundred dollars per year more than his female counterparts, the industrial school matrons) and assigned to visit in the Tompkins Square area. By May 1853, Mr. Smith was "very busy in his work," so Mr. Bogan, "a German Lutheran clergyman of excellent spirit," was retained to visit a few days a week "among the German families in Houston

St + that quarter." The understanding that it was beneficial to employ visitors who reflected the community eventually resulted in hiring an Italian visitor as well. Although the third visiting agent added in the early days was Elbridge Thomas Gerry, to canvass the Fourth Ward.

The trustees mandated that "every agent of this Society . . . keep a book of his transactions, as a visitor, showing the number of visits made by him, with such details of circumstances as shall inform the Board of Trustees of what he is doing." These reports were presented to the Trustees "at regular Meetings."[40] Agents' books became invaluable tools, not only for internal accountability but also for supplying the evidence with which to paint rich narrative portraits of the poor in newspapers, annual reports, public speeches, and sermons.

***

Board of Trustees

While Mr. Brace was experimenting with bringing CAS to life on the ground, the trustees were meeting monthly and making policy decisions that were giving shape to the new endeavor. Early on they resolved "that the agents of the Society be instructed, in all cases of taking charge of children, to obtain the written consent of the parents, where possible."[41] Children were never to be placed until "we are first satisfied as to . . . the advantage of the situation to the child."[42]

In April, the board of trustees set up a library at the central office stocked with books for "circulation among the poor children." The collection consisted of contributions "of all surplus books from the Trustees and such of their friends, as they can influence.[43]

They invited others to join the board, reaching out intentionally to a variety of religious denominations. In short order the board included Unitarians,[44] Congregationalists,[45] Presbyterians,[46] Dutch Reform,[47] Episcopalians,[48] Methodists,[49] and one come-outer.[50]

They met regularly during the winter evenings "to write and sign letters soliciting the help of friends whom they thought likely to take an interest in the work."[51] Much later they would joke, "The whole of the invested property of the Society . . . consisted in an office-desk and chairs."[52] Donations trickled in. In the month following publication of the first circular, $250 arrived.[53] The trustees insisted on hearing the names of donors at each board meeting and publishing the "subscriptions of moneys received" in the "public papers."[54]

The first large gift—a hefty fifty dollars—came from Mrs. William B. Astor. Mrs. Astor would remain a lifelong supporter and financial backer of CAS.

By year's end, the "aggregate amount received by the Society in donations" was $4,732.77.[55] After accounting for its expenditures, the fledging agency had a balance of $242.91 at the start of its second year. "We need a more liberal support from the moneyed community," Mr. Brace said, for CAS to make good on its grand plans.[56]

***

Exploration and Experimentation

As the first year of CAS work drew to a close, Mr. Brace noted that thus far, "our efforts among the poor and vagrant children of New York has been mainly one of experiment. We have been explorers, seeking the way to go, and the means to act." While Mr. Brace argued that "we have done no inconsiderable service," it was "very little in comparison with what we propose."[57] Mr. Brace pledged to "act upon the knowledge we have gained, and also to discover new methods" for intervention.

Mr. Brace's exploration had taken the form of collecting evidence from neighborhood residents and professionals including clergy, police officers, businessmen, tradesmen, and merchants. He compiled the data in tables and narrative accounts. He explored the physical environment, systematically moving ward by ward, learning about the living and environmental conditions in each. He acquired as much knowledge as he could about the practices and habits of street youth. It had involved day and night excursions to expose himself to their work and leisure habits. He talked with them and observed them.

Mr. Brace's experimentation had taken two distinct forms. First, he acted on ideas, testing them in practice. His shoe cobbling workshop served as an excellent reminder that that practices had to be adapted to meet the unique needs of street youth and that unworkable ideas ought to be abandoned altogether. However, his experimentation took a second important form as well. He borrowed ideas from familiar models of intervention employed by other societies and missions around him, such as workshops and industrial schools but each had to be modified to bring it under his overall working philosophy for CAS. Chief among his foundational elements was his unwillingness to isolate poor children from their physical and social environments by restricting them to asylums or prisons. As a natural extension of this position, while he was happy to accept voluntary referrals from police officers or prison keepers, judges, or other officials, he was unwilling to rely on coercive or legal mechanisms of control. The children and their parents needed to find CAS's work practical enough to be willing to walk into the office on their own accord. If CAS was going to survive and expand, it had to supplement and improve the lives of the people it served.

***

Bold New Plan: A Lodging House for Homeless Newsboys

On September 19, 1853, Mr. Brace made yet another night excursion to visit the newsboys, this time accompanied by Mr. Smith and a police officer from Chief Matsell's force. Mr. Brace wrote that he was "impressed more than ever with the want of a lodging house for such children. They are exposed to such wretched influences, sleeping in bad cellars—often under drinking cellars or in brothels—or in the streets." He noted that "of course, a man of excellent judgment is needed to take charge of it."[58] Mr. Brace was convinced that it was time to open CAS's first lodging house. He also recognized he needed to start with one that was likely to succeed, be embraced by the public, and serve as a role model and trailblazer for all the rest. Although the lodging house would be open to all vagrant boys, he felt sure this first experiment should be advertised as one for *newsboys*. In addition, he relied on the notion of a *lodging house*, not an asylum. This would dissociate the facility from those associated with the poor and with restrictive measures of control and supervision. The lodging house reference brought with it notions of middle class respectability. Finally, if the experiment was going to work, he would have to select the person to head the endeavor carefully. Mr. Brace knew working with street youth required special interpersonal skills and tolerance.

Writing to his father, Mr. Brace said, "This Newsboys' lodging-house is *the* thing, I hope. I am house-hunting for the year; rents are enormous. We want a half-house or a suite of rooms for three hundred dollars, if possible."[59] On February 13, 1854, just days after the first anniversary of the motion that gave birth to CAS, Mr. Brace reported to the trustees that "after extensive search for the proper real estate," he had "engaged the sixth story of the Sun building for a lodging room for newsboys."[60] What's more, Mr. Brace believed he had found the perfect superintendent for the new endeavor, a man by the name of Mr. Charles C. Tracy.

The board moved quickly to facilitate the alterations necessary to convert the open loft space into a housing facility and hired Mr. Tracy. The new initiative was slated to open in March 1854.

***

Belfast Revisited

By early 1854, Mr. Brace was successfully putting his plan for CAS into action, but he had one more important mission on his mind. The trustees granted him permission to travel to Europe early in the summer of 1854. The board resolved that a "leave of absence" be given Mr. Brace, "for the period of two months and an half and that his salary" be continued "as a testimonial of our value of his services such his connection with our Society, and our belief that his intended visit to Europe will aid the cause in which we are engaged."[61] Indeed, the official plan was to visit ragged schools, charitable institutions, and model lodging houses in London and Liverpool. To some extent, this public agenda was a ruse for a more covert one.

As the final plans for the NBLH were being put into place, Mr. Brace wrote to his father, swearing him to secrecy. "Do not mention about my going out to Europe," he wrote. "If I should bring L. back, I would try to land in Boston, so that we might be among our family first. You would meet us there." The anxious younger Brace wanted to ask Letitia Neill for her hand in marriage. He wasn't sure what her answer would be. As if that wasn't worry enough, he fretted to his father that if she said yes, it would "be close shaving for me to live with a wife, but it can be done, and L. is used to moderate circumstances, though vastly better than mine."[62]

In the spring, Mr. Brace dutifully conducted his business in England but as soon as possible traveled to Belfast. Apparently his concerns about rejection were ill founded. Letitia readily said yes. Others observed the fact that this young American "came from so far away" to ask for the Irish girl's hand "was stimulating to the imagination."[63] More to the point, the pair seemed ideally suited. After a short engagement, they were wed in Belfast on August 21, 1854. Several weeks later, the newlyweds set sail for Boston so Letitia could meet her husband's extensive family for the first time.

To the extent that anyone might have doubted that the pairing of Charles and Letitia was a well matched partnership, that worry was vanquished before day's end when the couple finally reached New-York. Within hours of arriving in the city, with luggage as yet unpacked, Mr. Brace burst into the room where his wife was entertaining new acquaintances. "'Well, dear,' the husband said, "I think we had better go now and see the Fourth Ward School."[64] To the jaw-dropping astonishment of those present, the new bride took her husband's arm and headed out the door to meet New-York's ragged street children. Unpacking could wait.

In Letitia Neill, Mr. Brace found a life partner who would work with him as a teacher at the industrial schools and as a visitor among New-York's poor. For her, "discouragement was not within the possibilities of her comprehension."[65] She possessed a "buoyant temperament" that seemed to steady her husband when he needed courage. She moved through life with a deep devotion to her husband and to his work. At the end of Mr. Brace's second year of employment, when he once again wondered if he should leave CAS to pursue loftier scholarly pursuits, Letitia counseled him not to go. With that, the matter was settled, permanently. Mr. Brace trained his intellectual powers on the field of philanthropy, and the Brace family would be forever bound to CAS.

Notes

1. William C. Russell would later become a professor of history and eventually vice president of Cornell University in Ithaca, New York.
2. Children's Aid Society, "Minutes of the Board of Trustees" (February 8, 1853), 3, in The Victor Remer Historical Archives of the Children's Aid Society (1836–2006). New-York Historical Society Archives. Guide to the Records of the Children's Aid Society, Series I.
3. Charles Loring Brace, *Short Sermons to the News Boys with a History of the Formation of the Newsboys' Lodging-House* (New York: Charles Scribner, 1866), 14; *Thirty-Eighth Annual Report of the Children's Aid Society* (New York: Wynkoop, Hallenbeck, 1890).
4. Boyer, *Urban Masses and Moral Order in America, 1820–1920* (Cambridge: Harvard University Press, 1978), 106.
5. Brace, *Short Sermons*, 14.
6. Brace, *Short Sermons*, 13.
7. Brace, *Short Sermons*, 13.
8. Children's Aid Society, "Minutes" (February 8, 1853), 3.
9. The Children's Aid Society was not officially incorporated until January 9, 1856. It was incorporated under the general act of the state of New York related to charitable associations. Interestingly, CAS had developed a corporate seal with an image of mother with three children surrounding and the words "incorporated 1855" included along the outside edge. The seal was used on one legal document but the

Board of Trustees resolved to replace the reference to the incorporation date with "New York 1853" that "being the date of the origin" of CAS. In addition to the early insistence that daily records be kept of virtually all activities associated with CAS and this tinkering with the foundational date of the agency, both Mr. Brace and the Board of Trustees seemed to demonstrate a recognition of the historic importance of the work and a commitment to preserving its records for the future; Children's Aid Society, "Minutes" (February 25, 1857).

10. Children's Aid Society, "Minutes," 3.
11. Children's Aid Society, "Minutes," 3.
12. Children's Aid Society, "Minutes," 3.
13. Charles Loring Brace, "Early Diary of Charles Loring Brace, Founder of the Children's Aid Society" (unpublished, February 10, 1853–September 1855), in the Victor Remer Historical Archives of the Children's Aid Society (1836–2006). New-York Historical Society Archives. Guide to the Records of the Children's Aid Society, Series IV, vol. 38, New-York Historical Society.
14. Brace, "Early Diary," March 7, 1853.
15. Charles Loring Brace, *The Dangerous Classes of New York and Twenty Years' Work Among Them*, 3rd ed. (New York: Wynkoop & Hallenbeck, 1880), 76.
16. Brace, *The Dangerous Classes*, 76.
17. Brace, *The Dangerous Classes*, 76.
18. By March 1854, four additional trustees had joined the original group. They were Judge John L. Mason; J. S. Phelps, MD; James A. Burtus; and J. Earl Williams. Also see: Children's Aid Society, "Minutes" (February 21, 1853); Emma Brace, *The Life of Charles Loring Brace*, ed. Emma Brace (New York: Charles Scribner's Sons, 1894), 489–492.
19. C. Loring Brace, comp., *The Children's Aid Society of New York: Its History, Plan, and Results/Compiled Writings and Reports of the Late Charles Loring Brace* (New York: Wynkoop & Hallenbeck, 1893), 4.
20. Brace, *The Dangerous Classes*, 9; emphasis in original.
21. Brace, *The Dangerous Classes*, 92.
22. Emma Brace, *Life of C. L. Brace*, 492.
23. Children's Aid Society, "Donation/Subscription Form with Overview of First Year of CAS Accomplishments" (1854), in The Victor Remer Historical Archives of the Children's Aid Society (1836–2006). New-York Historical Society Archives. Guide to the Records of the Children's Aid Society, Series VI, box 24, folder 1, New-York Historical Society.
24. Brace, *Children's Aid Society of New York*.
25. Children's Aid Society, "Chronologies of CAS Property and Facilities" (undated), in The Victor Remer Historical Archives of the Children's Aid Society (1836–2006). New-York Historical Society Archives. Guide to the Records of the Children's Aid Society, Series V, box 23, folder 15, New-York Historical Society.
26. C. Loring Brace, *Children's Aid Society of New York*, 11.

27. Brace, *The Dangerous Classes*, 95–96.
28. Brace, *The Dangerous Classes*, 96.
29. Brace, *The Dangerous Classes*, 96.
30. Brace, *The Dangerous Classes*, 96.
31. Charles Loring Brace, *The Poor Children* (New-York Daily Times, March 23, 1854).
32. *First Annual Report of the Children's Aid Society* (New York: C. W. Benedict, February 1854), 10.
33. *Second Annual Report of the Children's Aid Society* (New York: M. B. Wynkoop, 1855), 11.
34. *Second Annual Report*, 11.
35. *Second Annual Report*, 11.
36. Minutes of the Board of Trustees, April 4, 1853, vol. 2, 1853–1861, in the Victor Remer Historical Archives of the Children's Aid Society (1836–2006). New-York Historical Society Archives. Records of the Children's Aid Society 1836–2006, New-York Historical Society Archives.
37. *Fourth Annual Report of the Children's Aid Society* (New York: John P. Prall, 1857), 7.
38. *First Annual Report*, 11.
39. Children's Aid Society, "Minutes" (February 8, 1853–February 20, 1854), in the Victor Remer Historical Archives of the Children's Aid Society (1836–2006). New-York Historical Society Archives. Guide to the Records of the Children's Aid Society, Series I, box 1, folder 2, New-York Historical Society.
40. Minutes of the Board of Trustees, May 9, 1853, vol. 2, 1853–1861, in Records of the Children's Aid Society 1836–2006, New-York Historical Society Archives.
41. Children's Aid Society, Minutes (June 13, 1853).
42. Children's Aid Society, "Minutes" (April 4, 1853). Within a year, the trustees faced a significant test. They received word that "a girl sent from the Society" for employment with the family of a man named Samuel Richards in Connecticut had been "debauched." The board acted swiftly. Within two days of receiving the news, they held a special meeting. With seven members present, the men heard a report from Mr. Smith about Julia L., the girl in question and acted. They acknowledged that they had "heard with great pain" about Julia, a girl "who had been under the protection of this Society, and by us had been placed" with the Richards family. Significantly, the trustees declared, they wished "to have the case judicially examined, and that the said Richards [be] punished if guilty." They authorized the CAS president "to employ Counsel in Hartford County Conn." and "to use all proper means to have the complaint against Samuel Richards prosecuted."
43. Minutes of the Board of Trustees, April 4, 1853, vol. 2, 1853–1861, in Records of the Children's Aid Society 1836–2006, New-York Historical Society Archives.
44. William C. Russell, Benjamin Howland, and John Earl Williams were Unitarians.
45. William C. Gilman was a Congregationalist.
46. Judge John L. Mason, William L. King, and Cyrus W. Field were Presbyterians.
47. Mahlon T. Hewitt was Dutch Reform.

48. Howard Potter, Archibald Russell, George Bird, and A. S. Hewitt were all Episcopalians.
49. James L. Phelps was a Methodist.
50. Charles W. Elliott was a come-outer.
51. *Thirty-Eighth Annual Report*, x.
52. *Thirty-Eighth Annual Report*, x.
53. Minutes of the Board of Trustees, April 25, 1853, vol. 2, 1853–1861, in Records of the Children's Aid Society 1836–2006, New-York Historical Society Archives.
54. Minutes of the Board of Trustees, March 8, 1853, vol. 2, 1853–1861, in Records of the Children's Aid Society 1836–2006, New-York Historical Society Archives.
55. *First Annual Report*, 12.
56. *First Annual Report*, 13.
57. Children's Aid Society, "Donation/Subscription Form with Overview of First Year of CAS Accomplishments" (1854), in Guide to the Records of the Children's Aid Society, Series VI, box 24, folder 1, New-York Historical Society.
58. Brace, "Early Diary," September 19, 1853.
59. Charles Loring Brace Jr. to father, February 7, 1854, in Emma Brace, *Life of C. L. Brace*, 196.
60. Children's Aid Society, "Minutes" (February 13, 1854); Children's Aid Society, "Minutes" (February 8, 1853–February 20, 1854).
61. Children's Aid Society, Minutes (June 21, 1854).
62. C. L. Brace Jr. to father, February 7, 1854, in Emma Brace, *Life of C. L. Brace*, 197.
63. Emma Brace, *Life of C. L. Brace*, 197.
64. Emma Brace, *Life of C. L. Brace*, 198.
65. Emma Brace, *Life of C. L. Brace*, 198.

4
Opening the Newsboys' Lodging House
PROPOSAL TO PRACTICE, 1854

One night, it was a lucky hour,
Fatigued I had no wish to roam;
I sought the place, which oft before
I wish'd to see, the Newsboys home.
I climb'd the high and winding stair,
The newsboys cheerful laugh my guide,
I join'd the happy circle there—
And found that love at home denied—
My mind improv'd—my better part,
My soul was gladden'd, and my heart.
—WILLIAM COLOPY DESMOND, *Newsboys Lodging House* (ca. 1855)

THE OPENING OF the NBLH[1] was met with skepticism by the wary street lads.[2] Rumors abounded. Among other things they were suspicious about the society's motives. The buzz among the boys was that the entire project was "gaseous" and the NBLH's superintendent was probably "a street preacher," who was likely laying a "trap to get them to Sunday Schools!"[3] Worse yet—circulated another rumor—the entire thing was merely a ruse to whisk them off to the juvenile asylum. They whispered, "It's a House-o'-Refuge trap!," just "a 'pious dodge' for trapping them into some place of detention."[4] They were familiar with the religious and not-so-benevolent charitable efforts of the day all of which involved preaching or policing and were none too keen on intentionally interacting with them. The boys had some good reasons for being skeptical because what Children Aid Society (CAS) organizers were touting wasn't like anything then available in New-York's existing landscape of options.

It is impossible to say what motivated some of the street-savvy boys to climb the stairs on March 18, 1854, and give the brand-new shelter a try on its opening night. However, it couldn't have hurt that Jerry-the-Oysterman was willing to endorse the fledging efforts. Jerry was among a handful of adults who had great credibility with the boys. Not coincidentally, many of these credible souls were also purveyors of food products. Another was Mr. Glendinning, who worked at the Nassau Coffee Saloon, where the boys regularly congregated. He was always willing to provide "coffee-cake, oyster pie, and fish bowl" on credit to a hungry lad when he "had't got a cent." Mr. Glendinning trusted the newsboys to pay their debts and the boys knew it.[5] Like Mr. Glendinning, Jerry-the-Oysterman was equally generous with his clams when the boys got stuck short or on special holidays. Such kindnesses went a long way. So when the mollusk peddler informed the boys that "de shanty's on de dead level" and insisted "that de bloke wot runs it is straight-goods," this may have been all the vagrant boys needed to give it a try.[6] Besides, Jerry would be the first to hear their complaints if *his* information proved gaseous.

Jerry's praise for "de bloke wot runs it" may have been a reference to Mr. Brace or it may have referred to the lodging house's newly appointed superintendent, Mr. Charles C. Tracy. Both Messrs. Brace and Tracy were cut from the same cloth, and both were committed to the same plan. However, Mr. Tracy was the one charged with the immediate and difficult task of putting Mr. Brace's vision of applied Christianity and alternative to the House of Refuge into practice. It was going to be his job to implement that vision in a way that was palatable to a bunch of street savvy teenage boys.

Mr. Tracy's hurdles were many. Yet he proved his mettle and demonstrated the early seeds of considerable talent in working with vagrant teenage boys. Shortly after the lodging house opened, a visiting newspaper reporter noted that "no common man could successfully perform" the task of overseeing these boys, but concluded that "if the Society had searched the world over, they could not have found a man better suited to such a task than is Mr. C. C. Tracy."[7] Later, Mr. Brace's son would remember Tracy as a man who "showed remarkable ingenuity and tact in the management of these wild lads."[8] In all ways, his temperament, sense of humor, and "good judgment and patient kindness," as well as his genuine admiration for the youngsters, seemed to make him the ideal choice for the new endeavor.[9] All that said, on opening night, it was lucky Mr. Tracy got through his first twenty-four hours with the boys—and the building—intact. Within hours the unruly street boys began testing the new project and gauging Mr. Tracy's fortitude as well as assessing his responses.

That first night, Mr. Tracy let the boys into the Sun Building through the street-level door. The willing subjects scaled six flights of winding stairs to the uppermost floor to reach the newly appointed lodging house and gathered in a meeting room that would eventually serve as a classroom, concert hall, and gymnasium. Mr. Tracy addressed his would-be lodgers, "a motley congregation of ragged and rough boys," from a small, elevated podium located at one end of the room, "simply and kindly" telling the boys "the objects of the plan."[10] In essence it was "to prevent them from growing up vagrants, and to save them from exposure to the weather, and consequent disease, and to help them on in the world."[11] Technically, this was a place for boys without parents so they were supposed to be "friendless" or "orphans." No boy would be "harbored while under the influence of liquor."[12] In addition, "no fighting would be allowed in the bedrooms."[13] The rules were minimal but perhaps hardest one for the free-spirited boys to swallow was that there was to be a curfew, and "no boy could gain admittance after ten o'clock."[14] Finally, Mr. Tracy told his charges that one of the cardinal rules of the lodging house was that each lodger must pay "six cents for a bed."[15] He explained that the boys "were not objects of charity" but rather "each one a lodger in his own hotel."

In reality, Mr. Tracy would exercise enormous flexibility in how all these rules got implemented, particularly the one regarding the entrance fee. Nonetheless, the message itself was significant. Mr. Brace later wrote, "The great peculiarity of the New York News Boys Lodging house, as distinguished from similar European institutions, is the payment demands from the lodgers."[16] The fee was an integral part of the carefully crafted intervention design. He recognized that the boys had been independent and self-sufficient starting early in life and "felt strongly that they could be reached by recognizing *their* sense of independence and fair dealing."[17] This meant that CAS's goal would be to "cultivate the feeling of independence and self-respect" and to nurture the boys' fair dealing practices. Nothing in the agency mission should hobble or hinder these strengths.

More important, everything about the lodging house was designed to distinguish it from the child asylums associated with the poor. The NBLH was not conceptualized as being either an almshouse or a charity. Endeavors such as those weakened the character of the inmates, supported pauperism, and contributed to an ongoing cycle of poverty. Mr. Brace felt strongly that the six-cent investment would mean the boys would "value the place more from paying for it"[18] and that they would benefit from knowing they would "aid in the support" of the program itself. In fact, in the first five years of operation, the boys' lodging payments covered $2,156.56 of the program's $8,518.51 operating expenses, or about twenty-five percent of the total.[19] Although a drop in the bucket in terms of overall cost of running the lodging house, it put Mr. Brace's philosophy into practice. In short order, these numbers would also become a marketing tool for promoting CAS's lodging house model as a successful intervention to potential benefactors.

Taken together, the NBLH model merged the idea of charity, hotel, and boarding house. Unlike workhouses, CAS did not offer direct employment to the boys; nor did it require a particular kind of labor in exchange for shelter. Although called the *Newsboys'* Lodging House, it sheltered any boy, no matter what his employment. Framing the facility as a lodging house brought with it a projection of working class respectability and distanced it from poorhouses. The agency sought to walk a fine line between helping boys by providing for their basic needs while fostering independence and building character without subsidizing laziness or dependence. Mr. Brace noted, "The first thing to be aimed at in the plan was, to treat the lads as independent little dealers, and give them nothing without payment, but at the same time to offer them much more for their money than they could get anywhere else."[20] Its ultimate goal was to put into action Mr. Brace's belief that the boys could learn good behavior and be diverted from bad, without artificial constraints placed on their freedom by legal authority. This project took the active engagement and participation of the boys themselves.

Although other rules were developed with time, this short explanation brought Mr. Tracy's opening night address to an end. It had served as a sorting mechanism. Most of the boys stayed, willing to continue with the new experiment. However, another group, "those who had come merely 'to make a row,' left in disgust."[21] In doing so yet another novel feature of the lodging house was on display. The boys could come and go freely. No one was locking them in or baring their exit. Nonetheless, the exodus didn't last long, and the boys didn't go far. Instead, the leave-takers merely retreated and congregated to lay "their plans for a general scrimmage against Mr. Tracy."[22] As Mr. Brace described it, "There was 'larking' going on in the stairways by the outsiders." The boys attacked the gas line supplying the lodging house and "the gas-burner was twisted off."[23] Disrupting the gas source "might have been followed by serious consequences," but Mr. Tracy quickly cut the gas off inside the sixth-floor lodging house, averting tragedy.[24] Next, he escorted the "rough ring-leaders" down the remaining flights of stairs, where they "were politely dismissed to the lower door."[25]

Back in control, Mr. Tracy ushered the rest of the boys into the dormitory, where they were tucked into their beds for the evening. He then retreated and took up his place in his office, which contained a small window overlooking the tranquil scene of boys nestled in bed. The relative calm lasted only briefly. No sooner had he stretched out himself for the night when a projectile—in the form of a single boot— took flight across the room. Covertly, Mr. Tracy watched as a second boot was hurled from "a little fellow's bed." Having been surreptitiously identified as the culprit, the boy "found himself suddenly snaked out by a gentle but muscular hand, and left in the cold to shiver over his folly."[26] According to agency lore, the boys "began to feel that a mysterious authority was getting even with them, and thought it was better to nestle in their warm beds" than continue making a ruckus.[27] As they settled back down, they delivered an early assessment of this strange new place. Slats, the thinnest boy on the ward, murmured to Snowball, the only African American boy present, "No feller need freeze t'deat' in a doorway . . . while de hotel is dere."[28] "Yes, it's 'most as good as a steam gratin," joked one.[29] Yet another chimed in, "and there ain't no M.P.'s to poke neither!"[30] With that, the entire crew drifted off to sleep.

The next morning they were roused at half past six by Mr. Tracy.[31] Several of the lodgers joked that "they couldn't sleep, the beds were so soft!"[32] Compared with the sleeping in the overcrowded tenements, at the police station house, or on the docks, a single bed with sheets and blankets was an acknowledged luxury. One youngster later remembered, after a good night's sleep that, "we took up our baskets, and sallied forth to our day's trading."[33] Indeed, consistent with the agency mission to treat them as independent contractors, the boys were sent out to work, and the NBLH was shut down for the day.

That evening, there was one last test in store for Mr. Tracy, this one challenging the ten o'clock curfew. The boys, of course, had been "in the habit of keeping just such hours as they pleased, and consequently found it very hard to yield to the restrictive influence of a system that required a curfew."[34] So it was not altogether surprising that a small group of returning lodgers tested the rule on the second night of the NBLH's existence. About half a dozen of them knocked at the door, asking for admission at 10:30 PM. Mr. Tracy, "as in duty bound, refused to admit them." In fact, he told the boys gathered on the landing, "that 10 o'clock was the hour, not half-past ten, nor five minutes past ten, but ten." Predictably, the boys' response was to plead "'jest that once" and to promise "they'd never be late again."[35]

Clearly faced with yet another test, Mr. Tracy stood firm. He replied, "Boys, nothing in the world would give me greater pleasure than to let you in, if I could do so and at the same time preserve the rule, but I can't and I tell you now, as I told you at the commencement, that every rule of this establishment must be kept—let what will happen. You may rest as sure of that, as you are that the sun will rise to-morrow. So good night, boys, and I hope that you will find some other place as comfortable as this to sleep in."[36]

With his little lecture delivered, Mr. Tracy retreated to his office leaving the boys standing outside. However, he kept an ear on what was brewing beyond the door. "For a long time he heard them muttering curses 'not loud, but deep,' and presently one of them sang out, 'Mr. Tracy, if you don't let us in, we'll break the door down.'"[37]

The superintendent continued in his patient, balanced manner. "Do so," was the quiet response, "if you wish to gain admittance that way, I shall not try to prevent you, but I warn you against it—I am prepared for any such movement."[38] Mr. Tracy could hear "another low muttering" as the boys were "evidently holding a council of war—but they eventually left the premises without further trouble."

Having weathered these early storms, the NBLH was on its way. From the start, Mr. Tracy was willing to dismiss those who broke the rules—like the boot flinger. He was willing to deny entrance to those who knowingly violated clear rules, as the latecomers found out. In addition, for boys who threatened criminal acts or engaged in dangerous pranks, such as the boys interfering with the gas burners or those threatening to break down the door, Mr. Tracy was neither willing to be intimidated nor to tolerate misbehavior. However, he wasn't quick to turn them over to the police. In fact, being temporarily denied access to the program was the harshest sanction imposed. In the future, many seemingly hard-and-fast rules would turn out not to be immutable, but setting the tone, creating boundaries, and establishing precedent during those first twenty-four hours was undoubtedly critical to establishing Mr. Tracy's authority.

In general, the opening day's experiences went a long way in convincing a small band of street youth that the service might be all right after all. Aside from the pre-emptory evictions of a handful of troublemakers, Mr. Tracy's interventions on the first night were "bland and benevolent" and appeared to have been executed with surgical precision.[39] His actions were perhaps notable as much for what they were not as for what they were. The offenders were quickly and quietly dispatched without a "gaseous" lecture or sermon from Mr. Tracy. So far, no one had stuck a Bible in the boys' hands or uttered a word about God, Christ, or saving souls. Each boy had his own bed. For them, initial cost–benefit assessments suggested this might be a better alternative than sleeping in a hay cart or in a crowded tenant house over in the Five Points. The place didn't impinge too much on their freedom. There were no physical restraints nor corporal punishment like the child asylums. The boys could make their own decisions. In fact, the boys started referring to it as the "boys' hotel," or the "boys' Astor House," perhaps not fully aware of the irony of the latter name.[40] However, the very reference suggests that they saw the lodging house as a place available to them based on their own patronage. The lodgers were consumers and active participants, not inmates.

During the first year of its existence the NBLH would shelter as many as forty-one boys a night with an average nightly tally of about twenty-five lodgers.[41] These numbers would soar dramatically in years to come, but it was a promising start for the fledging agency.[42]

***

NBLH Facility

When the boys arrived that first night they found a space that had been neatly and efficiently fitted out for its new purpose. The open loft was punctuated with a series of structural supporting columns decorated with Corinthian capitals. Shutter-lined windows overlooked Nassau and Fulton streets. All the walls were "white-washed" and the hard wooden floors were "well scrubbed."[43] Everything about the place "betokens the most scrupulous cleanliness and neatness."[44]

The loft was divided into two distinct areas separated by a simple banister and sliding door. On one side of the sliding door was the dormitory. This room would undergo future expansions, and the furniture and the bedding would be constantly replaced and improved according to the best scientific information, evolving health standards, improved technologies, and the latest consumer products on the market. However, on opening night the dorm contained simple wooden double-decker bunk beds, precisely laid out in rows.[45] These wooden bed-stands were called "quadruples" and were "fashioned something like the berths in a steamboat, with two beds below and two above."[46] Initially, the bunks were fitted with "straw mattresses, and [were] quite soft and comfortable." Each bed was made up with bed linens, white sheets, a pillow, and a warm blanket.[47] All the bedding "had just left the laundry."[48] An early resident fondly recalled the "nice little bed with warm comforters and clean sheets."[49]

On the other side of the sliding door was the general multipurpose common room, where Mr. Tracy delivered his introductory lecture. This room was "not quite as large as the sleeping room, yet it was capable of accommodating one hundred boys comfortably."[50] In short order, this space would be smartly outfitted as a classroom with used school desks and chairs donated by the Public School Society. While primarily operating as a schoolroom, the space would serve other functions as well. At times it would be used as a lecture hall for guest speakers, a concert hall for choral performances, a meeting place for Sunday sermons, or—when the furniture was pushed to the side—a gymnasium for tumbling and wrestling or a dance hall for the occasional evening of Irish jigs.

At "the extreme end" of this common space was "the office of the superintendent and the wash-house, between which is the sliding-door opening into the lodging-room."[51] Mr. Tracy's office contained a window overlooking the sleeping space "from which he has a full view of those under his charge." In addition, there was a "couch upon which he sleeps," which was "close to the partition, so that upon the slightest call at night" he was "up instantly to attend to their wants."[52] Finally, the office also contained a secure desk. Each evening Mr. Trace received the boys' extra money for safekeeping, which was "done up in an envelope, with the owner's name marked thereon."[53] It offered another small service to the boys. They could fall asleep without worrying about the theft of their earnings. The coins were returned to their owners at the start of each day so they could purchase stock for the day's sales.[54]

Johnnie Morrow, an early resident of the lodging house, wrote of arriving with his brother late one evening and waking up the next morning. In describing his earliest impressions of the NBLH, he said, "We started up, rather bewildered at finding ourselves in so unusual a place" and concluded that the place "looked neat and commodious, while good ventilation was afforded by an ample supply of windows."[55]

CAS had selected the top floor of the Sun Building very deliberately, and it wasn't inconsequential that among the first things Johnnie noticed was the "good ventilation" and "ample supply of windows." The NBLH was located at the intersection of Nassau and Fulton streets. It was merely a short walk—approximately a half a mile—to the heart to the Five Points. The lodging house residents were intimately familiar with the densely packed tenant-house buildings with their poor ventilation and lack of light. By selecting the top floor of the Sun Building, CAS had ensured that the lodging house was far removed from the filth of the streets below. The building's height meant there was lots of natural light, and opening the windows provided ample cross ventilation and fresh air.

Added to these amenities was indoor gas lighting. Over in the Five Points and other poor neighborhoods, darkness reigned. Windowless rooms in tenant houses were illuminated with candles, hand-held gas lanterns, or coal-fueled stoves, all of which provided dim lighting at best. Gas fixtures were unusual for the poor in the 1850s, so its significance cannot be underestimated. It was a prerequisite for providing evening classes, a reading room, and a place to play cards or games like Fidchell, an Irish board game, after the workday ended.

Finally, perhaps the most significant amenity of all was the indoor washroom. Although bathing was a new experience and an acquired taste for some of the boys, it soon proved to be among the most important and popular of all the novel features of the boys' hotel. With a few quick draws at the indoor pump, cold Croton water was piped from the cistern and carted to the tub or sink. The "bath-room and water-closet" were "attached to the establishment . . . both of which [were] kept in the most perfect order."[56] Given the sorry state of the water supply and sewage disposal just a stone's throw away, these features were not only luxuries but indispensable to the health and well-being of the lodgers.

With its clean beds, natural light, ventilation, indoor gas lighting, fresh water, and sewage disposal, the NBLH offered luxuries almost beyond comprehension given the deplorable conditions in the tenant houses. Taken together, they implemented Mr. Brace's desire, when possible, to change the environment in which street children operated. In New-York, that meant improving on the quality of housing options open to them.

In 1854, this strange new "boys hotel" was a stunning new addition to the list of options for poor children. No matter what shortcomings the boys might find with some CAS rules, this was infinitely healthier, cleaner, and more comfortable than any of the alternatives. It was available for the price of six cents a night, a fee well below market value. It was free of the corporal punishment and physical restraints of the asylums. It didn't take very long to figure out that, all things considered, it was a pretty good deal.

***

Basic Service Structure

One of Mr. Tracy's most immediate challenges was that he had "to make the place attractive enough to induce these wild lads to make use of it and to behave in an orderly manner."[57] They were "to be kept in subjection solely by good management on the part of the Superintendent."[58] A reporter, visiting the lodging house during its earliest days, noted of Mr. Tracy that "he rules the impetuous little tradesmen with whom he has to deal, as easily as though they were the most tractable of children—a fact of which we must confess we should have had our doubts, from a slight knowledge of news boy peculiarities, had we not paid the Lodging-House a visit."[59]

Participation was voluntary, not coercive. As noted in one report, "there are no whips, or dungeons or other coercive measures to scare them into a proper observance of the rules laid down."[60] Boys were not sentenced by judges into the society's care for vagrancy or petty crime like the child asylums, almshouses or House of Refuge. A lad could walk away at any time of the day or night. In one of his reports, Mr. Tracy wrote, "I believe the Lodging-House and its arrangements are popular with the boys, but the temptations of a street life to such boys, and its excitements are so strong, that it is exceedingly difficult to get them here, and induce them to stay."[61] In short, the boys had to be willing to stay based on the value to them. CAS was not agenda-free but Mr. Tracy would have to disguise interventions in ways that made them palatable to street youth. He would have to be persuasive. As organizers were quick to note, "a large number of boys" had been "allowed, from their infancy up, to do pretty much as they please."[62] Mr. Tracy was on the frontline of developing a different form of practice with teenage children. It was his job to try to keep them from ending up in the House of Refuge.

The admission process was simple. Johnnie Morrow remembered the first day that he and his brother were granted entrance "on condition of our paying six cents apiece for the privilege, according to the rules of the establishment."[63] Each boy's name was entered into Mr. Tracy's ledger and had a brief intake interview in which he was asked his name, age, and something about his family background and personal circumstances. The boy's ethnicity and religion were often recorded, as were whether the boy could read or write or do both. The "code of rules and regulations" would then be "explained to the boys individually," as part of the society's plan to make each lad accountable for his own actions.[64] The boys "were given to understand that in no case would they be departed from, even in the slightest particular."[65] In reality, this was far from the truth; Mr. Tracy exercised considerable discretion in all aspects of managing the boys.[66]

The intake process seemed straightforward enough but information was not always easy to come by. Noted Mr. Brace, "It is difficult to arrive at their age. Many cannot tell how old they are. They average from eleven to fifteen, although we have some younger and older."[67] Many were foreign born, and their only birth records were located in the local parishes of the old country. Even for the native-born, regular birth certificates were not yet kept. The net result was that the exact date of birth and age of many of the boys was unknown and unknowable. For example, a suspiciously large number of children either reported being born on—or a CAS agent recorded their birthdays as falling on—March 17. For any Irish child, picking St. Patrick's Day seemed a better choice than most.

Names could be tricky as well. Street nicknames were common and often included ironic, descriptive, or comic tags, such Fatty, a rotund boy; Valise, a boy who earned his living carrying bags for passengers on the docks; Lush, so dubbed because of his attraction to girls; Roundhearts, named after a popular, small molasses cake of which he was fond; and the Professor, a particularly loquacious young man.[68] For some of these boys, the nicknames supplemented their birth names. Fatty was a lad named Matt Coleman, and the Professor's real name was Danny O'Sullivan.[69] According to Mr. Brace, "in a great many instances Mr. Tracy succeeds, by stratagem, in getting the real name, and when he does so, he quietly enters it on the book and says nothing about it, till the boy himself discovers it, and is puzzled beyond measure to ascertain how it leaked out."[70] However, in other cases even this information was not certain. "It is an interesting fact," CAS officials would later observe, "that some of these boys have not known their own names, so utterly vagrant have they been."[71]

For example, the first boy to sign Mr. Tracy's registry on opening night was Mickety. Mickety fell into the class of boys who didn't know much about his own personal history. His parents were dead, and he had no adult guardian. He had been on his own for a very long time. The society characterized Mickety as a "speculator" but not in the traditional sense of the newsboys' street parlance. For them, a speculator was a boy willing to assume a risk by buying a large stock of newspapers while commissioning younger boys to sell for him. However, CAS used the term *speculator* to describe Mickety because on the opening night of the NBLH, he shoved forty-two cents across Mr. Tracy's desk, paying for an entire week's lodging in one fell swoop. For Mr. Tracy, this confidence in the mission bode well. As a practical matter the boy was willing to play his part and pay for the services. As a philosophical matter he demonstrated his willingness to invest in the idea. It was a gesture that stood out. Years later, Mr. Tracy would reflect, it "created a great impression by paying at once his whole week's lodging in advance."[72]

***

The Bathing Requirement

One requirement that was quickly added to NBLH's short list of rules involved personal hygiene. It "was made a condition of lodging, that every boy should take a bath."[73] The demand was initially met with "great reluctance" by the boys, but it soon became "prized as a privilege."[74]

It was a requirement born of practical experience. In general, life in mid-nineteenth century New-York was a filthy business, particularly for the poor. For vagrant boys who made their beds sleeping out in hay carts, wagons, ash barrels, coal-boxes, cellars, barns, or on the docks, it was not unusual to come to the NBLH covered with vermin. Scrubbing from head to foot was not only critical for an individual's sake but was also necessary to ensure the overall health and well-being of other residents.

"How long is it since you had a clean shirt on you?" Mr. Tracy queried one new arrival.

"Three weeks ago, I put on one," was the answer.[75]

Mr. Tracy confiscated the boy's clothes and sent him directly to the bath. He was supplied with fresh apparel and his old rags were unceremoniously incinerated.

Another evening, a boy lingered in the bathroom after the others had gone to bed. He eventually emerged, tearful and "clearly in pain," and approached Mr. Tracy, who was sitting in the schoolroom. "May I have a plaster for my head, Sir?" the boy asked.

Upon investigation what Mr. Tracy discovered was "stomach-turning." The boy "looked as if he had been smitten with leprosy. The crown of his head was nearly bald and the hair had been eaten away down to his neck. There were large livid spots about his shoulders, and back where he had been bitten by vermin till his flesh had assumed a putrid appearance."[76] According to a witness of the event, Mr. Tracy, with "considerable strength of nerve, and unflinching perseverance," marched the boy back into the bathroom and spent the next half hour scrubbing the boy's scalp while the "boy winced in pain." Mr. Tracy bound up the wounds, wrapped the boy's head with "a clean linen cloth," dressed him in "a clean shirt, cap, and other clothes" and disposed of his existing filthy attire.

Only after tending to the boy's wounds had Mr. Tracy asked, "Where did you get that bad head?"

The boy recounted his story. He had left his job of running errands in New-York when he heard that there was "so much money" to be made by working on the canals. He lived on a vessel for two weeks and "slept out in his cloths, and in dirty places" and become infested with vermin.[77]

It only took a few such incidents before the NBLH began the practice of "incinerating clothes that crawled with vermin" and "trimming boys hair closely" on a fairly regular basis.[78] In later reports, they noted that "applicants for admission sometimes present so filthy an appearance as to require scrubbing to get them clean" and that "in such cases they are shorn of their long uncombed locks, their old clothes burnt or destroyed, and clean given to them in their place."[79]

In time, the boys came to appreciate the fresh, cold water, which seemed to have restorative powers for those who arrived depressed and in a bad way. One summer day when the evening temperature soared into the 90s, one regular lodger was observed pulling at the pump and then "hurried into the bathroom to enjoy the luxury and refreshment of soap and Croton."[80] At the other extreme there were evenings when the temperature dipped so low that water cistern froze solid, but an observer described the boys as "very willingly" passing the water pail "from hand to hand with great alacrity" to supply water, and "there was no appearance of an attempt to avoid this employment."[81]

**

Intake Dilemmas: Shaping Agency Policy

Despite the seemingly easy NBLH admission process, decisions associated with entry sometimes proved far from simple. Daily, Mr. Tracy was confronted with issues caused by urban poverty and forced to use his discretion when the society's values, mission, or rules collided with the realities of the boys' lives. He responded to specific cases and later CAS forged more consistent and clearer policies for broader application.

**

The Parent Problem

Initially, one of the explicit rules was that the boys were to be friendless, orphaned, homeless, or "houseless" and on their own. The society was almost immediately confronted with a complex array of family problems that necessitated flexibility in relation to the no-parent rule. The lodgers, like all poor children, came from complicated family situations, in part because illness, desertion, and death were so prevalent. Sometimes a boy did not know his parents' whereabouts. Parental abandonment was not uncommon. Furthermore, given the state of communication systems, locating parents, even if they existed, could be challenging, particularly if the parents had moved several times and a boy didn't have enough information to help track them down by mail or messenger. The society claimed that "a large majority" of the newsboys were orphans or "half-orphans," but noted "others have been cast off by unfeeling parents, whilst others have dissipated, vagrant, or otherwise unfortunate ones."[82]

For example, Stephen was only fourteen years old and described a father so violent that he had "stabbed his mother in the face with a knife" during a drunken rage. Stephen's abusive father had since died, but his mother was being hospitalized at New-York Hospital.[83] It is unclear how long Stephen stayed with the society. However, the NBLH would have taken him in temporarily or long term, depending on his mother's condition and situation. If necessary, CAS would have tried to find Stephen a permanent home or an alternative living arrangement. In any case, Mr. Tracy found himself helping boys whose parents were temporarily indisposed or permanently incapacitated.

Sometimes boys were constructively evicted from the family home because they were too old or the tenant-house apartment was too crowded. Other times boys rebelled against parental discipline or chafed at the demand that they contribute their meager earnings to the family. Some boys were turned out by parents or stepparents. One such boy came to the NBLH one evening "having a parcel of clothes with him." He approached the intake table and asked Mr. Tracy if he might spend the night. When asked about parents, the boy reported he had gone to the theater the night before and, after he returned home, his father told him "he might stop where he pleases but should not stop any longer" at home. The father handed his son his clothes and sent him on his way. Mr. Tracy "said a few words about the impropriety of paying visits to theatres"—to which the boy "concurred of course"—and allowed him entrance.

The most problematic cases were those involving physical abuse by parents. In a number of reports, some obtained from the boys themselves and others filtered through CAS agents, intemperance was often given as a root cause for the violence. While some staff condemned alcohol abuse and parents who, in their view, drank too much, they were not temperance workers nor were they associated with the temperance movement per se. Mr. Brace was far from a teetotaler himself, and there is ample evidence that he enjoyed a good beer or glass of wine in moderation. But Mr. Brace, like other reformers, occasionally linked heavy drinking to poor parenting. Whatever the relationship, violence associated with alcohol use and abuse was often noted.

It was Mr. Tracy who was confronted with decisions about how to handle the cases involving violence long before child abuse as a social issue received its first widespread public attention or sympathy.[84] As a practical matter, in 1854, Mr. Tracy needed to decide how to make accommodation to CAS's "orphans-only" policy, and he seemed to reach his threshold when boys demonstrated genuine fear of physical harm at the hand of a parent.

Angry parents occasionally presented themselves at the NBLH in search of children, much to the disquiet of all. For example, thirteen-year-old John, "an interesting dark eyed boy with a very animated expression," repeatedly ran away from a violent and abusive father. His mother had died three years earlier, but when she lived she "always wished John" away from "his drunken father." John tearfully recounted his history. According to the CAS agent recording the intake information, John's father "drinks very bad and beats John cruelly."[85] John reportedly said, "I can't stay at home," adding, "tis impossible father is too bad—liquor makes him savage and he carries a knife, and a pistol always about him outside.... He beats stepmother sometimes too."[86] The boy finished up his story by worrying that "father will say I disgraced him now for telling about his doing."

As if to prove the point John's father, "a stout roughish looking man," appeared at the lodging house one day, speaking "fiercely about his boy." The father "showed the fireman's badge" and the staff "could see that he had a pistol underneath" his coat.[87] With effort, CAS staff distracted him and while they "held an interview" with the father in one room, "John had taken the opportunity to make his escape" out the door.[88] The man was "turned away only with difficulty and not before the angry father issued a parting threat."[89]

Another example involved three brothers who arrived at the lodging house in March 1856, fleeing from an abusive mother. Even the eldest son, a seventeen-year-old, seemed to "fear her very much."[90] The mother was described by staff as "a large vulgar looking woman [who] pursues her children unrelentingly from place to place." She "caused considerable annoyance to Mr. Tracy a few nights ago at the Lodging House," reported one observer. The woman demanded her children, although staff believed that the reason was to lay claim to the boys' meager earnings rather than as an act of love or devotion. According to another lodger who witnessed an interaction between the mother and her youngest son, "she pulled him, and hauled him, yelling out that she would cut his throat, if he did not give up his money to her. She tore all his pants, and a confederate of hers held" her son "while she searched him all over."[91] The three brothers were allowed to stay, and their mother was fended off by agents of the society. However, even under these circumstances Mr. Tracy did not involve police officers or the court.

Johnnie Morrow's story is another example. As a precocious sixteen-year-old Johnnie wrote an autobiography and reported that he and his brother fled from an extremely violent and abusive father. He wrote that both his father and his stepmother drank heavily, often spending their children's hard-earned money on alcohol. The boys arrived at the NBLH seeking help but believed they would only be welcomed if they were true orphans. So Johnnie lied, giving Mr. Tracy an alias and asking, "Is this the place for boys to sleep who haven't got any father or mother?"[92]

Later, having developed a sufficiently guilty conscience, Johnnie confided, "I could find no relief, except in determination to see Mr. Tracy as early as possible the next morning, tell him the whole truth, and ask his forgiveness." In Johnnie's imagination, he "supposed that we should of course be told to leave the lodging house." Nonetheless, he "succeeded in summoning up courage to carry out [his] resolution." Johnnie approached Mr. Tracy's desk where he found the superintendent "was writing but in a moment or two laid down his pen, and looked at me inquiringly." Johnnie spilled forth the truth "at once before my resolution should fade out." He said, "Mr. Tracy, when I came here, I told you a *lie*, and now I am sorry for it; I said that I had not any father or mother but *I have*, and they drink so much brandy, and beat us so often, that we could not live with them!" Johnnie reported that he "went on to tell him the whole story." In recording Mr. Tracy's response to this outpouring Johnnie wrote, in some amazement, "Instead of getting angry and driving us from the building with a command never to return, as we expected he would," [93] Mr. Tracy "said that he was sorry that we had deceived him, but was very glad we had confessed it; from that day he has seemed a better friend to us than ever before."[94]

There is little doubt that Mr. Tracy was aware that many lodgers were initially stingy with the truth, particularly when it came to giving their names and family circumstances, but he also recognized gaining the trust of the boys was a process. It was all part of developing new interpersonal practice strategies for cultivating relationships with street youth so that they would continue to stick with the lodging house.

***

Coming Up Short

Boys often arrived at the lodging house short the pennies necessary to gain access. A fairly large number received shelter for free. Initially Mr. Brace worried about this.[95] He would later reflect, "I had always feared that we could not combine the system of half-pay and half-charity; that is, that some should be required to pay and other receive free." Looking back, he wrote, "We have done so, however, for years" and credited the superintendent with "great tact in discerning who are truly impoverished and unlucky, and who lazy or deceitful."[96] So among Mr. Tracy's tasks was to sort out the truthful boys from the artful scammers. It was part of the dual mission of CAS to provide concrete aid to needy children, but also to teach them responsibility and independent living skills that would serve them well the future.

One young lad "with a most rueful visage, made application for lodging, stating that he had been badly 'stuck' and had no money to pay, but would liquidate at some other time." Mr. Tracy allowed him entrance and off to bed he went. However, "the next night he had been 'stuck' again, and this time another boy had been equally unfortunate." This spreading misfortune "set Mr. Tracy to thinking, and by dint of close listening, he discovered that the youngsters had sewed their money up in their under-clothes, and intended, when they had gone as far as they could without paying, to 'slide on the shanty,' as they termed it." With this new information, Mr. Tracy again faced a novel management challenge.

Like many of Mr. Tracy's interventions, his response was understated. He decided to avoid a direct and accusatory confrontation. Instead, he "took the earliest opportunity to get a number of the boys together" at an evening meeting when the culprits were also present and "then he quietly asked 'the crowd' what they thought of a boy who was mean enough to sew his money up, and then tell a bare-faced lie for the sake of swindling his best friend out of sixpence?" The crowd of little laborers was quick to condemn such actions and declared such a swindler "was a sucker" and that they were "down onto him." Mr. Tracy nodded thoughtfully at their opinion, but "nothing further was said at the time." His initial approach was to see if some combination of peer pressure and personal sense of guilt would influence the boys' behavior without scolding or authoritative intervention. The ultimate objective was to steer the boys in the right direction without heavy-handed responses. Mr. Tracy's tactics must have worked because reportedly, "the next day the debtors squared accounts" and were not "stuck" again.[97]

Another frequent intervention when boys were "short" came in the form of a small, interest-free loan from Mr. Tracy. These coins were offered for the explicit purpose of getting the boy on his feet again, and the lad was eventually expected to repay the credited lodging as well as the funds loaned. For example, Little Con was out of money one night, and "Mr. Tracy gave him a shilling to start him in business, and trusted him for his lodging." He said, "Let us see what you can do with that." Overhearing the conversation, a fellow lodger piped in with some advice for the impoverished boy, encouraging him to buy a particular newspaper and telling him, "It is about the best investment you can make of a small capital."

Another frequently used method of dealing with those who were short the lodging rate was to take up a collection among the boys themselves. This approach allowed teaching lessons about generosity and built on the boys' natural tendency to help one another.

On one evening in 1855, an opportunity to teach the boys something about racial tolerance also presented itself. On this evening an African American boy named Jimmy arrived without six cents.[98] Some of the boys raised the question of whether Jimmy could be trusted with a loan. According to an observer, "after some delay, one of the large boys, Mick, spoke up. 'I say, Mr. Tracy, there's three cents to Jimmy's lodging!'" Mr. Tracy thanked Mick "and the evening passed quietly" until the moment came to actually settle the account. At this point Mick withdrew his offer, saying, "'Mr. Tracy! I ain't agoin' to pay that nigger's lodgin.'"

Mr. Tracy considered his response. "Very well," he said to his audience "of course Mick [can] do as he choose with his money," but Mr. Tracy continued, "this little colored boy is a respectable, well-behaved boy, as much as you—and you have no right to speak about him that way." Mr. Tracy drew a comparison: "I have taken you in, when you were much worse off than he—some of you were ragged and dirty and hungry—and you hadn't any one to care for you, and I was a father to you—and now you will talk in this way at the boy, because his skin is not so white as yours."

According to the observer, "Mick looked terribly ashamed." The other boys began to chime in. "Here's a cent, Mr. Tracy, for Jimmy!" said one. "Here's another!" said a second boy, and, "Here's another," said a third. This continued penny by penny until all six cents were collected from the lodgers to pay for Jimmy's shelter.

As the boys headed off to bed that evening, one pointed at Mick and said, "Ye'll have bad luck! Ye will, cause you didn't give nothin' to Jimmy's lodging."[99]

***

The Drama of the Theater

Perhaps one of the best places to see the practical problems facing Mr. Tracy as he tried to achieve a balance between the society's values and the real world involved intake decisions for boys who attended the theater but came up short when paying for lodging. On the one hand, Mr. Tracy was not in the habit of supervising how the boys conducted themselves outside of the lodging house, and CAS wanted to foster independence. On the other hand, he also wanted to guide the boys toward wise financial decisions. There were lessons to be learned about the consequences of bad choices.

CAS agents were of a somewhat divided opinion over the evils of the theater. For example, an CAS neighborhood visitor, Edward P. Smith, was largely sympathetic with the boys' need for entertainment. He recognized that the newsboys had to "keep a pretty sharp lookout all day if they wish to make any money," and that they had different ways of approaching relaxation at the end of the day.[100] For some of these boys, retiring to the NBLH with its structured evening activities—"washing, then reading, writing, or singing or some other exercise until bed time"—was "sufficient relaxation, sufficient engagement."[101] For others, Mr. Smith believed that "it is just the reverse." For these boys the lodging house activities were "quite a task" an "actual labour, such they must have a complete cessation of all this—a total change—and for a time feel under no restraint, no law, no rule."[102] For the boys who needed total escape, the theater was an obvious choice. "We are not all alike constituted," Mr. Smith concluded, "and ought not I suppose, to be measured by the same standard nor held subject to the same conventional law of morals."[103]

Mr. Tracy, on the other hand, took a less favorable stance relative to theater attendance. While his colleague, Mr. Smith could afford his philosophical view of the matter given his role as neighborhood visitor, Mr. Tracy was faced with the harder, real-world implications of these actions when the boys who were "short" pleaded their cases at his intake desk. He had to find ways that fairly balanced providing for the needy while fostering responsibility. His decisions also had to be perceived as fair among the boys themselves.

Mr. Tracy, Mr. Brace, and other members of CAS were concerned about the secondary consequences of theater attendance. First, they believed that the boys' hard-earned coins would be squandered on this entertainment instead of saved or spent wisely. Second, because the theater let out too late to meet the lodging house curfew, boys who attended often ended up frequenting saloons or coffee houses and sleeping on the streets. Third, even if the boys found alternative shelter, CAS was concerned that elsewhere they were "not likely to meet many good companions. Finally, the "low theater" or bawdy theaters that appealed to the boys arguably represented a threat to child's moral development and was perceived as a lure toward the criminal element. "Unfortunately," wrote Mr. Brace, "these low theatres seem the rendezvous for all disreputable characters" and here the boys "make the acquaintance of the higher class whom they so much admire, of flash-men, thieves, pickpockets, and rogues."[104] Mr. Tracy recognized that his jurisdiction didn't extend to policing the boys' actions outside the lodging house. His job was to try to influence their decisions while they were on their own by creating positive or negative incentives for various behaviors. His only tool in this regard involved the conditions of the boy's evening entrance into the lodging house.

One evening a young boy named Slattery approached Mr. Tracy's desk with his six cents for shelter. He had been absent from the NBLH the night before.

"You were at the theatre last night?" Mr. Tracy asked Slattery.

"No sir I had no money, so I did not come up," Slattery said, hanging his head.

"Where did you spend the night?" queried Mr. Tracy.

"In a hand-cart near the *Tribune* office—Sodger[105] saw me there—he can prove I was not at the Theatre," responded young Slattery.

Mr. Tracy responded with counterintelligence: "Sodger says he saw you about seven o'clock before the play began."

"Well, Sir," said Slattery earnestly. "I can assure you—I did not come up to the Lodging House, because I had no money."

"Well then, I will take your word for it—go, ahead to bed. It's a bad habit going to theatres," muttered Mr. Tracy. "When a boy goes once he likes to go again—like a cow that has got into a cabbage garden. She will try and get there again."[106]

It turned out that Slattery had, in fact, been to the theater the evening before, a fact learned later. On the other hand, he arrived at the NBLH with money in hand. While Mr. Tracy could signal his disapproval in general and perhaps be skeptical of Slattery's story, in the end, the boy was given shelter because he could pay for entrance. In the face of uncertainty, it was better to give the boy the benefit of the doubt and signal his faith in him.

The outcome was less successful for another lodger known as Booch when he arrived without his requisite pennies. Booch was a lodging house regular, and he well knew the lodging house rules. Even though he was short his fee, Booch decided honesty was the best policy but to little avail with Mr. Tracy. Booch admitted he had attended the theater. Unfortunately for him, Mr. Tracy was also well aware that Booch had "had three or four dollars worth of stock a few days ago—a large basket of matches and he has got rid of them all." To make matters worse, Booch was already in debt two shillings at the local coffee shop, the Nassau. Mr. Tracy had little patience for his combined set of circumstances. Booch was not permitted to stay that evening and retreated as far as the stairwell, where he sat crying.[107] While Mr. Tracy certainly encouraged and promoted honesty, this lesson was tailored for a different boy and was focused on financial responsibility. Mr. Tracy deemed the overall pattern of irresponsible behavior to be problematic in Booch's case.

In another similar case Mr. Tracy came to a different conclusion. In this matter, "a small boy McDonnell" arrived without six cents but confessed he had been at the theater the night before. McDonnell arrived "very dirty—his shirt, and pants looking as if he had lain in them in some filthy dew, and his whole appearance very unfavorable." The boy's story was he had been "coaxed away" to the Chatham Theater by another boy named Max. "After some cognition on the matter," Mr. Tracy allowed McDonnell to stay on credit but not before delivering a lecture appealing to the boy's sense of fair dealing. Mr. Tracy opined "that he was, and should be against this business of going to plays, and loafing round." He added, "Nor did [he] think it fair" that such boys "should have the privileges of boys who have the sense, and virtue to refrain from practices that tended to such unhappy results." McDonnell promised that he would not be so imprudent anymore.[108] Apparently this was good enough for Mr. Tracy. He was likely swayed by the boy's age, forlorn appearance, his contrite demeanor, and his pledge to be better behaved in the future. There is no doubt that Mr. Tracy would hold the boy to this promise in the months to come.

Similarly, Michael was granted entry even though he did not have his six cents after confessing to his whereabouts at the theater the night before and admitting "he was sorry." Michael was "in employment with a Mr. Davidson, and he carries parcels, and does other errands for that gentleman" and was well known to Mr. Tracy and other CAS staff. They did not believe Michael to be "one of those callous boys, who are inaccessible to repentance or remorse." So Mr. Tracy bombarded Michael with a longer lecture than most. "You spoil your clothes," scolded Mr. Tracy, "and you haunt, and skulk and dodge in those filthy dens, and so injure your own interests. The man for whom you work, will soon rid of you, if you continue in those evil ways, and you will find out too late that you have followed a wrong course." The guilty party withstood the onslaught in silence, with a look of self-condemnation. "Michael promised that he would not go to the theatre, any more, and that he will pay up on tomorrow evening." In the eyes of Mr. Tracy, "There was sufficient evidence of both in his countenance, as he promised . . . that he would behave better for the future, and avoid bad company and the Chatham," that he decided to give Michael the benefit of the doubt[109] and permitted him to stay. Perhaps as a gesture of gratitude—or out of a sense of guilt—Michael offered Mr. Tracy the names of the other newsboys who had been with him at the Chatham Theater. In the end, Mr. Tracy deemed those other boys "the hardest specimens of their class."

In short, Mr. Tracy's responses, while perhaps seemingly eclectic and inconsistent on their face, were individually tailored based on his assessment of each boy in front of him. There were competing values to be weighed when working with street children, among them were charity and compassion; however, he was also trying to steer them toward fiscal responsibility and truthfulness.

Just months after the opening, Mr. Tracy's concerns about the lure of theater were put to the ultimate test with the announcement of a new production at the Chatham Theater. Its title was the intriguing *Hell on Earth*. Mr. Tracy tried his best to discourage the boys' attendance in advance of opening night. Several days before, in a Sunday evening sermon Mr. Tracy "told the boys how very important the present time was to them. That whatever way we spent our early life it would have its effect on our after time." They were not, Mr. Tracy argued, "half thankful" enough "for what a kind providence had done for them." Resorting to another of his frequent farm animal analogies, Mr. Tracy likened this to seeing "a hog go into an orchard" where "it began eating the apples that were lying on the ground." It ate and ate "but never once looked up to see where the apples came from—so with many people, they take all that they can get ... but never look where it comes from."[110]

Nonetheless, despite "dozens of evenings" of sermons and lectures "about the theatre and its money wasting, and its immorality and its bad associations,"[111] and even "though Mr Tracy had expressed a wish that the boys would come up early"[112] in the end, the draw of this particular theatrical production "turned out to be too strong to withstand." Included as one of the "strong ingredients in the performance,"—as one might expect given the show's title—was considerable "fire and brimstone, thunder and lightening."[113] The boys were mesmerized. "Like most boys," Mr. Brace wrote, "they have a passion for drama."[114] The net result was that when opening night had arrived on Tuesday, July 10, the NBLH was "thinned" a number of lodgers"[115] because "some five or six of the boys" had gone to the theater.[116] This led Mr. Smith to conclude that "it is as clear as a sunbeam that we *must* have amusement, and the great point is to establish such as will be most innocent and harmless in itself and its tendencies."[117] The question for Mr. Tracy, who was developing the lodging house model from scratch, was what kind of evening entertainment might that be?

***

Intoxicated Youth

Another behavior of concern to CAS was alcohol consumption. While CAS couldn't regulate the boys' drinking habits when they were on their own, there was an express rule barring intoxicated youth from entering the lodging house.

One night a boy named Thomas arrived close to the 10 PM curfew.[118] He was visibly drunk. "Thomas," said Mr. Tracy in a mild tone, "I am very sorry to see you in this state; why didn't you wait to come here till you got sober? Don't you know that you are transgressing one of the rules, besides setting a bad example?"

Thomas claimed ignorance. "I don't know nothin' about it," was the reply. "All I know is, that I'm sleepy and I'm agoin' to bed. Here's your sixpence!" At the same time he took a coin from his pocket and tendered it.

"You can't go to bed here, Thomas," replied Mr. Tracy firmly, "till you are sober."

Thomas shot back, "Ain't my money as good as anybody else's?"

"Oh yes," was Mr. Tracy's answer. "Your money, no doubt, is very good, but your conduct, at present, is not, and you must go out, you can't stay here; do you understand Thomas? I say you *must* go out!"

By this time a crowd of youngsters had gathered around to watch the unfolding drama. They had "made up their minds that they were about to see some fun, and stood looking on with eager faces."

"I don't care a-wot you say," Thomas argued. "'I'm agoin' to bed,' and he moved towards the lodging-room."

"You are violating a rule, Thomas," Mr. Tracy repeated. At the same time, he laid his hand "upon the youth's shoulder" and began steering him toward the door. "Come, your road lies in this direction," he said, pointing the boy outward.

"Don't you put your hands on me," growled Thomas savagely. "If you do, I'll smash yer."

"I warn you not to attempt any violence, Thomas," responded Mr. Tracy, in the same mild manner that he often received a threat of violence. "I should be sorry to have to chastise you before the boys, but I must do so, if necessary to preserve the rules."

By this time, Mr. Tracy had ushered the boy "nearer to the door, till at length he got him outside. Once there, the boy jerked away from him, and exclaimed: 'Now you just come down stairs and see if I don't punch that good-lookin' head of yours!'"

"I have no business down stairs, Thomas," was the quiet answer. "This is my place; but I don't believe you'd hurt me if I did go. I know you wouldn't if you were sober, and I've too good an opinion of you to suppose that you would even in your present state. Good-bye, Thomas; at any time, when you are sober, you shall have a bed as quick as any boy, but I can't break through a rule to accommodate you."

In the aftermath of Thomas's display, Mr. Tracy chose not to deliver a lecture to the boys on the evils of drinking or frame the event as a moral issue. They would make their own decisions. Instead, "he read the boys a lecture on the propriety of always maintaining a strict observance of all necessary regulations." The house had rules and the boys' decisions to violate those regulations had consequences.

On another evening, a different boy came into the lodging house in even worse condition than Thomas. He "presented himself and with great difficulty came the length of the table and sat down."[119]

"What do you want?" asked Mr. Tracy.

"Lodging" he struggled to get out.

At this point, Mr. Tracy said, "We can't keep you. We allow no one here who comes as you are."

Again, the rest of the boys gathered to watch the spectacle. However, on this evening, they were unable to refrain from teasing the barely coherent boy. The group launched into a popular and frequently sung moral hymn known as "Temperance Glee" for the benefit of the newcomer:

> *Sparkling and bright in its liquid light,*
> *Is the water in our glasses;*
> *'Twill give you health,*
> *'twill give you wealth,*
> *Ye lads and rosy lasses!*
> *O then resign your ruby wine,*
> *Each smiling son and daughter,*
> *There's nothing so good for the youthful blood,*
> *Or sweet as the sparkling water.*[120]

At the conclusion of their impromptu concert, they offered the intoxicated lad the abstinence pledge. "Come now, sign the pledge?" said one, presenting him with a pen, while another produced a leaf of paper and another "offered his back for a table." The abstinence pledge had been the topic of conversation at the NBLH before. Many of the boys—with varying degrees of commitment—had voluntarily decided to sign it. For example, the Professor had pledged abstinence "forever" while Pat Comon agreed to abstain only until "the Fourth of July." Fatty, on the other hand, refused to sign it at all, "muttering something about Lager Bier" and holding out, saying he "was not quite ready." Of course, the choice was left to the individual newsboy. Nonetheless, the boys pushed the pledge toward the unfortunate would-be lodger in his drunken state.

At this Mr. Tracy intervened and said to the boys that a man in "such an inebriate state was not in command of his reason and was more an object of pity than of anything else." The older boy "staggered to the door and made his way down stairs and we saw no more of him,"[121] wrote Mr. Colopy, a CAS staff member who observed the incident. Overall, Mr. Tracy's position was one of tolerance. He refused to be overly moralist. While he insisted on adherence to the policies, but not to the point of lacking compassion. He recognized a boy's agency in making decisions for himself, but that decision might also have consequences. Mr. Tracy allowed peer pressure to operate by tolerating a limited amount of teasing but not at the expense of empathy. Thus was the nature of Mr. Tracy's job; it required balancing competing values, evaluating behavior in context, and tailoring individual responses which would be perceived as fair to all the lodgers.

***

Lodging House as Experimental Model

In short, the NBLH got off to a successful start from its inception. In part, this was because it clearly filled a niche for low-income housing. However, at least part of its initial success is also attributable to Mr. Tracy's talent for working with street youth. He was charged with the task of handling each crisis and new dilemma as it came his way. He made such day-to-day decisions without the benefit of existing guidelines or best practices. Among the early decisions were what to do with problem parents, penniless would-be lodgers, the pull of the theater, and lice-infested or intoxicated boys. Mr. Tracy dealt with those who violated rules and those who threatened violence. Yet he walked a careful line between confrontation and guidance. He was capable of the lecture or sermon, but he was also artful in deploying the boys' own sense of responsibility and leveraging their guilt. He appeared fair and evenhanded without being a pushover. He didn't need or expect absolute honesty and understood that each boy was on his own life path. Mr. Tracy's ad hoc but thoughtful decisions would eventually coalesce into more consistent agency policy, which was forged from his sensibilities and the discretionary power he wielded from the start. The fledging agency was feeling its way forward. CAS took shape as an organization while trying to stay true to its mission and, at the same time, confronting the realities of child poverty. In the end, Mr. Tracy was putting Mr. Brace's philosophical ideas into action.

Most significant, Mr. Tracy was creating a new type of social work practice and a entirely new form of intervention in congregate care housing that rested exclusively on the voluntary participation of the children under his charge. The NBLH was free from judicial involvement or the restrictive and disciplinary practices associated with the child asylums. Mr. Tracy was working on finding methods to help children internalize responsible and moral behavior, without resorting to threats, corporal punishment, or physical constraints.

The lodging house, as was true of all CAS interventions, was both innovative and experimental. Its design and operation would be the subject of constant tinkering, adaptation, and modifications made though trial and error over time. However, the NBLH was also a prototype. Its initial success rested on Mr. Tracy, but more important, his success (or failure) would be the determining factor in whether the *idea* of the lodging house for vagrant street children was viable at all.

The success of the NBLH gave rise to the use of lodging houses more broadly as Mr. Brace built CAS's interconnected network of services. For nearly a century, CAS would open—and close—dozens of lodging houses as needs arose and changed. These lodging houses would be for both girls and boys. They would be conveniently scattered around the city. However, the original NBLH would remain a constant for the next eighty-nine years.

Notes

1. Minor variations on the name of this facility appeared over time. In the CAS First Annual Report, issued in February 1854, Mr. Brace writes that, "a *Lodging-house for News-boys* is just being opened by the Society" (p. 11). In the following year's Annual Report (1855) Mr. Brace calls it, *The News Boys' Lodging House* (p. 13). By the third year, it has become *The Newsboys' Lodging-House*. Yet another variation occurred in the Fourth Annual Report (1857) where it is called *The News-boys' Lodging-House* (p. 17). Over time, the Society seemed to settle on *The Newsboys' Lodging House*, which is what I use in this book. *Third Annual Report of the Children's Aid Society*

(New York: M. B. Wynkoop, 1856). *Fourth Annual Report of the Children's Aid Society* (New York: John P. Prall, 1857).

William Colopy Desmond worked as a clerk in the office and at the NBLH from its earliest days. The boys called him Mr. Colopy rather than Mr. Desmond so I do the same in this book. The opening epigraph is from a seven-stanza poem written by Mr. Colopy and included with a note that "the foregoing was suggested by the perusal of a letter from a newsboy who had been sent to the country by the Children's Aid Society."

2. C. Loring Brace, comp., *The Children's Aid Society of New York: Its History, Plan, and Results/Compiled Writings and Reports of the Late Charles Loring Brace* (New York: Wynkoop & Hallenbeck Printers, 1893), 14. Charles Loring Brace's son later characterized opening night: "These little subjects regarded the first arrangements with some suspicion and much contempt."

3. Charles Loring Brace, *The Dangerous Classes of New York and Twenty Years' Work among Them*, 3rd ed. (New York: Wynkoop & Hallenbeck, 1880), 101; Charles Loring Brace, *Short Sermons to the News Boys: With a History of the Formation of the Newsboys' Lodging-House* (New York: Charles Scribner, 1866), 24.

4. Brace, *Short Sermons*, 24; Brace, *Children's Aid Society of New York*, 14.

5. William Colopy Desmond, "Incidents and Sketches Among the Newsboys," in The Victor Remer Historical Archives of the Children's Aid Society (1836–2006). New-York Historical Society Archives. Diaries and Journals of Agents of the CAS, circa 1853–circa 1864, vol. 47, p. 19, New-York Historical Society Archives.

6. C. Loring Brace (1898) "League for Social Service Pamphlet Series G. "Children's Aid Society of NY in Series III-Reports, Bulk, 1853–1942 1853–2006; Subseries III.2-Reports, Articles, and Addresses for the Public and Particular Audiences, 1857–1942; Box 12, Folder 9 in New-York Historical Society.

7. "News Boys' Lodging-House," May 28, 1854, reprinted in Brace, *Short Sermons*, 217.

8. C. Loring Brace, *Children's Aid Society of New York*, 14.

9. *Second Annual Report of the Children's Aid Society* (New York: M. B. Wynkoop, 1855), 14.

10. Brace, *Short Sermons*, 22.

11. Brace, *Short Sermons*, 22.

12. "News Boys' Lodging-House," reprinted in Brace, *Short Sermons*, 224.

13. "News Boys' Lodging-House," reprinted in Brace, *Short Sermons*, 224.

14. "News Boys' Lodging-House," reprinted in Brace, *Short Sermons*, 224.

15. Brace, *Short Sermons*, 23.

16. Brace, *Short Sermons*, 45.

17. C. Loring Brace (1898) "League for Social Service Pamphlet"; emphasis added.

18. Brace, *Short Sermons*, 45.

19. Brace, *Dangerous Classes of New York*, 109.

20. Brace, *Dangerous Classes of New York*, 100.

21. Brace, *Short Sermons*, 23.

22. Brace, *Dangerous Classes of New York*, 101.
23. Brace, *Short Sermons*, 23–24.
24. Brace, *Short Sermons*, 23–24.
25. Brace, *Dangerous Classes of New York*, 102.
26. Brace, *Dangerous Classes of New York*, 102.
27. C. Loring Brace (1898) "League for Social Service Pamphlet."
28. C. Loring Brace (1898) "League for Social Service Pamphlet."
29. C. Loring Brace, *Children's Aid Society of New York*, 15.
30. C. Loring Brace, *Children's Aid Society of New York*, 15.
31. John Morrow, *A Voice from the Newsboys* (San Diego: University of California Press, 1860), 63, Digital Archive, www.hathitrust.org.
32. Brace, *Short Sermons*, 23–24.
33. Morrow, *Voice from the Newsboys*, 64.
34. "News Boys' Lodging-House," reprinted in Brace, *Short Sermons*, 224.
35. "News Boys' Lodging-House," reprinted in Brace, *Short Sermons*, 224.
36. "News Boys' Lodging-House," reprinted in Brace, *Short Sermons*, 224.
37. "News Boys' Lodging-House," reprinted in Brace, *Short Sermons*, 224.
38. "News Boys' Lodging-House," reprinted in Brace, *Short Sermons*, 224.
39. Brace, *Dangerous Classes*, 102.
40. Brace, *Dangerous Classes*, 102.
41. *Second Annual Report*, 15.
42. During the first four years of the lodging house's existence, its number of residents per year doubled from 408 to 800. It would grow by leaps and bounds thereafter.
43. "News Boys' Lodging-House," reprinted in Brace, *Short Sermons*, 217–218.
44. "News Boys' Lodging-House," reprinted in Brace, *Short Sermons*, 217–218.
45. In keeping with CAS's tradition of staying abreast of new innovations, these wood bedframes, which could harbor bed bugs, would be replaced by iron ones as soon as they became available.
46. "News Boys' Lodging-House," reprinted in Brace, *Short Sermons*, 217–218.
47. "News Boys' Lodging-House," reprinted in Brace, *Short Sermons*, 217–218.
48. "News Boys' Lodging-House," reprinted in Brace, *Short Sermons*, 217–218.
49. Morrow, *Voice from the Newsboys*, 63.
50. Morrow, *Voice from the Newsboys*, 64.
51. "The News-Boys," *Frank Leslie's Illustrated Newspaper*, December 29, 1855.
52. "News Boys' Lodging-House," reprinted in Brace, *Short Sermons*, 219–220.
53. "News Boys' Lodging-House," reprinted in Brace, *Short Sermons*, 219–220.
54. "News Boys' Lodging-House," reprinted in Brace, *Short Sermons*, 219–220.
55. Morrow, *Voice from the Newsboys*, 63.
56. "News Boys' Lodging-House," reprinted in Brace, *Short Sermons*, 219.
57. C. Loring Brace (1898) "League for Social Service Pamphlet."
58. "News Boys' Lodging-House," reprinted in Brace, *Short Sermons*, 217.

59. "News Boys' Lodging-House," reprinted in Brace, *Short Sermons*, 217.
60. "News Boys' Lodging-House," reprinted in Brace, *Short Sermons*, 217.
61. *Third Annual Report*, 17.
62. "News Boys' Lodging-House," reprinted in Brace, *Short Sermons*, 217.
63. Morrow, *Voice from the Newsboys*, 62.
64. "News Boys' Lodging-House," reprinted in Brace, *Short Sermons*, 224.
65. "News Boys' Lodging-House," reprinted in Brace, *Short Sermons*, 224.
66. Virtually no rule at the NBLH was impervious to exception. For example, while Mr. Tracy's eviction of the boot thrower on the first night set a tone for behavior that was critical in the first hours, there was at least one other recorded incident of boot throwing where the guilty youngsters got away with his behavior without dismissal. In that case, the boots were directed toward a young man who had come into the shelter with particularly pretentious airs that annoyed the other lodgers. The boot incident, in this case, seems to have been interpreted as a relatively mild form of internal policing among the boys themselves. As another example, at least one intoxicated lodger was allowed to stay. This lodger was an older man, the only adult who was permitted to stay at the NBLH. It is not readily apparent why his exception was made, however, the man had spent a lifetime selling newspapers and had a number of physical infirmities. Instead of denying him entry, the other boys rallied on his behalf and suggested that he be allowed to sign an "intemperance pledge." Under the circumstances, Mr. Tracy deemed this acceptable. Younger, healthier lodgers would not have fared so well with Mr. Tracy.
67. *Nineteenth Annual Report of the Children's Aid Society* (New York: Wynkoop & Hallenbeck, 1871), 18.
68. Other colorful nicknames found in the records included these: Carrots, Oysters, Little Crutch, Luny, Wandering Jew, Pompey, Turkey, Toothless, Horace Greeley, Squintum, Gogle, Huckleberry, Sniffy, Butter-nose, Fat Jack, Cady, Sloberry, Bummer, Shapy, Blood-sucker, The Ghost, Picklenose, Country, Blue Jacket, Hobble Legs, Tumbler, Buck Tooth, and High Bridge.
69. Carolee R. Inskeep, *The Children's Aid Society of New York: An Index to the Federal, State, and Local Census Records of its Lodging Houses* (Baltimore: Clearfield, 1996), 3. In CAS records Danny O'Sullivan is often referred to as Danny Sullivan. However, according to Inskeep the 1855 census records of the NBLH have him listed as O'Sullivan. I have used the census record name, O'Sullivan in this book.
70. "News Boys' Lodging-House," reprinted in Brace, *Short Sermons*, 222.
71. *Eleventh Annual Report of the Children's Aid Society* (New York: Wynkoop & Hallenbeck, 1864), 16.
72. Brace, *Short Sermons*, 23.
73. *Second Annual Report*, 14.
74. *Second Annual Report*, 14.
75. Colopy Desmond, "Incidents and Sketches," vol. 48.
76. Colopy Desmond, "Incidents and Sketches," vol. 47.

77. Colopy Desmond, "Incidents and Sketches," vol. 47.
78. *Eleventh Annual Report*, 18.
79. *Eighteenth Annual Report of the Children's Aid Society* (New York: Wynkoop & Hallenbeck, 1870), 17.
80. William Colopy Desmond, "Incidents and Sketches," vol. 47.
81. William Colopy Desmond, "Incidentsc and Sketches," vol. 48.
82. *Eleventh Annual Report*, 18.
83. William Colopy Desmond, "Incidents and Sketches," vol. 49.
84. The case most frequently cited as pivotal for bringing public attention to the issue of child abuse was that of eight-year-old Mary Ellen in 1874. In this case a stepmother was criminally charged under "cruelty to animal" statutes because there were no such protections for children suffering from abuse by parents or guardians. This highly publicized case led to the founding of the first New York Society for the Prevention of Cruelty to Children in 1874 by Henry Bergh and Elbridge Gerry. It is important to recognize that this public outcry occurred two decades after Mr. Tracy first faced similar decisions at the lodging house, when there were no alternative services or legal precedents for intervention.
85. William Colopy Desmond, "Incidents and Sketches," vol. 49.
86. William Colopy Desmond, "Incidents and Sketches," vol. 49.
87. William Colopy Desmond, "Incidents and Sketches," vol. 49.
88. William Colopy Desmond, "Incidents and Sketches," vol. 49.
89. William Colopy Desmond, "Incidents and Sketches," vol. 49.
90. William Colopy Desmond, "Incidents and Sketches," vol. 49.
91. William Colopy Desmond, "Incidents and Sketches," vol. 49.
92. Morrow, *Voice from the Newsboys*, 61–62.
93. Morrow, *Voice from the Newsboys*, 65–66.
94. Morrow, *Voice from the Newsboys*, 65–66.
95. CAS was publicly criticized for charging the boys payment for the service; it is possible those critics were unaware of how often the rules were waived in specific cases.
96. Brace, *Short Sermons*, 45.
97. "News Boys' Lodging-House," reprinted in Brace, *Short Sermons*, 220.
98. *Second Annual Report*, 27, appendix.
99. *Second Annual Report*, 27, appendix. The NBLH had an open door policy when it came to children. It appears that the number of African American children who stayed at the NBLH were few enough to take special note of when they did appear. I don't doubt that children of color were not entirely comfortable in the facility; nonetheless, there is little evidence of overt discrimination and quite a bit to support the contention that CAS staff attempted to preach tolerance. This was true for racial difference but also ethnic and religious differences as well.
100. Edward Parmelee Smith, "Daily Journal" (unpublished manuscript, June 23, 1855), in The Victor Remer Historical Archives of the Children's Aid Society

(1836–2006). Diaries and Journals of Agents of the CAS, circa 1853–circa 1864, vol. 46, New-York Historical Society Archives.
101. Smith, "Daily Journal," June 23, vol. 46.
102. Smith, "Daily Journal," June 23, vol. 46.
103. Smith, "Daily Journal," June 23, vol. 46.
104. Brace, *Dangerous Classes*, 345–46.
105. *Sodgering* was a term used for someone who "is pretending to work, and accomplishing as little as possible." Frederick Law Olmstead, *Walks and Talks of an American Farmer in England in the Years 1850–51, Part II* (New York: George P. Putnam, 1855), 38.
106. William Colopy Desmond, "Incidents and Sketches," vol. 47.
107. William Colopy Desmond, "Incidents and Sketches," vol. 47.
108. William Colopy Desmond, "Incidents and Sketches," vol. 47.
109. William Colopy Desmond, "Incidents and Sketches," vol. 49.
110. Smith, "Daily Journal," Wed July 11, vol. 46.
111. Smith, "Daily Journal," Wed July 11, vol. 46.
112. William Colopy Desmond, "Incidents and Sketches," vol. 49.
113. Smith, "Daily Journal," Wed July 11, vol. 46.
114. Brace, *Dangerous Classes*, 345–46.
115. Colopy Desmond, "Incidents and Sketches," vol. 49
116. Smith, "Daily Journal," Wed. July 11, vol. 46.
117. Smith, "Daily Journal," Wed. July 11, vol. 46.
118. "News Boys' Lodging-House," reprinted in Brace, *Short Sermons*, 225–226.
119. Smith, "Daily Journal," May 22, vol. 46.
120. "Temperance Glee," published in 1842, was a song written by Mary Dana Shindler that became an anthem of the temperance movement. It was included in a song book (*The Northern Harp: Original Sacred and Moral Songs*) with sheet music and lyrics. The words were adapted to popular melodies for the piano and guitar by James B. Taylor. The publisher of this popular song book, Dayton and Saxton, happened to be located at the corner of Fulton and Nassau streets, right below the Newsboys' Lodging House.
121. Smith, "Daily Journal," May 22, vol. 46.

5

Eddying Point

MR. MACY'S CENTRAL OFFICE

It is remarkable how little can be known in each generation of those before who have done the most to make the present better than the past. The best workers for human good seem to be silent.

—CHARLES LORING BRACE, *The Silent Workers*

THE "PRACTICAL PHILANTHROPIST"—AS Mr. Brace liked to call his friend and colleague Jared Macy—was usually up to his ears in chaos and nothing made him happier.[1] The place of turmoil was the central office and the patient man managing it all was the society's assistant secretary.[2]

Just two years after founding CAS, the board of trustees extended the hours of the central office. Mr. Brace originally shuttered the doors at noon to attend to afternoon business in the city. However, in March 1855 the trustees resolved the office be open "not later than 8-1/2 o'clock A.M. and be not closed before 5 P.M." and the "months of operation extended into the summer, June, July, and August."[3] In short order the office had become the working center for the entire Society, a one-stop, social service agency. Each of the branches of service were coordinated through this central hub, and it served as the point of exchange. For example, although the NBLH was closed during the day, the boys were often sent up to Mr. Macy. Invariably he would extend CAS help to the boy in one form or another. Conversely, if a new needy boy wandered into the central office looking for evening shelter, Mr. Macy would send him down to the lodging house. So the central office was the site of a flurry of such exchanges between and among each of the branches of the Society as well as between CAS and the outside world. Mr. Macy was at the very heart of all the commotion.

Mr. Macy and Mr. Brace had worked shoulder to shoulder before the founding of CAS. Both had conducted Sunday "Boys' Meetings" in the lower wards of New-York. Mr. Macy accepted Mr. Brace's offer to be among the first of CAS's paid visiting agents. Like the other agents, he was assigned to a lower ward and charged with the "especial duty" of searching out "the deserted and vagrant children of the quarter," visiting "regularly from house to house" and scanning the "docks and lumber-yards and low lodging houses" or any other place where "children congregate."[4] There had been plenty of places to look and it wasn't hard to find homeless children or scare up society "business."

In fact, it was going so well that by 1856 Mr. Brace could barely keep up with his daily office tasks, so he turned to his friend and kindred spirit, Mr. Macy, to assume the role of his assistant. Mr. Macy spent the entire rest of his life—nearly twenty-eight years—in this second-in-command role. The two men were like different sides of the same coin. Mr. Macy was a practical Quaker and Mr. Brace, a practical Congregationalist. Mr. Macy meticulously attended to every aspect of the daily inner workings of the society while Mr. Brace was left to do the big thinking and the scholarly writing and appear as the society's public face. Mr. Macy, with his "bottled-up 'enthusiasm of humanity' under a very modest exterior," concluded Mr. Brace, "has become a sort of embodied Children's Aid Society in his own person."[5] No doubt for adults, Mr. Brace's name was synonymous with CAS, but arguably for thousands of children, Mr. Macy *was* CAS. To a large degree, it was he who participated in the most pivotal decisions in their lives.

Although Mr. Macy worked every day, all day, at the central office, his work among the poor wasn't over at quitting time. He and his two sisters founded the Cottage Place Industrial School for Girls in 1859, which was one of the many industrial schools associated with CAS, targeting poor children who were unable to attend public school.[6] In addition, with the help of CAS benefactors, Mr. Macy opened a free public reading room and hosted nightly gatherings for boys. These weeknight "meetings" sought to distract boys from less desirable evening alternatives. The idea was to keep the boys from "frequenting liquor-groceries and porter-shops, for the sake of being in warm and lighted rooms." So he was part of a nightly effort to provide alternative entertainment where boys could read, play cards or board games, or listen to a lecture. Occasionally, there were special performances, like the magic lantern shows arranged by Mr. Macy.[7] In addition, his commitment to the original boys' Sunday meetings never waned. He devoted particular attention to meetings at 23 Hamersley Street, near Varick on the lower West Side, where "the worst set of dock-boys and 'short boys'" could often be found.[8] Said Mr.

Brace, "There is probably no district in the city where so many boys are sent to the prisons and the House of Refuge."[9]

Buoyed by his faith and a notable sense of humor, Mr. Macy liked nothing better than to spend time among his little "lambs." The more recalcitrant and ill-behaved those little lambs were, the better. "In fact," wrote Mr. Brace of his friend, "he never seemed so well satisfied as when the roughest little 'bummers' of the ward entered his Boys' Meeting. The virtuous and well-behaved children did not interest him half so much."[10] Mr. Macy was "known to address these urchins in his usual calm and beatific tone, while brick-bats were smashing the windows."[11] There was no bigger challenge than trying to keep these children from the House of Refuge and lure them toward the NBLH.

All the evening activities and Sunday meetings were an addition to Mr. Macy's daytime job of running the central office. As CAS grew in size, complexity, and stature over its first decades, his day-to-day responsibilities grew proportionately. He met the challenges and managed the expansion with hard work, selflessness, and devotion. He also gave shape to the way CAS was creating an interconnected network of services that worked in combination with each other. Like CAS as whole, given the voluntary nature of its overall practices, the office was the place where services could be sought, referrals made, and, in some cases, direct aid provided on a walk-in basis.

In short, Mr. Macy lived with and among poor children nearly all day long, every day of the week for his entire life. Mr. Brace said of him, "Most men take their charities as adjuncts to life or as duties enjoined by religion or humanity. Mr. Macy lives in his."[12]

***

A Place for Rich and Poor

The central office was located at No. 11 Clinton Hall, on East Eighth Street between the Bowery and Lafayette Place, about two miles north of the NBLH. The location was a particularly symbolic spot.[13] No matter which direction you walked from the little office, it marked a dividing line of one kind or another. Walk uptown on the Bowery and you quickly reached the emerging regimented grid of the city's 1811 street plan. Walk downtown and you entered the chaotic streets laid down by the island's earliest inhabitants. Walk westward on Fourth Street and you reached affluent neighborhoods near Washington Square Park. Walk east and you entered the poorest wards of New-York. So the office marked scrimmage lines in all directions: new to the north and old to the south; rich to the west and poor to the east.

Mr. Brace called the central office the "eddying point" between the two distinct classes in New-York, the place "where two streams of the fortunate and the unfortunate classes seem to meet."[14] On the one hand, Mr. Macy entertained the wealthy—"ladies [who] enter to find the best object of their charities, and the proper field for their benevolent labors; liberal donors; 'intelligent foreigners,' inquiring into our institutions, applicants for teachers' places, agents, and all the miscellaneous crowd who support and visit agencies of charity."[15] CAS's increasing national and international reputation made it a destination spot for some visitors to the city and other philanthropists, as well as those seeking volunteer opportunities or employment. On the other hand, there were the desperately poor—those seeking food, clothing, shelter, employment, or help in any form that could be mustered. At the center was Mr. Macy, "holding himself perfectly cool and bland in this turmoil"[16] and exhibiting "all the tact of a diplomat ... getting on as well with the lady as the street-vagrant, and seldom ever making a blunder."[17]

***

Referrals to the Central Office and the NBLH

One day two boys with heavy Irish brogues spoke over one another as they jostled to tell their story to Mr. Macy. They explained that their names were William and Howard King, aged twenty and fifteen. They had just arrived on the ship Driver from Liverpool. The boys had passed through Castle Garden,[18] the recently commissioned immigration center that opened in 1855 in an attempt "to protect newly arrived immigrants from predatory con artists," including unscrupulous money changers and others willing to exploit bewildered newcomers.[19] The boys had arrived "friendless," knowing no one in New-York, let alone the U.S. However, on board Driver, a man had recommended that they look up Mr. Pease at the Five Point Missionary. So they immediately acted on the stranger's recommendation to seek out Mr. Pease. In turn, Mr. Pease directed the boys straight to the central office of CAS, so now they found themselves in front of Mr. Macy seeking help a few hours after stepping on U.S. soil for the first time.[20] These boys presented no problem for Mr. Macy. He gave them a referral card and sent them to Mr. Tracy at the NBLH, promising they would receive all the aid they needed.

Referrals from Mr. Pease at the Five Point House of Industrial were common. In fact, early on the trustees had explored the possibility of merging with Five Points. As practical matter, not only would that have extended the service from children to adult women but the board reasoned that Five Points had a "well planned building judiciously situated in the most destitute part of the city, but no system of out door organization by which to increase the number of beneficiaries" while CAS had "such out door agency in efficient operation but have no central depot to facilitate its business."[21] Nonetheless, after exploring the idea the decision was made to keep the charities separate, in part, because "more good" would be accomplished and "greater means secured" by working independently. The board resolution had continued "it is believed that the two can cooperate with great advantage." This had been the case, and both worked in close cooperation. However, a secondary consequence was that the central office had become the point of exchange for all CAS business. While Mr. Macy received a healthy number of referrals from Five Points, it was not the only source of referrals. In fact, Mr. Macy received children who had been sent by other charity organizations, by police officers, jail wardens, clergy, immigration officers, and businessmen. Not surprisingly, as word spread of CAS's work, these referrals increased from all parts of the city.

Although the focus of Mr. Macy's office was "out door relief," in other words services offered in the community and outside institutional care, like the asylums and poorhouses, he oversaw a steady flow of referrals from his office to CAS lodging houses, in particular the NBLH. CAS refused to characterize its lodging house facilities as indoor relief for the poor. Despite the similarity to child asylums in terms of congregate sheltering, NBLH was still deemed a form of out door relief as far as CAS was concerned. The boys were free to come and go as they pleased.

So no sooner had Mr. Macy dispatched the King brothers when the next boy wandered into his office. He would also be destined for the NBLH. Another Irish immigrant, Denis O'Driscoll, was no longer "green" like the Kings, having been in the U.S. for about a year. Nonetheless, he was desperate. Denis had come from Skibbereen, County Cork. Mr. Macy estimated that he was about fifteen years old, although Denis himself was unsure of his age. Even guessing was sometimes hard, as life on the street tended to age children beyond their years. Denis was a "tall boy, with a rich brogue, and harsh features." He told Mr. Macy that both his parents were dead and that he had "worked as a laborer in the old country." "It was," the boy said sadly, "awful to see how many died there for the want of something to eat." Denis and his family were yet another casualty of the potato blight.

Denis's route to Mr. Macy had been much more circuitous than that of the King boys. Leaving Ireland in a barque,[22] Denis landed in New-York but couldn't find work. So he went to Boston briefly and from there spent the summer in the country feeding "hogs an' cattle." That job came to an end, so finding himself unemployed, he moved on to Newark, where another farmer hired him for six dollars a month. "But," he told Mr. Macy, the farmer, "licked me with a horsewhip." After enough beatings, Denis fought back. In a fit of anger, he hit his tormentor, claiming, "I lets the flail go ale the ways." In Denis's telling he got the better of the fight but fled in the aftermath. His next employment was as a stone cutter, leaving there only when his employer "didn't want me no longer." Denis ended up back in New-York and landed in the hospital with a heart ailment. He concluded his story by saying, "Well here I am out again but I have no imployment an' the heart is sick witin me."[23] As he had with the King brothers, Mr. Macy referred Denis to the NBLH and hoped that Mr. Tracy would help stabilize the boy's housing, health, and work situation.

Mr. Macy had entertained three Irish boys in rapid succession, but he helped American children as well, not to mention German, Italian, Prussian, Jamaican, Scottish, and Dutch, or any others that walked through his door. The number varied day by day but the stream of referrals to the NBLH was a constant. By year's end, it would total in the thousands.[24] However, the movement of boys wasn't unidirectional. Mr. Tracy also sent boys *back* to Mr. Macy for assorted routine reasons such as job referrals, want of clothing, or screening for country homes. He also sent them when there were occasional glitches, such as that which occurred with a deaf boy named Edward.

***

Difficult Cases

Mr. Macy had sent the boy with impaired hearing over to the NBLH just the day before. He had hoped that a bathtub filled with Croton water would rejuvenate the depressed lad. Edward had dutifully gone but spent a lonely night. The other boys didn't pay much attention to him. Now he was back looking as filthy and forlorn as he had when Mr. Macy sent him off.

Despite some difficulty in communicating, Mr. Macy learned that due to the frigid January temperatures, the NBLH cistern was frozen solid. So

Edward had been "unable to perform an ablution."[25] He had been sent back to the central office to rectify the problem. With that understood, Mr. Macy "secured the office door," had Edward remove his vermin-infested cloths and sent him off to bathe. In the meantime, Mr. Macy dug up, "a clean shirt, and new suit" from the donated clothing bin. He even found a trendy "black silk stock" collar which he helped fix on for Edward. The transformation was stunning; clean and clothed, Edward "was wholly changed—comfortable and refreshed." He was also smiling from ear to ear, signaling to Mr. Macy that his "life [had] been saved."[26]

Mr. Macy dispatched Edward back to the NBLH. Chances were that he would fare better among the boys, given his cleaned-up appearance and happier mood. The newsboys were usually welcoming of others, and, if not, Mr. Tracy would invariably intervene with one of his creative lessons on tolerance. Mr. Macy probably worried about Edward, though. He was going to face more difficulties locating employment than the others. Although the boy was intelligent, his deafness had already proven an impediment to employment. Edward had been in the U.S. for nine months but "he could not get on here, had no money, and was soon a homeless and friendless wanderer—he had slept in the Station House for several nights before he had the good luck to discover the office of CAS."[27]

Edward was reminiscent of another boy Mr. Macy had referred to the NBLH. That lad's father had died some years ago, so he had found work as a cabin boy "on board a topsail schooner."[28] "The boy made several voyages in this ship, but had the misfortune to fall from the yard arm, during a storm in the Gulf of Florida, and had the fingers of both hands driven up half ways to his wrist."[29] The boy spent "four days insensible" as the schooner made its way up the East Coast. When the vessel finally docked in New-York, "he was put into the Hospital."[30] When he regained his physical health, the hospital discharged him, but he was "turned adrift . . . without any resources in the streets of New-York."[31] With his "limbs crippled" he could not return to life on the vessel nor find other employment easily. Mr. Macy initially sent him over to the Seamen's Home, the best fit for the maimed young man. However, "there was no place vacant for him" so he had returned to the central office.[32] Mr. Macy then sent him over to the NBLH, where he could stay as long as needed. Nonetheless, it was a harsh environment for surviving with physical limitations, and the boy's best hope would be a bed at the Seaman's House.

Mr. Macy's next distraction was Adolphus who dropped by the office just to say hello and pay a friendly call. Adolphus also had been referred to the NBLH a while back. After first arriving in New-York, the boy had traveled upstate to Troy, where he tried to find work. When his money ran out, he returned to the city. Like Edward, Adolphus ended up sleeping at the police station house, a common spot for vagrant, penniless men. The station houses were notoriously dank, dreary, and overcrowded. When the Ladies of the House of Industry of the Friendless had suggested Adolphus try CAS, he leaped at the chance and found his way to Mr. Macy, declaring it was a stroke of "good luck."[33] In turn, Mr. Macy sent him to Mr. Tracy, where "he stayed a few nights at the Lodging House."[34]

Among the lodgers, the earnest Adolphus was well liked. However, due to a crippling back injury, he eventually found it impossible to negotiate the six flights of stairs up to the lodging house quarters. It was a problem that CAS was unable to fix.[35] Although in 1854 Elisha Otis had introduced his contraption called the "safety hoister" at New-York's World's Fair—a novel innovation and curiosity—it would take years to evolve into a workable elevator that could be used in building construction. Unable to negotiate the walk-up, Adolphus had quit the NBLH and was now at a boarding house. He dropped by the central office occasionally to stay in touch with Mr. Macy and say "he was getting on very well" although he had to carry coal to fourteen other residents in exchange for room and board. Unfortunately, he said, "the pain in this back came hard."[36]

The long-term outcomes for these boys with special needs—deaf, maimed, with heart ailments, or in chronic pain were dim. The world was not an easy place for impoverished youth under the best of circumstances. But Mr. Macy—and by extension, Mr. Tracy—faced tougher challenges with boys like Adolphus and Edward. Life had dealt them an unlucky hand.

***

Central Office as Employment Agency

Mr. Macy knew how hard the world would be for boys with disabilities on first-hand experience. Among his jobs at the central office was that of essentially running an employment agency. He routinely entertained—either in person or through written correspondence—prospective employers.[37] These people were looking for boys or girls for any number of jobs, such as running errands, doing farm work, providing domestic services, delivering messages, working in offices in New-York as well as in the surrounding states. Invariably these potential employers wanted "perfect children"—whatever that meant to their individual sensibilities and prejudices.[38] Mr. Macy tried to dissuade them from having unreasonable expectations. The street children with which Mr. Macy was familiar and CAS worked, required coaching, guidance, and patience. They needed adults who understood their developmental level and were willing to tolerate their mistakes. What Mr. Macy looked for in employers were those willing to offer a hybrid situation that entailed fostering, apprenticing, supervising, and training. The point was to help the child transition to adult occupations and labor markets.

Mr. Macy was also charged with the final screening of children before placement. Many a poor child seeking work was referred to Mr. Macy from some area of the CAS network—a lodging house, an industrial school, or a boys' meeting—or by a visitor. Sometimes, there was no work to be had but the child's need for cash was immediate. So Mr. Macy was known to create work for children. He would employ one boy "to throw wood down" only to hire "the other to pile it up."[39]

Mr. Macy relied heavily on the recommendations that the boys carried with them from Mr. Tracy and others but in the end, it was his job to do all the final match-making between children and employers. He hated the idea of getting it wrong. The society had learned early on about badly matched placements when a sweet little Irish girl had been dispatched to a prospective employer only to have the tearful, disappointed girl returned to the office with a note reprimanding CAS for sending a Catholic child. It was a lesson learned. Although CAS essentially maintained an open door policy serving children of all faiths—Protestant, Catholic, Jewish—and all races and ethnicities—black, white, American-born, and immigrant—the truth was that the children faced the reality of an outside world less universally tolerant. The society didn't operate in a vacuum. Within months of opening, the board of trustees had resolved "that we will not entrust the care of any child to any person or institution until we are first satisfied as to their character and the advantage of the situation to the child." No matter what the political leanings of the individual agents working at CAS, a misplaced child hurt not only the child but the agency as well.

***

To the Country: Transfer Point and Temporary Lodging

In a variation on the theme of serving as an employment clearing house, the central office was also the launching and transfer point for the society's inaugural efforts to place children "in the country." Many of the older, homeless, or orphaned boys from the NBLH volunteered for the "emigration parties" themselves, actually seeking employment in the west. Like all children sent to the country, the boys were screened by Mr. Tracy and Mr. Macy.

In contrast, there were also parents, relatives, and other custodians who requested that their children be placed out. For them, the central office was the access point for applying for placement. In addition, it served as a transfer point when dropping off children. For example, right before a scheduled trip, two boys aged ten or eleven were brought to the office by their mother. The boys were "chubby faced, and good humored" and were "as like each other as 'twin cherries on a stem.'" They had been born in Londonderry, Ireland, and their father was dead. After coming to the U.S., they lived with an aunt for a while when their mother couldn't maintain them. However, the aunt herself was no longer able to provide for the boys and their mother, having exhausted her family networks, now turned to CAS for help. She brought them to Mr. Macy requesting that they be sent to a family that could care for them.[40]

Mr. Macy, like Mr. Brace, believed children were better off in the country—anywhere outside New-York. However, he wasn't immune to the sadness of separating parent and child. This was particularly true in cases like this one, where a mother lacked any other viable options.

Children in other situations trickled in, like Philip Krohn and his German mother. Philip had been born in the U.S. of a Norwegian father. He was "a bright slender little boy" who spoke and read "the English language very well" and was "remarkably intelligent and observant." Philip's mother wanted a place for the boy in the country, and he was scheduled to depart the following day.[41] Similarly, a young adult, James Van Buskirk, brought in his two younger cousins, Alfred and Henry Taylor. It was unclear why this young man was caring for his cousins, but the brothers were slated to go to a country home, and James requested that he be allowed "to spend the night with them" so "he [might] bid them farewell in the morning."[42] Mr. Macy sent the entire lot of young men—the twin cherries from Londonderry; Philip; Alfred; Henry; and their cousin, James—over to Mr. Tracy at the NBLH, where they would all spend the night. For these boys, the lodging house served as overnight hotel before an early departure.

***

One Hundred Miles, Due North

Among other things, Mr. Macy was responsible for "disentangling all the complicated threads" in the various applications for service and helping those who presented themselves. This made him, in the view of his supervisor, Mr. Brace, "an expert in paidology," or "the science of boys."[43] Mr. Macy's colleagues were in awe of his ability to sort through fabrications and fibs without losing compassion for the truly needy.

Over the years, he developed what appeared to be a sixth sense for detecting deception but may have been better attributed to a finely honed sense of observation and unique expertise. Working with street youth demanded a set of unusually skills. One of them was to sort fact from fiction. For example, "the runaway from a good home" who was requesting services was "soon betrayed to this experienced friend of boys."[44] Where the untrained eye might see a ragged boy, Mr. Macy was apt to see "amid his rags, a neatly-sewed patch, or note that his naked feet are too white for a 'bummer.'"[45] Once Mr. Macy spotted a fraud, rather than the sympathy the boy was likely expecting, he was more often confronted with a direct question, such as "Where is your mother?" When the information was finally successfully extracted, Mr. Macy would send the boy back home.

According to Mr. Brace's daughter, Emma, "Mr. Macy's sense of humor" was at "his strongest" when he detected "cases of fraud and deceit."[46] As legend had it, one day two older boys—claiming great need—arrived at the office. Mr. Macy listened patiently to their stories of woe, but he smelled trickery and believed they were attempting to con him. Mr. Macy's response to the boys would be gleefully recounted by his friends for years to come. He "conducted them politely to the door" and "pointing amiably to third avenue" he said, "Now, my boys, just be kind enough to walk right north up that avenue for one hundred miles into the country, and you will find plenty of work and food."[47] Apparently, "the boys departed mystified,"[48] with Mr. Macy's jolly "Good-bye! Good-bye!"[49] ringing in their ears.

***

A Man of Good Humor

Mr. Macy was cheerful and "always ready with his joke or quaint apothegm," and his "salvation in these exhausting and nerve-wearing efforts" was "his humor."[50] The boys liked Mr. Macy in part because they could pull a prank on him without raising his ire. Not infrequently, the boys incorporated Mr. Macy's own preaching on topics such as the evils of spending evenings in the liquor shop or engaging in petty theft into their antics.

For example, on one bitter cold winter's evening, Mr. Macy arrived at the hall for the nightly boys' meeting only to find "the lock of the room picked" and a group of boys already gathered inside the building. Mr. Macy accused the older boys of this mischief, to which they responded, "No, sir—no: it couldn't be us; because we was in the liquor-shop on the corner; *we ain't got nowheres else to go!*"⁵¹ In this context Mr. Macy could only be delighted the boys had chosen to jimmy the lock rather than gather in a drinking den to stay warm.

On another night, Mr. Macy ventured into an infrequently used storeroom attached to the meeting hall. The topic of his most recent Sunday sermon was the impropriety of stealing, so he could only be amused when he discovered that the "private room" had been "employed by the boys for some time as a receptacle for stolen goods."⁵² It was a story Mr. Macy told with delight for the rest of life. Mr. Brace observed of his friend, "some peculiar exhibition of mischief or wickedness always seemed to act as a kind of tonic on him and restore his spirits."⁵³ Nothing delighted him more than the boys' devious behavior. Where other city charity workers might see juvenile delinquency, Mr. Macy only saw a worthy challenge.

Mr. Macy could give as well as he could take. For example, there was the way he outmaneuvered the boys at a meeting on the evening of the pepper prank. The boys had surreptitiously placed pepper on the coal stove, which was used to heat the meeting hall. As the pepper fumes began permeating the room—seeming to displace all the available oxygen, "until they were half suffocated"⁵⁴—the boys began to squirm. However, Mr. Macy droned on and on, finding ever more creative ways of extending his remarks without showing any sign of succumbing to the pepper assault himself. Mr. Brace recalled, "I think the contest of wits among them—they for mischief and disturbance, and he to establish order and get control over them—gave a peculiar zest to his religious labors, which he would not have had in calmer scenes and more regular services."⁵⁵

All told, Mr. Macy demonstrated an attitude toward working with the boys that was evident with Mr. Tracy at the NBLH as well. In fact, it seemed to pervade the entire Society. Neither man displayed any indication of being a strict disciplinarian nor wed to rigid formality. The interactions with the boys were, playful, informal, light-hearted, and good natured. The boys themselves seemed comfortable engaging in a tolerable level of mischief and without fear of harsh reprisal or a call to the police. All this undoubtedly contributed to fact they continued to return for more day after day, week after week. CAS would measure its success by the value the boys placed in the program each time they returned.

***

Endless Errands and Odds and Ends

Luckily the busy Mr. Macy had the help of other CAS staff and volunteers. Among the most notable was a clerk, Mr. Colopy. His real name was William Colopy Desmond but, for whatever reason, the boys simply called him Mr. Colopy. Mr. Colopy served as a human bridge between Mr. Macy in the central office and Mr. Tracy at the NBLH (although Mr. Tracy appeared at the central office himself and Mr. Macy, at the NBLH, periodically). Mr. Colopy spent considerable time during the day running errands around the city for Mr. Macy, escorting boys, picking up donations, and the like. In the evenings, he helped at the NBLH and would wrangle the boys through their nightly routines. It was a job without set description since the day's unique needs inevitably dictated his role.

On the unusual side of the continuum was the day a gentleman associated with Castle Garden arrived at the office. The man had come to discuss "three young Emigrants who arrived . . . after a passage of five weeks from England in the ship William Rathbone." It turned out the lads had been sent from the Kingswood Reformatory School in Bristol by their schoolmistress, Mrs. Mary Carpenter. The boys' ultimate destination was Pennsylvania, where they were to stay with Mrs. Carpenter's cousin. However, during their transit through New-York, the boys were "consigned to the care of Mr C. L. Brace, who is to forward them as soon as possible."[56] This was news to Mr. Macy but he dispatched Mr. Colopy to pick up the young trio at Castle Garden.

When the boys arrived in the office, they claimed that although many at Kingswood "had been placed there as bad boys, under reformatory treatment," they were different.[57] Their parents had paid for their placement, and they had been sent to the U.S. Whatever Mr. Macy thought about this story, he referred them over to the NBLH for the night. The next day the boys were escorted by Mr. Colopy to a railway car for transport to Pennsylvania. It was just one more referral from the public that passed through the office to the lodging house and then onward.

***

Cash: In and Out

In addition to handling the flow of humanity that passed in and out of Mr. Macy's office, he also managed donations—cash and in-kind—that sustained

CAS, a job that increased in size and complexity with each passing year. Cash donations from benefactors—either through subscriptions or as one-time gifts—streamed in. They ranged in amount from pennies collected during children's Sunday school classes to large donations from some of New-York's wealthiest families. The cash might come in the form of U.S. currency—dollars, dimes, and pennies—or it might come in as British coinage—pounds, pence, and shillings.[58] All these funds would ultimately end up in the hands of the society's official treasurer, James Earl Williams, at the Metropolitan Bank. Nonetheless, donations were not only "gladly received by the Treasurer," CAS publications advertised, but "by the Secretary of the Office."[59] As a practical matter, that meant Mr. Macy. By the end of his tenure as assistant secretary, CAS estimated that three million dollars had passed through his hands without a penny going astray.

Some of these funds were used to pay the salaries of the gradually increasing numbers of CAS employees. Mr. Macy was in charge of paying these workers and recording the transactions. For example, in 1857 his salary receipt book included notes on his own salary as well as that of Mr. Brace, four permanent visitors, an "agent for country," Mr. Tracy, Mr. Colopy, and Mr. Cerqua from the Italian School.[60]

Each man showed up in the waning days of the month or in the earliest days of the next, seeking pay for services rendered as well as any authorized expenses associated with society work. So, for example, Mr. Tracy might arrive to collect his sixty-five-dollar salary along with thirty dollars for NBLH expenses and fifty dollars' rent for the Sun Building loft. Each amount was dutifully recorded in the receipt book along with a signature of acknowledgment.

***

In-Kind, Comings and Goings

The cash was relatively easy to manage compared with the flood of in-kind donations that passed through the CAS central office. Once again, it was Mr. Macy who was charged with receiving it, accounting for it, thanking donors according to their individual wishes, and distributing it in accordance with the donors' desires. Given the number of gifts and their variety, it was a daunting part of his job.

As early as 1855, CAS had formalized its request to the public. "Donations of Clothing are much needed, and can be sent to the Office, No. 11 Clinton Hall, Astor Place," read a note on the second page of CAS's annual report.[61]

By the next year, the society extended its plea for clothing to "shoes, stockings, &c." and noted that "old clothing will be called for, if the address be sent to the Office."[62]

Sometimes, Mr. Macy received a note in advance of a gift: "Dear Sir, I send by local express today a valise and two packages of clothing for CAS. The valise need not be returned—Please acknowledge receipt—... but don't publish my name in any printed acknowledgment."[63] In cases such as these, Mr. Macy needed to record the contents of the donation, mail a handwritten thank-you note to the sender, and record a note that it should be acknowledged as an anonymous gift from a "friend" in next year's annual report. Other times, a note arrived in the central office requesting a donation pick up, such as this: "Please call at 142 West 16th St for 1 Pkg of clothing." It was Mr. Macy's job to find someone to retrieve the package.[64] He might hire a boy from the NBLH who was down on his luck. He might send a visitor or Mr. Colopy. Or he might make the call himself. It was just one more thing that filled the days of the busy assistant.

Clothing donations came from many sources: individuals, ladies' sewing circles, and manufacturers. Articles came by the piece but also by the bundle, in parcels, packages, bags, and baskets. For example, in 1859, Mrs. Addie sent a bundle of clothing; Mrs. Jones sent a package containing stockings, drawers, and other items; and an unknown friend sent a bundle of clothing containing jackets, vests, and hats. The amount and variety of gifts was duly noted by Mr. Macy.

Once the clothing donations arrived and were processed, there was the pleasant task of distributing them to people in need. Appeals for dresses, pants, blouses, shirts, shoes, stockings, coats, hats, or mittens for ragged street children flowed in regularly from every artery of CAS's branches of service. Visitors and other agents or employees stopped by the office to pick up clothing for poor children in their wards. All of the transactions were recorded. For example, Mr. Trott "took from Office for 14th In. School 12 pairs shoes, 2 pairs pants, 3 jackets."

Technically, as with virtually all CAS efforts, clothing was distributed as a reward for effort not handed out as matter of pure charity. On the other hand, if being without was an immediate impediment to a child's education, CAS filled the need. Much like the small entrance fee at the NBLH, which was expected but could be waived, so too with clothing distribution. It was offered as a mixture of charity and earned privilege. Written requests flowed in from CAS agents, teachers, and superintendents explaining a family's need, reporting that the children had earned the right to an article of clothing through good attendance at industrial or evening schools or would otherwise not be able to attend classes. "Please to send 3 pair of pants, one pair for a boy 12 years old, 2 pairs for small boys . . . [and] . . . one large jacket suitable for a boy 13 or 14." The writer added, "These boys have not been absent, since school commenced, and have earned them, and they are members of a large family."[65] While CAS's focus was on poor children, there is no doubt that services such as these benefited poor families.

Another note to Mr. Macy read as follows: "Please to send shoes for these children, they have earned them and are in want of them," and the request was followed by a list of nine children's names.[66] Yet another said, "Please to send me shoes for these children they are in great want, and can not attend school without them," followed by names of seven girls. "These children have earned their shoes and are very destitute," said yet another with nine names listed. In particularly bad weather—or more difficult economic times—the pleas increased and the needs become more graphic. "I would like to have some clothes for this boy Peter Healy, also some for a boy about 14 years old . . . also 3 pair of pants, and 3 jackets . . . The boys are increasing in number, and very destitute so you must do all you can, as I am afraid I can scarcely cover them so as to render them decent to make their appearance."[67]

In each case, Mr. Macy did the best he could to fill the endless requisitions with the desired items. Although clothing was received in great quantity, Mr. Macy often gave items out "soon as they [came] in."[68] Another bit of agency lore involved a particularly cold winter day when Mr. Macy was confronted with "a needy young man who had been unfortunate" and was asking for a warm winter coat. Mr. Macy had none on reserve. So he gave the young man his own "best one" and Mr. Macy himself "went in an old overcoat" for the rest of that winter."[69]

In short, Mr. Macy ran a clothing swap shop on top of his other responsibilities. CAS's annual report of 1856 claimed that "at least 10,000 garments have been distributed among the poor, this last year from this office" in addition to "200 pairs of new shoes; 240 pairs of new stockings."[70] Clearly, the volume of items that passed through Mr. Macy's hands and reached New York's poor was not insignificant and must have gone a long way in meeting a critical basic need for poor children and their families.

Clothing was not the only in-kind donations offered to CAS. Almost immediately other kinds of contributions began to pour in. They were often earmarked for one branch of CAS service or another. For example, in one year alone the NBLH received at least four dozen copy books, reams of paper, books, and magazines—including a pile from Mrs. J. J. Astor—but also some "choice books" from the editor of the *New York Observer*, Sabbath-School Bell picture books, and Sunday school manuals. In addition, manufacturers like Colgate & Co. sent boxes of soap. A variety of individuals contributed coal—six tons of it in total—in 1858. Food came often, particularly at the holidays. That year, the NBLH alone received a basket of cross-buns from Mrs. Carlton and another from Mr. Higgins and ten turkeys, two hams, a bushel of potatoes, eight loaves of bread, and a box of oranges from two prominent New-York hotels. This was in addition to a barrel of potatoes and a box of celery from other sources. There were plenty of donated comforters and there was lots of donated bed clothing. Not to mention miscellaneous other things, such as a pin cushion, a ball of twine, bolts of calico, flannel, muslin, and half a stick of Griswold's Salve, in its iconic brown paper rolled up like a Tootsie Roll. Also, J. L. Mott & Co. sent over a "bathing-tub." All of it, from books to bathtubs and bedding, was accepted, dutifully recorded, and gratefully acknowledged by Mr. Macy on behalf of the society. The items were earmarked for the NBLH and then transferred there.

At the end of the day, in addition to all his other responsibilities, Mr. Macy's central office served the important task of receiving and distributing a large variety and massive amount of goods. Either directly as in clothing distribution, or indirectly as in sending books and bedding to the lodging house, these benefits flowed to poor children and supplemented CAS's overall support and services.

***

A Veritable Ringmaster

Mr. Macy, a calm, good-humored religious man, was happiest when he was confronted with dozens of pressing demands at the CAS office. This probably meant he was happy most of the time. Like a traffic cop at the center of a busy intersection, Mr. Macy was at the heart of this congestion, and he regulated the flow of all of the society's charitable business and transactions for nearly twenty-eight years. He handled mischievous children and wealthy women with equal grace. He referred boys and girls for employment and fielded requests from potential employers. He received money and in-kind donations and directed them to their proper place. He paid salaries and managed correspondence. He made arrangements for picking up children or clothes. He listened to, and consoled, children. He offered them a bath, food, clothing, or shelter when needed. He "comforted their broken-hearted mothers, or rebuked their drunken fathers."[71] Mr. Macy attempted to sort through all the children and families in need as they arrived. He looked for immediate solutions within CAS's increasingly sprawling network of services. Under his watch the office became a one-stop social service center for the public. However, significantly, the central office also served as the ultimate connection point through which all CAS work was mediated. It was the point of intersection for multiple branches of CAS's decentralized services in its neighborhood based programs, including lodging houses and schools. Mr. Macy was the ringmaster of it all.

Notes

1. Most of the empirical evidence for this chapter is from the period of 1855 to 1859. However, I have taken the liberty of using the best evidence available from later years to illustrate activities that were occurring in the earliest days of CAS if there was a dearth of available records and/or documents from the 1850s period. Not all CAS record books have survived, so there are limitations to what information exists. However, there is no reason to believe that the composition of a brief donation letter from the 1870s, for example, is significantly different from one that would have been received in 1856. Furthermore, I have focused on Mr. Macy's work with boys, specifically those directly referred to and from the NBLH in keeping with the focus of this book. However, Mr. Macy also dealt with other boys as well as girls and young women who passed through the office.
2. Charles Loring Brace, *The Dangerous Classes of New York and Twenty Years' Work Among Them*, 3rd ed. (New York: Wynkoop & Hallenbeck, 1880), 212.
3. Minutes of the Board of Trustees, March 14, 1855, vol. 2, 1853–1861, in The Victor Remer Historical Archives of the Children's Aid Society (1836–2006). New-York Historical Society Archives. Records of the Children's Aid Society 1836–2006, New-York Historical Society Archives.
4. *Third Annual Report of the Children's Aid Society* (New York: M. B. Wynkoop, 1856), 7.
5. Emma Brace, ed., *The Life of Charles Loring Brace* (1894; facsimile of the first edition, New York: Arno Press, 1976), 382.
6. By 1856, CAS was connected to five industrial schools. In addition, the society had opened the Italian School in December 1855, which was housed in Mr. Pease's House of Industry in the Five Points. Although CAS would open new industrial schools over the years and occasionally close old ones, in 1856, the five industrial schools associated with CAS included the Fourth Ward School, the German School on Avenue C, the Hudson River School on West 28th—which was mostly for German, Irish, and American children—the East River School at 40th Street near 3rd Avenue (which had many children who were "swill gatherers, rag-pickers and beggars from Dutch Hill"), and finally the Calvary Church School for German

girls (*Third Annual Report*, 16). Although the industrial schools were primarily run by ladies who volunteered, over the years CAS helped with hiring "salaried teacher[s]—assisted by the ladies volunteering" (*Third Annual Report*, 9).
7. *Third Annual Report*, 12.
8. *Third Annual Report*; Seventh Annual Report of the Children's Aid Society (New York: Wynkoop, Hallenbeck & Thomas, 1860), 21.
9. *Seventh Annual Report*, 21.
10. Brace, *The Dangerous Classes*, 274.
11. *Thirtieth Annual Report of the Children's Aid Society* (New York: Italian School Printing Department, 1882), 62.
12. Emma Brace, *Life of C. L. Brace*, 382.
13. This same plot of land was the site of the deadly Astor Place Riot of 1849, although the theater was dismantled in 1853 (see Chapter 1 of this volume). Given the location's history as the site of class and nativity tensions, it seems appropriate to have placed CAS's central office in the vicinity. The trace remains of this spot can still be seen by New-York subway riders of the downtown 6 train. The "Clinton Hall" lintel is embedded in the tilework.
14. Brace, *The Dangerous Classes*, 271.
15. Brace, *The Dangerous Classes*, 273.
16. Emma Brace, *Life of C. L. Brace*, 382.
17. Brace, *The Dangerous Classes*, 278.
18. Castle Garden, opened on August 3, 1855, was the first "official immigrant processing center" and as such represented a significant shift in American immigration policy (National Park Service, Castle Clinton, History and Culture, retrieved 2016, https://www.nps.gov/cacl/learn/historyculture/index.htm). It operated until 1892, when Ellis Island opened (National Park Service, U.S. Department of the Interior, National Monument, New York, Castle Clinton, 2016).
19. Castle Garden was purportedly a place where the arriving immigrants could receive "lodging and travel information, medical attention, and honest currency exchange" (https://www.nps.gov/cacl/learn/historyculture/index.htm).
20. William Colopy Desmond, "Incidents and Sketches Among the Newsboys, Part III" (September 6, 1855–November 22, 1855), 121, in Guide to the Records of the Children's Aid Society, Series V, vol. 47, New-York Historical Society.
21. July 17, 1857 (Special Meeting of the Trustees).
22. The barque, also spelled *bark*, was a popular vessel known for its three masts.
23. William Colopy Desmond, "Incidents and Sketches Among the Newsboys, Part IV" (November 22, 1855–February 11, 1856), 42–45, in Guide to the Records of the Children's Aid Society, Series V, vol. 48, New-York Historical Society.
24. For example, in 1860, a total of 1,003 boys were referred from the central office directly to the NBLH (*Seventh Annual Report*, 12).
25. Desmond, "Incidents and Sketches," vol. 48.
26. Desmond, "Incidents and Sketches," vol. 48.

27. Desmond, "Incidents and Sketches," vol. 48.
28. Desmond, "Incidents and Sketches," vol. 47.
29. Desmond, "Incidents and Sketches," vol. 47.
30. Desmond, "Incidents and Sketches," vol. 47.
31. Desmond, "Incidents and Sketches," vol. 47.
32. Desmond, "Incidents and Sketches," vol. 47.
33. Desmond, "Incidents and Sketches Among the Newsboys, Part V," (February 18, 1856–May 7, 1856), entry dated February 19, in Guide to the Records of the Children's Aid Society, Series V, vol. 49, New-York Historical Society.
34. Desmond, "Incidents and Sketches, Part V," February 19, 1856.
35. CAS would eventually develop special services for "crippled" children. The NBLH welcomed children with disabilities, nonetheless its location on the uppermost floor made it difficult for children with mobility problems. Nonetheless, the records show NBLH at times entertained blind, deaf, physically ill, or injured children.
36. Desmond, "Incidents and Sketches," vol. 49.
37. Correspondence was in writing only. This period predates the telephone by about two decades.
38. Brace, *The Dangerous Classes*, 273.
39. Emma Brace, *Life of C. L. Brace*, 383; Brace, *The Dangerous Classes*, 278.
40. Desmond, "Incidents and Sketches," vol. 47.
41. Desmond, "Incidents and Sketches," vol. 49.
42. Desmond, "Incidents and Sketches," vol. 49.
43. *Thirtieth Annual Report*, 61.
44. *Thirtieth Annual Report*, 61.
45. Brace, *The Dangerous Classes*, 276.
46. Emma Brace, *Life of C. L. Brace*, 383.
47. Emma Brace, *Life of C. L. Brace*, 383.
48. Emma Brace, *Life of C. L. Brace*, 383.
49. Emma Brace, *Life of C. L. Brace*, 383.
50. *Thirtieth Annual Report*, 61; Brace, C.L. 1880, p. 275.
51. Brace, *The Dangerous Classes*, 277.
52. Brace, *The Dangerous Classes*, 276–277.
53. Brace, *The Dangerous Classes*, 276.
54. Brace, *The Dangerous Classes*, 277.
55. Brace, *The Dangerous Classes*, 277.
56. Desmond, "Incidents and Sketches," vol. 47.
57. Colopy Desmond, "Incidents and Sketches," vol. 48.
58. The American Revolution took place roughly eighty years earlier. British currency was still used in New York.
59. *Second Annual Report of the Children's Aid Society* (New York: M. B. Wynkoop, Book & Job Printer, 1855), 2.

60. *Fourth Annual Report of the Children's Aid Society* (New York: John P. Prall, Printer by Steam, 1857), 2.
61. *Second Annual Report*, 2.
62. *Third Annual Report*, 2.
63. Children's Aid Society, "Donation Correspondence" (August 1873–November 1873), in Guide to the Records of the Children's Aid Society, Series VI, box 27, folder 9, New-York Historical Society.
64. Children's Aid Society, "Donation Correspondence."
65. Children's Aid Society, "Requests for Shoes and Clothing from Schools and Lodging Houses" (1864–1866), in Guide to the Records of the Children's Aid Society, Series VI, vol. 66, New-York Historical Society.
66. Children's Aid Society, "Requests for Shoes."
67. Children's Aid Society, "Requests for Shoes."
68. *Third Annual Report*, 20.
69. *Thirtieth Annual Report*, 62.
70. *Third Annual Report*, 20.
71. *Thirtieth Annual Report*, 61.

6

The Earliest Lodgers

THE GOOD AND THE BAD, 1855–1856

We hear him at very early hours in the most distant parts of the city, and across the ferries, with his song of "Here's the Herald!" "Times!" "Tribune!" and then in a lowered tone, "Morning papers, sir?"
—JOHNNIE MORROW, *A Voice from the Newsboys*, 1860

AT THE NBLH,[1] Mr. Tracy's voice always rang out at half past six in the morning, "Up, boys, up!"[2] The lodgers' responses were undoubtedly varied: some grumbling and reluctant; others sprang up ready for the day. Some beds had already been vacated. Their occupants had quietly slipped out, at four or five o'clock, to be first in line for their daily stock of newspapers. They might have to wait, but they would beat their competition to the street. The boys who were lingering at the lodging house would have shaken off the last vestiges of sleep, gotten dressed, gathered up whatever wares or money they had left with Mr. Tracy for safekeeping the night before, and scrambled down the zigzagging flights of stairs to street level.

Invariably, Valise was at the head of the pack. He was the lodging house's resident "baggage smasher," a term he had explained to Mr. Colopy one night. "Some calls it breaking baggages," he said. "It means baggage carrying though. Fellers as carry baggage are called baggage smashers." Valise had adopted this line of work four years earlier, when "I seed a little feller one day a carrying a big trunk an' I sed—says I—why shouldn't I be able to do the same?"

Valise's trade required him to be fleet of foot. The faster he was, the more he could carry in a day, and the more shillings he earned. However, he had originally developed his sprinting ability for an entirely different reason. He had had Charley Wood to contend with. Officer Wood was on Chief Matsell's Municipal Police Force. This particular copper had snared Valise no fewer than three times for failing to possess a license. Valise admitted to Mr. Tracy, "I spent five days in The Tombs and I tell you it was an ugly place to live in. I hopes as how I shan't get in there any more." Luckily for Valise, Officer Wood had been replaced with another officer who had a "big pot belly," an attribute Valise had likely underscored with expansive hand gestures to demonstrate the man's girth. "He gets out of breath if he only walks half ways through a block. He hasn't got no chance of catching us," reported Valise with obvious satisfaction. Nonetheless, to stay in shape, the boy still took the lodging house stairs two at time. There was no telling when Officer Pot Belly might be replaced by a leaner, more agile police officer. More generally, the boys had an uneasy relationship with the police who could whisk them off to a magistrate for the most minor offenses. The Tombs, the House of Refuge, or the Randall Island Nurseries were all predictable outcomes of such an encounter and could result in lengthy terms of incarceration.

If Valise had been at the front of the gaggle of boys darting down the stairs, inevitably Fatty, a proud Irish Catholic boy, would have been toward the back. Fatty's real name was Matt Coleman but everyone always called him Fatty. It was a nickname he readily embraced. He had only drawn the line one day when his peers tried to rename him "Galvanized Beer Barrel" after he had gone on a "burst" of heavy drinking. It was true that Fatty had a great fondness for lager beer, and he occasionally imbibed stronger spirits—much to Mr. Tracy's dismay—and, as a general rule, he accepted his peers' ribbing with good humor. However, he had balked at the beer barrel reference, threatening "assault and battery on the individual as insinuates I bears any resemblance to any such odious vessel." The boys quickly desisted, more from genuine fondness for Fatty than from any fear of imminent harm at his hand.

Similarly toward the back of the pack descending the lodging house stairs were likely two English Protestant boys and a smaller Dutch lad. Johnnie Morrow would have been slow because of his bum leg. As a small child in England, Johnnie had been playing a game of "flying swing" with schoolmates[3] and had been thrown off, shattering his leg in several places. His damaged limb never fully healed, leaving it three inches shorter than his healthy leg.

Johnnie's physical disability in no way diminished his resilient spirit. He was a great favorite with CAS staff. Not only was he well educated, studious, and pious, but he was honest, too. It was this later characteristic that had particularly impressed Mr. Tracy when Johnnie confessed to having lied about being an orphan at intake. In any case, Johnnie descended the lodging house stairs with difficulty.

Johnnie sometimes called his fellow Protestant, Danny O'Sullivan, "English" because of their shared heritage. Everyone else in the world seemed to refer to Danny as "the Professor." The Professor had been born in England of Irish parents but had emigrated to the U.S. when he was young. Once, when the Professor was asked by a visitor to the lodging house if he was a "Yank," Mr. Tracy had quickly stepped in and responded that he was "quarter English-Irish-Yank and Kentuckian," a true American mix for anyone but the diehard nativists who were making waves in New-York at the time.

Johnnie had once opined that because "the Protestant boys were outnumbered" by the Catholics, "we kept together."[4] Yet the Professor was a great favorite with all the boys at the lodging house. The Professor had two noteworthy characteristics, the first of which contributed to his popularity across religious denominations: his legendary generosity. The "Professor's real forte," according to Mr. Colopy, was "doing the Samaritan" (or, as Fatty had once said after misunderstanding a lodging house lecture, the "good martin"). The Professor frequently paid the way for less fortunate boys. One evening, a group of newsboys had been discussing his generosity over steaks at the Nassau Coffee Saloon. Little Booch testified, "Danny is the best feller in New York—many a feller would have starved but for him. Whenever a feller is short there is no one as can put in for him like Danny. He is a first rate feller is Danny."

This generosity occasionally got the Professor in trouble with CAS staff.

The Professor once visited Mr. Macy at the office, informing him that he had spent thirty-three cents on two poor boys, treating them to two meals of thick cuts, toast, and tea. As a result, the Professor reported abashedly, he now found himself short on cash. Could Mr. Macy reimburse him for his troubles?

"Well Danny," Mr. Macy had said gently, "Mr. Colopy will square up with you on this occasion, but for the future you will permit Mr. Colopy to feed the boys from the office—some of them, you know, may be bad boys, and we would not wish that they should be so high fed as your indiscriminate generosity might prompt."

With this mild rebuke delivered, Mr. Colopy reimbursed the Professor from the office coffers. As popular as the Professor was, his indiscriminate gifting also led CAS staff to note that he was both generous but at the same time "an inveterate beggar." Mr. Colopy concluded, "Danny's habit of giving everything away predominates over every other."

In any case, one object of the Professor's charitable efforts was a small, homeless Dutch boy who rode on his back, slowing his progress down the lodging house stairs. The Professor had found this particularly unfortunate little lad on the street one day. He had promptly taken him to the Nassau Coffee Saloon, buying "a feast of oyster pie and fish ball . . . and cakes and coffee for two!" With bellies filled, the pair climbed the lodging house stairs to meet Mr. Tracy and the lodgers. To Mr. Colopy's eye, the Professor had dragged in a "miserable looking boy . . . a street outcast, dirty and ragged, with a great wound on his nose, and a most woe-worn look." The lodgers took note and immediately dubbed this newcomer "Broken-Nose," although his real name was Jack.

Given his sorry state, Broken-Nose had required an extra allotment of Croton water to scrub him clean. After his nose was "plastered up" with an "India rubber bandage" and his "hair was trimmed," the Professor sought to ensure his immediate financial security. He passed his cap around to the newsboys, seeking donations and putting three pennies toward the boy's lodging himself. Little Booch immediately contributed the additional three cents Broken-Nose needed. Three or four other boys also donated to Broken-Nose's care and upkeep. In the end, the Professor "collected fifteen cents which he said would help to get Jack his breakfast and start him in the newspaper business tomorrow morning." The Professor's "genial kind-heartedness" could often be parlayed into alms raising for himself or others.

Although the newsboys had temporarily dubbed Johnnie's little charge Broken-Nose, they churned through a series of nicknames in short order. As Jack's nose healed, the boys began calling him "Dutchy." As a recent immigrant, the boy retained a heavy accent. However, Dutchy became "Friday" when another lodger observed that the Professor and "his little footboy" were virtually inseparable, "just like Friday to Professor's Robinson Crusoe." Surprisingly, the Professor wasn't familiar with "this world famous story." So he asked Mr. Colopy how Robinson's man came to be called Friday. When he learned it had to do with the day on which Crusoe first came upon his underling, the Professor had pondered this briefly, finally announcing, "Then, that is a reason why little Dutchy should not be called Friday . . . because I found him on a Sunday." Reaching the logical conclusion, the Professor made a pronouncement: "Let his name be Sunday." So Jack had been rechristened by the newsboys, in rapid succession, "Broken Nose," "Dutchy," "Friday," and, finally, "Sunday."

The Professor's second noteworthy trait had to do with his inclination to wander. With regularity, he announced plans to travel to a distant state, but then, with equal regularity, he reappeared at the lodging house or the central office after a one- or two-month absence. Invariably, he explained his departure and return—as well as any movements in between—as having something to do with the comparative price of broiled mackerel. He had once complained to Mr. Tracy, "The times are so hard in New York, that I couldn't break them with a sledge-hammer. I am getting disgusted with this city—I will soon start for Louisville. Mackerel is one shilling and sixpence a pound and I am so fond of that fish, that I must hunt up a place where I may be high enough to reach it." The Professor extolled the virtues of this "very fine fish" to anyone who was willing to listen. It seemed an odd choice of seafood in New-York, given that the city was virtually awash in oysters. "In the business streets of New York," an English visitor had observed, "the eyes are greeted continually with the words 'Oyster Saloon' painted in large letters on the basement story."[5] You could find several people, "usually blacks," she wrote, shucking fresh oysters at one end of the saloon's counter.[6] Customers could also order their oysters cooked up in stews, pies, and puddings, or simply pickled. Nonetheless, given a choice, the Professor always ordered mackerel.

Aside from the lure of mackerel, there was no telling what might divert the Professor in his travels. For example, his proposed trip to Louisville started with a steamboat ride up the Hudson River to Albany. He stayed six weeks before moving eight miles further north to Troy. From there, he turned around and headed back to New-York, showing up at the lodging house once again. No matter where his journeys took him, he always returned with a new collection of colorful tales about his adventures and misfortunes. His travel junkets were, in part, about gathering new material; these tales would serve as fodder for his street performances for New-Yorkers for months to come.

Little Booch, the Professor's admirer, would also have been in the pack of boys heading downstairs to begin work on any given day. He was among the most hard working of all the lodgers. In fact, Mr. Colopy noted, he "appears to be one of the most successful traders among the boys. He surprises them all sometimes by his display of silver when the day's business is over, and he takes it from his pockets to count it over." Booch sold "fancy matches." What made his matches "fancy" was the fact they came with Booch's pledge that they were "guaranteed not to smell of brimstone." It was a dubious claim; nonetheless, he did a brisk business. His success may have had less to do with his sales pitch than with his hustle. In a single day of match selling he was known to run up staircases; knock on doors; visit basements and cellars where women tended babies and knit stockings; engage people sitting on door stoops; and run into office buildings to visit "the quills," over to the hotels to sell to guests and staff, and up to the garrets in the tenements. It was a lot of bustling about for $2.50 a week but that was an excellent profit for a young peddler.

Like Little Booch, Johnnie Morrow also sold matches. Both boys got their inventory in the match district, where there was a single, large factory on Thirtieth Street. It supplied over seventy distributing branches in the vicinity. One of these was a business run by two German brothers, Jake and John, on Twenty-Ninth Street between Seventh and Eighth avenues. In Johnnie's estimate, "Not less than fifty boys and girls lived by peddling matches bought from Jake and John."[7] Since they owned "only one of the six dozen branches of the Thirtieth street factory," Johnnie speculated, "each branch has probably as many customers as they have."[8] He concluded, "It would startle some people to know the number of families in this great city who gain their whole support from the sales of matches."

In a city that needed a daily supply of matches to keep candles, gas lanterns, wood stoves, and coal furnaces lit, the match sellers with their door-to-door sales were critical to the well-being of the city's residents. Match selling, like newspaper peddling, rag picking, errand running, baggage smashing, and all the other street-based jobs, were indispensable to the overall operation of the metropolis.

For a mere twenty-four cents Johnnie could buy two packs of matches containing thirty-six boxes per pack. With an additional penny, he purchased some cord or twine and repackaged the matches in smaller bundles to sell at a profit. Although it would have been possible to repackage the matches in "fancy boxes"—Johnnie knew of "two families who supported themselves by making paper boxes to hold matches for eight cents a gross"—their fancy boxes were too dear for Johnnie's business, so he stuck to securing his bundles of matches with a simple twine lace. Johnnie's initial twenty-five-cent investment could yield ninety cents in profit. It was a far cry from Booch's $2.50, but it was a respectable yield, particularly given his physical disadvantages.

As all the NBLH lodgers hit street level, they would have scattered like so many billiard balls to the match district for matches, printers row for newspapers, or the docks looking for totable luggage. However, a sizeable group stayed on Nassau Street, heading a little more than a block uptown. They were aiming for a squat six-story building that housed a variety of businesses including magazine publishers, book binders, and Charles Scribner & Co. Yet on reaching 114–115 Nassau Street, the boys would have descended a steep flight of cellar stairs into a basement cavern, one of the hundreds of "subterranean abodes" that housed saloons of varying degrees of respectability in the Five Points area.

***

The Nassau Coffee Saloon

The Nassau Coffee Saloon was a favorite among the newsboys and CAS staff alike. Mr. Tracy was known to join his lodgers for a meal. Mr. Macy sent boys from the office, often accompanied by Mr. Colopy. Mr. Colopy himself was a regular. He once said the place reminded him of this saying: "The warmest welcome is often to be found at the inn." Mr. Colopy had actually put pen to paper and composed a little poem called "The Nassau" in honor of the place. Its opening lines included these:

> *Snug in a basement, sinking from the street,*
> *The Newsboys find a welcome, and retreat...*
> *Their freedom here is under small restraint,*
> *Welcome alike, the sinner and the saint.*

The Nassau was always busy. It would fill up as the boys emerged from the lodging house, but these boys would be replaced soon by the earliest rising lodgers who had already finished selling their first morning papers. With every table occupied, "little Frank, the waiter," wearing "his best apron," would have scurried to meet the demands of his customers while the assistant manager, Mr. Glendinning, lent a hand. The menu included the usual fare: griddle cakes, coffee, and tea. For lunch the boys could get a six-cent steak, corned beef and cabbage, or, if they had enough change in their pockets, calf's head, venison, or woodchuck, with sauces.[9]

Given the Nassau's popularity among the newsboys, Mr. Tracy was thoroughly amused one day while sitting at one of its tables with the Professor and Booch, who were deeply engaged in a debate over the "best dining saloon in New York." The topic came up because the Professor had just visited a new place near Washington Market. Predictably, he had sampled the broiled mackerel, finding it to be very good.

It turned out Booch had strong opinions on the matter. His preference ran in favor of Mr. Crook, who ran three saloons in New-York. "Mr. Crook," declared Booch, "is a perfect gentleman. He keeps the best, and has the cheapest table in New York: and he is a perfect gentleman."

The Professor had to agree on this point. Turning to Mr. Tracy he had said, "Aye that he is.... Booch is not stretching a bit.... Mr. Crook's saloons, they be as good as the Astor House every one."

While the Professor might well have been basing his assessment on the quality of the mackerel, Booch seemed more taken with Mr. Crook's perfect gentlemanliness. Mr. Crook was inclined to buy Booch's fancy matches, giving him "more than double the price and a piece of pie" at the same time. You couldn't really beat Mr. Crook's combination of patronage. So Booch had ended the debate decisively in favor of Mr. Crook. "Let that be the last of it—I guess we don't want any more evidences."

With all due respect to Mr. Crook's generosity, it would have been easy to find boys who would similarly vouch for the Nassau's Mr. Glendinning. As Mr. Colopy once noted, he "knows the Newsboys very well and makes considerable allowance for their caste. He sees them every day, industrious, and self-dependent, and if they happen to be unfortunate in the sale of papers or other speculations—he trusts them and they very rarely 'step out.'"

One of the lodgers most frequently in debt at the Nassau was none other than Fatty. This was true despite the fact that Fatty was "constantly employed in a newspaper office folding papers." This was another one of those indispensable jobs. Someone had to manually fold the massive sheets of newsprint in half to make them manageable for carriers and customers alike. Fatty was skilled at this task, folding upwards of "3,300 newspapers in less than a day at four cents a hundred." He was so well known among the publishers that he often brought along an unemployed comrade from the lodging house, vouching for the boy when a luckless lad needed help finding work.

Yet despite Fatty's steady income, he wasn't known to be particularly frugal with his earnings. Compounding the problem was the fact that Fatty had an unusual talent for losing money. One night he had whispered to Mr. Colopy about two new lodgers from Massachusetts. "The Bostoners are scoundrels, they 'stept out' on me this afternoon. I gave them papers to sell for me and I haven't seen 'em since." This practice, of employing younger boys, usually resulted in profits for all concerned. However, on this occasion Fatty managed to lose fifty cents in the deal.

On another night, Fatty arrived at the lodging house complaining bitterly that "some folk have hearts no bigger than pea-nuts." When Mr. Tracy inquired about the specific evidence for this assertion, Fatty reported he had spent a good part of the day leading "nine horses from the livery stables up Courtland Street" and held "the reins of a waggon-horse" for a man from the country. "And how much do ye think I was paid?" he asked Mr. Tracy incredulously, throwing in some ethnic and religious slurs for good measure. "The countryman took out of his purse a three cent piece—an' after holding it between his fingers an' thumb, as carefully as he would a pinch of snuff, he handed it to me axin' for the change." Fatty was indignant. "Well if that wasn't impertinence, I don't know wot's wot!"

One evening, Fatty had proudly entered the NBLH and threw "six cents on the table" before Mr. Tracy. He then "set his arms a kimbo" and declared triumphantly, "There's six pence for you. Put down my name," he said, tapping the lodging house registry. "I'm squared up for tonight and that makes me as independent a man as there is in New York." Earlier that day, Fatty had earned fifty cents selling newspaper extras.

"Well," Mr. Tracy said in response, "This is a kind of miracle. I fear we will have a thunderstorm after an incident like this of Fatty's saving money, or of having any to save."

That same afternoon, when Fatty had arrived at the Nassau and feasted on "five plates of cakes and a cup o' tea," Mr. Glendinning rejoiced at the fact that Fatty produced the silver to pay for it. For Fatty to be fed, full, and debt free not only at the NBLH but also at the Nassau was indeed a stunning accomplishment.

Mr. Glendinning, in addition to being the boys' benefactor, was also known as "something of an artist." It was in this capacity that he "volunteered to paint a scene on the sliding door that separates the school-room from the dormitory" up at the NBLH. Fatty seized on this offer with particular zeal. That evening at the lodging house, Fatty mounted the platform in the common room space and "let up the gaslight, so that it shone with more brilliancy" upon himself and—according to the observer—"harangued the newsboys at some length" in a long-winded speech.

"Now boys," said Fatty, "I have a move to make the man wot is a going to paint the door, is a friend of ours. We take our coffee-cake, oyster pie, and fish bowl at the Nassau." Fatty had then launched into a vivid description of the proposed mural.

"Now I heard all about this painting. The star spangled banner is to be on the right, the captured flag of England in the middle, and the green flag of old Ireland at the t'other side standin' up for the glory of the Great Republic." The mention of the Irish flag was met with a great deal of "cheering and clapping of hands" from the Irish contingent in the room.

Fatty's oratory ended with a proposed resolution. "Well then my resolution is that every strange gemman as passes through that door after it has been painted must pay for peeping," said Fatty, "and when the Newsboys sing for the entertainment of these here strangers they pay a shilling a piece as they should do at the Bowery or the National [theaters]." In fact, the NBLH hosted visitors on a nightly basis, and the boys often sang or recited for these strangers. So Fatty's proposal of making them pay an entrance fee for this privilege made good sense to the newsboys. They passed the motion with one lone dissent, perhaps from Johnnie objecting to the "captured flag of England."

Unfortunately, Mr. Tracy was absent from the lodging house on the evening of this parliamentary action, so he had not been able to weigh in on it. It created a bit of dilemma. On the one hand, he had encouraged the boys to operate using democratic principles and parliamentary procedures. Fatty's motion was carried according to the rules they were learning. On the other hand, Mr. Tracy needed the newsboys to reconsider because there was no way CAS was going to charge visitors an admission fee. He decided on the following approach.

"Something was said the other night on which I want to speak a little," Mr. Tracy began on the evening of his return. "It was proposed that visitors should pay for hearing the boys sing." Mr. Tracy speculated on his own response if he were faced with an entrance fee. "Now if I were a visitor on such an occasion as that I would put on my hat and walk downstairs." To make the significance of this reaction clear, Mr. Tracy added a small lesson on fundraising. He suggested that visitors to the lodging house, after hearing the boys sing, "might perhaps in writing to Mr. Brace, express their pleasure" and they might "on leaving feel so grateful that they would send a donation. 'Those boys,' they would say, 'are worthy of being befriended. They are not beggars.'"

"But," Mr. Tracy warned ominously, "if you should be sharp on them, and require money they would say those are greedy fellows. We will have nothing further to do with them." He concluded, "The results of this would be bad to yourselves, and bad to the Society—it would, in the words of the old adage, be penny wise and pound foolish."

With the fund raising portion of the lesson delivered, Mr. Tracy moved on to business accounting. "It has cost to sustain the lodging house for one year $1,431.82 and the receipts [from the newsboys] were $391.26. So you see what a difference there is in the numbers." He quickly solved the shortfall problem for the boys, saying, "There are plenty of gentlemen to keep it going, and assist us if they see that we are acting right." In the end he returned to their resolution and weighed in with his own assessment. "Now it would be very unwise if this resolution of yours should be acted on." Significantly, however, Mr. Tracy left the final decision of what to do next with the boys. "I felt it was necessary to make these remarks as you had not understood those things, but I hope you will consider them, and see the error that misled you."

In light of what they had just heard the newsboys then "seemed to think with Mr. Tracy, that they had been hasty in passing a very foolish resolution."

They proceeded to rescind their previous act. In the end, Mr. Tracy's mission was accomplished. Without imposing his will on the boys from his position of power he had managed to influence them to change their minds on their own accord. It was exactly that kind of teaching through persuasion that animated his entire approach with the boys.

Shortly thereafter, Mr. Glendinning painted a mural on the sliding door of the boys' dormitory. Wisely, he shied away from Fatty's suggested political themes and instead portrayed "a clever landscape." Like so many benefactors of CAS, Mr. Glendinning rendered his artistic services to the NBLH for free. When the boys sang in front of his pastoral backdrop for visitors, they did the same.

***

The Professor Mentors Sunday (and Mr. Colopy)

Leaving the Nassau with the Professor and Sunday on a bitterly cold winter's day, Mr. Colopy was treated to the opportunity to be mentored by a master in pragmatic street survival strategies, as the trio strolled along Broadway. The best of child street sellers could parlay their charm or their plight (or both) into profit. However, few were as effective selling pure personality as the Professor. On this occasion, Mr. Colopy had the opportunity to observe "how Danny plies his trade and how it happens that he is so successful."

Ostensibly, the Professor made a living peddling merchandise. He always carried a little wooden portfolio—a neatly painted red box with a strap that could be worn around his neck—brimming with trinkets, novelties, and books. At any given moment it might hold pencils, pen-knives, twine, or stationery. It always contained a variety of books and magazines: "cookery books" for the ladies, periodicals such as pocket almanacs, pictorials, and action books for young readers. More often than not the latter included books about pirates or notorious English highway robbers such as Dick Turpin or Claude Duval.

The Dick Turpins did as much to satisfy the Professor's reading tastes as those of his customers. There was nothing the Professor liked better than to escape into the world of highway robbers. Johnnie Morrow recalled a particularly dramatic incident in which the Professor and two other lodgers ventured into an empty room in the *Sun* building, a floor below the NBLH. According to Johnnie, the Professor had gotten it into his head that he wanted the "two newsboys [to] *hang* him" and that he "wanted to die just like an English robber."

One boy was designated sheriff and the other, hangman. The Professor saved the starring role of highway robber for himself. The trio took the Professor's "red comforter... made a slip-noose at one end, and threw it around his neck, while they passed the other [over] one of the beams overhead." Next, the sheriff said prayers over the condemned man and "the hangman adjusted the noose, and they hauled him up," keeping him suspended "till his face turned almost black." They finally "let him down" and "threw a pitcher of water in his face." Apparently the water was enough to bring the robber back from the dead. Johnnie reported that the Professor "returned to the lodging house that night; in all probability he was thoroughly cured of his desire to experience the hanging process."[10] Presumably he had also learned some cautionary lessons about re-enacting scenes from his favorite books.[11]

As Mr. Colopy followed the Professor along Broadway, it wasn't the content of the red box that fascinated him half as much as the Professor's unique sales strategies. When the Professor spotted two gentlemen, he gathered up "a few loose papers in his hand." He approached the men and presented them with the papers, declaring them to be "very amusing." Rather than offering them for sale, the Professor urged the men to take them for free. Both did, but one felt compelled to make a small donation in return. As soon as the men were out of earshot, the Professor explained to Mr. Colopy, "I give away those gratis... [but] there are very few take them without giving me something."

The Professor was less successful with his next target, "a gouty choleric-looking old man." Once again he thrust a free paper in the man's hands, this time reporting it contained "three columns of medical news" including "how to cure corns." It was unclear if any of this was actually true. Nonetheless, the elderly man took the paper but failed to offer a coin in return. The Professor was unfazed. "I'd a got something from old choleric too," he explained to Mr. Colopy as they walked on, "but he couldn't take his hands out of his mittens for the cold."

Given the "raw weather," the Professor and Sunday were actually heading toward the Astor House Hotel. The Professor explained that a hotel was a lot more profitable environment on a rainy or snowy day. In general, bad weather, snow, ice, or rain could have a dismal impact on business for child vendors. Customers didn't want to dig for change. Newspapers got wet. Lugging trunks in snow drifts was difficult. Canal boys were frozen out of employment altogether. Wisely, however, the Professor could move his outdoor sales techniques inside.

On such brutal days, his helper, Sunday, retired by the stove—much to his delight at having a day off from carrying the Professor's box—while the

Professor did all the work. Mr. Colopy was mildly critical of this arrangement, given that Sunday had very little to do to earn his keep. But the Professor defended his man, saying, "He is a useful one, when I gets among the Dutchmen with my box, and papers—he does all the talking then."

The Professor's indoor strategy was much like his outdoor one. "I go in where there are a lot of 'em sittin' and they are smokin' and chewing round. I scatter my compliments, and my papers round about 'em, and then out come the purses." Like text in a cartoon thought bubble, the Professor imagined his customers' responses aloud: "This is a funny feller, I must give him something for his wit." Or, "He is a very generous fellow. The little newsboy gives his papers away, without asking for any money. We must help him on a little."

In short, the Professor's entire technique rested on earning donations—essentially a glorified form of begging—rather than peddling wares per se. Yet the Professor's far more lucrative occupation was as a street performer. Mr. Colopy reported the Professor had learned "by heart several historical passages—anecdotes of celebrated men—speeches made on remarkable occasions, comic songs and droll stories: his mind is, in fact, an Olla Podrida of these things."

The Professor's most notable and recurring performance piece was known as "My Grandfather." It was a comic routine so popular that the Professor was frequently asked to perform it for visitors at the lodging house. Johnnie Morrow called it "a curious medley of verse and of prose" and recorded the lyrics for posterity. The Professor would begin singing as follows:

> *My grandfather was a most wonderful man,*
> *He could do, or invent, a most wondrous plan,*
> *He travelled around through vast regions unknown,*
> *And always found out the philosopher's stone.*
> *And just like a duck or a goose he could swim . . .*

At this point the Professor interrupted the song with some comic vamping about his grandfather. "Talking about *swimming*, once he swam from Albany to New York, and beat the steamboat by two hours and a half!"[12] Then the Professor would revert back to the song. If things were going well, the entire routine could be stretched out for the better part of an hour. In the end, the professor peddled wit and charm as much as anything else.

***

An Incorrigible Rogue

There is little doubt that the Professor was a favorite among the CAS staff even if he appeared to be an "an inveterate beggar" at times. For the most part he worked hard and was thoughtful, kind, and very smart. Clearly, his good characteristics outweighed the bad. That said, CAS was concerned about boys who displayed some of these same characteristics but had few redeeming ones to balance things out. Society staff were doing their best to keep the boys from following a path of delinquency that would land them in the House of Refuge or city prison. In the process, very few boys lost favor permanently with CAS, but one who did was an Irish lad named Michael Cogan. Mr. Colopy eventually called him an "incorrigible scapegrace" who was "adept in all kinds of roguery" and a "hard specimen of the vagrant boy."

Although Mr. Brace and other CAS staff routinely visited New-York's prisons and removed children who had been committed because they were homeless or placed there because of extreme poverty, Cogan found his way to CAS office of his own volition. He came straight from the Jefferson Market Prison. When he arrived, the boy was dressed in filthy rags and bruised and bloodied. Mr. Macy listened attentively to the boy's story; however, privately he must have been a bit dismayed as Cogan regaled him with tales of the "first rate fellas in the prison," which included a man held for capital murder, two housebreakers, and a bunch of pickpockets. Mr. Macy—not one to discourage honesty—had managed to sputter out, "I like your frankness; Now if you were only clean."

A first indicator of problems emerged as Mr. Macy directed the boy to a private washroom to clean up and change his clothes, only to have "a number of the office cards" that the boy "had abstracted from the drawer" tumble from the holes of his tattered rags. When asked how in the world the cards had managed to leap from Mr. Macy's desk drawer into Cogan's pockets, "he did not appear to be much abashed or confused, saying with great coolness" that he had taken them to "distribute among the boys uptown." Attempting to buttress his credibility, Cogan showed Mr. Macy that "he had purloined nothing else of consequence." This was true in terms of value. Nonetheless, he did possess "a roll of paper" he had taken from the "waste paperbox." While Mr. Macy didn't care much about items in question, he did appear to be bothered by behavior associated with this appropriation of property. After a rather uncharacteristically stern reprimand from Mr. Macy and a warning about the longer-term consequences of "such habits of thievery," Cogan promised reform. Such pledges went a long way in satisfying CAS staff.

So Mr. Macy next commissioned Mr. Colopy to walk the new boy downtown to the lodging house and introduce him to Mr. Tracy. As the pair walked toward Fulton Street in a heavy downpour, Mr. Colopy heard a thud behind him. He looked back and saw that yet another "parcel of loose cards" that Cogan "purloined from the office" had tumbled onto the wet cobblestone.

"Well," said Mr. Colopy, "after all Mr. Macy's kindness you have made a sorry return."

"Oh!" replied the boy. "Mr. Macy gave them to me to distribute among the boys up at 14th street." Mr. Colopy countered that this was a "barefaced lie" and it "would not go down." Mr. Colopy then delivered a rare lecture of his own, telling the boy that dishonesty was "the worst policy and that falsehood would, if persisted, lead him first to the Refuge and finally to a more dreadful place."

Cogan assured him that he had genuinely intended on reform when he had made his promise to Mr. Macy back at the office, but, he said, "Tis harder to keep a good resolution than to make it." Cogan continued, "I dunno how it is but there are some things I cannot help laying hands on when I see 'em, though they are of no value to me; but I will be honest for the future and will keep my promise to Mr. Macy and tell no more lies. I'll hold on to the truth. . . . I'll take after General Washington for the future. Wasn't that a beautiful story about his cutting down the cherry tree and telling the truth about it?"

Cogan rattled on by way of distracting Mr. Colopy from further scolding as the pair continued down Broadway. However, within blocks of Cogan's latest pledge to reform, the pair passed an apple cart temporarily abandoned by the vendor, who had retreated to a nearby door stoop to take shelter from the rain. A single apple had fallen from the cart and rolled a short distance. Cogan snatched it up and "took a large mouthful from the forbidden fruit" before Mr. Colopy "could snatch it from his lips." At the same time, the owner, an older woman, emerged from her shelter "shrieking her maledictions on the head of the scapegrace."

Mr. Colopy was losing track of the number of rebukes this boy had received in the few hours he had been in the society's presence. This time, the boy hung his head theatrically and again pledged reform, promising he would give the apple seller "a cent tomorrow when I go up Broadway or when I have money."

En route to the lodging house, the pair made a brief stopover at the Nassau Coffee Saloon after Cogan claimed to be "nearly starved out" since "I got nothing in the prison since last night when they gave me a little rice, and molasses. And I had nothing today but the loaf of bread I got from Mr. Macy an' that unforthenat' apple I hooked. An' that didn't do me no good wid the scolding." So at the Nassau, Mr. Colopy treated Cogan to "a shillings worth of cakes and coffee" and he refrained from further lecture.

Once at the lodging house, Cogan continued in his ways such that "Mr. Tracy was soon out of all patience with him—and somehow he got into disfavor with the Newsboys" as well. The next morning Cogan hopped "out of bed about 5 o'clock" and was "stealthily pacing up and down the dormitories, to the no small annoyance of the Newsboys." A bit later, he was discovered trying to pilfer a couple of pairs of boots from a storage room, insisting he was directed to take them by one of Mr. Tracy's assistants. This was another lie. Cogan was "unceremoniously put out of doors" before he could lay hands on anything else.

That evening Cogan once again appeared at the NBLH but this time—and probably to the surprise of no one—he "made his appearance... accompanied by an M.P. who had taken him under his especial guardianship." The police officer had picked the boy up after he was "discovered under very suspicious circumstances" in which it appeared "he had design on a stranger's pocket."

At the boy's request, the officer brought him to the NBLH and discharged him into Mr. Tracy's custody and supervision. However, even this act wasn't accomplished without a scene. The newsboys, who had been singing for a group of visitors, were interrupted. One of the boys shouted out in surprise that Cogan was wearing "my neck tie and my vest," items Cogan had apparently pilfered earlier in the day. This was followed by "a murmur of indignation among the boys," who cried, "we won't have no thieves among us."

Mr. Tracy took the "culprit into the dormitory" for a private conversation that took a good deal of time. In the end, Mr. Tracy believed Cogan was "quite callous" and "unconcerned." By mutual agreement, the boy "made his exit" from the lodging house. Seeing him go, one of the lodgers expressed displeasure that he had gone "without a court martial." The boy added, "He should have been expelled by a vote of the house, and we'd have drummed him away into the bargain." In the end, Michael Cogan was not only banished from the NBLH, but Mr. Macy also told him not to return to the CAS office, either. It was unusual for anyone associated with CAS to exclude a boy from its services, but it is notable that Michael was not turned over to the police for his thefts.

***

Curbing the Drift to Delinquency

Giving up on a boy like Cogan was highly unusual. More commonly, a boy was given months to choose the right path. External intervention was extremely rare, although Billy Patterson was an exception in this regard.

Patterson's association with the NBLH was sporadic over an extended period of time. Messrs. Tracy, Macy, and Colopy welcomed the boy back time and again; however, they worried about the fact that on each return, he seemed a little worse for wear.

One morning Mr. Colopy was walking past Barnum's Museum of Sensational Curiosities. Despite the "very noisy band" that seemed always to be advertising the "gaudy" museum, he heard his name called above the din.[13] There, "standing on the steps of the Museum, each with a cigar in his mouth" was Billy Patterson and another former lodger, the Flying Dutchman. Neither boy had been to the lodging house in several months. Both boys were filthy and appeared to have slept out in the open.

As he crushed the stump of his cigar on the flagstones, Billy explained that they "had had to spend several nights on the street" because they had been turned out of the Seaman's Home. They had been working odd jobs, including blacking boots, selling papers, smashing baggages, and driving an ass and cart. Mr. Colopy assured the boys they would always be welcome back at the NBLH should they wish to return.

In response to the invitation, the pair turned up at that lodging house that evening, and Mr. Tracy "spoke very kindly to the truants." The newsboys greeted the Flying Dutchman "with a cheer." Billy Patterson "was welcomed but not so warmly as his companion." Characteristically, the Professor sent around his cap to collect funds for the newcomers. The Flying Dutchman had happily settled in, but Billy "did not appear so much at ease" and slipped out the door of the lodging house and drifted off into the night without notice.

On another occasion when he had returned to the NBLH, Billy tried explaining his long absence to Mr. Tracy by saying that "he had been at work husking corn for a farmer on Long Island—at a place called Cold Springs." However, when Mr. Tracy "cross examined him about the whereabouts of this locality," he received so many "conflicting replies" that the superintendent questioned the veracity of the entire account. Mr. Tracy "warned him that he would do no good by dodging from place to place." Mr. Tracy permitted the boy to stay at the NBLH that night, merely grateful that the boy had returned.

Billy reappeared at the lodging house again for the fourth or fifth time, after months of absence, in filthy clothes that barely covered him, infested with vermin, and smelling intolerably. On this occasion, the other newsboys felt they "[could] not recognize him as the Billy Patterson of a year ago." Privately Mr. Tracy expressed fear that Billy was "beyond hope" and noted that "his folly and recklessness have transformed him sadly." A bath and new set of clothes perked Billy up considerably, but this success was, once again, short lived.

For unknown reasons, Mr. Tracy finally lost patience—at least temporarily—with Billy in March 1856 after over a year and a half of comings and goings from the lodging house. Normally, sporadic attendance wasn't grounds for concern. However, in Billy's case, with each arrival he seemed to be sinking deeper and deeper into trouble. On this occasion he showed up worse for wear to the point that Mr. Colopy likened Billy's face to that of "a chimney sweep's."

On this occasion, Little Booch was bold enough to tell Mr. Tracy that "we newsboys don't want to have Billy Patterson among us—he begs pennies." The source of Mr. Tracy's information is unknown, but he said, "Billy Patterson has been doing worse than begging pennies—he has been stealing." Turning to Billy, Mr. Tracy asked, "What have you to say for yourself? Are you not ashamed of the course you have been pursuing?" Billy, sullen, displayed an air of defiance.

Mr. Tracy was uncharacteristically worked up that evening, perhaps out of sheer frustration. "I have warned you before, and counseled you," said Mr. Tracy. "I feared it would come to this. The House of Refuge is now the place for you. Boys like you leading to ruin must be rescued because to save yourself is nearly impossible. It is the only chance left, so I am going to try."

The newsboys listened quietly but without much sympathy. Later, to the surprise of virtually every one present, Mr. Tracy made good on his threat. A police officer suddenly materialized. Billy "was very much startled" by the arrival of the officer and "had not imagined that Mr. Tracy would so soon have put his threat into execution." It was such an uncharacteristic move that it had caught the lodgers by surprise, including Billy. The little boy's response was to weep bitterly, plead hard, and throw himself at Mr. Tracy's feet, begging forgiveness and promising reform. Having gone so far as to initiate this unusual action, Mr. Tracy was resolute. The police officer took the boy to The Tombs for a night in jail before his arraignment.

Mr. Tracy's resolve lasted only as long as the next morning, when he joined the arresting police officer and the little prisoner before the court magistrate.

The officer had aggressively advocated for sending Billy Patterson to the House of Refuge. Mr. Tracy, now seeing the boy in court, regretted his actions of the previous night. He ended up pleading with the judge to give the boy another chance at freedom. In the end, the judge delivered a compromise. Billy was to be banished from New-York. He was to immediately return to his parents in New Jersey. If he was "discovered within the precincts of New York," the police had "orders to secure him, and convey him to the refuge."

Billy and Mr. Tracy walked from the courthouse back to the lodging house together. Mr. Tracy would make Billy's travel arrangements and see to it he got on a ferry heading to New Jersey. However, before the boy's banishment, Mr. Tracy "had several daguerreotypes taken" of him. The pair might have stopped at T. Lewis' Daguerreotypes and Ambrotypes near the courthouse on Chatham Street. Or they might have gone to a studio around the corner from Barnum's Museum and just a few blocks from the lodging house. This studio occupied a shady corner on the second floor of the building and offered one-dollar portraits. It was a far cry from Mathew Brady's extravagant studio and Miniature Galleries across the street but much less expensive.[14]

Mr. Tracy added the new images of Billy Patterson to the growing collection of newsboy daguerreotypes that were filling a glass case on the lodging house wall. Despite his banishment, Billy Patterson would hold a place in the hearts of CAS staff and be remembered by the other boys. It was simply impossible for Mr. Tracy to stay angry at his little charges—miscreant though they might be—for very long.

**

Pickpocketing

There were very good reasons for Mr. Tracy and the rest of the CAS staff to worry about boys like Michael Cogan and Billy Patterson. Crime was rampant in mid-nineteenth-century New-York. In fact, the criminal subculture was so well developed that Police Chief Matsell took the time to write a 147-page lexicon for the public on the "rogue fraternity's" unique language.[15] One of the major goals of the NBLH was to prevent delinquency; nonetheless, the draw of street life and the lure of easy money could be made pickpocketing was a constant threat. Getting caught could land the boy in a prison or House of Refuge.

For many New-Yorkers, the most nettlesome of all the criminal activities was pickpocketing, in part because no one was immune from victimization.

It was as lucrative as it was common. Skilled pickpockets specialized, working at exclusive locations such as markets, street corners, theaters, steamboat landings, railroad stations, race tracks, or specific kinds of events such as church services, charity sermons, funerals, or public rallies.[16]

They would steal anything they could get their hands on, including pocket watches and jewelry, which were quickly disposed of in one of the scores of pawnbroker shops. What made pickpocketing particularly lucrative in the nineteenth century was that the entire city operated on a cash-only basis. Few people "entrusted their money to banks."[17] Even fewer merchants conducted transaction with anything but currency. It wasn't just ordinary citizens who carried cash. So did businessmen of various sorts. This included bank messengers shuttling enormous amounts of money between banks and employers carrying the payroll for entire factories.[18]

Arrest records indicate that boys between the ages of fifteen and twenty-four were the most likely perpetrators.[19] While they were rarely caught, sentences could be extremely harsh when they were. A teenage boy who stole as little as fifty cents could be sentenced to one to three years in The Tombs or sent to the House of Refuge.[20]

From CAS's perspective, however, most troubling of all was the link between pickpocketing and vagrant street youth. A whopping thirty-five percent of boys arrested for pickpocketing were newsboys, bootblacks, messengers, errand runners, and the like.[21] The pathway from newsboy to pickpocket was a route followed by some of the notorious pickpockets of nineteenth-century New-York, such Danny Driscoll and George Appo.[22] The classic pickpocket profile fit squarely within the boys being served at the NBLH. It was exactly these boys that Mr. Brace wanted to divert from criminal practices. The NBLH was his attempt to stabilize their lives, provide better influences, and offer healthier alternatives. The goal was to lessen the lure of the street subculture.

***

A Pocket Picked!

On the afternoon of January 16, 1856, Mr. Tracy boarded the railroad cars on his way to work at the NBLH. He was wearing "his large cape closely folded round his person" and was carrying $68.56 belonging to CAS in a sketchbook in his "pantaloons pocket." To some extent this was a protective measure. During winter months, many New-Yorkers placed their money in overcoats with external pockets leaving them particularly vulnerable to picking. Mr. Tracy had buried the agency funds deep in a pocket covered by outerwear. Nonetheless, in a blink of an eye, "a row had been purposely got up by a gang of pickpockets inside" the car. This was a common tactic among the "carbuzzers," who specialized in robberies in railroad car settings.[23] Some boys created a disturbance while another picked Mr. Tracy's pocket. The boys then scattered. Mr. Tracy immediately recognized that "they had lifted his pocketbook containing the lodging house funds." He leaped from the cars in pursuit. When he finally caught up with a "suspicious looking fellow" his search of the boy turned up nothing.[24] This was part of pickpocketing teamwork. The most obviously fleeing boys merely served as decoys while the boy with the cash melted into the crowd, unnoticed.

For the CAS board of trustees, this loss of agency funds was the first of its kind. At their evening meeting, the trustees briefly debated whether Mr. Tracy should be held personally liable for the loss and the money deducted from his salary. Given the fact that Mr. Tracy's income was a mere sixty-five dollars a month, replacing the lost funds would have been a substantial penalty.[25] Instead, the trustees passed two resolutions that evening. The first was that Mr. Tracy need not "make good the amount so lost."[26] The second was that henceforth, Mr. Tracy would be required to deposit daily with the secretary "all sums of money received by him on account of this Society exceeding the sum of Ten Dollars." So in the end, the event was chalked up to a lesson learned and a new policy was enacted.

However, even with this rule in place, the risk of losing CAS cash to pickpockets remained great. Mr. Tracy routinely picked up cash to pay lodging house bills from Mr. Macy in the central office. On January 30, 1856, just two weeks after he had been pickpocketed, Mr. Tracy signed Mr. Macy's ledger book acknowledging receipt of $151 in cash. This included his salary of sixty-five dollar, fifty-six dollars to pay for the lodging house rent, and thirty dollars for current lodging house expenses.

***

Pugilists and Politics

As annoying as pickpocketing was to the general public, there was an even more serious problem brewing in mid-nineteenth-century New-York. Increasingly, gangs of fighting men were ruling the streets, and their influence was extending to political, economic, and social control as well. Among these gangs was the infamous Bowery Boys and one of its legendary members, William ("Bill the Butcher") Poole. There is no better illustration of the stewing social and political tensions than the story of the life and death of Bill Poole. He was murdered in early 1855; however, his reputation preceded his death and its impact was felt long after.[27]

Poole owned a butcher shop in Market Square (as well as several saloons and gambling dens), but he was best known as a "sporting man" or a "fighting man." By the mid-1800s the lines between sport boxing, street fighting, and barroom brawling were fuzzy, at best. Whether the fights were bare-knuckled or with weapons, they were bloody and brutal. These fights were usually fueled by ethnic and religious animosity accompanied by heavy drinking and gambling.

In New-York, Poole was a standard bearer for the Know-Nothing nativist movement and its related political arm, the American Party.[28] As a national political movement the Know-Nothings didn't hold uniform views; nonetheless, they tended to share some common beliefs. Among them were that "Protestantism defined American society," that "Catholicism was not compatible with the basic values Americans cherished most" (in particular because it was deemed autocratic rather than democratic in nature, given Catholics took direction from the pope via his clergy), and, finally, that "Catholics had attained political power disproportionate to their numbers."[29]

Given their views, in New-York the Know-Nothings had grounds for concern. By 1855, "only two New York City wards were completely secure for native candidates," and half of all voters were naturalized citizens.[30] In light of this perceived threat, Poole used his talent as a pugilist to function as a strongman during primary meetings, political conventions, and city elections.

Rival gangs on the other side of the immigrant divide were equally active in asserting control of the political machinery. They were known to "browbeat and bully individuals" until campaign donations were produced; they surrounded "the polls on election day, and beat off honest and timid voters of the opposite party" and helped supporters "vote over and over again."[31] Reverend Hare opined, "The fighting men of New-York have hitherto, to a great extent, controlled and carried its elections by mere brute force."[32]

It was in this context that Bill the Butcher was shot in the earliest morning hours of February 25, 1855 after an evening of trading escalating insults with Irish-born pugilists. All of the players in this incident were young men in their twenties. Most were inebriated. Although accounts differ, what is certain is that in the end, Lewis Baker, an Irish fighting man and former police officer, shot Poole, the nativist. Fatally wounded, Poole lingered for eleven days before finally dying on March 8, the slow death only adding to his mystique. Legend has it that as death approached, Poole's final words were "I think I am a goner. If I die, I die a true American; and what grieves me most is, thinking that I've been murdered by a set of Irish."

In the meantime, Lewis Baker had fled, "by connivance of some of the police."[33] To make matters worse, he not only received help from a bevy of police officers, but his escape was also facilitated by a city councilman. While strongmen functioned as front-line enforcers of party politics, they operated for the benefit of "men who are considered more respectable politicians and office seekers" who were only too happy to shield them from prosecution.[34]

While his assailants were getting away with murder, Poole's funeral turned into a public spectacle of legendary proportions. George Templeton Strong wrote sympathetically in his diary, "A vast 'demonstration' at the funeral of our lamented fellow citizen, Bill Poole. Two hundred thousand people, they say, were in Broadway; the street was crowded from Bleecker Street to the Ferry."[35] More conservative estimates put the crowd at six thousand but noted that the funeral included "a grand marshal, a fifty-two piece band, local politicians, members of fraternal organizations, volunteer firemen, militia companies."[36] Poole had become a martyr for the entire nativist cause.[37] Sympathetic newspapers worked overtime, "glorifying Poole and portraying him as the innocent victim of an Irish conspiracy."[38]

Baker was finally arrested on April 16, 1855, but the news didn't reach the city until May 15, when the ship carrying the captive, returned to New-York's harbor. CAS staff noted that news of Baker's arrest "has kept most of the boys out till a late hour" selling extras. The fact was that the boys at the NBLH made a small fortune peddling the daily papers—as well as a plethora of extras—for virtually every aspect of the Poole affair. It was a cash cow for them, and the arrest of Baker was only another chapter. In the end, the Poole murder fueled strong sales for the newsboys for nearly a year.

Although George Templeton Strong was prophetic on a number of topics in his diary, his predictions about the reception of Baker by New-Yorkers was not one of them. Prior to Baker's arrest, Strong had written, "Should [Baker] be captured and brought here while the present feeling exists, I don't think he'd live to reach The Tombs."[39] Nonetheless, in December 1855, when the prisoner was conveyed from The Tombs to the courthouse he was "warmly greeted by those who had been associated with him as police officers, and by many others who were connected with him in his rough and tumble exploits." As part of the aristocratic upper class, Strong failed to understand the depth and breadth of immigrants' reach and power. It was about obliviousness like this that Mr. Brace continually warned monied society. They ignored the simmering divisions around them at their own peril.

All told, the assorted trials of Baker, the other assailants, and accomplices stretched on for months and spilled into 1856.[40] In the end, no one was convicted for Poole's murder or any lesser offense associated with it. The entire affair provoked one critic of the day to note that the "state of crime and ruffianism in our city ... is truly startling. The inefficiency of our present police system, the delays of justice, the frequent escapes from punishment of well known offenders, call loudly for reform."[41]

A week after Poole's extravagant funeral, Reverend George S. Hare delivered a sermon at the Methodist Church on John Street.[42] It was a scathing critique of New-York's fighting men. Reverend Hare summarized in disgust, "The elections of a great City in the nineteenth century; the largest City in the world's largest and most flourishing republic; a city teeming with intelligence, refinement and wealth, carried by brute force, and controlled by gamblers and gougers."[43]

Indeed, had Poole been alive to see it, the mayoral election of November 1855 would have infuriated him. Fernando Wood won the first of his two nonconsecutive terms in office.[44] He accomplished this by courting immigrants. He was experimenting with a new brand of politics, soon to be perfected by Boss Tweed and his cronies. George Templeton Strong wrote shortly after Wood's election, on November 11, 1855, that "our antipathy to the Pope and to Paddy is a pretty deep-seated feeling. Were I about to enter political life, and selecting an available set of principles, I should be very apt to cast in my lot with the Natives. I could very honestly pronounce in favor of material change in the naturalization laws."[45]

At the national level the Know-Nothing movement and its American Party were also making waves. Among other things their candidates ran on a platform that included supporting "a twenty-one-year naturalization period for immigrants, Bible reading in public schools, deportation of foreign paupers and criminals, and elimination of Catholics from government office."[46] Know-Nothing candidates, while united on their intolerance for Catholic immigrants, differed in their levels of tolerance for slavery.

Slavery had been creeping to the fore of national dialogue as a political matter for several decades. However, with the passage of the Kansas–Nebraska Act (1854)—which permitted "popular sovereignty," or the right of each territory to decide whether to permit slavery within its borders—the question of slavery catapulted into public and political discourse. It added two new states to the union, Missouri as a slave state and Maine as a free one, maintaining a delicate political balance of twelve states in each category. The Missouri Compromise of 1820 had barred slavery, restricting its spread above the latitude line of 36.30 (or the southern border of Missouri). The passage of the Kansas–Nebraska Act breached this provision prohibiting the spread of slavery, thus reopening the question of slavery for the entire western expansion. Passions on all sides of the issue were unleashed with new force and a sense of urgency.

In Kansas, militant abolitionist John Brown and his sons murdered five proslavery settlers. The battles between antislavery and proslavery groups were violent enough for the territory to be dubbed "Bleeding Kansas." Americans were beginning to demonstrate a willingness to go to war. Disagreements within the Democratic Party were driving many Democrats to the newly emerging Republican Party. The question of slavery was equally divisive within the American Party.[47]

New-York had its own uncomfortable relationship with the institution of slavery because of its extensive commercial ties with the South. The city, as a shipping and industrial center, was heavily reliant on tobacco and cotton. New-York had a thriving cigar rolling industry. Cotton was even more important. According to the statistics of Mr. M. P. Wright, a New-York cotton broker, the number of bales of cotton that went to market in 1855–1856 was 3,527,845, the largest quantity ever sold in a single year.[48] He compared this to the mere 857,744 bales sold in 1828–1829. In 1856, most of the cotton was for export; nonetheless, 652,739 bales were destined for northern factories, many of these in New-York.

So into the mix of New-York's already complicated landscape, with its religious tensions and fighting men doing battle between nativist and immigrant groups, the question of slavery was introduced. As everywhere else in the country, citizens of Gotham were divided in their opinions. On one hand, people like Charles Loring Brace saw it as a moral issue. On the other, there were those like Mayor Wood, who saw it as an economic one.[49]

All told, the tensions brewing in New-York were complicated and contentious. The hoopla around William Poole's murder was a harbinger of things to come. American society was irreparably fragmented and hurtling toward an inevitable civil war.

***

Mr. Tracy's Complicated Peace Work

To some extent the fractured and heated political environment was lucrative for the boys at the lodging house. One evening Fatty dozed off during a lecture, but a fellow lodger argued he should be excused because he had been up two nights past folding *The Tribune*. The boy opined that the "abolitionists will have to give him a good supper" given all the employment they had provided him. He continued, "I am on a paper myself that is down on niggers." Each side of every issue had its proponents in the press. The boys sold them all.

Of course, the boys were not without their own political opinions. One evening a group of the nonnative-born lodgers had attended a Know-Nothing rally. When darkness fell, the nativist organizers had handed out torches to light the venue. Slyly, several of the foreign-born boys volunteered to hold the torches but did their best to "hold their torches down" so that they would "burn fast." Another group of lodgers came upon a cart crowded with torch-bearing nativists, listening to the speeches emanating from a makeshift stage. The crowded cart was secured with stones. The boys surreptitiously removed these anchors and as the cart rolled off, "out fell the torch bearers into the mud." The lodgers retold the story, giddy with delight.

At the same gathering, someone in the crowd "shouted out something as didn't go down with the Greeks," who then made "shillelaghs of the torches in quick time." The boy reported, "The Greeks had the victory. The torches instead of throwing light on the meeting, darkened two or three fellers eyes . . . an' the Know Nothings had their dander aggravated." The boy had turned to his companions in confirmation: "Didn't we have fun?"

The boys' story was received with amusement, not scolding, by the NBLH staff. As good natured as these pranks appeared to be, and as sympathetic as Messrs. Macy, Tracy, and Brace would have been to the boys' opposition to the nativists, there lurked a danger of which CAS staff was acutely aware.

The lodging house was filled with children of all kinds. They were Catholic, Protestant, and occasionally Jewish; native born and immigrant; white; and occasionally black boys. The NBLH staff preached and practiced tolerance within the lodging house walls, but the lodging house wasn't immune to tensions simmering around it. Nor was it free from the institutional racism and societal prejudices that shaped the organizations of the day. The boys who entered the lodging house came with their own world views. The philanthropists and visitors who supported CAS mission were not monolithic in their opinions, either. The families, farmers, and employers to which Mr. Macy or Mr. Tracy sent the boys were of diverse minds as well. The NBLH had to function and survive within this fractured and contentious landscape.

In this context, the question posed by the lodging house visitor who wanted to know whether the Professor was a Yank or not doesn't seem quite so humorous or so innocent. Mr. Tracy had stepped in to answer for the

Professor, and his characterization of the Professor as a quarter Irish, English, Yank, and Kentuckian may have been diplomatically inclusive or inflammatory, depending on the visitor's political sympathies.

Within the lodging house, Mr. Tracy had to manage the tensions and prejudices between and among the boys. Proudly Irish Catholic Fatty was known to needle English Protestant Professor on occasion, despite their generally amicable relationship. Fatty wasn't above using racial or ethic slurs about blacks, Dutch, or Jews. There was no way of knowing how tempers might flare on a given issue.

Michael Cogan, the Irish boy who was permanently expelled, may have been too completely enmeshed in the criminal and gang subculture for CAS tastes. Within twenty-four hours of his release from prison, he had lifted CAS property, hooked an apple, stolen a vest and tie, attempted to steal a pair of boots, and been arrested for attempted pickpocketing. CAS staff looked the other way for any one of these behaviors if they deemed it possible to divert the boy from ongoing criminal activity, even after small thefts. Yet there was something in the totality of Cogan's behavior and the remorselessness in his responses that was too much. He may have been just too close to the Irish gangs ruling the streets.

Similarly, Billy Patterson's case had pushed Mr. Tracy to an extreme, but he only reached that point after nearly two years in which the boy seemed to be increasingly vagrant and sinking more deeply into a criminal subculture. Mr. Tracy warned Billy repeatedly but to no avail. Mr. Tracy worried that it seemed "nearly impossible" for Billy to save himself and that he "must be rescued." At wit's end, Tracy threatened Billy with the House of Refuge only to waiver in his resolve the next day. The entire point of the NBLH was to keep boys out of facilities such as these. Undoubtedly the judge's decision to send Billy back to rural New Jersey would have been a relief to Mr. Tracy. Getting the boy out of the urban environment and away from the enticing pull of street culture was exactly what CAS advocated. However, in general, the boys had to want to leave the New-York voluntarily. They would be encouraged by CAS but not coerced.

Many New-Yorkers deemed boys like those at the NBLH threatening not only because they were different but also because they were going to be eligible to vote. Given that reality, one can better appreciate Mr. Tracy's artistry in undoing Fatty's motion about Mr. Glendinning's mural. Not only had Tracy modeled the democratic process by honoring Fatty's motion, but he had engaged the boys in the process of thinking an issue through for its political, social, and financial ramifications. In the end he both taught them about the democratic process and engaged them in it.

As a group, the early lodgers were a colorful cast of characters. Captured in daguerreotypes hanging on the lodging house wall were the likes of wayward Billy Patterson; hard-working Booch; the hobbled match seller, Johnnie Morrow; the proud Irish expatriate, Fatty; and the Good Samaritan and inveterate beggar, the Professor. All of them were industrious children trying to gain traction in a difficult environment.

On the night Mr. Tracy's pocket was picked of CAS funds, he had been on his way to the NBLH. When he finally arrived and told the boys what had happened, "the newsboys were very much concerned, and felt great sympathy for his loss." No sooner had he finished telling the boys his story than the Professor ran up to him, "opened his pocketbook, thrusting it forward impulsively and pleaded, 'Oh! Mr. Tracy, won't you take a quarter from me to pay your way home in the cars?'"

Later that evening, Mr. Tracy confessed to Mr. Colopy that the Professor's gesture of kindness "affected him more powerfully than any other in connection with the unlucky affair." The spontaneous and self-sacrificing generosity of Danny O'Sullivan, the good Professor, had touched Mr. Tracy perhaps because it was an indication of the good being done by CAS in a troubled time.

Notes

1. The narratives about the boys in this chapter derive largely from three volumes in the New-York Historical Society Archives. The collection is generically called *Incidents and Sketches Among the Newsboys*. Volume 47 part III covers the period from September 6, 1855 to November 22, 1855; volume 48 part IV covers the period from November 22, 1855 to February 11, 1856; and volume 49 part V covers the period from February 18, 1856 to May 7, 1856. The vast majority of entries were written by Mr. William Colopy Desmond, a man the boys called "Mr. Colopy." Toward the end of volume 49, the penmanship is markedly different, suggesting a different author.

   The diaries are interesting both for what they are and what they are not. They are nearly daily "sketches" of the boys. Clearly some have been written with the public in mind. Some of the sketches ended up as newspaper stories or in the annual reports of CAS. Indeed, some of the entries in the notebooks have lightly penciled initials "CLB" next to an otherwise inked story. Undoubtedly this was a note to bring the entry to the attention of Charles Loring Brace. While the spin placed on the anecdotes by Mr. Colopy must be taken with a grain of salt, there is also a real-time truthfulness to the narrative accounts as they follow the boys' ups and downs. Mr. Colopy documented their failures and lapses as well as their successes. In doing so a researcher can follow the strand of a particular boy over time and a portrait emerges of that child. With the exception of Michael Cogan, the boys featured here are the subject of many entries over nearly two years. In addition, the exchanges recorded are indicative of the nature of social work practice that was being conducted in the NBLH specifically and CAS more generally.

My accounts of these early lodgers are drawn primarily from the sketch books. I have taken some liberty with dates and combinations of boys present on a particular evening. Where possible, information has been corroborated. However, I admit to taking many of Mr. Desmond's sketches at face value.

The only place where Mr. Colopy addresses the question of his purpose in writing the sketches and his intended audience is at the beginning of Volume 49, where he writes the following:

> In those sketches and incidents among the Newsboys I am giving the details, with as much as possible of the naiveté and conversational case of the remarkable personages themselves. The sayings and doings of the newsboys will bring them bodily before the reader, in more definite shape than any description would do. The little narratives may be thus more graphically delivered, and the characters will develop themselves.

In some cases, I have made minor changes to the structure of his sentences, changed British English spellings to American English spellings, and occasionally translated some of Mr. Colopy's attempts to capture the boys' accents or use of language into versions more easily read.

2. John Morrow, *A Voice from the Newsboys* (San Diego: University of California Press, 1860), 63, Digital Archive, www.hathitrust.org.
3. Morrow, *Voice from the Newsboys*, 19–20.
4. Morrow, *Voice from the Newsboys*, 67.
5. Isabella Bird, "The Englishwoman in America" (1854), in *Empire City: New York Through the Centuries*, edited by Kenneth T. Jackson and David S. Dunbar (New York: Columbia University Press, 2002), 236.
6. Bird, "The Englishwoman in America," 236.
7. Morrow, *Voice from the Newsboys*, 41–42.
8. Morrow, *Voice from the Newsboys*, 42.
9. Morrow, *Voice from the Newsboys*, 130–31.
10. Morrow, *Voice from the Newsboys*, 69–70.
11. The idea that Danny O'Sullivan might be inspired to experience dying like an "English robber" by Dick Turpin and Claude Duval novels, popular as juvenile action literature and definitely books read by the boy, seems like a plausible interpretation of the event. This story was reported in the writing of a fellow newsboy, sixteen-year-old Johnny Morrow, and he described it humorously. However, I could not find any record of this event in CAS documents. Several other incidents that Morrow recounted, about himself and about O'Sullivan, can be corroborated by the CAS records. It is unusual to have this kind of external corroboration of CAS internal records.
12. Morrow, *Voice from the Newsboys*, 68.

13. Bird, "The Englishwoman in America," 237.
14. By 1855, Brady had been experimenting and perfecting the art of the daguerreotype for over a decade and was unrivaled in the field. His photographs, with their creative use of light and shade, were already being heralded as works of art, earning him comparisons with Rembrandt, Raphael, and Corregio "Brady and His Art Triumphs," *Frank Leslie's Illustrated Newspaper*, October 25, 1856, 310; "M. B. Brady, Esq.," *Frank Leslie's Illustrated Newspaper*, January 10, 1857, 86; "Brady's New Photographic Gallery, Broadway and Tenth Street," *Frank Leslie's Illustrated Newspaper*, January 5, 1861, 10.
15. Matsell, George Washington, *Vocabulum; or the Rogue's Lexicon* (New York: R. Worthington, 1859), iii.
16. Timothy J. Gilfoyle, *A Pickpocket's Tale: The Underworld of Nineteenth-Century New York* (New York: W. W. Norton, 2006), 61.
17. Gilfoyle, *A Pickpocket's Tale*, 67.
18. Gilfoyle, *A Pickpocket's Tale*, 66. By way of dramatic illustration of the kind of money to be made pickpocketing, according to Gilfoyle, one bank messenger was relieved of fourteen thousand dollars by a pickpocket and a "carpet manufacturer lost sixteen thousand dollars, which he was 'carrying to pay his workers wages.'"
19. Gilfoyle, *A Pickpocket's Tale*, 63.
20. Gilfoyle, *A Pickpocket's Tale*, 68–69.
21. Gilfoyle, *A Pickpocket's Tale*, 25.
22. Gilfoyle, *A Pickpocket's Tale*, 25, 179.
23. Gilfoyle, *A Pickpocket's Tale*, 61.
24. Minutes of the Board of Trustees, January 30, 1856, vol. 2, 1853–1861, in the Victor Remer Historical Archives of the Children's Aid Society (1836–2006). New-York Historical Society Archives. Records of the Children's Aid Society 1836–2006, New-York Historical Society Archives.
25. Record of Payments to Staff for Salary and Expenses, vol. 59, March 1854–June 1860, in Series VI, Financial and Fund-Raising Records, Records of the Children's Aid Society 1836–2006, New-York Historical Society Archives. The surviving financial records of CAS employee salaries are far from complete. However, a staff salary receipt book indicates that Mr. Tracy's salary was fifty dollars a month from April 1854 to September 1854. He was given a raise of fifteen dollars in October, making his November 1854 paycheck sixty-five dollars. In April 1857 his salary was raised to $83.33 a month. It is important to note, however, that he was increasingly devoting more time to the Emigration branch of CAS, taking children west. Starting in 1858, probably in April or May, his salary was raised to $91.66 a month, where it remained until the last of the recorded receipts in May 1860.

    The salary receipt book notes that Mr. Tracy received reimbursement on January 30, 1856. The receipt book reads: "$68.56 Rec'd New York Jan'y 31/56 of J. Macy Sect'y eight + 56/100 Dollars being the amt of money belonging to the society which was in my pocket when it was picked." The entry was signed by C. C. Tracy.

26. Minutes of the Board of Trustees, January 30, 1856, vol. 2, 1853–1861, in the Victor Remer Historical Archives of the Children's Aid Society (1836–2006). New-York Historical Society Archives. Records of the Children's Aid Society 1836–2006, New-York Historical Society Archives.
27. Bill ("the Butcher") Poole's life and death have taken on nearly mythical proportions. It makes it difficult to sort fact from fiction, particularly because even the original sources—such as newspaper accounts at the time—filtered information through the publisher's own political agenda. The details in these accounts vary. The story was also told in Herbert Asbury's classic book, *The Gangs of New York: An Informal History of the Underworld*. This book was immortalized in the Martin Scorsese film by the same name, with the Poole character played by Daniel Day-Lewis as William Cutting. Details of Bill the Butcher's life were changed to accommodate the movie story line, the most significant being the year of his death. Poole was murdered in 1855. The Cutting character dies during New-York's draft riots of 1863. By far the most carefully crafted scholarship on these events can be found in the article written by Elliott J. Gorn in 1987 and entitled "'Good-Bye Boys, I Die a True American': Homicide, Nativism and Working-Class Culture in Antebellum New York City."
28. Like much about his life, there are conflicting reports about William Poole's official political party affiliation. Nonetheless, he died a martyr for the nativist cause.
29. Tyler G. Anbinder, *Nativism and Slavery: The Northern Know Nothings and the Politics of the 1850s* (New York: Oxford University Press, 1992) 105–106.
30. Elliott J. Gorn, "'Good-Bye Boys, I Die a True American': Homicide, Nativism and Working-Class Culture in Antebellum New York City," *Journal of American History* 74, no. 2 (1987): 398.
31. "Sermon on the Death and Burial of William Poole," *New York Daily News*, March 19, 1855.
32. "Sermon on the Death," *New York Daily News*, March 19, 1855.
33. George Templeton Strong, *Diary*, March 13, 1855, in *The Diary of George Templeton Strong*, eds. Allan Nevins and Milton Halsey Thomas (New York: MacMillan, 1952), 1:214–15.
34. "Sermon on the Death," *New York Daily News*, March 19, 1855.
35. Strong, *Diary*, 214–15.
36. Gorn, "Good-Bye Boys," 391.
37. Gorn, "Good-Bye Boys," 395. According to Gorn, "The accounts of Poole's murder brought these themes together, most poignantly expressing the Know-Nothings' sense of victimization, their feelings of powerlessness before social changes they neither desired nor understood. . . . The sense of powerlessness that cut so many native-born Americans stung even more sharply when they pondered the strength of the foreigners in their midst."
38. Kenneth T. Jackson, "Poole, Butcher Bill (William)," in *The Encyclopedia of New York City*, 2nd ed. (New Haven, CT: Yale University Press, 2010), 1015.

39. Strong, *Diary*, 214–215.
40. "The Poole Murder: Further Action of the Coroner," *New York Daily Times*, March 20, 1855, 1. The principals charged in this case were Lewis Baker, Jim Turner, and Patrick McLoughlin. Accessories to murder before the fact included Charles Van Pelt, Cornelius Linn, John Hyler, John Morrissey, and James Irving. Accessories to murder after the fact included John Lyng, George Burns, Councilman Kerrigan, Daniel Linn, and Harvey Young. None were convicted.
41. Alfred Henry Lewis, *Nation-Famous New York Murders* (New York: M. A. Donohue, 1912), 61.
42. "Sermon on the Death," *New York Daily News*, March 19, 1855.
43. "Sermon on the Death," *New York Daily News*, March 19, 1855.
44. Fernando Wood was mayor of New York from 1855 to 1857 and from 1859 to 1861.
45. Strong, *Diary*, 241.
46. Gorn, "Good-Bye Boys," 394–395.
47. The American Party is often referred to as the Native American Party. In this case, *native* is a term used to refer to American-born citizens, not the original indigenous natives. I have dropped the word *native* to avoid confusion. However, this is an excellent example of the relative nature of being an American "native."
48. "Cotton Production of the United States," *The Spectator*, October 4, 1856, 32.
49. Jackson, "Poole, Butcher Bill," 1,410. In 1861, Mayor Wood—serving his second term—would famously suggest that "New York City become a 'free city' and during the Civil War walk a fine line between loyalty and treason, eventually becoming the city's leading Copperhead."

7

Advancing the Lines

BUILDING AN ANTI-POVERTY AGENDA, NEWSBOYS'
LODGING HOUSE, 1855–1861

The natural drift among the poor is toward virtue.
—CHARLES LORING BRACE, *The Dangerous Classes*, 1880

ONE EVENING, WHEN the newsboys arrived at the lodging house, they discovered that Mr. Tracy had placed a "heavy table of solid walnut about five feet by three and a half feet" between his office and the washroom. The boys gathered around. On closer inspection, it was no ordinary table. One hundred and ten squares had been marked off on the top. Each of these squares had been labeled with a number and a narrow incision had been pierced through the top of the table. Below the tabletop there was one large drawer, which was locked shut. The boys must have watched intently as Mr. Tracy unlocked and opened the drawer, exposing a "series of boxes or compartments; one compartment corresponding to each of the registered squares above."[1] Mr. Tracy let the suspense build as the boys gawked, pointed, and hypothesized. Finally—having sufficiently primed the pump—he announced the grand opening of the Newsboys' Savings Bank.

This grab their attention first and then peddle an otherwise improbable idea to the street youth was a hallmark of Mr. Tracy's efforts. He had used similar tactics before. For example, there was the night he baited the boys with a job offer. "Boys," Mr. Tracy announced, "there was a gentleman here this morning, who wanted a boy in an office, at three dollars a week." The boys had crowded around Mr. Tracy, practically jumping for joy, enthusiastically volunteering their services and extolling their individual virtues. "Well," said Mr. Tracy thoughtfully, as he seemed to muse over a small puzzle. "But he wanted a boy who could write a good hand." The smiles quickly faded as few boys in the crowd could successfully meet this employment criterion. "Well now, boys," Mr. Tracy said, as if suddenly stumbling upon a solution to the perplexing dilemma. "Suppose we have a night-school, and learn to write—what do you say, boys?"[2] The lodgers had taken the bait, heartily embracing the idea, given that its application had become so readily apparent. Thus the Newsboys Lodging House (NBLH) night school was born.

Then there was the evening when the boys were assembled at their desks in the common room, and Mr. Tracy had said, "I want to start with a question, boys." The lads listened expectantly. "Which man exerts most influence? A rich bad man, or a poor good man?"[3] Pat Comon piped up, "A poor good man." He was immediately challenged by Booch, who suggested a rich bad man could do good with his money. The Professor had picked up this thread: "Couldn't the rich man buy a poor one a plate of broiled mackerel on occasion?" Mr. Tracy steered the conversation back to a poor man who "may do good by visiting the sick, by sitting by the bed of the dying when a man likes to have a friend to talk to him."

Once the boys were sufficiently engaged deliberating the question, Mr. Tracy again seemed to ponder a new thought. "What do you think, boys, of forming among yourselves a debating society?" Within minutes the Newsboys' Debating Society was born. Mr. Tracy was elected president; the boys chose debate captains from among the lodgers. The newly minted president scheduled the first debate for the following week, to allow the boys sufficient time to prepare. With the officers elected and rules in place, Mr. Tracy took a moment to highlight the benefits of this activity, in case they had missed its more obvious applications. He argued for the value of being able to construct well-reasoned arguments and developing public speaking skills. He then announced the first question for debate: "Which is the greatest rogue, the lawyer or the doctor?" Of course the single, greatest rogue of the evening may well have been Mr. Tracy himself. He had managed to slip yet another educational initiative and value-laden activity past the boys with apparent ease.

The NBLH, which had been promoted to the boys as a cheap place to sleep, was stealthily becoming a well-rounded social service agency. Nonetheless, each new initiative had been part of Mr. Brace's grand plan. Education, broadly defined, would be beneficial for many reasons. In the short term, it would distract the boys from other objectionable evening activities, such as the theater, drinking, or gambling. In the longer term it would enhance their employment prospects. It would help produce informed citizens at a time when democratic processes were under attack due to the city's widespread corruption and democratic participation mattered because the issues facing the city and country were enormous.

Mr. Tracy displayed an obvious talent in introducing activities that might otherwise have been unpalatable to the street-wise boys and disguising them so artfully that the boys seemed to eagerly acquiesce without being fully aware of what hit them. As Mr. Brace recalled of his lodging house superintendent, "quietly and judiciously did Mr. Tracy advance his lines among them."[4]

***

An Educational Plan: Night School

When the boys first arrived at the lodging house, they were always asked if they could read or write. The responses varied dramatically, from well-educated boys such as the Professor and Johnnie Morrow to children who had no education whatsoever. Most of these children had not attended any public school classes.

The Free School Society, a private charity, had operated free schools in New-York since 1829. In 1843 these school programs (and property) were subsumed under a newly established Board of Education, resulting in the first true public school in the city. Nonetheless, there was no compulsory public education so no requirement that poor child attend.[5] Many poor children, like the newsboys and other street venders, needed to work to survive and were to ill-clad to be welcomed in the public system and among working-class children anyway.

In addition, the Free School Society employed well-established Lancasterian approaches to pedagogy, relying on "rigid and mechanical" principles. Mr. Tracy knew such a discipline-bound system was not likely to appeal to the free-spirited newsboys. Nor would it be consistent with Mr. Brace's overall institutional philosophy. Just as he rejected the strict and mechanical techniques employed by the juvenile asylums, Mr. Brace also worried that educational programs that relied a routine were prone to becoming mechanical in nature.[6] Instead, CAS would favor an "object teaching system" with "allowed the children a significant amount of freedom within the framework of formal instruction."[7] Mr. Brace believed children needed to play a more active role in the classroom. This is what Mr. Tracy intended to implement. There was little doubt that a more flexible and participatory approach would make night classes more enticing to the street boys, and they would be more likely to voluntarily engage in the evening activity instead of just arriving in time for curfew.

The NBLH began offering evening classes in the elementary branches of a common school education. Initially, Mr. Tracy taught all the subjects. His instructional efforts were supplemented by two regular volunteers, Mr. Van Meter, who taught singing, and Mr. Jacques, who taught spelling and reading. Visitors to the lodging house were often invited to help as well. The boys were not required to attend the evening classes. Some did so religiously; others, irregularly. So participating in educational activities, while encouraged, was not a requirement of shelter. Classes needed to be engaging enough to entice the boys.

Sometimes the boys listened to a lecture or sermon in a large group. Other times, the instructors du jour divided the boys into skill levels or by subjects. For example, one evening a volunteer taught a writing class while Mr. Tracy opened an "infant class in reading." Other times, the boys worked at their desks on individual assignments. For example, one observer watched a boy who "had his slate full of figures; he was making calculations, and summing up at a great rate" while another was "making very large round letters on his slate," practicing his orthography. "Every one seemed anxious about his own lesson, and they did not compare handwritings or examine each other's studies very much."

Prizes were frequently awarded to one or more of the pupils, although they didn't necessarily go to the best scholar. Hard work, application, interest, and effort were equally prizeworthy. Mr. Jacque, for example, had made a pledge designed as incentive that "he would give no reward to any boy who would not be punctual in attending... and is [not] anxious to learn.... To a boy who may spell well but is not constant in attendance, I will not give the shilling." Prizes could be small change, food, or clothing. One night Mr. Tracy "bestowed an apple" on a small boy when he had "no other prize" to give. On another evening, he gave a jacket to the boy with the highest savings.

**

One-Room Schoolhouse

The little one-room schoolhouse at the lodging house was surprisingly well equipped. The Public School Society had donated old, used school desks and chairs.

In front of these individual work stations were long benches, which could be used during lectures or sermons. There was a small, elevated lectern for the instructor or guest speaker. A large "conspicuous" blackboard hung on the wall "to facilitate the study of arithmetic and writing."[8] The classroom contained a "pair of splendid globes."[9] Simple framed artwork, maps, and prints, which had been "presented by various donors," decorated the walls.[10] A glass "case containing fifty daguerreotype portraits of newsboys"—including the image of little Billy Patterson before his exile to New Jersey—also hung on the wall.[11] In addition, there was a slightly outdated framed portrait of the first thirteen U.S. presidents, right up to Millard Filmore but not yet containing Franklin Pierce or the sitting president, James Buchanan. One evening during some boisterous play, this print was accidently knocked from the wall. "Oh well!" exclaimed a lodger in mock dismay, "America is ruined."

"How's that?" Mr. Tracy had asked.

"There is a fall of the Presidency!" was the boy's reply.

In hindsight—given the fact that the country was a mere four years shy of a civil war that would not only divide it in half but also generate two presidencies—the boy's quip was prophetic. It was also indicative of the easy good-humored banter between children and adults that infused evening activities.

The schoolroom was abundantly stocked with supplies, including school books, writing paper, newspapers, and musical instruments. Each boy was loaned his own slate board, rimmed with a wooden frame. Schoolbooks included *Peter Parley's Tales*, which were favorites.[12] Peter Parley was an alias for Samuel Griswold Goodrich. He wrote a series of popular short chapter books with stories such as "The Runaway," "The Faithful Dog," "The Little Soldiers," "Digging Potatoes," and "Chopping Wood."[13] The books contained etched illustrations and the text often narrated these pictures, helping the beginning reader along. Mr. Goodrich had also authored instructional books on other subjects, such as *Peter Parley's Spelling Book, with Engravings*. The little volume included lists of spelling words at various levels, short sentences, and finally more advanced reading lessons as well as poetry.[14] These were among several schoolbook options available to the newsboys and their instructors.

***

Library and Reading Room

In addition to the instructional books, the lodging house had its own library, so the schoolroom also functioned as a free reading room. Although it contained a few select volumes at the beginning, it grew continuously, evolving into a collection of "three hundred instructive and interesting books." New contributions arrived on a regular basis from "liberal publishers" and donations from the public. At any given moment, "an unopened package of books" might be sitting on a bench waiting for shelving. The boys had "free access to the library" and even after the first decade, Mr. Brace would say that "it is creditable to them to say that, thus far, not a single volume has been missed.[15]"

The popularity of various books, of course, changed with the times. Although Mr. Tracy preferred that the boys pick up a work of history, a biography, or, for that matter, the Bible, he certainly didn't prevent the boys from reading what they wanted. So in addition to educational books and literary classics, there was "yellow colored literature"—books about pirates or highway robbers, such as the Dick Turpin books so loved by the Professor (at least before his experiment with hanging). Later, Horatio Alger's rags-to-riches books, occasionally featuring stories from the NBLH itself, would also be added to the collection of popular juvenile literature.

Given the number of volumes the little library contained, it was not surprising that it was in a constant state of disarray. Mr. Colopy once noted, "The readers of the week past, had left [it] not exactly in Bodleian order." One evening, Mr. Tracy declared an end to the mess. "Now boys," he had said, "I've got a few words to say about the library. I told boys every night that I wanted those books adjusted when you have done with them." Mr. Tracy then pointed to the current state of disaster; there were books scattered everywhere. His solution was to appoint a committee of three or four boys "who have clean hands" to rectify the problem. Their assignment was to "set them in order tomorrow night."

One of the three boys assigned to this task was Fatty. The next day, in accordance with the resolution, he and two other lodgers set out "to arrange the library." Fatty had taken the opportunity to mingle business with pleasure, "hunting up something amusing while he fixed the books in their places." "Here's the life of General Washington!" he cried out after finding the volume buried at the bottom of a pile.

"Well arrange the books before you begin to read," growled one of his fellow shelvers, who was standing on a library ladder, "and hand me up that set to the second shelf." The boys worked diligently to "set to right" the library, and they had "time to read a while" before the evening's end. So Fatty, the Irish immigrant, nestled in with George Washington, a tale that started with a felled cherry tree and ended in the presidency of a new nation.

***

Common Education

Mr. Jacque's spelling and reading classes were a fixture from the first days of the night school. Mr. Jacque was "an especial favorite with the Newsboys," an affable man who was as far removed from a stodgy disciplinarian as might be found. Learning should be fun, particularly if it was going to succeed at engaging these savvy street youth. In fact, spelling classes with Mr. Jacque could be downright hilarious. There "was considerable laughter at each other's blunders among the spellers," said Mr. Colopy, but also plenty of support for those who struggled.

For example, one evening, the Professor's man, Sunday, with his heavy Dutch accent, managed to spell *Broadway* with three *w*'s and he threw in one *v* for good measure. The boy "got another chance" and, with help and encouragement from his peers, "succeeded in spelling it correctly." The boy was diligent enough in his studies that later that year, Mr. Colopy declared that Sunday was "climbing aloft on the ladder of learning."

Mr. Jacques' assigned words ranged from easy, like *wig* and *pig*, to harder ones like *magnanimous, dogmatical, nonentity,* and *hypothesis.* Most words were followed by a question about its meaning.

"What is the meaning of supposition?" Mr. Jacque had asked one evening.

"To suppose a thing," responded the Professor.

"Suppose I get the shilling?" piped up another lodger, Pat Comon, from a back corner.

Occasionally the entire class would be stumped with a word such as *psaltery*, even with Mr. Jacque's hint that "it meant a collection of psalms." Raspberry was another puzzler. *Courtesy* went "round several times with every conceivable way in which the letters could be placed" until it was finally spelled correctly. This led Mr. Colopy to note that "some of the spelling would cause a laugh at a funeral" but he also suspected when a boy could not "spell the word correctly they go the whole augural and make an outlandish word of it." The playful educational environment supported the occasional diversion into silliness.

Some of the boys were superb spellers, such as the Professor and Pat Comon. The Professor had easily handled *equilibrium, quadrillion, ague,* and *occiput*. Pat conquered *obstreperous* although he had stumbled on the word *arithmetic*, missing a letter. He quickly explained he had missed the letter "because I have lost a tooth." Although the connection between the missing letter and tooth wasn't altogether clear, it didn't stop the boys from laughing heartily in response.

If the Professor and Pat were at the top of the class, at the other end of the spelling spectrum was Fatty. His struggles were legendary but often provided comic relief for the evening. Good natured in character, Fatty took the ribbing in stride. When he was successful in "spelling a word of three or four letters, his winks and grins were formidable." For reasons that will remain a mystery, Fatty had particular difficulty with the letter *t*. One evening when Mr. Tracy was substituting for Mr. Jacques, Fatty was asked to spell the word *doth*, with its irksome *t*. When he came to the third letter, Fatty had "shifted about and scratched his head."

"Is it in the alphabet Mr. Tracy?" he asked, as the boys exploded in laughter.

"Yes," Mr. Tracy assured him, bending over his book to conceal his own inclination to laugh out loud. Straightening up, and hoping to aid the floundering Fatty, Mr. Tracy had asked helpfully, "What do you take at the Nassau?"

"Coffee and cakes," came the quick response.

"Nothing else?" queried Mr. Tracy.

Fatty immediately added, "Oyster pie" and then, as an afterthought, "I have tea sometimes." He was about to explain that "he never took molasses in his tea" when Mr. Tracy interrupted.

"Yes, 'tis a *T*!" exclaimed Mr. Tracy, sensing Fatty didn't recognize that he had accidentally stumbled onto the mysterious letter and would continue to rattle off the menu options of the Nassau's cuisine.

***

Reading

Reading classes usually followed spelling. Mr. Colopy marveled at the fact that there seemed little correlation between the boys' ability to spell and their ability to read. However, in keeping with his nickname, the Professor excelled at both. The reading lesson often involved a lengthy historical passage, usually on American history, such as the one chosen on the evening when Mr. Jacque asked the boys to read about John Andre and Benedict Arnold. After the boys finished, they were verbally quizzed on their comprehension.

Mr. Jacque peppered them with questions: "Where did Arnold command? What led him to think of betraying his country?" This particular story allowed Mr. Jacque the opportunity to moralize on gambling, extravagance, and betrayal. He introduced a geography lesson as well. "Have you ever been to West Point?" he asked. The evening concluded with a description of

Andre's execution, a theatrical climax guaranteed to hold the boys' attention to the end.

That evening, George Clark, known to the lodgers as Yank, was awarded a shilling from Mr. Jacques as the best reader. He was a good, hard-working, reliable boy but not much of a scholar. By all accounts, including his own, his penmanship was atrocious. So Yank was not so lucky with the prize when it came to writing class.

***

Writing Class

One evening a visitor, Mr. Cary, "volunteered to form a writing class." Most of the boys quickly agreed to participate. To keep the boys engaged, Mr. Cary assigned each one a newspaper headline. The boys were to pretend they were journalists and to write a story that went with the headlines. Yank received "The Boy of the Fire Department." Billy Patterson—who had made one of his sporadic appearances at the lodging house before his banishment—was prophetically assigned "Bound to Hoboken." Fatty was assigned "Who hit Billy Patterson?" This piece required a bit of investigative journalism to explore an earlier incident.

The boys immediately took to the task, bending over their slates, writing furiously. Yank had "perched himself on a stool apart from the reading desks." He claimed to need "more elbow room" for his task. He began "slyly sketching something on his slate." Half an hour later, the boys were ready to reveal their essays. Pat Comon had written an award-winning piece of journalism.

Yank, in contrast, when asked to read his essay aloud, held up his slate for the boys to see. It contained a drawing. "See," he said proudly, "it is of a woman in distress with the newsboys in the distance." Unsurprisingly, Yank's artwork was not awarded the shilling for writing that evening. Nonetheless, the newsboys got a hearty laugh at his creative journalistic approach to the assignment. He may have been inspired by *Frank Leslie's Illustrated Newspaper*. Just five years old, the weekly magazine was richly illustrated using wood engravings, a novelty at the time. Yank had merely decided to illustrate, rather than narrate, his headline.

***

Singing and Voice

Singing was a regular part of evening affairs at the lodging house. In general, music was an important evening activity for the well-to-do and a form of nightly entertainment. Mr. Van Meter regularly organized formal voice and choral classes. However, the boys often sang informally as well. Their repertoire was extensive and eclectic. They sang religious hymns, patriotic songs, temperance songs, traditional folk songs, Irish jigs, and popular music. Early on, CAS received a donation of a melodeon, which was carefully hoisted up the lodging house stairs, adding to the musicality of the evening.

Occasionally, a lodger appeared with a particular skill. This was true of Harry Loomis, who showed up at the lodging house with his fiddle and a talent for playing it. To capitalize on the moment, that evening lessons were canceled and the classroom turned into a concert and dance hall. Harry began with "two or three quiet solemn tunes" but eventually ended up playing reels, hornpipes, waltzes, and jigs, until virtually all the boys were dancing. They "struck out their feet, and capered if not with much grace of posture at least with a great deal of energy and humour," reported Mr. Colopy. The evening ended with a request for "Planxty Kelly," a soulful Irish tune, and several Irish famine songs.

At the end of the concert, the boys claimed this to be "better than the Chatham." "We needn't go to the theater tonight. Three cheers for Harry!!" "Put in for the fiddler," said Fatty. His call echoed around the room: "Put in for the fiddler." And "while Henry loosened his bow," Fatty collected "loose change from the newsboys" to pay the artist for his performance.

***

Physical Activities

In addition to the occasional evening of dancing, the NBLH staff appreciated the need for the boys to blow off steam with physical activities. New-York was decades away from its first accessible public playground, although Fredrick Law Olmsted had included a "kinderberg" or a "children's mountain" for children in his 1850s designs for Central Park. However, "in practice areas for free play were restricted."[16] In general, the boys played on the filthy, crowded streets or around the docks. Given that, Mr. Tracy occasionally took the opportunity to turn the schoolroom into a gymnasium. "There was a grand cavalry fight this evening," reported Mr. Colopy. "The big boys represented the prancing steeds—the others on their backs tilted against each other." Fatty made a fierce charge but went down in the melee, and in the end "the field of battles was strewn with the riderless warriors."

Other times the boys played "a game of leap-frog." On these occasions they "tumbled over each other in their play and came down in every imaginable shape, sometimes with their limbs strangely intertwined, at other times all in a heap." When any boy played foul, he was made to "run the gauntlet." Fatty usually sat out leapfrog but added to the sound track for the evening with vigorous laughter, particularly when a lodger's pants split along a seam.

***

A Moral Educational Plan: Sunday Meetings

In addition to the boys' scholastic education, of critical importance to CAS was their moral and religious training. Mr. Brace and Mr. Macy had been involved with the Boys (and Girls) Sunday Meetings even before the founding of CAS. However, with the successful opening of the NBLH, they began to supplement their program by offering Sunday options at the lodging house itself. Like all the other evening activities, boys were invited to attend but not required to do so. Mr. Tracy launched the Sunday meetings "in a similarly discreet manner" as he did all his other educational initiatives.[17] One day the boys had returned "impressed and full of questions about a public funeral they had witnessed." Mr. Tracy "suggested their listening to a little reading from the Bible," and so the regular instruction began.[18]

From the start, these religious teachings were tailored for the newsboy audience. No matter who delivered the lecture or sermon, the goal was to translate the story into material that vagrant boys could understand, or to animate it with examples from their own lives to produce "suitable services." Mr. Tracy or Mr. Macy might lead these services. However, on a regular basis, Mr. Brace himself arrived for Sunday meetings at the NBLH.

One evening in the fall of 1855, Mr. Brace delivered one of his guest sermons. He had crafted a story about a "good-hearted woman who lived away up in a garret." She was "remarkable for her kindness to every living thing that was in want of it, which came in her way." This included a "poor beggar boy," a "lame dog," and "an old starving horse which she fed with Indian meal."

After Mr. Brace left the lodging house, it became clear that Fatty had been particularly delighted by this story. "Wasn't she good? To feed the old horse, and tie up the poor dog's leg? It was so droll. I could hardly help laughing before Mr. Brace."

Mr. Tracy then asked the other boys if they knew who the man was who had told them this story. "Mr. Brace. The founder of this place," came an answer from the floor.

"Who is neighbor to the Newsboy?" asked Mr. Tracy.

"Mr. Brace, I guess," said one of the boys tentatively, making the connection between the stories.

"Yes, it was Mr. Brace who first started the idea of this place and who first set it going—carry out those principles of which Mr. Brace spoke tonight," Mr. Tracy said. Then, extending the lesson still further, he continued, "Help your fellow creatures who are all fellow travelers with you. Mr. Brace always loves to hear of your kind acts to each other. You have no idea how those things please him."

Another night, Mr. Macy read aloud from the scriptures, focusing on the story of the Good Samaritan. When he finished, he turned to the boys for his example.[19] "Does not the Professor," he asked, "when he picks up a little fellow in the street, takes care of him, and after giving him his supper, brings him up to the lodging house resemble in part the Good Samaritan?" The boys had to agree that the generosity of the Professor to strangers looked a great deal like the Good Samaritan story they had just heard.

The Good Samaritan was just one of the popular recurring biblical stories that made its way into Sunday sermons or evening lectures where Mr. Tracy introduced wise sayings, parables, or similar moral teachings. Other recurring themes included the Golden Rule,[20] "Am I my brother's keeper?"[21] and "The kingdom of heaven is like a mustard seed."[22] They offered a particularly rich and relatable moral curriculum for the vagrant newsboys.

***

A Fiscal Educational Plan: Banking and Saving

The "contrived table" Mr. Tracy introduced to the newsboys as their savings bank was a custom-built piece of furniture of Mr. Tracy's own design and manufacture. Mr. Tracy's prior trade as a carpenter had come in handy. Although Mr. Brace's original idea included having the boys deposit money in a real bank, as he had written in CAS's first annual report, "We design, too, to have an arrangement by which the boys can deposit money in the Sixpenny Savings Bank, through the Superintendent."[23] The project proved too ambitious. The leap from pennies earned to direct bank deposit was a bit too steep for the vagrant and ever-hungry street boys. So, like all of Mr. Brace's big ideas, it was adapted to work in practice. If CAS couldn't get the boys to the bank, Mr. Tracy would bring the bank to the boys.[24]

Initially, the bank opened and closed on a daily basis. But it quickly became apparent that allowing the poor boys to make nightly deposits and daily withdrawals was not producing the kind of longitudinal fiscal lesson on savings and asset building that CAS had in mind. In fact, "the boys could hardly be induced to leave their money, to accumulate, for twenty-four hours together."[25] So, as usual, CAS modified the practice.

Mr. Tracy's new plan involved making a "proposition to close the bank . . . for a certain length of time."[26] How Mr. Tracy actually sold this idea to the boys is unknown, but whatever his methods, on January 8, 1855, the boys voted to close the bank and not reopen it until the following month, on February 1.[27] Henceforth, the bank would open on the first of every month or, if the first fell on Sunday, on Monday the second.[28] No matter how much the stock market fluctuated in the outside world, the lodging house would conduct a "safe business."[29] (However, Mr. Tracy did have to fortify the bottom of the drawer with a sheet of metal to prevent unrecorded withdrawals by would-be bank robbers burrowing in from below.)

When February 1 arrived the boys could hardly contain their excitement. It had been building for a full month, as their deposited coins slid through the little slots and disappeared into the depths of the drawer. At around 8:30 that evening Mr. Tracy announced the moment had come. The boys crowded around the table or perched on stools in the common room. One mounted a desk and yelled out a motion "that the boy as has most tin in the bank gives a treat of oysters to all the rest." This was greeted with "immense applause" but no further action was taken.[30]

"First, the by-laws," said Mr. Tracy, settling them down. "Boys are all to keep their seats quietly while their number is called."[31]

"Yes," responded one, "just like what is up in the stages," referring to common practice on public stage coaches. "No conversation with the drivers. So boys, no conversation with the bank man."[32]

With that Mr. Tracy—a.k.a. the bank man—took his seat, opened the record book and unlocked the till. The bank was officially open. One by one, Mr. Tracy called the numbers in the register.

"Number 1?" Mr. Tracy called out.

A chorus of voices responded, "Snoozing out tonight!"

"Number 2?" called Mr. Tracy.

"That's Roger!" exclaimed a group of boys in unison.

"Roger, step forward," said Mr. Tracy solemnly. Roger raced toward the table in excitement until it dawned on him that this was a dignified event, and he slowed to a stately walk as he approached the teller.

Mr. Tracy carefully pulled the accumulated copper coins from his compartment and asked Roger to count the pieces. The audience of youngsters were now straining in their seats to get a better view. As the boy added his pennies aloud, the excited hum of the crowd began to grow.

"Why my eyes, Roger," said Mr. Tracy proudly. "This is great, I didn't think you had half that amount," he said, subtly highlighting the evening's lesson.

Roger gazed at Mr. Tracy in some astonishment. "I didn't think myself I had so good."

"Put out the gas someone, now's a chance for a grab," yelled a lodger from the crowd.[33] He was shouted down by a chorus of other depositors—presumably those who had money to lose in a bank heist. Mr. Tracy called the room back to order, hiding his delight at the early reaction to his banking lesson. Although the total sum was small, the point had been made. Roger retreated to his seat with his newly fattened purse.

"Number 3?" called Mr. Tracy.

In response, an earnest, hard-working boy known as Barney stepped forward. As if by design, an even more dramatic lesson was about to unfold. Mr. Tracy reached into the little compartment of the bank and withdrew a large pile of coins. This one contained copper and silver. As he had with Roger, Mr. Tracy encouraged Barney to add up his savings in front of the eagerly watching group of ragged newsboys.

Barney began to count. He counted and counted. "$14.75!" he finally called out, reaching the end of his stack of coins. He turned to Mr. Tracy in astonishment. "$14.75," he repeated in amazement.

A chorus of excited boys weighed in on Barney's savings. "Such a pile! Oh! Golly."

"I'll swap banks. Barney!" called out a boy from the floor.

Barney denied that request, but added, proudly, "Some of the exchange offices haven't that amount."[34] With his stash in hand, Barney retreated to his seat, as the others watched the nouveau riche boy, with a mixture of admiration and jealousy.

In contrast, when Fatty stepped forward, his pot was a relatively meager $1.90. "How is it that you have not saved more Fatty?" asked Mr. Tracy gently.

"My grub costs me 25 cents a day and I hadn't much work this week," explained Fatty. However—perhaps feeling the pressure of being publically exposed—Fatty promised more diligence in the future. "Twill be $2 next time," pledged Fatty to Mr. Tracy.

There were other low savers among the newsboys. Not surprisingly, the Professor had even less than Fatty. He explained that the situation was due to the "hard times" in which he had to feed and shelter all those needy boys around him. Valise, who had accumulated a mere ten shillings, was accused by his fellow lodgers of having too great a fondness for the Chatham Theater.

Mr. Tracy allowed the boys like Barney to serve as role models, but he didn't chastise those who hadn't saved much. In fact, he routinely reminded them that the end of the month was "a break in the chain," one that offered renewed opportunity, as the future was "now fresh before us." Always quick with a parable, Mr. Tracy said it was like a swimmer "confident in his strength" but taking "a moment to rest the muscles" before starting again. The opening of the bank was merely one of those "stopping places" meant to replenish resolve.

"Now," said Mr. Tracy encouragingly. "Put three dollars a month in the bank and see what an amount you'll have in a year." To the boys, Mr. Tracy's idea of saving for a full year sounded overly ambitious, but some began to see the logic in his general argument. "Yay!" bellowed three or four boys in unison. "Let's put in and see how much we'll have in Patrick's day!" True, St. Patrick's Day was merely a month away. Nonetheless the value of actively saving over the course of a month began to gain some traction. Little did they know that Bill the Butcher's shooting was going to enhance their fortunes before the holiday. At the end of the evening, Mr. Tracy calculated the cumulative savings of the all the boys and commended them on their efforts.

With the bank money fully distributed, Mr. Tracy and the boys faced another decision: What next? Mr. Tracy refrained from telling them what to do with their money. The boys could spend it. "Unless," Mr. Tracy added thoughtfully, one preferred "to let it remain awhile longer in the bank."[35]

In the aftermath, a number of boys did redeposit some or all of their savings. There was also a flurry of small money exchanges among the boys, paying off debts owed to each other. Some boys spent money on items normally outside their reach without the semi-forced savings. For example, some bought clothing. One boy returned to the lodging house the next day strutting around in "a pair of double breasted pants, good cashmere, English cloth."[36] Another group took a full pocket of coins to the Nassau where they had "Thanksgiving night on a small scale." One boy declared, "I'm getting a shilling's worth of shampooing."

Even Fatty, who fared so poorly in the first round of banking, mastered the art of small savings over time. After a bank opening about a year later, he returned to the lodging house in a newly purchased coat and "twirled on his heels like a dancing Dervish in the exuberance of his pleasure" while the other boys joked, "Mr. Tracy has made a gentleman of Fatty!"

***

An Employment Plan: Situations and Emigration Parties

One evening, Tom Dolan came up to the NBLH with a revelation. He announced he thought he was "getting too big to continue selling papers with the little boys." This was a fact of life for the newsboys. Street-based jobs were often best performed by younger children. Most would eventually outgrow them since sales were partly dependent on their youthful appearance. At that juncture, CAS agents worried that boys would drift into vagrancy and, ultimately, crime. Tom declared that he wished "to have some trade or to go into the country, or into top boots and the army." Tom was getting ambitious, eying an alternative future, exactly according to Mr. Brace's plan.

CAS was experimenting with two options for these boys. The first was finding an "employment situation" for the youngsters, preferably in a trade with future potential and preferably outside New-York. While some were in the city itself, most were nearby in the tri-state area. The second option was even more experimental. It was to include the boys in one of the emigration parties going to the western states or territories, where families would either take them in as farm hands or possibly as family members. Mr. Macy's office served as the central clearinghouse for both efforts.

Tom Dolan was essentially asking for help of this nature, so Mr. Macy and Mr. Tracy began to look for a specific employment situation that would be appropriate for him. In mid-November 1855, just the right one came along. The editor and proprietor of the *Clyde Times* wanted a boy to "learn the printing trade and to work as 'devil in the office.'" Clyde was a tiny little hamlet in Upstate New York just south of the shores of Lake Ontario. Tom jumped at this chance. He was fitted up and shipped off to Clyde.

Similarly, the editor of the *Milwaukee Sentinel* contacted CAS looking for "two regular built newsboys to sell papers at the cars and elsewhere." Milwaukee paper selling was a far cry from that on New-York's congested streets. Mr. Tracy touted the benefits of "becoming a man in the thriving city of Milwaukee." He pointed out, "Now, those publishers would not go to the expense of paying for those boys if they did not mean to deal fairly with them." Mr. Tracy was looking for adventurous volunteers who would want to travel days to reach this distant and unknown place called Milwaukee.

The Professor, the consummate traveler, eagerly volunteered. Mr. Tracy demurred, suggesting that the Professor would make a poor fit. Mr. Tracy joked kindly that the Professor "was such a changeable genius he would turn druggist in a week." Mr. Tracy was looking, he said, "to send two straight forward, up and down boys." In the end, Eddie Comon and George "Yank" Clark were selected. The boys bid a fond farewell to their lodging mates—by punching them in the arms, as boys are wont to do—and headed off on a long journey.

All three boys—Tom, Yank, and Eddie—wrote back to the lodging house and the central office on a regular basis. They reported their progress, sent copies of the local newspapers, and requested letters in return. Mr. Macy and Mr. Tracy regularly corresponded, sending New-York newspapers and CAS annual reports. The newsboys also stayed in touch with their former mates. Among the regular correspondents was Eddie's younger brother, Pat Comon, who had zealously dedicated himself to his studies ever since his brother left town so he could write a good letter.

Tom wrote from Clyde that he liked his boss "very well," although he occasionally found the weather to be an irritant. "I have had to go out on the telegraph line, when the line is down, in frost or snow, wet or dry; just the same; and I tell you that it is not the pleasantest of work ever found out by a 'long odds." But then again, New-York newsboys complained about bad weather themselves, and Tom had reported that they "had pretty fine sleighing" in Clyde. Although his letters were sometimes laced with signs of homesickness, he also reported, "I can set type now pretty fair." It was exactly that kind of apprenticeship experience that Mr. Brace had hoped for. Fixing the telegraph line—which was the only way the isolated little town was going to receive news—and learning to set type—which was how that news would be produced—were both trade skills that could serve Tom well in the future, anywhere in the country. Both Messrs. Brace and Tracy believed they would likely be better off in the long run in areas where labor was in short supply rather than trying to make ends meet in the competitive city streets. In addition, they could learn trades that would serve them better as adults.

Letters arrived from Yank and Eddie as well. They were usually jointly written and Yank always apologized for his handwriting. Among other things the boys were earning a princely sum of eight to ten dollars a week in profit after paying for board. They wrote that in one particularly good week they had "made twenty-two dollars" and were "saving money up like blazes." Apparently the two had learned their Newsboys' Savings Bank lessons well and Milwaukee was making them just as prosperous as Mr. Tracy had predicted.

All these letters were read aloud to the boys at the lodging house. In part, this was to share news from friends. However, the letters also served as advertisement for alternatives to street trading and life outside Gotham. One evening, Mr. Tracy showed the boys "the size of the *Western Extra*," which had been sent from Milwaukee. It immediately sparked a conversation on pricing and earnings. Mr. Tracy also reported that the editor was so pleased with Eddie and Yank that he would be looking for two more boys in the spring. Suddenly, the remaining lodgers had employment to aspire to and friends in the distant location already set in place.

***

Into the Country

From the first days of CAS, Mr. Brace's plan included sending children "into the country." CAS's earliest efforts included sending individual children like Tom to fairly nearby destinations, like Upstate New York or New England, or across a river to Long Island or New Jersey. However, Mr. Brace's sights were really set on the vast expanse of land to the west. The colonization project associated with manifest destiny seemed to open infinite opportunities for poor children. The Midwest was just being settled. The state of Michigan was about twenty years old, Wisconsin had been admitted to the Union about twelve years earlier, and Minnesota was a mere one year old.[37] In addition to Ohio and Indiana, these states offered enormous possibilities with their high demand for labor, nearly limitless natural resources, and untapped potential. Removing children from the poverty, filth, and crime of New-York's Five Points seemed optimal to Mr. Brace. For him, it was a simple supply-and-demand issue. The West needed workers, and New-York was oversupplied. Ever one to capitalize on any technology, industrial advancement, or scientific breakthrough at hand, Mr. Brace eyed the complex maze of railroad tracks being laid helter-skelter throughout the Midwest, creating an increasingly dense web of transportation opportunities. Mr. Brace directed CAS to set its sights on these prosperous and newly accessible midwestern states. Doing so conformed to his scientific approach to charity, complied with natural laws of economics and was consistent with childhood development.[38]

To some extent, this response was Mr. Brace's best effort at a wholesale solution to complex problems of his day. The idea of creating a scaled-up solution was innovative. Finding individual employment situations for boys like Tom, Yank, and Eddie, one by one, was a time consuming and labor intensive process. There were thousands of poor children at risk in the city. So sending groups of children in parties, and inviting matches to be made in situ, would be considerably more efficient than arranging placements individually.

As CAS took its first tentative steps toward what would become its most publically touted efforts, its Emigration Branch, Mr. Brace anointed one of his most talented staff members to test the waters. That turned out to be none other than Mr. Tracy. In one such early expedition, Mr. Tracy left New-York on November 18, 1856, with a group of fifty children (boys and girls), for a journey that was to end in Kalamazoo, Michigan. The Kalamazoo community had already been alerted of the pending arrival. They had heard about it "from the pulpit" and read about it in the local press.

The journey was a long one. The group started on a steamboat up the Hudson River to Albany. In Albany they transferred to the New York Central Railroad line, which they took to Niagara Falls. The children marveled at Lake Ontario—which to them seemed more like an ocean than a lake—as they took the Great Western Railroad line through Canada and then traveled back into the U.S., arriving in Detroit, Michigan. From Detroit, they took the Michigan Central Railroad to Kalamazoo. Mr. Tracy had managed to talk each of the captains and conductors into free passage for his entire entourage. His band of fifty poor children was a novelty and created quite a buzz, although over time the scene of these emigration parties headed by CAS—as well as other philanthropic societies—would become much more commonplace.

Mr. Tracy was persuaded to leave three children in Detroit with families who made "very favorable applications," but the remaining forty-seven who traveled to the intended destination of Kalamazoo found homes or work within forty-eight hours. According to Mr. Tracy they "went off like hot cakes." One farmer had driven fifty miles for the opportunity to find a boy. In Mr. Tracy's view—Pollyannaish though it may have been—each child was adopted "into the family of some well-to-do respectable family, in one of the most prosperous States in the Union."[39] Before leaving, Mr. Tracy talked of CAS efforts to three church congregations and the children sang for the gathered crowd.[40]

Ostensibly each child had a right to weigh in on the placement process. Sometimes, prospective parents or employers would take a child home for a trial night or two and then either keep or return the child to a CAS agent. Under any circumstances, however, the child could walk away from a placement after the fact if she or he was unhappy. Mr. Brace was quick to remind the public of this on every occasion he could. "It should be stated here, as has been done often before," he wrote in CAS's Fourth Annual Report, "that we do not indenture children to anyone, and that they are only sent with the consent of their parents or guardians, or, if they have none, with their own consent, and that where a child does not suit a person, or becomes only a burden to his employer, we are willing to receive him back again."[41]

It was common practice to indenture children. Although Mr. Brace could have initiated that practice in his Emigration Branch, as did other charity organizations and child asylums, he firmly rejected the idea that impinged on free will. Some have noted that "the whole arrangement was exceedingly casual" and that "no legal commitments" altered any of the various relationship be that parental and employment.[42] The notion of contracting children to strangers was deeply abhorrent to Mr. Brace and much too close to slavery for his abolitionist sensibilities. Either party in these emigration efforts—child or adult—should be able end the relationship at will.

Significantly, Mr. Tracy's party of fifty children had included a "clever little black boy." The boy had become something of a "company standard bearer," proudly leading the group with an American flag that he had been given before leaving New-York. The boy had arrived at CAS Central Office shortly before Mr. Tracy's trip. Mr. Colopy reported watching the boy gaze at a statuette in Mr. Macy's office. It was a portrayal of a guardian angel, cradling a child in one arm and fending off evil with the other. The "little colored boy" took a long look at the figure and finally turned to a white boy who was also in the office at the time and asked, "Have I a Guardian Angel?"[43] Mr. Colopy had stepped in and assured the boy that both white and black children were dear to God, and both had guardian angels. As long as they had faith, their "angels [would] be near."[44]

It is unclear whether Mr. Tracy left this child of color in Detroit or Kalamazoo. However, either way, he had left the boy in a free state with a protective buffer of free states surrounding it, far from the slave-holding south and the sparsely settled Kansas–Nebraska territory to the west, where disputes over slavery were taking a bloody turn. The boy was undoubtedly as safe as he was going to be in any state in the Union.[45] Mr. Brace's opposition to indenturing children—particularly a black child—must be understood in this historical context. Although he was opposed to indenturing any child, the idea of indenturing a black boy as a farmer in Michigan, or anywhere else for that matter, was likely unfathomable to him.

After Mr. Tracy's visit, Mr. Brace received a letter from a gentleman in Kalamazoo praising both Mr. Tracy and CAS's work. "We wolverines will never forget Mr. Tracy's visit," he wrote, adding that Mr. Tracy was "peculiarly and eminently fit to prosecute" this work and that he left "a good impression upon the community with respect both to the work and to himself." The writer had also made note of the fact that all the children had been taken up by "our best citizens" and that they had collected an additional fifty applications from others requesting children. He hoped Mr. Tracy would make a speedy return "to us with the new company of destitute children, for whom good homes are even now prepared."

Mr. Brace must have appreciated this letter for several reasons. For one, it showed that the trip was an unmitigated success from his point of view. Second, people were lining up to provide homes for the next batch of children, confirming his hypothesis that midwestern families were an untapped resource. Third, although it wouldn't have surprised him, he must have welcomed the letter writer's rave reviews of Mr. Tracy. All told, the enthusiastic response bode well for his fledgling emigration program and confirmed that his intuition to entrust Mr. Tracy with the effort was spot on.

***

Newsboys' Lodging House's Instability

Mr. Tracy's success as a western agent created problems back at the NBLH. Mr. Brace recognized that Mr. Tracy was doing "excellent service" but also noted that for almost a year Mr. Tracy had "devoted his time and energies to the transportation of companies of children to the West." As a consequence the NBLH—while still operating—had floundered without Mr. Tracy's vigilant oversight.[46] It was clear that he could not do justice to both jobs at the same time. So Mr. Brace promoted him to the position of "agent for the country" in 1857. It was a job he would hold for the next twenty years, eventually relocating to Michigan to be of better service locally.

In October 1857, Mr. Brace hired a new superintendent for the NBLH, Mr. Conrad Wiegand. He was "energetic" and revitalized the program, doing active outreach in the marketplaces and docks for lodgers, but his tenure was short. Mr. Wiegand's greatest contribution was introducing new statistical tables that would be used by CAS to collect data and adorn public reports for decades to come. Having left his particular mark, Mr. Wiegand moved to California in 1858 to take a job with a branch of the U.S. Mint.[47]

Once again, the NBLH's head position was vacant. However, Mr. Brace would fill it with yet another of his loyal and dedicated workers. He promoted one of CAS's "visiting agents." Mr. Charles O'Connor, a veteran of the Crimean war, and his wife, Mary, as superintendent and matron of the NBLH. Like the other lifetime employees of CAS, Mr. O'Connor would hold this position until his death in 1887. Although less is know about Mrs. O'Connor, she served as den mother to thousands of lodgers over the next decades. The couple became a stable fixture, bringing to maturity not only the boys under their guardianship but also the program that Mr. Tracy had so artfully sketched out in its infancy.

***

Return Visit to NBLH

In 1860, Johnnie Morrow paid a visit to the NBLH.[48] The lame boy had first arrived, as an eleven-year-old, on a snowy evening six years earlier. Since leaving the lodging house, Johnnie had struggled with the instability that comes with poverty but he had also shown the grit and determination that CAS staff so admired.

Johnnie had his sights on becoming a missionary or a preacher. In short succession he spent time at the Union Theological Seminary on University Place in New-York and later moved to New Haven in the hope of eventually attending the seminary there. In the meantime, he supported himself by "selling to the students articles of stationery." The seminary students had taken a shine to the likeable Johnnie and often engaged him in "controversial points of theology" such that he became a "theological pet." Johnnie also had proven his intellectual mettle, one evening suggesting a topic for the students to debate: "Which is a greater sin, to lie or to steal?" The question had come to him from his own experience of having lied to Mr. Tracy to gain entrance to the lodging house and avoid an abusive father, who insisted that he steal wood and coal for the family's benefit.

In keeping with his precocious nature, Johnnie published an autobiography entitled *A Voice from the Newsboys* as a sixteen-year-old. He wrote about his childhood in Great Britain and New-York, his life as a street peddler, sleeping outside, his violent and intemperate parents, the fate of his siblings, as well as his interactions with CAS, the NBLH, and its lodgers. Johnnie hoped the sales of this little book would fund his education, a plea he made directly in the little tome. His book had, in fact, achieved a measure of success, and he was in the process of making his dream a reality.

When he returned to the NBLH for a visit, Johnnie found it much changed. Most notably, Mr. Tracy was gone although both of the O'Connors greeted the former lodger warmly. The savings bank was still there in the exact same location. However, the lodgers—who had been in the process of enacting a scene from *Macbeth*—were all new to him. Johnnie took note of the addition of "a row of receivers or boilers on a stout shelf raised a few feet from the floor" and asked about them. Mr. O'Connor said they were "for holding tea and coffee; and that now instead of charging the boys six cents for lodging alone, they charge eight cents, and give them a supper in addition." Mr. O'Connor said that this was "strong inducement to keep the boys from theatres; for if they go, they lose their supper." In addition, Johnnie learned that they also had "a Sunday dinner for boys who prefer a quiet day in the Lodging-House to working on the Sabbath." Johnnie explained to his readers, "I am sure that those who have paid any attention to the matter must notice that there is much less noise in the streets on Sunday, from the newsboys, than formerly—and although it may partly be owing to the vigilance of the Metropolitan Police, I think it is owing still more to the effects of the Sunday dinner."[49]

***

Metropolitan Police, Sabbath Selling, and Free NBLH Suppers

Certainly Johnnie was right to see these three things—the Metropolitan Police, the crying of the newsboys, and the NBLH Sunday dinners—as being related in 1860. The dinner was the product of a confluence of factors that had been in play for four years. The bigger battle had less to do with poor street children than with politics.

In a few short years of dramatic political struggle, the Municipal Police Department had been replaced by the Metropolitan Police Department. One key event in this struggle had been the infamous Police Riot of 1857 that occurred on the steps of city hall between the two warring factions—both claiming authority—and the subsequent arrest of Mayor Wood by the Metropolitan force. The Metropolitan Police Department had been created by the Republican-controlled New York State legislature and was a direct attempt to rein in the power of the city government. Its authority was legally established by an appellate court order. Nonetheless, the Metropolitan Police had considerably less credibility on the streets of New-York than its Municipal Police counterpart.

The Metropolitan Police were allied with pious, wealthy, mostly native-born New-Yorkers who were eager to establish authority in this belligerent and independent-minded metropolis controlled by immigrant politics and ward aldermen. They launched a multiyear campaign to enforce the Sunday Blue Laws. Their primary targets were the numerous immigrant-owned saloons and beer gardens that sold liquor on Sunday. However, over the years, fueled by both politics and puritanical agendas, the restrictions had expanded beyond drinking establishments, eventually reaching the newsboys. Among those leading the charge against the newsboys was a group of wealthy citizens calling themselves the "Sabbath Committee." The committee included a prominent banker, Mr. William A. Booth, who would assume the position of president of the CAS board of trustees two years later. At the time, however, the Metropolitan Police General Superintendent, Frederick Talmadge, issued an order to his captains to arrest the boys who were crying out the headlines on Sunday for disturbing the peace and causing a public nuisance.

The attack on poor children who were trying to eke out a living sent members of the Fourth Estate into overdrive. Besides, the publishers' profits were partly dependent on the boys' lung power. In particular, *The Sun* and the *New-York Herald* jumped to the defense of the newsboys.[50] *The Sun* poked fun at the entire proposition. "Instead of endeavoring to put a stop to the Sunday amusements of the burglars, thieves and assassins who infest the metropolis," it editorialized, the police have "directed a wholesale crusade against the poor boys who earn a livelihood by vending newspapers."

The *Herald* was even more persistent in its attack. Its arguments ranged from the logical—for example, that Jews and Quakers didn't observe Sunday Sabbath—to the sarcastic. "Very injurious to the peace, quietness and comfort of the Sabbath" the paper opined, "were things like funeral parades, false fire alarms, milk delivery and [the] wheezing of the ferry boat engines." It argued all these should be immediately prohibited as well. One city alderman went so far as to propose extending restrictions to Sunday church bell ringing, which, he argued, surely disturbed the peace to as great an extent as the newsboys.

Although the *Herald's* assault on the Blue Law enforcement was relentless, the editor was also quick to point to what he believed to be the true motivating factor behind these skirmishes. He argued that it was "a political trick to get the white cravats to go the Black Republican Seward abolition ticket at the polls."[51]

The object of this concern was William Seward, Governor of New York and an early advocate of the Republican party. Indeed, the country was careening toward the 1860 presidential election, which would see the first Republican president elected, Abraham Lincoln, and the splintering of the Democratic Party into northern and southern factions. The same year, New-York City would yet again elect Mayor Woods, a Democrat sympathetic with the South. In any event, the year before that fateful election, as the metropolitan police again attempted to enforce the Sunday Blue Laws, the *Herald* wrote, "At the moment they are strongly and stealthily pushing their policy over our city through the black republican Police Commission, made to order at Albany, and imbued with all the spirit of the three thousand political black coats which that party boasts of possessing."

At the insistence of the CAS board of trustees, Mr. Brace was cautious about leading CAS into a visible position on the political fracas of the day despite his own deeply held personal beliefs. Nonetheless, Mr. Brace and Mr. O'Connor had immediately recognized that CAS could capitalize on the Blue Law controversy. They were of like mind about the Sunday selling of newspapers. They urged the boys not to sell on Sundays; however, neither one faulted the boys for doing so. Sunday sales were extremely lucrative. The boys often earned more on that day than during the entire rest of the week. So CAS understood, and even respected, the financial incentive working against their professed wishes. Now they saw a golden opportunity. Mr. Brace began a targeted fund-raising campaign among wealthy and religious New-Yorkers for donations to underwrite a free Sunday dinner for the newsboys. It allowed pious, Puritan philanthropists to earmark their contributions to this particular endeavor.

Mr. Brace was successful enough that on June 12, 1859, the NBLH began to offer a free "substantial supper" of bread and molasses, coffee, and tea to any boy who refrained from selling Sunday papers. It was a good design on a number of fronts. First, CAS could advertise its role in decreasing Sunday nuisance and use it as a metric for touting the importance of its work. In fact, in 1860 Mr. Brace proclaimed that "2,400 boys have been saved from the necessity of working on the Sabbath" by being offered a Sunday meal.[52] Second, donors could feel good that their contributions were not only feeding hungry children but also helping them observe the Sabbath. Mr. Brace wrote that it exerted "a very salutary effect." Finally, CAS could offer an incentive (beyond moral persuasion) to entice the boys not to sell. A free meal gave the boys pause in their calculus. It was yet another small example of Mr. Brace's genius and uncanny skill in moving his broader agenda forward, play by play, capitalizing on the social and political chessboard in front of him.

***

Untimely Deaths

On May 23, 1861, news arrived at the central office that quickly spread from Mr. Macy to Messrs. Brace, Tracy, Colopy, and Van Meter. Johnnie Morrow had died at the age of seventeen. His death, mourned by the CAS family, was also felt by seminary students and members of a small but devoted public fan club who had read his book. The Saturday paper carried news that "little Johnny Morrow," the newsboy, was dead, reporting that "many who have been brought in contact with him during his short but eventful career, will drop an honest tear to his memory."[53] Accounts of Johnnie's death varied, but it appears that he had undergone surgery in the hopes of improving the deformity of his lame leg. During his recovery, something went terribly wrong. He died shortly thereafter.

On Sunday, May 26, 1861, a fairly large group gathered—given his lowly status—at a Brooklyn church. Elegies were offered by the doctor who had performed his surgery and several clergymen, including Mr. Brace. The devoted group traveled to Ever Green Cemetery, where Johnnie was laid to rest.

On the same day, there was another funeral procession in New-York, although this one garnered national attention. The body of twenty-four-year-old Elmer Ephraim Ellsworth was slowly transported down Broadway before "thousands who with aching hearts and tearful eyes came to pay the mournful tribute."[54] He had died the day after Johnnie Morrow, on May 24, just outside Charleston, South Carolina, at a fort known as Sumter. Mr. Ellsworth had become the first U.S. Army casualty in what would be a grueling civil war.

Young men nationwide, from the North and the South, would be called to duty. This would include many of the poor, teenage boys from NBLH.

Notes

1. John Morrow, *A Voice from the Newsboys"* (San Diego: University of California Press, 1860), 80, Digital Archive, www.hathitrust.org; *Twenty-Third Annual Report of the Children's Aid Society* (New York: Wynkoop & Hallenbeck, 1875), 20; "The News-Boys," *Frank Leslie's Illustrated Newspaper*, December 29, 1855.

2. Charles Loring Brace, *The Dangerous Classes of New York and Twenty Years' Work Among Them*, 3rd ed. (New York: Wynkoop & Hallenbeck, 1880) 102–3.
3. William Colopy Desmond, "The Newsboys' Debating Society,", in Diaries and Journals of Agents of the CAS, circa 1853–circa 1864, vol. 49, 118–21. New-York Historical Society Archives.
4. Brace, *The Dangerous Classes*, 102–103.
5. Henry W. Thurston, *The Dependent Child: A Story of Changing Aims and Methods in the Care of Dependent Children*, (New York: Columbia University Press, 1930). 97.
6. Thomas Bender, *Community and Social Change in American: Ideas and Institutions in Nineteenth Century America* (Baltimore: Johns Hopkins University Press, 1975), 150.
7. Bender, *Community and Social Change*, 150.
8. "News Boys' Lodging-House," May 28, 1854, reprinted in Charles Loring Brace, *Short Sermons to the News Boys with a History of the Formation of the Newsboys' Lodging-House* (New York: Charles Scribner, 1866), 218.
9. "The News-Boys," *Frank Leslie's Illustrated Newspaper*, December 29, 1855.
10. *Second Annual Report of the Children's Aid Society* (New York: M. B. Wynkoop, 1855), 14.
11. "The News-Boys," *Frank Leslie's Illustrated Newspaper*, December 29, 1855.
12. *Sixteenth Annual Report of the Children's Aid Society* (New York: Wynkoop & Hallenbeck, 1869), 20.
13. Samuel Griswold Goodrich, *Peter Parley's Juvenile Tales* (Philadelphia: Tomas, Cowperthwait, 1836); Samuel Griswold Goodrich, *Peter Parley's Picture Book* (New York: Samuel Colman, No. 8 Astor House, 1834).
14. Samuel Griswold Goodrich, *Peter Parley's Spelling Book: With Engravings* (Philadelphia: Henry F. Anners, 1834).
15. "News Boys' Lodging-House," reprinted in Brace, *Short Sermons*, 218.
16. New York City Department of Parks & Recreation, "History of Playgrounds in Parks" (New York: The City of New York), https://www.nycgovparks.org/about/history/playgrounds.
17. Brace, *The Dangerous Classes*, 103.
18. Brace, *The Dangerous Classes*, 103.
19. Luke 10:25–37, *The New Oxford Annotated Bible,* Revised Standard Version (New York: Oxford University Press).
20. Luke 6:31.
21. Genesis 4:9.
22. Matthew 13.31.
23. *First Annual Report of the Children's Aid Society* (New York: C. W. Benedict, February 1854), 12.
24. *Second Annual Report of the Children's Aid Society* (New York: M.B. Wynkoop, Book & Job Printer, 1855), 14.

25. *Third Annual Report of the Children's Aid Society* (New York: M. B. Wynkoop Book & Job Printer, February 1856) 18.
26. *Second Annual Report*, 14.
27. *Second Annual Report*, 14.
28. The boys could reopen the bank upon their own motion but for the most part they did not do so. There was one notable exception when a visitor arrived at the lodging house promoting an Irish charity. The boys initiated a motion to open the bank so that they could contribute to the charity.
29. Vol. 46 Daily Journal 1855, July 2.
30. "The News-Boys," *Frank Leslie's Illustrated Newspaper*, December 29, 1855.
31. Edward Parmelee Smith, "Daily Journal" (unpublished manuscript, July 2, 1855), in The Victor Remer Historical Archives of the Children's Aid Society (1836–2006). New-York Historical Society Archives. Diaries and Journals of Agents of the CAS, circa 1853–circa 1864, vol. 46, July 2. New-York Historical Society Archives.
32. Smith, "Daily Journal," vol. 46, July 2, 1855.
33. Smith, "Daily Journal," vol. 46, July 2, 1855.
34. Smith, "Daily Journal," vol. 46, July 2, 1855.
35. Morrow, *Voice from the Newsboys*, 81.
36. Smith, "Daily Journal," July2, 1855.
37. Michigan was granted statehood in 1837; Wisconsin, in 1845; and Minnesota, in 1858.
38. Joseph M. Hawes (1971). *Children in Urban Society: Juvenile Delinquency in Nineteenth-Century America*. NY: Oxford University Press, 110.
39. C.C. Tracy to My Dear Mr.____, in *Fourth Annual Report of the Children's Aid Society* (New York: John P. Prall, Printer by Steam, 1857), 28–29.
40. This practice of singing for western audiences drew harsh criticism from Hastings H. Hart, who witnessed such an event as child in Ohio on the 1861 or 1862. In a letter to Henry W. Thurston, he reported "I have never forgotten the impression I received from the pathetic singing of these homeless children." Hart, who grew up to become the Secretary of the Board of Charities in Minnesota, a leading prison authority, and president of the National Conference of Charities and Corrections in the last quarter of the nineteenth century, was a fierce lifelong opponent of CAS and placing out practices in general.
41. "Agents in the Country," in *Fourth Annual Report of the Children's Aid Society* (New York: John P. Prall, Printer by Steam, 1857), 19.
42. Paul Boyer, *Urban Masses and Moral Order in America, 1820–1920*, (Cambridge, MA: Harvard University Press, 1978) p. 100.
43. William Colopy Desmond, "The Guardian Angel and the Children," in *Fourth Annual Report of the Children's Aid Society* (New York: John P. Prall, 1857), 57.
44. William Colopy Desmond, "The Guardian Angel," 57.
45. Had the boy been left in Detroit, he was only a short river's crossing into Canada. In Kalamazoo, the Underground Railroad was active. Dr. Nathan Thomas and his

wife were said to have aided over a thousand fugitive slaves over a twenty-year period from their home base in Kalamazoo County.

46. *Fifth Annual Report of the Children's Aid Society* (New York: Wynkoop, Hallenbeck & Thomas, 1858), 24. It appears that Mr. Tracy retired from CAS around 1873. CAS's twenty-first annual report contains a long entry under the heading, "A veteran western agent's report." Mr. Tracy had taken a three-week trip, searching for some of the thousands of children he had taken west over twenty years. This included those originally placed in 1859. As with all the emigration efforts, his findings were mixed. He found a former CAS child who introduced him to her own children as "grandpa." Other adoptive parents did not want their now-grown children reminded of their past. Mr. Tracy insisted that many "have become so blended with the community that the facts of their early history are forgotten." He closed by saying "the fact that I have seen and heard of so many good results from our work, so many who have been made better and happier by it, has made this one of the most pleasant trips I ever made in this work." Although my search may not have been exhaustive, it was last trace I found of him in CAS records.
47. Charles Loring Brace, *Short Sermons to the News Boys With a History of the Formation of the Newsboys' Lodging-House* (New York: Charles Scribner, 1866), 40–41.
48. For several variations of John Morrow's life and death, see the following: Tyler Anbinder, *Five Points* (New York: A Plume Book, 2002); "A News Boy's Funeral" in Brace, *Short Sermons*, 238–44; "Johnny Morrow, the Newsboy," *Farmer's Cabinet,* June 21, 1861, reprinted from the *New York Observer*; Morrow, *Voice from the Newboys*; and "Johnny Morrow, The Newsboy," *The Evangelist*, June 6, 1861, Morning edition, 2.
49. Morrow, *Voice from the Newsboys*, 120–21.
50. For stories on the crusade against the newsboys published in the *New York Herald* see the following: "Observance of the Sabbath," March 19, 1858; "A Caution to Newsboys—Policemen at Churches," March 21, 1858; "Proper Observance of the Sabbath," April 8, 1858; "Religious Revivals—The War against the Newsboys," March 21, 1858; "Much Ado about Nothings," May 8, 1858; "Desecration of the Sabbath Day," May 12, 1858; "The Poor Newsboys and their Persecutors," June 6, 1858; "Municipal Affairs," June 8, 1858; "The Sunday Newsboys Agitation," June 12, 1858; "The Modern Crusade against Newsboys," June 21, 1858; "Progress of Puritanism," June 23, 1858; "Metropolitan Police Inconsistency on the Sunday Law Question," August 14, 1859; and "Sunday Laws and Black Republican Popes—The Time for a Rational Sunday Movement," August 20, 1859.
51. "Sunday Laws," *New York Herald*, August 14, 1859.
52. *Seventh Annual Report of the Children's Aid Society* (New York: Wynkoop, Hallenbeck & Thomas, 1860), 14.
53. "Johnny Morrow, The Newsboy," *The Evangelist*, June 6, 1861, Morning edition, 2.
54. "Johnny Morrow," *Evangelist*, 2; Brace, *Short Sermons*, 239.

8

Mr. Macy's Record Books

NEWSBOY LODGERS AND THE EMIGRATION BRANCH,
1861–1866 AND BEYOND

> *A vast correspondence is kept up by Mr. J. Macy, the Assistant Secretary, and the clerks, with the employers of the children and the children themselves. Only a few of the thousands of encouraging letters received can be printed, owing to want of space.*
> —Twenty-Fourth Annual Report of the Children's Aid Society, 1876

MR. MACY OFTEN reached for the large accounting book on his office shelf.[1] Unlike the book next to it—which tracked salary receipts—this one was far more precious. In it, he attempted to keep track of all the children sent out on emigration parties. The question of how to set up such a system of case record keeping was an evolving one. In early 1861, all Mr. Macy had to work with was a large blank book, a stack of writing paper, a small bottle of India ink, and a fountain pen.[2] He also had a stack of perforated, three-cent postage stamps clearly marked "U.S.," although the U.S. postal system would soon to be thrown into chaos, along with the rest of the country.[3]

Although many lodgers never left New-York, spending as long as six years or more at the NBLH; others used it as a more temporary shelter. According to Mr. Macy's books, between 1861 and 1866, CAS "placed out" 708 boys from the lodging house through its Emigration Branch.[4] The task of keeping track of them—along with all other children sent west—fell primarily on Mr. Macy.[5] The record book was his answer to that challenge.

By 1861—six years into the emigration process—Mr. Macy had worked out a bit of a rhythm. When a new boy indicated his interest in going to the country, Mr. Macy located the next blank page in his book. In his mind's eye, the page was divided into sections to record answers to three basic questions: where the boy came from, where he went, and what happened to him. In response to the first of these questions, Mr. Macy tried to jot down some initial information systematically, including the boy's name, age, religion, ethnicity, his family situation, a bit about his background, and perhaps something about his appearance, if anything stood out. After this, Mr. Macy inscribed the date the boy left and the name of the CAS agent, other charity worker, or missionary who accompanied the "emigration party." Later, when the agent returned to New-York, Mr. Macy amended his ledger for the third time, adding the city and state where the boy was placed and the name of the family, employer, or farmer who received him.

The third—and often largest—section of the page was left blank, in hopes that it would fill with updates about the boy's progress over time. Given the state of communication, Mr. Macy happily received news from any source. That might be brought by a CAS agent returning from a trip; more often, it came in the form of a letter. These letters made their way slowly across the country, traveling by some combination of horseback, stagecoach, train, steamboat, and letter carrier. It could be a frustrating process. Mr. Brace would note, "It is sometimes only after a year or two of writing that we can discover where some of the older [boys] are."[6]

The letter writer might be the boy himself, his adoptive or foster parent, an employer, a neighbor, a church or community elder, or a boy's biological relative. In addition, the local postmaster was an invaluable source of information on relocations, disappearances, or deaths. Occasionally the postmaster offered helpful corrections, such as this one: Did Mr. Macy mean *Mr. Timmerman*, when he had written to *Mr. Zimmerman*? Mr. Macy probably found it particularly discouraging when problems arose from preventable error. This occurred in the case of a thirteen-year-old boy named Thomas, who had been left somewhere in Ohio. Mr. Macy's inquiry was returned "for better directions" by the postmaster because "there is not any such place in Ohio." The original information must have been conveyed or recorded incorrectly. On the other hand, new information occasionally surfaced unexpectedly. Sometimes—years after last hearing from a boy—a fully grown man would walk into Mr. Macy's office and reintroduce himself as a former lodger. No matter the source or the timing, Mr. Macy located the boy's page, entered the date, and recorded what he learned.

This loose system of oversight produced a variable and inconclusive record. It was impossible for Mr. Macy—and, by extension, Mr. Brace—to give an accurate report. Simple demographic questions, such as how many

Catholic children were sent, or outcome questions, such as how many boys ended up in reform schools, were unanswerable.

Yet Mr. Macy and Mr. Brace shared a sense of eternal optimism, and there was enough positive anecdotal evidence to keep it fueled. Such was the case when Mr. Brace received a letter, in November 1858, from a clergyman in Albion, Michigan, who had been charged with general supervision of children left in a large swath of the state, including Albion, Battle Creek, and Kalamazoo.[7] The man was enthusiastic and estimated that "not three in one hundred" children were not doing well. However, he admitted he had removed about ten children from their initial homes and relocated them in new families. He was quick to add, "The fault—if fault there was—making the change necessary, was as often that of the parents, as the children."[8] This was exactly why Mr. Brace wasn't in favor of indenturing children in the first place.

Despite this welcome news, Mr. Brace took note of the clergyman's impetus for writing. The man had received "inquiries" from a New-York institution, soliciting information "from those who are on the ground" and could testify as to CAS "daily operations and effects."[9] It was ominous; Mr. Brace suspected those poking around in CAS business were a group he labeled collectively as the "asylum interest."

***

Critics: Asylum Advocates, 1859–1860

On the evening of November 2, 1859, the CAS board of trustees called an emergency meeting to discuss "statements and rumors said to have been circulated" by Reverend Mr. Samuel B. Halliday, that were "prejudicial to the operation of the Society."[10] Mr. Halliday was the superintendent of the House of Industry in the Five Points, a successor to Mr. Brace's mentor, Mr. Pease.[11] That night, the CAS trustees appointed Mr. Brace, among others, to investigate the matter by visiting their accuser in person.[12] The visiting committee was less than satisfied when Reverend Halliday "declined giving them any information in relation, to the charges said to have been made by him."

Not willing to let the matter drop, the board took two major actions. First, in December 1859, it entertained a motion on "the question of appointing an agent to reside in the West."[13] The following year, agents were so placed. The first was Mr. Tracy, who relocated to Michigan. Second, the board directed Mr. Brace to prepare "a pamphlet of publication" defending CAS. Mr. Brace tackled the project with his usual zeal. The resulting pamphlet—approved by the board in December and published in January 1860—laid out a forceful argument for CAS's placing out system and contained forty-nine letters of support collected from residents in Michigan, Indiana, Illinois, Ohio, Pennsylvania, New Hampshire, Connecticut, Massachusetts, New Jersey, and Upstate New York. Mr. Brace's ultimate goal was to persuade the public that his method was preferable to that of the asylum interest, which placed poor children in congregate care facilities such as reformatories, refuges, or poor houses.

Mr. Brace was particularly interested in correcting widespread public misconceptions. One was that "all methods of treatment are equally good for reforming vicious children, or for preventing crime among them." Equating poverty and vagrancy with crime and viciousness was another common misconception, held by proponents of asylums from the start. In fact, when the New York State Legislature established the House of Refuge in 1824, it was managed by the Society for the Reformation of Juvenile Delinquents. The managers were empowered to receive and place in the House of Refuge "all such children as shall be taken up or committed as vagrants, or convicted of criminal offences" following a conviction in any one of a number of courts, including the Court of General Sessions and the Court of Oyer and Terminer, or a conviction before police magistrates. Once children were committed to the House of Refuge, the managers could "bind [them] out" (technically, with their consent) "as apprentices or servants."[14] Indentured servitude had been widely adopted as common practice among asylums and orphanages.

Asylum advocates held pessimistic views of about the interconnectedness of poverty, vagrancy, and crime. They saw "viciousness" in poor, vagrant children, although Mr. Brace argued that this was "often only an external habit and soon eradicated by pure and kindly influence." Poor children, he declared were merely "victims of circumstance."[15] Work by NBLH superintendents such as Mr. Tracy and Mr. O'Connor demonstrated that while poor, vagrant boys might commit some bad acts, they could also be guided to better behavior and make good choices. All they needed was stable living environments, positive incentives, education, and good role models. There was no need for heavy-handed legal intervention.[16] All this was consistent with Mr. Brace's understanding of child development and his deeply held belief that with minimum supervision children could be coached to good behaviors that would be internalized as they grew. While asylums relied on legal coercion and physical restraint, CAS's method relied on this coaxing. Or, as Mr. O'Connor said of the NBLH, it relied on "persuading rather than compelling its inmates to be virtuous and industrious."[17]

A skilled advocate, Mr. Brace started his written defense by seizing a dramatic example straight from newspaper headlines. Recently, a teenage inmate at a reform school in Westborough, Massachusetts, had set fire to the institution, burning it to the ground. That's what happens, Mr. Brace intimated, when you lock children up and fail to take into account their individual needs. He reframed the problem as one of prevention, asking, "How to prune dangerous impulses and yet not plant mechanical virtues?"

Mr. Brace rested his thesis on several progressive assumptions. First, "children of the poor are not essentially different from the children of the rich."[18] Second, the public saw poor children through "too rigid [a] *classification*" system. In doing so, they failed to recognize, "the grand truth" that "each poor, deserted, unfortunate little creature in the streets is an *individual*, like no other being whom God has created." As such, he argued, each boy "has his own tastes—his own habits—his own peculiar temptations—his especial weaknesses, and his own virtues."[19] Honoring this uniqueness required individual attention. Third, the only way to cultivate virtues that actually "spring from the heart" was to allow a boy to "be exposed to the strain of temptation."[20] Finally, Mr. Brace argued that "America has the accidental, but immense advantage of an unlimited demand for labor, especially juvenile labor" in the country.[21] The comparative advantage was held not only by the U.S. over Europe but also by the western states over eastern cities. Poor children were expected to work no matter where they lived, yet homeless youngsters in New-York struggled to survive.

For Mr. Brace, the answer was easy.[22] First, simply "connect the supply of juvenile labor of the city with the demand from the country."[23] Second, realize that children's individual needs were better met by families than institutions. In fact, he would often say, "The family is God's Reformatory."[24] In his view, this led to the inevitable conclusion that the best solution was "to place unfortunate, destitute, vagrant and abandoned children at once in good families in the country."[25]

This theoretical and practical approach appealed to Mr. Brace's sense of scientific reasoning. For him, placing out conformed to both the natural laws of supply and demand and well as those on human development. In addition, it was consistent with his attempts to integrate Darwinian principles of evolution into charity work. For Mr. Brace, natural selection applied to "the moral history of mankind, as well as the physical," and evolutionary drift must be toward virtue.[26] Environment was central to his thinking, not because it determined "the pattern of evolution" but because it provided the "challenge against which the natural variations struggled." Removing children from the inhospitable influences of urban slums, and placing them in the relatively more favorable environment of the country, enhanced chances of successful survival.[27] Similarly, isolating children in asylums and reformatories removed them from the natural environment from which character should be forged.

For Mr. Brace, everything about the "asylum interests" arguments were wrong. He became one of the leading advocates of his day railing against them. Asylums, he wrote, "managed numbers of persons" but failed to address the "peculiarities of the individual." Furthermore, disciplining children into submission only taught them "technical virtues," "drill virtues," and "tread-mill goodness."[28] Virtues acquired in this manner would only mimic good behavior on a temporary basis. These asylums failed "in not following the natural laws which Providence has established for human nature."[29] He wrote, "in applying these various errors of principle—namely, the want of individuality of treatment, the disregard of natural laws, and of the economic advantages peculiar to America—to our reformatory and preventive systems in this country, we shall find that great mistakes have been committed" by those favoring reformatories or asylums.[30] In stark contrast, Mr. Brace's placing out system "secures an individual management for the child, it brings him under the great natural impulses which train the character most vigorously; it is in harmony with economic laws."[31]

Mr. Brace's critics were neither persuaded nor appeased. Reverend Halliday doubled down in his efforts against CAS. He solicited additional complaints by publishing "private circulars" in western newspapers. Again, the CAS Board of Trustees confronted these allegations head on. In April 1860, they dispatched Mr. Tracy and Mr. Brace to "visit the place at the West where the letter to Mr. Halliday had been written to "investigate the allegations in person."[32]

Other rumors surfaced, ostensibly coming from Mr. Apollos R. Wetmore, president of the New-York Juvenile Asylum, alleging "conclusive evidence" that CAS was "doing injury by its operations in the West." In response, Mr. Brace and his board badgered Mr. Wetmore for weeks, repeatedly demanding that he produce his evidence. Eventually CAS threw down the gauntlet, challenging the juvenile asylum to join together in a joint committee to "investigate the general effects of both systems."[33] The beleaguered Mr. Wetmore eventually conceded that he had "delayed an answer because I was unwilling to enter into any controversy with your Society and am still not disposed to do so." Nonetheless he agreed to put the matter of a joint investigation before his own board of trustees.[34]

All told, these aggressive and vigorous responses to critics would be a hallmark of CAS efforts for decades to come. Mr. Brace insisted that allegations against the society be backed by evidence. Once that evidence was produced, it was investigated as thoroughly as possible. This often included sending agents to the western location where complaints had arisen and reporting the findings to the public. In addition, CAS continued to explore ways to evaluate its own services and practices, although how best to accomplish this would be a matter of ongoing public debate. Even so, proof of the Emigration Branch's successes (and failures) lay largely in Mr. Macy's hands and resided in his record books.

***

Mr. Macy's Update

Back in the privacy of the central office, Mr. Macy's system rested on hope that news would eventually waft in his direction. Sometimes it did. Such was the case on March 17, 1862. On this day, Mr. Tracy had returned from a trip to Ohio, bringing a report on a boy named Solomon. It had been a year since Mr. Macy had heard anything of the boy. Mr. Macy located reference to Solomon on page 201 in his book. He likely paused to reread the sketch he had written in early April 1861, although it is unlikely that he would have forgotten this unusual boy.[35]

Solomon was a Prussian Jew. He had only been in the country for four months when Mr. Macy first met him. The sixteen-year-old had emigrated to the U.S. by himself and worked in a New-York cigar factory but was eager to find employment in the country. Mr. Macy had been only too happy to oblige. He placed the boy in Mr. Smith's group heading west on the Ohio-Pennsylvania Railroad.

Immediately on arriving at the hotel in Massillon, Ohio, a "Jewish clothing dealer" named Samuel Oppenheimer claimed he knew Solomon to be a Jew "at sight," given his "prominent Jewish features." The boy had already told Mr. Macy as much, although he confessed he sometimes attended church as well as synagogue. In any case, the clothier offered to give Solomon a home although "he had nothing for him to do." At that moment, another gentleman, a carpenter, stepped forward and offered to teach Solomon his trade. Carpentry was lucrative in the thriving state with its abundant timber: birch, cherry, black walnut, oak, and buckeye. But Mr. Oppenheimer countered that Jews "must get a living by trading not by a trade" and argued that "all Jews are bound by a religious law to take care of each other." That argument won the day and Solomon went home with the man who shared his faith.[36] With that, Mr. Macy's passage on Solomon ended.

The story that followed was all too common. One week after Solomon went home with Mr. Oppenheimer, the Confederate army attacked Fort Sumter. Eight states—Virginia, South Carolina, Mississippi, Florida, Alabama, Georgia, Louisiana and Texas—had already seceded from the Union. On April 15, newly sworn President Lincoln issued a proclamation calling forth 75,000 "loyal citizens" to volunteer to help suppress the rebellion. Ohio Senator John Sherman called the response to the president "the most remarkable uprising of a great people in the history of mankind." Among those to answer President Lincoln's call to arms in Senator Sherman's home state was one of its newest residents, a sixteen-year-old Prussian Jew named Solomon.

Mr. Macy picked up his fountain pen, filled its bladder with ink, and began to write what he learned from Mr. Tracy. Days after his arrival in Massillon, Solomon had volunteered with the Thirteenth Regiment of the Ohio Infantry. Sometime between when the regiment mustered out, heading to Parkersburg, West Virginia, on June 30 and before it was ordered to Kentucky in December, Solomon was shot and killed, most likely at the Battle of Carnifex Ferry.[37]

When Mr. Macy finished this written update, he drew a solid black line below the entry. He placed his pen in the center of the page, immediately below, and in his very best penmanship, he wrote the word *Dead*. The single word rested heavily on the page, entombed in a sea of white space that would never be filled with updates.

Unlike Mr. Macy's helter-skelter chicken scratches above the line—or, for that matter, in the rest of the record book—this word was not written in haste. Frequently in subsequent years, Mr. Macy—and others who placed notes in the record books—would take extra time, letting the ink flow heavily to create boldfaced script, and write **Gone to War**, or—in awkward attempts at calligraphy—pen the single word *Enlisted*. It was unlikely that anyone would ever read these business records or even notice these gestures, but Mr. Macy—in his own private and personal way—nearly always paid tribute.

***

Gone to War

Like Solomon, most of the NBLH boys placed out in 1861 were immediately swept up in the war. By 1864, Mr. Brace wrote, "It is estimated that there are now *over a regiment* of our boys in the armies of the Union."[38] Unfortunately, Solomon was not the only NBLH alumnus who would sacrifice his life, although not all died in battle. For example, seventeen-year-old Stephen ended up succumbing to "camp fever." The fever that claimed his life seemed nearly preordained. He had arrived at the NBLH a vermin-infested, ragged mess. The boy, orphaned at age nine, had lived with his grandmother for two years before she, too, passed away. With the complete loss of family, Stephen's life became unstable. He worked on a farm for a bit then picked up work as a canal boy, an occupation that nearly always resulted in flea, lice, tick, or other parasitic infestation. At the NBLH, the O'Connors cleaned him up and tended to him for eight months. Then Stephen decided he wanted to go west. Once there, he had promptly written to Mr. Macy to say that "he had the best home in Ohio." However, three years later, he found himself caught up in the devastating war that would claim his life.

Although Stephen and Solomon were technically too young to volunteer for the Union army, it didn't seem to matter much except in the most extreme cases. Even then, underage children volunteered as drummer boys, beating out the military commands above the din of battle. Some of the youngest lodgers contributed to the war effort by making "flying visits to Washington and the camps," following the army and pursuing "their avocation" of peddling papers."[39] A *New York Herald* war correspondent called it "perhaps one of the most curious features of the day" to have "the presence of the newsboys upon the battle field, with the latest papers." He described the "ragged urchins on horseback . . . calling forth, '*New York Herald*' in stentorian tones" while "the musketry was at its loudest . . . the artillery was most sonorous, and when the passing bullet, with its deadly 'chirp' compelled one involuntarily to duck his head." The journalist concluded, "It was an incident of this curious and cruel war which I shall not soon forget."[40] Of course, neither the battlefield newsboys nor the drummer boys were immune from the dangers associated with the war.

Some younger lodgers were persistent in their efforts to enlist. John Reily, a sixteen-year-old Catholic boy, tried to serve as a captain's waiter but was discharged for being "too small." Although not a true orphan, the boy arrived at the NBLH seeking help because his mother had suffered bad burns and was confined to Bellevue Hospital. Denied his chance to serve, John went to Ohio with Mr. Tracy and lived with a farmer for two years. At first opportunity, John enlisted in the infantry. In February 1864, he wrote to Mr. Macy that "he [had] just returned from the war" and that he had "seen hard service" but was pondering re-enlisting. Mr. Macy recorded this shred of information—as he always did—but it would be the last he ever heard from John.

Several former lodgers ended up as professional soldiers, including an American Catholic boy, eighteen-year-old James O'Brien. The young man worked in a hoop skirt factory in New-York, eventually asking to go west. Mr. Macy sent him over to the NBLH until the next trip was scheduled to depart. The boy's foster family said he was doing well in his new home. However, later that spring he volunteered as a drummer boy with the Ninth Regiment of Indiana Infantry. James fought at the Battle of Shiloh, among others. In 1864 he was reported as being "a good soldier and hard drinker when off duty." A year later, Mr. Macy recorded a rumor that James had been taken prisoner at the Battle of Munford in Alabama. To his delight, in July 1868, James walked into his office, saying he had been in the army in Georgia, Alabama, and Texas and that he had come to "see about his mother and found her dead." This slightly surprised Mr. Macy because seven years earlier, the boy had claimed his mother was already deceased. But James was hardly the first boy to misrepresent himself at CAS intake.

Nine other former newsboys enlisted—information Mr. Macy gleaned from one source or another—but that is where his trail ended. It particularly saddened him when he had known a boy well. For example, another boy named James was only thirteen when he first arrived at the NBLH, living there for three years and charming the O'Connors. After being placed with a family in Indiana he had seemed happy, writing Mr. Macy several times, always reporting that he as "well satisfied" with his place and wished that some of his friends at the lodging house would "come out now" because "they would get good homes." However, in February 1865, his adoptive mother wrote to Mr. Macy saying that James had "joined the army" and that was the last anyone heard from him.

The Civil War also disrupted fragile families in New-York. With men off fighting, those they left behind struggled. Although the Union army paid decent wages, the money didn't always make its way back to dependents. As a practical matter, the number of orphans and half orphans seeking help from CAS increased. Boys applying to the NBLH often had little information about their fathers' whereabouts. For example, neither fifteen-year-old William—who ran errands for a living—nor twelve-year-old Patrick—a baggage smasher who "lived round in cellars, and boxes"—was able to identify his father's regiment. Patrick's father had been killed in battle. A veteran's pension system was in place for disabled vets and included small payments to dependents of Union soldiers killed in battle. So Patrick, as well as another boy named Michael, whose father was killed at Bull Run, were both receiving small stipends.

The first battle of Bull Run—or the Battle of Manassas, to the Confederate army—was waged on July 21, 1861. As fate would have it, while Michael's father lay dying on a the battle field down below, witnessing the bloodshed on a hillside above was another Union loyalist volunteering his services: Charles Loring Brace. Mr. Brace later predicted that 1861 would be remembered as "probably the most disturbed and disastrous which will ever occur in the history of the Republic."[41]

***

Challenges and Changes, 1861: War, Leadership, and NBLH Growing Pains

Mr. Brace, thirty-five years old at the time of the war's outbreak, did not enlist. Nonetheless, he sought ways to help. He spent the early war serving as a "civilian" journalist for two newspapers, the *New York Times* and the *Independent*, an abolitionist paper. In July 1861, he traveled to Virginia, catching up with the advancing army and eventually reaching Manassas Junction. "I suppose," he wrote to his wife, Letitia, that night, "they will fight at the Junction." Indeed, fighting erupted the next day. Although Mr. Brace was safely perched on the hillside, he wrote that they "suddenly had the cannon-balls flying among [them]" and that "the first experience of a round shot whirring over one's head, is a sensation." He added, "Don't be frightened. We escaped all right."

Mr. Brace sought additional ways to aid the Union cause. In 1862, he reached out to his childhood friend, Fredrick Law Olmsted, who was head of the Sanitary Commission, a relief organization that tended to sick and wounded Union soldiers. Mr. Brace wanted to volunteer. Mr. Olmsted's warm "Dear Charley" response quickly sharpened in tone as he summarily rebuffed his old friend's offer. "I employ three classes, surgeons, nurses and women—the first and last of two grades, but in neither of either would you yoke." Declaring that nurses and mercenary soldiers were infinitely more helpful than volunteers, Olmsted wrote, "I have therefore abandoned volunteers. Don't want them. Consequently, in the way of business, I don't want you."

He softened the rejection slightly, adding, "Any man without a clearly defined function about the army is a nuisance."[42]

Doggedly, Mr. Brace turned to another private relief agency, the newly formed U.S. Christian Commission (USCC), in which Mr. Edward P. Smith—an early CAS worker and emigration agent—was acting as a field secretary. USCC had both home front as well as field branches. In New-York, Mr. Brace's friend and colleague, William E. Dodge, was in charge of the home branch. However, Mr. Brace had volunteered for the field branch, putting him closer to the action.[43] USCC was far less structured than Olmsted's Sanitary Commission. Among other things, it delivered supplies to Union troops.[44]

Mr. Brace also continued to wheedle and needle prominent New-Yorkers over the issue of slavery. This included his friend, Horace Greeley, publisher of the influential *New York Tribune*. In a personal letter to Greeley in 1861, Mr. Brace prodded him to publish more on the antislavery cause. Greeley, a vocal Republican supporter, resisted, writing back that the slavery issue would be solved by "the war, and not what you and I may say about it."[45] In addition, Greeley prophetically added, "The real question is not, 'shall emancipation be recommended as the true antidote to rebellion?' But who shall do it?"[46]

***

Leadership

In 1861, Mr. Brace also suffered a personal and professional loss unrelated to the war itself. Judge John L. Mason, one of the founding members of CAS and its only board of trustees president, died "in the course of nature and the fullness of years."[47] Back in the early days, Mr. Brace had been wary of the jurist, fearing he would be "too conservative in opinion and too hard" to work among street youth.[48] Over the years, Mr. Brace's opinion changed, and the two became close working colleagues.

The relationship had not always been conflict-free. Early on Judge Mason expressed concern about Mr. Brace's outspoken, and controversial, views on religion, science, and politics. Nonetheless, the two came to amicable agreement that Mr. Brace would "never in any report or document or speech, in behalf of the society or about it, or anywhere as officially as its secretary, broach any controverted religious or political subject."[49] Mr. Brace could continue to express his radical ideas as long as CAS was not directly implicated in the process. Judge Mason had lived by this agreement even as the Civil

War approached and Mr. Brace wrote passionately and "incessantly through the religious and secular papers over my signature" on the "anti-slavery question . . . calling out some bitter controversies." These included defending "old John Brown" as well as opining on highly contentious mayoral, gubernatorial, and presidential campaigns.[50]

Immediately following Mason's death, the board appointed a new president, Mr. William A. Booth.[51] Just two years earlier, Mr. Booth had made a name for himself by helping to lead the charge of the conservative Sabbath Committee, with its anti–Sunday-selling campaign against the newsboys. His position on that matter stood in direct contrast with Mr. Brace's more tolerant, less authoritative view that each boy needed to make his own decision. Although that issue was now settled, when Mr. Booth became board president, the men clashed again. Mr. Booth bristled at Mr. Brace's political outspokenness, fearing it would damage the reputation of CAS. He also questioned Brace's fitness to continue as secretary.

Mr. Brace responded with restrained fury. In a letter to Mr. Booth defending his position, he acknowledged that "your and my opinions are probably diametrically opposed on many questions," but he reminded Booth of the care with which he had always managed to separate his personal and professional life and the truce he had worked out under Judge Mason's leadership.[52] Mr. Brace insisted that his various beliefs were "entirely individual," and were "so understood by the public." As proof he offered the fact that all "shades of religious and political opinion have always approved our charitable work." In the end, the new president accepted Mr. Brace's reasoning and allowed him to stay on as secretary. Nonetheless, Mr. Brace's outspoken political views had nearly cost him his job at the very agency he created.

***

NBLH Growing Pains

CAS had grown exponentially under Mr. Brace's charge. Nowhere was that more evident than its flagship New-York program, the NBLH. Under the firm control of Mr. O'Connor and his wife, it had not only stabilized but grown. Since it's opening, the NBLH had occupied the sixth floor loft space of the Sun Building, with its sleeping quarters outfitted with forty double-decker beds. The residence could comfortably handle seventy to eighty boys a night. However, by 1860 the census was reaching as high as ninety boys with "the overplus being obliged to sleep on the benches."[53]

Mr. O'Connor began waging an internal campaign for more space. His wish was partially granted in 1861 when the NBLH expanded by taking over an additional level of the Sun Building on the fifth floor.[54] The "new dormitory" was "fitted up" with sixty additional beds, which meant CAS could "now lodge, in both sleeping apartments one hundred and thirty boys."[55]

Mr. O'Connor and others knew the move offered only an imperfect, temporary solution to the growing demand. Mr. O'Connor's wish list had included also having enough space for a "gymnasium and reading room."[56] However, by far the most pressing and yet unsolved problem had to do with water.

CAS had always prided itself on the ventilation, light, and water available to the lodgers. The fifth floor expansion still offered light and allowed for sufficient cross-ventilation when the windows were open. However, the water tank and washroom facilities remained the same. They would be strained to the brink. The water tank was "not at all equal to supply the demand." Mr. O'Connor argued that "our bath and washing-rooms are not sufficiently large and commodious, now that the number of lodgers has so much increased." In addition, Mrs. O'Connor had scarcely sufficient water "for the purposes of washing the bed-clothing and keeping the rooms clean." In the end, the water tank was "soon exhausted and [had] to be constantly refilled."[57] The O'Connors would have to make do with what they had during the war years, even though "they still fall far short of all we need."

The demand for shelter for vagrant and homeless boys continued to rise. Within the next two years, even the 130 beds proved inadequate. The nightly census frequently reached above 150. Mr. O'Connor noted that "on some nights" he was compelled "to place two in a bed."[58]

***

Complications of 1863: Draft Riots, Catholic Critics, and a Board Resolution

On January 1, 1863, Mr. Greeley's question about slavery was answered when President Lincoln signed the Emancipation Proclamation. Although it would have little practical effect, the official act finally brought to the fore the real reason for the Civil War. It also lit a fuse on what would be an explosive year in New-York.

Among other things, the Emancipation Proclamation inflamed New-York's already agitated and concerned Irish Catholics. Archbishop John

Hughes fueled the discontent when he acknowledged that while the "U.S. had given asylum to Irish refugees fleeing British oppression, and they would fight to preserve the Union," he insisted they would not go to battle "to free the slaves."[59] So while Catholic New-Yorkers were willing to fight in a war to preserve the Union, they were less willing to do so to dismantle slavery.

Tensions between poor Irish immigrants and black New-Yorkers had long simmered. From the Irish perspective, while Irish men went to battle, blacks were taking their jobs. Exacerbating this tension was the fact that black citizens were often hired as strike breakers. In 1863 alone, this included replacing three thousand striking stevedores—most of them Irish—with black workers.[60]

Adding kindling to the flames, the U.S. Congress passed the Enrollment Act on March 3, 1863, imposing a mandatory draft on every male between the ages of twenty and thirty-five (and all unmarried men between thirty-five and forty-five).[61] Congress justified the law by pointing to declining enlistments and increasing desertions.[62] For young men who had rushed to volunteer at the start of the war, their two-year commitments were coming to an end. Not all were eager to re-enlist. By 1863, casualties were mounting and those who returned maimed and disfigured were graphic reminders of the war's brutality.[63]

Several former NBLH lodgers added to the ranks of the permanently disabled, including fourteen-year-old William, who was disabled by a malfunctioning gun. Rather than return to civilian life, he had joined Ohio's Invalid Corps. Similarly, seventeen-year-old John returned to Mr. Macy's office sporting "an artificial arm." His earlier correspondence included vivid descriptions of his experiences in a battle near Shiloh, from which he escaped unscathed, but he was not so lucky as time wore on.

In addition to casualties, desertion rates were soaring. At least one former lodger was among them. Frank had stayed at the NBLH for four months, selling papers and working in Center Market, before Mr. Macy sent him west with an emigration party. Mr. Macy had scrawled a fairly long and colorful description of the boy's abusive past, which included being held against his will and denied food. This may have been true, but when his farm family learned of Frank's desertion, they wrote to Mr. Macy that he would "make a good actor, but not a farmer."

As if mandatory draft weren't controversial enough, embedded in the Conscription Act was an even more contentious provision that permitted any man to buy his way out of military obligation for a three hundred dollar substitution fee. Not surprisingly, this was a prohibitive amount for the poor and, in New-York, that largely meant the Irish. Taken together, the Emancipation

Proclamation, the Conscription Act, and the labor situation in New-York all aggravated existing tensions. Implicated were questions of class, race, ethnicity, and religion. By early summer 1863, tensions were again reaching a breaking point as implementation of the draft approached.

Saturday, July 11, the first day of the draft, passed uneventfully, but officials had not finished their work so the process was set to resume on Monday morning. This left all day Sunday for draft-aged men to stew about it in taverns and saloons. On Monday morning, intoxicated, agitated mobs began attacking people and property deemed associated with the Republican cause. The next day, crowd anger morphed into a full-throated, indiscriminate assault mostly on black New-Yorkers. Victims were mutilated, lynched, drowned, beaten, and burned. Their property, including homes and businesses, was torched.

Among the institutions burned to the ground was the Colored Children's Orphanage. Miraculously, the several hundred children escaped unscathed.[64] In the immediate aftermath, both Mr. Brace and Mr. Macy worked with the orphanage's managers to shuttle some of the displaced children to Cottage-Place Mission, which had been founded by Mr. Macy and his sisters five years earlier.[65]

On July 16, after three days of uncontrolled rioting, New-York was finally wrestled back to order. The property damage was extensive, and the estimated death toll ranged from 105 to 150.[66] Mr. Brace would reflect on the riots, writing of the "inconceivable barbarity and ferocity of the crowd toward an unfortunate and helpless race." He placed the blame squarely on "a great, ignorant, irresponsible class, who were growing up here without any permanent interest in the welfare of the community or the success of the Government." It was about this very class, scolded Mr. Brace, that "the agents of this Society have incessantly warned the public for the past eleven years."[67] He noted that his first annual report had "contained a prophecy of a terrible outbreak which might be expected in nine or ten years, from the masses of untrained, and neglected boys and girls then wandering our streets."[68] Mr. Brace had used this initial prediction to motivate wealthy New-Yorkers to support the fledgling society, and he now used the riot to scold them for failing to adequately heed his words.

For Mr. Brace, the Draft Riots confirmed the danger of leaving street children, particularly teenage boys, unattended. He pointed out that in "every crowd attacking houses or torturing negroes, were a large number of lads and young men. These sackers of houses and murderers of the innocent, are merely *street-children* grown up," he wrote.[69] "They are boys whose only home has been the corner grog-shop, who have slept in barges and boxes, whose wits have been sharpened by the incessant 'struggle for existence' in the streets, while their animal passions have been without control or restraint."[70]

***

Catholic Critics, 1863

As Catholic New-Yorkers flexed their muscles in response to the Conscription Act, they also began to organize on other fronts. As a practical matter, poor Catholics had to turn to the existing, mostly Protestant societies when in need of help. In large measure, that meant CAS. Catholic officials became increasingly vocal in their objections to this arrangement.[71] So 1863 saw the founding of the Catholic Protectory.

The Catholic Protectory had been established only after intense political battle. State legislators had argued that existing institutions in New-York, including the House of Refuge, Juvenile Asylum, and CAS, were sufficient. Furthermore, they were "loath to recognize a sectarian institution."[72]

To a large extent the Protectory was the result of the work of Levi Silliman Ives. A former Episcopalian bishop who had converted to Catholicism, Dr. Ives became a zealous advocate for children of Catholic immigrants in New-York. Nonetheless, his beliefs could not have been more different than those of Mr. Brace on a number of fronts.

First, Dr. Ives was basically supportive of slavery, which he found preferable to factory labor. In part, this was because "religion was made a disciplinary part of the life of the slave" and produced "a common bond that . . . joined master and slave into a brotherhood."[73] Ives didn't engage with moral questions about slavery while Brace's deep-seated opposition to slavery rested almost exclusively on its inhumanity.

Second, Dr. Ives's initial work with the Society of St. Vincent de Paul in New York, brought him in contact with Protestant-leaning agencies including CAS. This influenced his decision to experiment with the placing out of "untrained and destitute Catholic children" in western homes.[74] It had been a disaster. Ives reflected "I succeeded in finding places for many," but noted "I can call to mind only a single instance where the child either did not abscond or prove utterly ungovernable and worthless."[75] In addition, he had equally bad luck apprenticing children reporting, "we have apprenticed a considerable number of orphans to good Catholic masters, selected with great care, and we are pained to say that a majority of these orphans have proved to be wholly unmanageable." Of course, Brace not only favored placing out, and opposed indenture, but he generally took a more positive view of the capacities of the children with which he worked.

Third, Dr. Ives's experiences led him to believe that homeless "children needed a long period of training and of strict discipline, before they should be returned to their own homes or sent to foster homes in the west."[76] For him, the natural conclusion was that institutional asylum care was preferable to placing out. Mr. Brace, firmly believed that good behavior was cultivated only through trial and error and better learned outside institutional care. He was loath to trod on children's free will and he could not be more strenuously opposed to the asylum model.

Finally, for Dr. Ives and his fellow Vincentians, their "all-consuming thought ... was to save the children of the immigrant to the Catholic faith."[77] His opposition to Protestant agencies was inherently connected with his commitment to preserving Catholicism. Catholic leadership had little interest in converting others, and "were more concerned with the foundation of their own church. ... As a matter of fact, the Catholic effort was consumed largely in the mere struggle for existence."[78] Mr. Brace not only saw CAS as nonsectarian, he didn't believe that children should be indoctrinated. Mr. Brace was much more concerned with their exposure to basic Christian values than adherence to any formal religious traditions.

Although it will take a full decade to come to fruition, the Catholic Protectory would ultimately open its own bricks and mortar institution. The protectory's decade-long evolution eventually resulted in a "reformatory for Catholic juvenile delinquents" that was "modeled after the House of Refuge."[79] The original plan was to receive three types of children, " those entrusted to it by their own parents, those committed by the courts and those transferred by the commissioners of public charities"[80] As a practical matter, due to limited funding, the Protectory largely restricted its care to children committed by the courts.[81]

However, given their diametrically opposed views on everything from slavery, asylum care, placing out, indenture, child discipline, court intervention, free will, and role of religion in children's lives, it is not surprising Mr. Brace ended up in conflict with these Catholic child welfare pioneers.

Although Mr. Brace was already well practiced in fending off the critics promoting the "asylum interest," Catholic critics added a new religious twist to the old critique. Among other things, CAS was accused of proselytizing.

Although Mr. Brace was no fan of Catholicism, he flatly denied the allegations. "We know no sect or race." He insisted that "both Catholic and

Protestant homes were offered freely to the children. No child's creed was interfered with." Mr. Brace was quick to point out that CAS worked with supervising committees in the west, composed of local citizens who oversaw the care of the children, and Roman Catholics were frequently "on the committees themselves in the Western villages."[82] "Our action" Mr. Brace claimed, "in regard to these waifs, has always been fair and open."[83] According to Mr. Macy's record book, 103 of the boys sent west were Catholics.[84] Yet that statistic was dwarfed by the 530 boys for whom no religion was recorded at all.

On a case-by-case basis CAS always attempted to correct problems as they arose. So it was with an Irish Catholic boy named John McGregor. John told Mr. Macy that his father had gone to war and his mother had been run over by a wagon in the busy city streets and was confined to a hospital in Brooklyn. Mr. Macy made no attempt to confirm John's story, a process that would have been cumbersome at a time before telephones. Besides, the story seemed plausible enough. At John's request, he was sent to Michigan. But no sooner had he arrived than it became evident that his entire tale was fabricated. John McGregor was actually James O'Connor and his Catholic parents were very much alive, well, and living in Brooklyn. They reported James was truant from school and had run away from home. The boy was promptly returned to Brooklyn.

Later, Mr. Brace would look back on this period and complain that "the poor were early taught, even from the altar, that the whole scheme of emigration was one of 'proselytizing,' and that every child thus taken forth was made a 'Protestant.'"[85] He chafed at the gossip that "children were re-named in the West and that thus even brothers and sisters could marry!" Even more galling to Mr. Brace were rumors "that the little ones 'were sold as slaves,' and that the agents enriched themselves from the transaction."[86] Given Mr. Brace's opposition not only to slavery, but also to its first cousin, indentured servitude, the rumors seemed particularly abhorrent to him. Nonetheless, faced with this public attack by fellow Christians, Mr. Brace retreated. Later, he claimed that "a class of children, whom we used thus to benefit, are now sent to the Catholic Protectory, or are retained in the City Alms-house on Randall's Island.[87]

***

A Board Resolution

If President Lincoln's Emancipation Proclamation opened the tumultuous year of 1863, an action taken by the CAS Board of Trustees created its own kind of havoc at year's end. On December 16, 1863, the board of trustees passed a resolution that "a company be sent once in every three weeks through the year beginning January 5, 1864 and that no causes should delay or prevent (except with the consent of the President and Secretary) their departure, whether ready for emigration be few or many" children.[88] In one fell swoop, the trustees institutionalized and routinized the Emigration Branch.

A number of factors probably motivated the board's action. Certainly, the recent violence was fresh in mind. In addition, the numbers of orphans and half-orphans seeking help during the war was increasing. The NBLH was bursting at the seams, often sheltering between 130 and 150 boys a night. In addition, lodgers were living at the facility for longer periods of time, treating it as a permanent home rather than a temporary, transitional shelter.[89]

Whether the trustees understood the implications of their action for Mr. Macy's central office is debatable. Nonetheless, with one resolution his job got exponentially more difficult. Until then, Mr. Macy sent parties to the west at unpredictable intervals, whenever he had enough children on the list, an agent available, a western community expressing interest, and sufficient funds in CAS's coffers to cover expenses. The number of boys sent out was relatively modest—twenty-five in 1861, nine in 1862, and thirty-two in 1863—and therefore manageable. However, with this resolution institutionalizing the Emigration Branch, the numbers swelled. In 1864, a total of 133 boys went west; in 1865, it was 214, and by 1866, the number leaped to 293. Mr. Macy's record books showed immediate signs of the strain. He began omitting information that was routinely collected on the boys—including ethnicity, religion, and family background.

Adding to his burden was the fact that CAS was placing boys further west. Until 1863, all the boys found homes in one of three states: Indiana, Ohio, or Michigan. The circumscribed geographic area allowed returning CAS agents to collect follow-up information after placement. Beginning in 1864, CAS pushed westward, first to Illinois and Wisconsin and finally as far northwest as Minnesota, over a thousand miles away.

In the end, of the 708 newsboys placed out, CAS maintained relatively complete records on the earliest groups sent from 1861 to 1863, and many of those boys were caught up immediately in the Civil War. After 1863, the numbers of boys sent out soared and information about them grew sketchier. Nonetheless, taken as a whole, Mr. Macy's records paint a picture of how the services linking the NBLH and the Emigration Branch worked toward the overall mission of the society and breathed life into Mr. Brace's comprehensive vision.

By definition, lodgers were teenage boys or young men. Only eight of those sent west were eleven or younger and another twelve were over nineteen. The vast majority of boys—447—were between the ages of fourteen and sixteen. They represented the very population most likely to be traveling, living, and working independently of adults. For them, the boundaries between family-like placements and employment situations were fuzzy. In fact, Mr. Brace capitalized on this ability to market the initiative flexibly depending on his audience. Work situations ranged from vocational training, apprenticeships, and seasonal labor to full-time employment. In Mr. Brace's mind, none of these constituted discrete categories but they rather created a spectrum of opportunities for youth that provided support, guidance, education, training, shelter, and employment. No demographic group better reflects the nature of this hybrid system of family and work placements than that of teenage boys.

***

From NBLH to Emigration Outcomes

The former residents of the NBLH followed various paths after leaving New-York. Some boys returned to New-York or to their families. Others never got to their intended destinations. The stories of some boys suggest their placements were spectacularly successful and the boys were engaged in a broad variety of employment situations. Others left their placements (possibly returning to a vagrant lifestyle), committed petty thefts, or ended up in institutions. The state of Michigan, for example, took a particularly aggressive approach to homeless children.

***

Returning Home

It's not surprising that many teenage boys stayed in contact with their biological families and often returned home, either on their own volition or because they were called back by relatives. At least forty-three did.

For some, the initial trip may have been a mistake because they returned almost immediately. For example, fourteen-year-old Henry returned to New-York, with money sent by his parents, after only two weeks in Indiana. A sixteen-year-old Scottish boy spent a single week in Wisconsin before his mother in Philadelphia sent for him.

More often, the call of relatives came after the boy seemed settled. John, a thirteen-year-old, went looking for work with the blessing of his mother in New-York. He was taken in by a butcher in Ohio. Mr. Macy received several letters from the butcher over the course of the year stating that John was "still with him doing well" and that he "goes to school and is a very good boy." However, a year later, Mr. Macy received a final note saying that John had been "persuaded away by his uncle who lives in Illinois" and moved on. Similarly, Denis, a fifteen-year-old Irish boy whose father died at the battle of Antietam, went to Ann Arbor, Michigan, but at the "urgent request of his brother" returned to Boston. The Michigan family reported being "sorry to part with him."

Some boys who returned ended up regretting the decision to do so. For example, sixteen-year-old John lived in Wisconsin for two years earning fifteen dollars a month but returned to Charleston, South Carolina, at the behest of his father and brother. He later wrote to the farmer who had taken him in that he "was sorry he did not take his advice and stay at the West." Seventeen-year-old Andrew spent six weeks in Ohio, where he "conducted himself well while there," but returned to New-York to see his brothers and sister. Andrew expressed a desire to return to Ohio.

At least one boy was sent back to biological relatives because of difficulties faced by the host family. Ten-year-old George went to Ohio with the blessing of his mother. He was "doing very well," went to school, was "learning well," and attended Sunday school regularly. George was reportedly a "very good boy" and "happy as a lark." A year later, however, when his adoptive father's business failed, the man sent George back to his mother, who told Mr. Macy she was "anxious to have George go west again."

**

Not Getting There

Another group of boys never got to their intended destinations for one of three reasons. A few changed their minds even before leaving the city. Early on, Mr. Brace scrawled in his diary that "very many of the boys engage to go to the country and then become frightened + back out."[90] Such was the case with twelve-year-old James, an American Catholic, who had the consent of his father in writing but decided he didn't want to leave home. Mr. Macy scratched the boy's name from the emigration log. A second group got on the ferries and steamboats leaving the city only to disappear somewhere along the way. For example, thirteen-year-old Louis was a Protestant of German ancestry. After being discharged from a New-York orphanage as a twelve-year-old, he ended up at the NBLH. Louis got as far as Cincinnati but than vanished into thin air. Similarly, two eighteen-year-old boys, George and Thomas, traveled as far as Ionia, Michigan, and then "walked off" together. Most concerning was the third group of boys—albeit small in number—who were put off the train by a CAS agent along the way for disciplinary reasons.

***

Spectacular Successes

Nothing pleased Mr. Macy or Mr. Brace more than spectacular successes.[91] The best documented of these rested in dozens of letters sent over a fifteen- or twenty-year period, tracing a boy's transition to manhood. For example, Hugh was an orphan of eleven when he spent several weeks at the NBLH before being placed in Indiana. Hugh's foster father was a faithful correspondent, writing Mr. Macy about the boy's progress and always saying he was "well and getting along nicely" or "doing very well." Even thirty years later, he wrote that Hugh was married and had three children and had "done very well." Similarly, Hugh's daughter wrote on behalf of her illiterate father, saying Hugh had stayed with his adoptive family until he turned twenty-three and had always been "treated as their own child." On leaving home, Hugh was given a horse, which he still owned. After getting married, he and his family lived on a farm in Bedford, Indiana, for fourteen years and had "done nicely." She noted that her father was a member of the Methodist Church and the Independent Order of Odd Fellows and that he had asked after the O'Connors at the NBLH. She also reported there were two or three other New-York boys still living "in his neighborhood."

Similar glowing reports of happy childhoods, successful transitions to adulthood, and gainful employment poured into the central office for boys such as Michael and James. Michael stayed with his Illinois family for nine years before turning twenty-three and getting "married to a nice girl," having been "a good boy." By the age of twenty-eight he was a deputy sheriff, and he was "well liked by every body and [was] a fine gentleman." James spent two months at the NBLH as a thirteen-year-old before deciding to go to Minnesota, even though his mother lived in Connecticut. His adoptive family stayed in touch with Mr. Macy for twenty years, heralding James for being "quite a man for work" and "doing well." James was "very steady," "[saved] his money," and was working "at logging in the woods."

In general, dozens of other positive accounts drifted back to Mr. Macy, even if he received word for shorter periods of time. Sometimes, the boys wrote that they were "getting along first rate" or were "treated as one of the family." "I am enjoying myself hugely," they sometimes wrote. More often, foster families wrote updates, reporting that a boy attended school and church and was making "good advancement." The writers often provided positive assessments of the boy: He "will grow up to be a man of good principle and good workman." The boy was "a good, sober, honest, and industrious boy," "dutiful, pleasant and trusting," "a superior boy," and "faithful, kind and honest." The family "would not wish to have a better boy."

**

Employment Opportunities

Many older boys worked as farm hands, staying for a season or two before moving on. For example, eighteen-year-old Joseph went to Ohio, stayed with a farmer for three months but "left on good terms with all the family." Similarly John, an eighteen-year-old American boy, stayed until after the first harvest even though he was promised eight hundred dollars if he stayed for two years. Nonetheless, the farmer reported John was "a good boy on the farm." Thirteen-year-old John found a home in Oshkosh, Wisconsin. He worked on Mr. Reynolds's farm for a year and then on neighboring farms for several seasons. He eventually left for the Dakota Territory (now Wyoming), where he was "getting good wages and doing well." By 1870, John had moved on to California, where he worked in a store receiving seventy-five dollars per week in wages. According to reports, he was a "smart man" and was likely to become "one of property."

Given the burgeoning rail industry, dozens of boys found employment on the railroad. This included Patrick, an orphan who stayed at the NBLH for five years before being placed in Minnesota as a thirteen-year-old. His adoptive parents wrote regularly, including a decade later, in 1876, to say he was married, "gainfully employed," and "doing well on the Rail Road." Another orphan, Josiah, was placed with the Porters in Illinois. They wrote often, eventually reporting he was "grown to manhood" and was "well employed in the freight business at the depot of the Missouri Pacific Rail Road" in Independence, Missouri. William lived at the NBLH for eight months before going to Michigan as a sixteen-year-old. He immediately wrote, saying "he wished he could find words to express his happiness." Twenty years later, he wrote from Saginaw, telling Mr. Macy he was married, employed as an "engineer on the Rail Road," and "doing nicely."

Since many former lodgers had hawked newspapers, it wasn't surprising that some turned to publishers for employment. Edward, a fifteen-year-old Canadian orphan, was placed in Illinois and dutifully reported his progress to Mr. Macy over decades. Early on he claimed that "he has the best home of any boy that went west." Two years later, he wrote that "the west is the place for every young person to live" and that he was "thankful." His adoptive father wrote that "for one of his age [Edward] exhibits good taste and judgment" and that Edward had "a great deal of ambition." As an adult, Edward was employed as a proof reader, working his way to city editor in Lawrence, Kansas, and eventually "given charge of a paper" in St. Louis.

In addition to publishing, working on railroads, or working as farm hands, a variety of trades were open to the boys. Charles, a sixteen-year-old, was "learning the shoemaker's trade" in Ohio. In Michigan, thirteen-year-old John was learning the "machinist trade," and sixteen-year-old Michael was learning the "harness makers trade." Three other boys ended up as blacksmiths. In Wisconsin, fourteen-year-old August eventually began "learning the miller's trade." In Minnesota fifteen-year-old Thomas, an American orphan, was doing well, ending up as a "clerk in a wholesale hardware store in St. Charles." Equally glowing reports came from Ohio, where fifteen-year-old James was "getting along nicely." He thanked the society for "getting him such a nice place." A year later his foster father reported that James was attending school and "working in his shop cutting marble." "If he continues," the man predicted, he would "make one of his best workmen."

***

What to Make of Vagrancy?

A question often asked of western agents by prospective adoptive families was, "Won't the boy run away?" Given the fact that many boys had lived a nomadic, homeless life before arriving at the NBLH, it wasn't an unreasonable question. Mr. Brace, who dubbed Mr. Tracy "our most successful agent" and noted that he had "a certain quaintness of conversation and anecdote, and a solid kindness and benevolence, which won his way with the Western farmers," was fond of recounting Mr. Tracy's response to this question. "Did you ever see a cow run away from a haystack? Treat him well, and he'll be sure to stay."[92]

Yet, despite these assurances, large numbers of boys did leave without warning. In fact, 136 fell into this category. In these cases, Mr. Macy's final entry ended abruptly, albeit colorfully, with a note that the boy had "run away," "left," "absconded," or was "on the hook" or had "skedaddled." At least three boys ran away with the circus as it passed through town.

From a distance, Mr. Macy was hard pressed to see clear patterns in this kind of behavior. Some of the boys left almost immediately after arrival, staying a single night or a few days. Others stayed months and the reasons they vanished were a complete mystery to the host family. For example, a farmer in Ypsilanti, Michigan, where Robert was placed, seemed both baffled and miffed by his disappearance. The man wrote that the boy had "proved untruthful," telling him that he "liked his place" but then leaving home in the fall without word or cause, and he had "not seen him since." Most often the boy took off alone. However, sometimes groups of boys from New-York ran off together. After all, many had known each other before leaving the city, and they stayed together afterwards. Some left home more than once. For example, Charles ran away from his Michigan home almost immediately. He returned and received a "lecture" from his new father but five months later he fled again. That was the end of Mr. Macy's trail.

What to make of these disappearances is difficult to determine. Critics of CAS found this continued vagrancy a source of irritation and Mr. Brace was not unsympathetic to their concerns. That said, flexibility in placements, which allowed parties on either side, boy or family, to break the initial deal if unsatisfied, was a hallmark of Mr. Brace, who disliked indentured servitude and other binding contractual arrangements. He hated impinging on a child's free will.

For example, Peter remained with a farmer for ten months but "became dissatisfied," was paid for his services, and left for Cincinnati, where he worked on river boats. George, sixteen, left a farmer in Ohio because he was unhappy with his wages. Henry, a fourteen-year-old, was left with a tailor in Indiana but declared "he did not like the tailor's trade" so he "went to live with a farmer." Walter, an eighteen-year-old American Protestant, was "a good boy," but he only stayed in rural Illinois for "three months at $10 per month" before leaving because he "found better employment in Chicago." Mr. Brace would likely have seen all these moves in a favorable light.

Occasionally, it was the family or employer who broke the agreement. William, fourteen, was returned by a farmer in Ohio who said he was " a lazy bad boy." The boy was given "money to pay his fare to NY" and "put on the cars." A farmer in Flint, Michigan, wrote of Thomas, his sixteen-year-old Irish boy, that "he could not do anything with him" and did not know where he was. Joseph, a seventeen-year-old Irish immigrant, went to Ohio but vanished, and the farmer wrote that he was "lazy insolent disobedient and a loafer." Some were unhappy enough to demand a refund from CAS for money spent on the boy. For example, a farmer in Ohio wrote that eighteen-year-old Albert "was a bad boy and left" and that he desired a refund for the amount he had paid for Albert's transportation. It wasn't clear if CAS reimbursed the man; nonetheless, it routinely took responsibility for unwanted teenagers if they were being sent back to New-York. However, this young man had just wandered off.

***

Petty Theft and Worse

In general, CAS had a high tolerance for boys' bad behavior. It was a message that agents attempted to convey to potential families in the west. One of Mr. Brace's favorite stories was that of the "bland and benevolent manner" with which Mr. Tracy replied to "an irritated employer" who complained that "the 'New York boy' had knocked over the milk-pail, pelted the best cow, let the cattle in the corn, left the young turkeys in the rain," or some such. Mr. Brace gleefully declared Mr. Tracy's response to such complaints was "delightful to behold." "My dear friend," Mr. Tracy would coo, "can you expect boys to be perfect at once? Didn't you ever pelt the cattle when you were a boy?"[93] Mr. Brace was quick to note that even "children of the more favored classes" were not immune to bad behavior, asking, "How seldom is it that any large proportion would be entirely free from bad habits?"[94] CAS consistently recognized the development capacity of children and urged those taking child in to do the same.

CAS tolerance even extended to petty theft, as long as individual incidents didn't turn into patterns of problematic behavior. Mr. Brace argued that "even those who have committed criminal offenses—thefts or the like—are not necessarily hopelessly gone."[95] Some western families understood Mr. Brace's position and were sympathetic. One Ohio farmer wrote that their fifteen-year-old boy, Albert, "stayed the winter but left as the weather grew warm without letting them know." He had taken several things that "never belonged to him" but the farmer remained supportive, writing Mr. Macy that "these little disappointments must not detract" CAS from continuing the "good work."

At least forty-six of the former lodgers were accused of taking something, although most were not formally charged with a crime.[96] Sometimes the boys stole money and fled immediately. For example, a fifteen-year-old orphan named James "took some money" from the Indiana farmer with whom he was placed and "left for parts unknown." Other times, boys stayed for a while but ultimately ran off with cash. A sixteen-year-old German orphan, Charles, stayed for about six months with an Illinois farmer before he "stole some money" and ran away. Edward, an eighteen-year-old, spent three weeks in Ann Arbor, Michigan, and then stole a wallet and some money and left.

Sometimes the earliest signs were that things were going well, as with eleven-year-old Joseph, a half-orphan, placed in Indiana. Shortly after his arrival Joseph wrote that his foster family was "very kind to him" and that he "[attended] Sunday school." He added, "It is so splendid and we have such nice things here." He reiterated that sentiment in a letter dated a year later. Joseph wrote that he liked "the country very much and finds there is considerable work to be done." Nonetheless the final entry in Mr. Macy's case log was that "he took some money" and "has since left."

Sometimes both boy and money were recovered, and no further legal action taken. For example, Thomas, a fourteen-year-old Irish Catholic immigrant, was placed in Indiana and ran away twice. The second time, he "stole $22," but the money was recovered and "on account of his extreme youth was not imprisoned but has a good place with a Baptist man five miles from Columbus." Frank, a sixteen-year-old orphan, went west to Illinois, leaving quickly and taking "a pocketbook with him." The teenager was overtaken and surrendered the pocketbook and its contents. Fifteen-year-old Edward was placed in Wisconsin but Mr. Macy received word that Edward had left, stealing "as much as he could carry." He was "caught and property returned" but vanished shortly after and was not heard from again.

In addition to cash, boys stole property, including an assortment of small but valuable items. An Indiana famer reported that fifteen-year-old Alexander had fled, "taking his wife's jewelry and $27 in money." John, a boy of the same age, stayed in Ohio for five days before taking "a gold pen and $10."

Other times, the theft was far more serious. A farmer in Michigan wrote to Mr. Macy that "my boy stole about 30 lbs. of honey and left." Even worse, Gilbert, a nineteen-year-old, was with a farmer in Indiana who reported he had stayed only two weeks before taking a horse and fleeing. The farmer wrote that "he [had] no farther knowledge of horse or boy." Horses were valuable commodities and had the boy been caught, a conviction would have resulted in serious prison time.

For the ever-optimistic Mr. Brace, the only cases he deemed failures were when boys "have become a burden or nuisance to society."[97] For example, fourteen-year-old James had been "a good boy for two months" but then "stole two watches" and was sentenced for grand larceny and sent to the state prison for six months in Wisconsin. Henry, a sixteen-year-old Scottish immigrant, allegedly stole "$7000" and was "sent to a State prison in Elyria." Within days of placement, fifteen-year-old Charles, a half-orphan, had "skedaddled," and the following month Mr. Macy learned he had been "arrested and put in jail for larceny." John went to Illinois but once there "formed a band of thieves" and was ultimately confined to "jail." It was this kind of outcome that worried Mr. Brace the most, despite conceding that "of course, in an enterprise of this nature, failures must occasionally occur."[98]

***

The Michigan Problem

In Michigan, a spate of boys ended up in state-run facilities, suggesting Michiganders had comparatively low tolerance for bad behavior. The state had established its first juvenile refuge in 1853. Like New York, Michigan had passed state legislation to create facilities for boys "where the milder course of treatment, more especially adapted to their reformation, can be employed" than the common practice of incarcerating "boys and youth among the more hardened criminals in the state prison."[99] So state training and reform schools received boys under fifteen who had been convicted of crime "where less than a life penalty would apply" or to boys fifteen to twenty years of age at the judge's discretion.[100] Boys usually ended up confined in juvenile facilities in Flint or Lansing, although more serious offenders were incarcerated in the state prison in Jackson.

A cluster of boys ended up in Lansing's House of Correction. Fifteen-year-old James successfully lived with a farmer in Michigan for two years before taking $550 in government bonds from the farmer's sister. He was caught and sentenced to the "Reform School at Lansing till of age." Daniel, a fifteen-year-old American Catholic orphan, arrived in Michigan in the spring of 1865. However, the farmer wrote back shortly thereafter: "Daniel stole some money" and was "now in the house of correction at Lansing." William, an American Catholic boy, was a half orphan. His mother was dead and his father lived in Bergen, New Jersey, but had "turned him out of doors." After staying at the NBLH, William went west with Mr. Tracy. Once there he "ran away" and changed homes several times. Eventually he stole "$30 and a watch and left." This final act resulted in William being "sent to the House of Correction." The writer concluded that this was "the best place for him."

***

Critics Again, The Prison Attack: Spreading the Seeds of Vice

It was only a matter of time before another generation of critics would emerge voicing objections to CAS operations. In the mid-1870s, the "asylum interest" again leveled the charge that CAS was "scattering poison over the country."[101] Mr. Brace steadfastly insisted that "our children were not criminal, but simply destitute and homeless boys and girls."[102] Mr. Brace tried to draw a distinction between poverty and criminality, which was not one that many other charity workers of the day recognized. For Mr. Brace, childhood vagrancy and homelessness could lead to criminality. He argued, "This class is the very one to form criminals, though not yet criminal in habit."[103] His focus was always on preventing that development.

Nonetheless, the ferocity of the attack in 1874 caught even Mr. Brace off guard. At the National Prison Reform Congress, which met in New-York that year, "two or three of the Western members asserted that the homeless children sent out to the West by the Children's Aid Society of New York, were 'crowding the Western prisons and reformatories;' one lady being understood to say that 'their prisons and houses of refuge were half full of these children.'"[104] Taken aback, CAS employees present responded that this "did not correspond" with their information, and "that the number of 'failures' under our plan was less, proportionally, than under any other for juvenile reform."[105] Mr. Brace insisted that "we do not believe, going over the whole field of our work, that the failures would reach ten per cent; in many States they would not exceed four per cent."[106]

However, faced with these new allegations, Mr. Brace and the CAS board of trustees did what they always did when under attack. They launched investigations. CAS immediately dispatched one of its most experienced agents to investigate the claims, Mr. C. R. Fry. He traveled to fifteen state prisons and reformatories in twelve cities in three states: Indiana,[107] Illinois,[108] and Michigan.[109] Mr. Fry spoke to wardens, deputy administrators, superintendents, former prison personnel, bookkeepers, and inmates (in some locations, speaking to every person in custody). He examined records books containing information on the inmates' backgrounds, combing them for any indication the child had been born, or ever even lived, in New-York. For those with any connection to the city, Mr. Fry summoned the youth for personal interviews. The sum total of his investigation produced a grand total of five institutionalized children possibly sent west by CAS: one girl who had gone west (but couldn't name the society that sent her) and four boys.

Mr. Brace wrote of these efforts that Mr. Fry's "investigations have been, in each case, as thorough as it is possible to make them, and I think, clearly demonstrate the fact that the children sent to the west by the New-York Children's Aid Society do not fall into criminal habits, and cannot be found in the penal institutions in the West."[110]

Mr. Fry's efforts appeared to have been nothing short of Herculean. However, even this investigation didn't quell the critics, who found fault with CAS methodology, claiming "poor sampling methods" that "lacked objectivity."[111] They voiced these concerns at the 1887 National Conference of Charities and Corrections not only about the rigor of CAS's scientific methodology but in the ongoing debated over methods of practice.[112] That said, none of the criticism deterred CAS, which continued to send its parties out on a regular basis.

**

Mr. Brace's Muscular Orphan Problem

Mr. Brace maintained his belief in the basic soundness of the Emigration Branch. Each department of CAS service (including evening school, industrial schools, lodging houses, and emigration parties) was yoked through Mr. Macy's central office and aligned with Mr. Brace's grand vision. The link between the NBLH and the placing out system would remain strong. Rapidly expanding communities in the western territories needed all kinds of labor, from farm hands to carpenters, harness-makers, blacksmiths, lumberjacks, marble cutters, and office clerks. To Mr. Brace, the opportunities appeared nearly limitless. Employment of almost any sort was available for any hardworking individual, and life free from poverty seemed assured.

Despite Mr. Brace's confident and defiant public defense of CAS work, quietly he began to express concern about one group of young people that he referred to as "muscular orphans." In the mid-1860s, a doctor in Michigan had written of a boy who ended up in prison in Jackson that he thought the boy "was too old to go to the west." Mr. Brace worried that the writer was essentially right. Older teenage boys or young men posed a unique set of challenges.

Mr. Brace understood that in many ways, these urban-raised teenagers were ill suited to suddenly take up rural life. In addition, they were hard to keep track of. Said Mr. Brace, "With the larger boys, the exact results are more difficult to attain, as they leave their places frequently."[113] He was concerned that they had a tendency to drift "into the western cities, and take up street-trades again."[114] However, as was the case with all Mr. Brace's initiatives, signs of problems only served as an invitation to experiment with new solutions. Mr. Brace began to explore other avenues for his muscular orphans.[115]

Notes

1. *Methodological note on the case records.* The case studies used in this chapter are all drawn from Mr. Jared Macy's record books from 1861 to 1866, located in the Victor Remer Historical Archives of the Children's Aid Society (1836–2006). New-York Historical Society Archives in Guide to the Records of the Children's Aid Society at the New-York Historical Society (Series XI, Sub-Subseries XI.4.B, Emigration/Placing Out Department, access restricted). This included Record Book 8, vol. 413; Record Book 9, vol. 414; Record Book 10, vol. 415; Record Book 11, vol. 416; and Record Book 12, vol. 417. The records are restricted, and I had permission from CAS to examine them. Because of their confidential nature, I have used the first names from children's records, but not their last names. I scoured the record books and extracted the subset of cases with notations indicating that a boy had spent some time at the NBLH before going west. The resulting 708 cases served as the sample for my analysis. It must be remembered that this represents a small subset of the all the children—boys and girls, young and old—sent west by the CAS through its Emigration Branch. I have used this sampling strategy to highlight the relationship between the NBLH and the Emigration Branch of the society's work.

   It is unlikely that my sample is complete. Although Mr. Macy often recorded something about the boys' stay at the NBLH, it is probable that he did not always mention this connection. His primary purpose in writing these records was to keep track of children being sent out, not to document the relationship between CAS branches of service. For example, in 1863 Mr. Brace wrote, "The number of emigrants furnished by the Newsboys' Lodging-House this year is 180, nearly one-fourth of the whole (*Tenth Annual Report of the Children's Aid Society* [New York: Wynkoop, Hallenbeck & Thomas, 1863], 37). Using Mr. Macy's record, I located a mere thirty-two that referenced a stay at the NBLH. This discrepancy is illustrative of how difficult it is to draw any firm conclusions about the overall numbers.

   These record books were never meant for external examination. They are internal documents and business records. For this reason, it seems fair to assume that Mr.

Macy recorded faithfully both good and bad outcomes without an eye to public scrutiny. Nonetheless, there are reasons to question the veracity of some of the reports he received, which included rumors, second-hand information, and opinions. That said, I have primarily relied on these as truthful accounts.

The quality of cases varied dramatically. In the worst records, there was nothing more than the boy's name and age with no follow-up information at all. Other records contained minimal information gleaned from second-hand reports. However, in the richest case records, there were dozens of entries based on communications received from the boy, his foster family, or others making observations over decades.

Interestingly, Bruce Bellingham used a similar methodology and evidence in his study of child abandonment and family life in nineteenth century New York. His work is based on 383 usable case histories from CAS's Record Book 1. This record book contains evidence from CAS's first year, covering April 1853 to September 1854. Although my evidence is from a later period, and I used a subsample of entries restricted to boys linked to the NBLH, our findings are remarkably similar. Significantly, like Bellingham, I independently found CAS supported normative family practices (both labor and custodial care) and that there is little evidence of hostility toward parents and no abrupt disruptions in family relationships. In fact, for the older boys, there was a fair amount of evidence of ongoing correspondence between biological family youth placed out.

2. Mr. Macy set up these record books decades before modern inventions like typewriters and telephones would make the job slightly easier. It wasn't until 1874 that the first commercially successful typewriters were introduced in the U.S., although it would take longer before the CAS began to use them regularly. Alexander Graham Bell placed the first telephone call to his assistant in the next room in 1876. Therefore, Mr. Macy was mostly dependent on the U.S. postal system.

3. Smithsonian National Postal Museum, "Arago: The Complete Collection of U.S. Postage Stamps on Arago," https://postalmuseum.si.edu/research/topical-reference-pages/the-complete-collection-of-us-stamps.html

4. Of these 708 boys, 40 lived at the lodging house for over a year, and another 57 stayed over a month. The vast majority stayed less than a month.

5. For the most part, CAS referred to placing children "in the country" and "in the west," using these phrases interchangeably. I do so in this chapter. The vast majority of these placements were in the western states. However, a small number of boys were placed closer home, in Upstate New York, New Jersey, or in the New England states.

6. Charles Loring Brace, *The Best Method of Disposing of Our Pauper and Vagrant Children* (New York: Wynkoop, Hallenbeck & Thomas, 1859), 14–15.

7. Other children were left in Ann Arbor, Jackson, Dawagiac, and Niles. Current train riders might recognize this string of cities as the sequential stops on the Wolverine line operated by Amtrak between Detroit and Chicago.

8. *Sixth Annual Report of the Children's Aid Society* (New York: Wynkoop, Hallenbeck & Thomas, 1859), 37–38.
9. *Sixth Annual Report*, 37.
10. Minutes of the Board of Trustees, November 2, 1859, vol. 2, 1853–1861, in the Victor Remer Historical Archives of the Children's Aid Society (1836–2006). New-York Historical Society Archives. Records of the Children's Aid Society 1836–2006, New-York Historical Society Archives.
11. Because of failing health, Mr. Pease retreated to Westchester, where he purchased a farm for the employment of boys (B. K. Pierce, *A Half Century with Juvenile Delinquents; or: The New York House of Refuge and Its Times* [New York: D. Appleton, 1869], 213). CAS would soon follow suit with its own farm school, which became another major branch of CAS's services.
12. Minutes of the Board of Trustees, November 2, 1859.
13. Minutes of the Board of Trustees, December 21, 1859.
14. An act to incorporate the Society for the Reformation of Juvenile Delinquents in the City of New York (March 29, 1824), reprinted in B. K. Pierce, *A Half Century with Juvenile Delinquents*, 320).
15. Brace, *The Best Method*, 14.
16. Understanding this distinction between court-ordered coercive services imposed on poor children as distinct from the CAS system that relied on youth voluntarily seeking out, and participating in, services also helps explains Mr. Tracy's extreme ambivalence in calling the police and last-minute decision not to testify against Billy Patterson (see Chapter 6 of this volume).
17. *Twelfth Annual Report*, 20.
18. Brace, *The Best Method*, 4.
19. Brace, *The Best Method*, 4.
20. Brace, *The Best Method*, 5.
21. Brace, *The Best Method*, 6.
22. Mr. Brace pondered a number of important questions, both privately and publically, in designing the Emigration Branch. In his own words, they included the following: How were the demand and supply for children's labor to be connected? How might the right employers be selected? When the children were placed, how were their interests to be watched over, and acts of oppression or hard dealing prevented or punished? Were they to be indentured, or not? If this was the right scheme, why had it not been tried long ago in our cities or in England?
23. Brace, *The Best Method*, 12.
24. Brace, *The Best Method*, 12.
25. Brace, *The Best Method*, 12.
26. Richard Hofstadter, *Social Darwinism in American Thought*, (Boston, Beacon Press, 1944, repr. 1992), 16. Bender has noted that Brace "spoke in Darwinian imagery of the struggle for survival" and that he "felt that if 'children of the streets' were trained 'to the habits of industry and self-control and neatness.' If they were given

'the rudiments of a moral and mental education.' They would have a real chance for respectable lives." (Thomas Bender, *New York Intellect: A History of Intellectual Life in New York City from 1750 to the Beginning of our Own Time* [Baltimore: Johns Hopkins University Press, 1987], 198. All of Mr Brace's programs were designed to do just that.

27. Joseph M. Hawes, *Children in Urban Society: Juvenile Delinquency in Nineteenth-Century America* (New York: Oxford University Press, 1971), 110.
28. Brace, *The Best Method*, 5.
29. Brace, *The Best Method*, 5.
30. Brace, *The Best Method*, 6.
31. Brace, *The Best Method*, 12.
32. Minutes of the Board of Trustees, February 28, 1860; Minutes, April 10, 1860.
33. Letter from Charles Loring Brace to Apollos R. Wetmore, March 28, 1860, in Minutes of the Board of Trustees, April 2, 1860.
34. Letter from Brace to Wetmore, March 28, 1860, in Minutes of the Board of Trustees, April 2, 1860; Minutes of the Board of Trustees, February 22, 1860.
35. Jared Macy, "Record Book 8" (1861), 201, in the Victor Remer Historical Archives of the Children's Aid Society (1836–2006). New-York Historical Society Archives. Guide to the Records of the Children's Aid Society, Series XI, Sub-Subseries XI.4.B, vol. 413, New-York Historical Society.
36. Interestingly, another "unusual" case (by CAS standards) concerned a twelve-year-old black boy named Thomas, sent west in 1866. Thomas went to Wisconsin, where he was placed with a black family. Over the course of the next five years, CAS received reports that Thomas was "learning a trade and doing well" and that he was "a fine boy." The family was so happy with Thomas that they asked CAS to send out a little girl as well.
37. National Park Service, The Civil War/Battle Unit Details: Union Ohio Volunteers, 13th Regiment, Ohio Infantry, https://www.nps.gov/civilwar/search-battle-units-detail.htm?battleUnitCode=UOH0013RI01; National Park Service, The Civil War/Soldier and Sailor Database, https://www.nps.gov/civilwar/soldiers-and-sailors-database.htm.
38. *Eleventh Annual Report of the Children's Aid Society* (New York: Wynkoop & Hallenbeck, 1864), 9.
39. *Tenth Annual Report of the Children's Aid Society* (New York: Wynkoop, Hallenbeck & Thomas, 1863), 20.
40. "Newsboys upon the Field," *The New York Herald*, October 30, 1864, 1.
41. *NinethNinth Annual Report of the Children's Aid Society* (New York: Wynkoop, Hallenbeck & Thomas, 1862), 21.
42. Frederick Law Olmsted to Charles Loring Brace, 1862 in Emma Brace, ed., *The Life of Charles Loring Brace* (New York: Charles Scribner's, 1894), 248.
43. Robert H. Bremner, *The Public Good: Philanthropy & Welfare in the Civil War Era*, (New York: Alfred A. Knopf, 1980), 57.

44. Mr. Brace stayed in the south until, at least, the summer of 1862.
45. Horace Greeley to Charles Loring Brace, October 3, 1861 in Emma Brace, *Life of C. L. Brace*, 246.
46. Emma Brace, *Life of C. L. Brace*, 246.
47. *Eighth Annual Report of the Children's Aid Society* (Wynkoop, Hallenbeck & Thomas, 1861), 31.
48. *Eighth Annual Report*, 33.
49. Emma Brace, *Life of C. L. Brace*, 264.
50. Emma Brace, *Life of C. L. Brace*, 265.
51. Mr. Booth served as CAS Board of Trustee president until 1892. Stepping down from the presidency, he continued in his capacity as a trustee until the expiration of his term in 1896.
52. Charles Loring Brace to a Trustee, August 7, 1864, in Emma Brace, *Life of C. L. Brace*, 264.
53. *Seventh Annual Report of the Children's Aid Society* (New York: Wynkoop, Hallenbeck & Thomas, 1860), 14.
54. The expansion had not been cheap, costing CAS $1500 to both "fit up and enlarge" the facility. "Treasurer's Report," *Eighth Annual Report*, 14, 29.
55. *Eighth Annual Report*, 14. In addition to the extra beds, the boys were also offered a new amenity in the form of a "private lock closet." Although the possessions of vagrant street boys were meager, the lads relished having a private safe in which to stow what they did own.
56. *Eighth Annual Report*, 15.
57. *Seventh Annual Report*, 14.
58. *Twelfth Annual Report*, 22
59. Kenneth T. Jackson, *The Encyclopedia of New York City*, 2nd ed. (New Haven, CT: Yale University Press, 2010), 377.
60. Edward K. Spann, *Gotham at War: New York City, 1860–1865* (Wilmington, DE: Scholarly Resources, Inc., 2002), 96.
61. Iver Bernstein, *The New York City Draft Riots: Their significance for American Society and Politics in the Age of Civil War* (New York: Oxford University Press, 1990), 8.
62. Edwin G. Burrows and Mike Wallace, *Gotham: A History of New York City to 1898* (New York: Oxford University Press, 1999), 888.
63. Spann, *Gotham at War*, 95.
64. Stephen O'Connor, *Orphan Trains: The Story of Charles Loring Brace and the Children He Saved and Failed* (New York: Houghton-Mifflin, 2001), 214.
65. O'Connor, *Orphan Trains*, 214. Mr. Brace often told the story of an incident which occurred shortly after the riots when, "a deputation of hard-looking, heavy-drinking Irish women, the mothers of some twenty or thirty of the children" arrived at the door of Cottage Place, demanding the "exclusion of some colored children." According to Mr. Brace, Miss Macy, "In the most amiable and Quaker-like manner,

but with the firmness of the old Puritan stock from which she sprung, she assured them that, if every other scholar left, so long as the school remained it should never be closed to any child on account of color." The Irish women, "withdrew their children," but "soon after returned them." Charles Loring Brace, *The Dangerous Classes of New York and Twenty Years' Work Among Them*, 3rd ed. (New York: Wynkoop & Hallenbeck, 1880), 214.

66. Burroughs, 887–899; *Gotham: A History*; Spann, *Gotham at War,* 93–105; Jackson, *Encyclopedia of NYC*, 377–378.
67. *Eleventh Annual Report*, 3.
68. *Eleventh Annual Report*, 3.
69. *Eleventh Annual Report*, 5.
70. *Eleventh Annual Report*, 5.
71. See O'Connor, *Orphan Trains*, 168–171; Marilyn Irvin Holt, *The Orphan Trains: Placing Out in America* (Lincoln: University of Nebraska Press, 1992), 106–7.
72. John O'Grady, *Levi Silliman Ives: Pioneer Leader in Catholic Charities,* (New York: P. J. Kennedy, 1933), 65–66.
73. O'Grady, *Levi Silliman Ives*, 9–10.
74. O'Grady, *Levi Silliman Ives*, 63.
75. O'Grady, *Levi Silliman Ives*, 63.
76. O'Grady, *Levi Silliman Ives*, 62.
77. O'Grady, *Levi Silliman Ives*, 62.
78. O'Grady, *Levi Silliman Ives*, 72.
79. Joseph M. Hawes, *Children in Urban Society: Juvenile Delinquency in Nineteenth-Century America* (New York: Oxford University Press, 1971), 103; "The New Protectory for Destitute Catholic Children: Laying of the Corner-Stone at Westchester Village Yesterday, Addresses by Archbishop McCloskey and Dr. L. S. Ives," *The New York Times*, July 24, 1865; Holt, *The Orphan Trains*, 106–7.
80. O'Grady, *Levi Silliman Ives*, 80
81. O'Grady, *Levi Silliman Ives*, 81.
82. Brace, *The Dangerous*, 244.
83. Brace, *The Dangerous Classes*, 244.
84. The remaining boys were listed as seventy-one Protestants, two Methodists, two Jews, and a single Presbyterian.
85. Brace, *The Dangerous Classes*, 323.
86. Brace, *The Dangerous Classes*, 323.
87. Brace, *The Dangerous Classes*, 265.
88. Minutes of the Board of Trustees, December 16, 1863, vol. 4, 1861–1872, in Records of the Children's Aid Society, New-York Historical Society.
89. For example, in 1864, in the immediate aftermath of the resolution, twenty-one of the boys sent west had stayed at the lodging house for more than a year, including four that had lived there for over six years. Another twelve had lived there between two and four years.

90. Charles Loring Brace, "Early Diary of Charles Loring Brace, Founder of the Children's Aid Society" (unpublished, February 10, 1853–September 1855), April 28, 1853, in the Victor Remer Historical Archives of the Children's Aid Society (1836-2006). New-York Historical Society Archives. Guide to the Records of the Children's Aid Society, Series IV, vol. 38, New-York Historical Society.
91. An often-repeated story is of two boys who went west in the same emigration party in 1859. Both men eventually became governors of their respective home states, John Brady of Alaska and Andrew Burke of North Dakota.
92. Brace, *The Dangerous Classes*, 26.
93. Brace, *The Dangerous Classes*, 267.
94. Brace, *The Best Method*, 16.
95. Brace, *The Best Method*, 17.
96. While duly noting the problematic aspects of the CAS record books, it is interesting that of the 708 boys sent west from the NBLH, only 46 records, or about six percent, report any transgressions in the form of theft of either property or cash. This number includes every recorded incident whether serious or not and whether the boy was punished through legal intervention or merely scolded by the foster family. In short, the total number is within Mr. Brace's range of four to six percent failures.
97. Brace, *The Best Method*, 16.
98. Brace, *The Best Method*, 16.
99. William J. Phelps, *Michigan Comprehensive Plan for Juvenile Justice Services* (State of Michigan Office of Juvenile Justice Services, 1977), 1. According to Henry W. Thurston, Michigan would become the first state to "establish an exclusive state system for the care of all destitute children who became public charges" in 1874. Up until that point, the problem of delinquent, destitute or dependent children was left to local communities.
100. Phelps, *Michigan Comprehensive Plan*, 1.
101. Brace, *The Dangerous Classes*, 235.
102. Brace, *The Dangerous Classes*, 235.
103. Charles Loring Brace, The "Placing Out" Plan for Homeless and Vagrant Children. *Conference of Boards of Public Charity* (September 7, 1876), 136.
104. *Twenty-Fourth Annual Report of the Children's Aid Society* (New York: Wynkoop & Hallenbeck, 1876), 8.
105. *Twenty-Fourth Annual Report*, 8.
106. Brace, *The Best Method*, 16–17.
107. In Indiana, Mr. Fry visited the North Indiana State Penitentiary (Michigan City), South Indiana State Penitentiary (Jeffersonville), House for Friendless and Woman's Prison (Richmond), Orphan Asylum (Richmond), Home for the Friendless (Richmond), Reformatory Institution for Woman and Girls (Indianapolis), and Indiana State Reform School (Plainfield).

108. In Illinois, Mr. Fry visited the State Penitentiary (Joliet), State Reform School (Pontiac), House of Correction (Chicago), and House of Refuge (Chicago).
109. In Michigan, Mr. Fry visited the Michigan State Public School for Dependent Children (Coldwater), State Reform School (Lansing), Michigan State Penitentiary (Jackson), and Detroit House of Correction (Detroit).
110. *Twenty-Fourth Annual Report*, 58.
111. Martin Wolins and Irving Piliavin, *Institution or Foster Family: A Century of Debate* (New York: Child Welfare League of Merica, 1964), 7.
112. Henry W. Thurston, *The Dependent Child: A Story of Changing Aims and Methods in the Care of Dependent Children* (New York: Columbia University Press, 1930), 127–28. In finding fault with Brace's methodology, Thurston has argued that absent definitive proof that placed children were "paupers or criminals in the clutches of the law," he believed "their lot was certainly better than it would have been had they remained in New York City." This is undoubtedly true. In addition, Brace possessed at least as much evidence of the emigration branch's success as its failure. Other concerns raised at these conferences had to do with CAS's national reach. Many delegates believed that each state ought to responsible for the care of its own dependent children.
113. Brace, *The Dangerous Classes*, 242.
114. Brace, *The Dangerous Classes*, 242.
115. Mr. Brace began exploring other avenues for older boys although not all of them came to fruition during his lifetime. First, he became a vocal critic of New-York's trade unions which refused entry to poor boys, systematically excluding them from their ranks by denying them apprenticeship training and employment. Second, he began developing plans to open a CAS-run farm school, to train boys in agricultural and livestock practices before trying to find them employment as farmers. The farm school would eventually grow into another major arm of CAS operations after Mr. Brace's death. In the longer term, there is also some evidence CAS forged a relationship with Cornell University's cooperative extension program, seeking to further boys' practical education.

9

A Permanent Place

BUILDING, BRIDGING, AND POLICY ADVOCACY IN THE
GILDED AGE

> *How to make our legislation, our reformatory expedients, and our charity, not exceptional and temporary, but in harmony with the great principles of political economy and the great impulse of human nature?*
> —CHARLES LORING BRACE, *The Best Method of Disposing of Our Pauper and Vagrant Children*, 1859

ON OCTOBER 16, 1867, Mr. Brace launched the next major phase in the evolution of the NBLH when he presented a resolution to the CAS board of trustees asking that "the Society endeavor to raise a fund for the purpose of procuring a building for a permanent Lodging House for the News Boys."[1] The resolution contained a proviso that "no funds intended for the general work of the Society be diverted to this object." From the start, the trustees had been financially conservative, unwilling to invest in real estate "till firmly established." As CAS was now confident in the success of its lodging house model and the financial footing of the entire organization, the time seemed right to take this next bold step. With the resolution unanimously passed, CAS launched its first major capital campaign.

Mr. Brace made two basic arguments for investing in real estate. The first was programmatic: "We need a building of our own, fitted up expressly for the work we are called upon to perform." Converting loft space in a commercial building had worked for a while, but it wasn't really adequate for feeding, sheltering, and educating hundreds of boys. Mr. Brace's second argument was economic. Continually adapting the rental space was expensive. He argued that a new building "would in a few years, pay for itself by saving many expenses, such as rent, repairs, and alterations, which we are daily incurring."[2]

The fund-raising campaign, and the subsequent hunt for a new location, would take seven years. During that time, CAS encountered a new reason for investing in its own property when the NBLH received a "notice to quit" from the landlord of the Sun Building. For the O'Connors, this wasn't altogether unwelcome news. Even with the makeshift expansion to the fifth floor, the facility was still "too small and inconvenient for the great number of homeless lads gathered there."[3] Nonetheless, caught between the building campaign and the eviction notice, the NBLH had to find a temporary home. The trustees leased the top four floors of a nearby property at 49 and 51 Park Place for five years. Renovating the premises was costly and the move, disruptive. Mr. Brace complained that it "greatly crippled . . . our work during the months of May, June, and July" of 1869.[4]

Nonetheless, Park Place was a "great improvement upon the cramped accommodations of the Sun building."[5] The upper two floors "were reserved for the sleeping quarters" and could comfortably "accommodate 260 boys a night."[6] More important, the building had an adequate supply of water, with three baths and several washrooms, all "supplied with hot and cold water" capable of meeting the needs of hundreds of grimy, sweaty street boys.[7] Heat and hot water were supplied by new technology, "a steam boiler on the lower story," and there were large "water-vats into which the many barrelsful used daily by the lodgers" were "pumped by the engine."[8] In addition, Mrs. O'Connor had a separate laundry room.

The Park Place facility offered other improvements. One floor contained a kitchen and a dining hall that comfortably sat 150 boys. There was "a large lecture-room" for the night school and an additional room fitted up as a gymnasium.[9] No longer must the schoolroom double as exercise space, something Mr. O'Connor had complained about for years. The best part—from the O'Connors' perspective—may have been the separate superintendent's apartment, located on the premises. There was a servant's room for the increasing numbers of employees who helped the O'Connors wait tables, clean, cook, and perform night watchman duties. Despite these improvements, the society's trustees remained convinced that CAS ought "not be at the mercy of landlords."[10]

**

Real Estate Investment

Mr. Brace and other CAS officers, particularly Mr. John Earl Williams, its treasurer, worked hard on the capital campaign. They promoted the project in circulars, newspaper articles, annual reports, and private appeals. "It seems now the time to put this excellent charity on a permanent basis," Mr. Brace argued. "Some benevolent person may feel it a privilege to endow such an Institution as a Home for homeless lads, for all future generations."[11]

In addition to appealing directly to the public, the trustees also "petitioned the Legislature."[12] Their efforts were rewarded in May 1868, when the legislature appropriated "*Thirty Thousand Dollars*" for "the erection of a LODGING HOUSE FOR THE NEWSBOYS" to be paid "out of the Excise Fund" of the city as long as "a *like sum of Thirty Thousand Dollars* shall be raised by the CHILDREN'S AID SOCIETY." The guaranteed matching fund became a marketing tool. Shortly after the announcement, one donor responded, "My Dear Brother Macy . . . now a law has been passed appropriating $30,000 . . . provided other gifts are made to an equal amount. My wife and I want the privilege of placing something there. Accept then from us for that object the enclosed fifty dollars, and oblige us."[13]

Many donations were more modest and subscribers expressed regret that they couldn't afford more. A single dollar came with this note: "Your work is a noble one, and I would be glad to do much more than I can."[14] Ten dollars came from Illinois with a message that said, "Hoping that it may aid, though it be but little."[15] Another ten came from two sisters in Kalamazoo, who were not rich in "worldly goods, but feeling that each should contribute as God hath given us in store, to provide for the homeless among us."[16] Although small in size the donations also reflected the growing national presence of CAS and its fund-raising reach well beyond New-York's city limits.

Mr. Brace welcomed the show of support demonstrated by each small donation. Nonetheless, he and his trustees also turned to New-York's increasingly ostentatious monied class for more substantial gifts. He circulated a pledge book among them. Mr. J. J. Astor responded with a note on family letterhead, adding his "name to those already in it, for $500," but declining to further forward the request. "I regret that I cannot present the book to my Father, but he is so constantly applied to, that I make it a rule to lay nothing before him, if I can possible avoid it."[17]

Mr. Theodore Roosevelt Sr., a new CAS trustee and chair of the committee on the building fund, actively promoted the cause among his family and friends. Mr. Roosevelt had joined the board in 1868 and immediately taken a special interest in the newsboys. The building committee would be the first of his many efforts on their behalf. On June 11, 1868, he sent a note to Mr. Brace: "Enclosed is check for $250.00 from Mrs. William E. Dodge for News

Boys Lodging House." He added, "This need not interfere with Mr. Booth's effort to obtain a large subscription from Mr. William E. Dodge."[18]

It took CAS less than two years to reach its target goal. In 1869, Mr. Williams announced that thirty thousand dollars had been "contributed, and paid into the Treasury by individuals, towards securing a Newsboys' Lodging-House."[19] He promptly applied for the matching funds "entitled the Society, by Act of the Legislature" and, thus, the additional amount "was duly paid to the Treasurer."[20]

Even with sixty thousand dollars in the CAS coffers, the trustees were hesitant "to purchase any property at the present prices of real estate."[21] Instead, Mr. Williams invested the money in "first-class securities," keeping the fund "separated from the ordinary assets of the Children's Aid Society."[22] One happy result was that "the interest on the fund" was "about equal to the rent now paid" of five thousand dollars per annum for the "excellent quarters at 49 and 51 Park Place."[23] Contributions continued to be added to the principal, and eventually the account balance crept up to ninety thousand dollars.

In the meantime, Mr. Brace, Mr. Roosevelt, and the building committee searched in earnest for the perfect site at the right price. The search continued until 1872, when, after considerable haggling, CAS purchased the old Shakespeare Hotel on William Street at the corner of Duane and [New] Chambers, at a cost of sixty-five thousand dollars."[24] Fortuitously, a second property, the "lot and house" at 7 Duane Street "in the rear of the Shakespeare Hotel" at the "corner of Duane and Reade," also became available. Although its purchase was not part of the original plan, the trustees immediately capitalized on the opportunity. Driving a hard bargain for the adjoining property, they purchased it "on very favorable terms" for an additional fourteen thousand dollars.[25] The net result was that by combining the adjacent properties and demolishing the two existing structures, CAS could construct an entirely new lodging house, designed specifically for its purposes, on a large wedge of prime New-York real estate.[26]

Taking yet another financial plunge, the trustees hired a prominent architect, Leopold Eidlitz—whose works included churches, synagogues, and commercial and civic spaces—to design the building.[27] They entered into a contract "for the erection there of a Newsboys' Lodging-House, at an expense of about ninety thousand dollars."[28] Despite the financial burden, the trustees were delighted. Mr. Brace claimed that "a better location, it is believed, could not have been found, if the Society had had a whole city to choose from." He triumphantly concluded that "this building may be considered as making a fixture of the Newsboys' Lodging-House for a century to come."[29]

***

A Permanent Lodging House for Newsboys

The grand opening of the new facility in July 1874 was a feted affair. In attendance were some of CAS's most prominent benefactors. Notably absent were the boys themselves, although that ended up being a source of amusement for the entire evening. Several speakers came prepared to address a younger audience, resulting in a rash of apologies and "dexterously" altered remarks.[30]

When the boys finally moved in, they found a spectacular facility. As always, safety, security, and sanitation were the highest priorities. CAS remained committed to proper ventilation. Having taken down two buildings to erect the NBLH, the new facility was "central, on high ground" and "open to air and light on three sides." Most innovative of all, CAS declared the building "perfectly safe in case of fire" and that "its means of exit [were] ample."[31] They went to extra lengths in this regard, incurring an additional expense of $3,300 to contract for "a fireproof stairway" and two points of egress, "one public and one private," with "the public entrance" being "fireproof."[32]

Fires remained a serious problem, and the NBLH had had one close encounter. On the night of February 14, 1860, thirty-one volunteer firemen responded to an alarm at "eight-thirty in the evening" at "Fulton and Nassau."[33] Johnny Morrow, a lodger at the time, recalled the fire occurring "when tired and weary newsboys were in their beds." He reported the lodgers woke up to screams of "Fire! FIRE! FIRE! The Sun Building is on fire! Rouse up! Wake up, boys!"[34] Chaos ensued. Many boys tried to grab their meager possessions and one suggested that the savings bank be "carried down."[35] Eventually, the lodgers received word that their "own part of the building [was] yet safe" and returned to bed.[36] Nonetheless, the next morning, they discovered the structure next door had been "consumed to the ground" and "there was nothing in its place but a smoking heap of ruins."[37] So it wasn't altogether surprising the trustees went to extra expense to fireproof its facilities.

The new NBLH was enormous. Each of its seven floors encompassed 6,540 square feet of space. The basement and ground floor were designed as commercial space to be rented out so the income would "contribute in some measure to render the establishment self-supporting."[38] Mr. Williams observed that "it is not—it never has been—the policy of the Children's Aid Society to have a permanent debt."[39]

The rest of the building was specifically designed with program needs in mind. On the second floor was a kitchen and a dining hall with tables capable of accommodating four hundred boys. In addition, there was an apartment for the superintendent's family and a servants' hall. The third floor contained a large schoolroom, sometimes called the "audience-room," which had a "seating capacity for 500 boys."[40] Attached to this space were the boys' bath and washrooms, as well as water closets. Dormitories were located on the fourth and fifth floors and could accommodate six hundred boys.[41] To upgrade the residence, all the old wooden bunk beds were replaced with double-decker iron bed stands and arranged with "ample space between them." Servants' rooms were also located on the fifth floor. The top floor contained a "well-fitted gymnasium."[42] It also housed laundry and drying rooms.

A *New York Times* reporter observed that the building was "in all respects suitably furnished with every modern improvement."[43] Mr. Brace concluded that it was "probably the most complete structure for its purpose anywhere existing."[44] There is no doubt that this facility stood in stunning contrast to other congregate care facilities for poor children, including the city's asylums, reformatories, and prisons, even though the NBLH promised to shelter, feed, educate, and care for hundreds of very similar children every night.

***

The Charles and Mary O'Connor Years

Despite two moves and a new home, the NBLH continued to serve much the same clientele,[45] and its program structure remained basically the same. The lodgers were admitted to the building by a watchman at 5:30 every evening and climbed the stairs to the third-floor audience room. Here they paid six cents for their room and another six cents for board.[46] Mr. O'Connor had also initiated an "upper ten" option for the older boys. The fifth floor contained a separate dormitory with "16 small rooms" with "curtains drawn on walnut bars" to offer some privacy.[47] Boys in the "upper ten" could rent these relatively private spaces at ten cents a night.

As always, the point of the payment was "to create a feeling of independence." However, "a large number of needy and worthy boys" who could not "afford to pay" were "received gratuitously."[48] In addition, the long-held practice of extending loans to impoverished boys was formalized. In the early 1860s, the Howland Loaning Fund was established with a gift from trustee Benjamin J. Howland.[49] Most loans were under twelve cents, although a single youth could be awarded as much as fifty dollars with unanimous approval of the fund's executive committee.[50] As was so often the case, data obtained from this initiative were used to CAS advantage. Mr. Williams kept close track of the monies loaned and repaid and the profits made. For example, in 1863, he reported that seven hundred boys had borrowed $282.71 and only "seventy-five cents remained uncollected" although he believed that "not a cent [would] eventually be lost." Even better, the boys "made a profit of

$428.97 in the use of it!"[51] So yet another outcome measure was used to sell the advantages of CAS's program to the public, minor investments generated considerable profit.

Whatever his financial situation, each boy who entered the NBLH received a "check" for lodging and meals as well as a key to a small locked closet where he could store his coat, cap, and possessions. After registration, the boys retreated to the schoolroom, where they could mingle or read or play a game of chess, checkers, or mills until dinner. The regulars knew to grab the front-row seats, assuring that they would be first in line when the dinner bell rang at seven o'clock.

At suppertime, several hundred boys lined up to go downstairs to the dining hall. Dinner, while often only a simple meal of baked beans with pork, bread, butter, pie, and coffee or tea, was plentiful and each boy could eat "as much as" he wished.[52] One resident claimed it was "a splendid meal for six cents." The meals were served by waitresses, a fact so notable that one evening, when the boys were charged with writing an essay describing their day at the lodging house, the scholars took note. One wrote, "Three happy + obliging girls . . . wait on us with style." Another wrote, "4 handsome young ladies (names omitted)" were the "pride of the House."[53]

After dinner, the boys returned to the third floor schoolroom. Evening classes were taught by several salaried, professional educators.[54] The teachers were licensed by either "City or State authorities" and the school was "under the supervision and control of the Board of Education."[55] By this time, CAS was mixing state and municipal financial support with private donations. Mr. Brace believed that "the best course for permanently and efficiency of a charity" included this mixed support, "to make it depend in part on the state, that it may have a solid foundation of support, and be under official supervision, and in part on private aid, so that it may feel the enthusiasm and activity and responsibility of individual effort."[56]

The once-a-month opening of the newsboys' savings bank continued to provide entertainment of the highest order. Mr. O'Connor had sweetened the pot—and extended the financial lessons—by awarding "5% interest on savings deposits."[57] Yet another CAS trustee, Robert J. Livingston, had established an account to provide a prize to the boy who saved the most in any given month. Mr. Brace observed that the prizes "created a feeling of emulation, and induce a saving spirit."[58] All of these initiatives built on CAS's primary design of offering incentives and providing positive reinforcement to shape behavior. The number of depositors increased so dramatically—by 1870 there were over 1,065—that they far outgrew Mr. Tracy's original custom-built walnut table.

Mr. Brace noted that it would "require us to build a larger one."[59] At evening's end, the boys recited the Lord's Prayer and at nine o'clock they retired to what one lodger described as their "elegant beds" (although the *New York Times* described the beds as "plain, but at the same time shapely and durable").[60]

The boys were roused first thing in the morning by the night watchman, who made sure they were washed, dressed, and down the stairs by 6:30 for an unlimited breakfast of bread and butter with coffee or tea. Then they were out the door to work. All told, "the house," declared one of the residents, was "the best of any of its kind in the world."[61]

***

New Directions: Inspirations from a Charity Fair

In May 1865, Mr. Brace had attended the International Reformatory Exhibition in London, hosted by the Prince of Wales.[62] It was a "world fair" of charity work with delegations from Germany, France, Italy, Great Britain, Egypt, Syria, and Portugal. As Mr. Brace addressed his international colleagues, he voiced his characteristic refrain against asylums, refuges, and work houses. As would be expected, he promoted CAS's lodging houses, industrial schools, and placing out system, arguing that they were consistent with both "natural" and "economic laws of nature."

In his presentation, Mr. Brace described New-York as "the sink of all nations," noting that poor children were often "cast adrift on the streets" due to parental poverty or death.[63] "We know," he argued, "that the very existence of a republic depends on its having 'no dangerous class'—no lower stratum of ignorance, poverty, and vagabondism, such as becomes at last fixed and not to be reached by ordinary moral and social influences." This argument contained traces of Darwin's influence on Mr. Brace's philanthropic thinking.[64] He rejected the notion that "bad traits" were inherited by poor children as fixed characteristics. Instead, he asserted that they developed when children were exposed to poor environmental conditions, such as overcrowded urban neighborhoods. The solution, he told his colleagues, was to "elevate and educate this great class of poor and street children." To that end, he informed his audience, CAS had been opened as "a preventive movement against these evils."[65]

In addition to making his usual argument about the unique economic advantages of the United States due to its "unlimited demand for labor," he offered an evaluation of American society. He insisted that its "ruling class... the great forces of the nation—[those] which govern its councils and rule its foreign policy, as well as shape its domestic character"—were not to be found in a wealthy aristocracy as in Europe. They resided rather "in the class of small rural freeholders—the farmers... as by a misnomer we call them."[66] CAS's charity work was designed to give poor children access to this stratum of American society.

Once back in the United States, Mr. Brace's took stock of what he had learned from his international colleagues. He felt confident that CAS's programing was superior to that of its European counterparts because of its primary focus on prevention, promoting self-sufficiency and independence. However, he had to admit that the United States lagged behind Europe in two areas: the sanitary improvement of its cities and legislative reform.[67] Inspired, Mr. Brace began steering CAS toward more active participation in policy advocacy.

***

Policy Advocacy: Child Labor, Education, and Housing

CAS joined the fight for legislative reform in education, child labor, and housing. During the 1870s and 1880s, its efforts would be only moderately successful. In general progressive reformers faced powerful political headwinds. They were also confronted by several interconnected social problems that needed to be thoughtfully untwined. While *enforced* education seemed an obvious solution, it immediately gave rise to the related issue of child labor. Poor families were dependent on their children's earnings. This economic reality kept children from attending school regularly, if at all.

New York State had, in theory, embraced compulsory education in 1853 when it passed a truancy law. However, in the same legislative session, it failed to pass any factory regulations.[68] As Mr. Brace noted, no "Police Judge would sentence a lad or young girl to punishment who was supporting by steady industry a poor old mother or starving brothers and sisters." Moreover, not even "the police themselves" could "be depended upon for executing any law which was so oppressive on a hard-working class of children."[69] The net result was that in reality, there was no truancy enforcement in New-York. For a compulsory education measure to be successful it would have to be tied to child labor regulations. Mr. Brace's evaluation of workable policy, like all of his endeavors, was grounded in a realistic appraisal of the conditions of the poor and the search for practical ways to support them while also promoting his objectives, education being one of them.

The complexity didn't end there. Child labor itself was a triple-headed hydra, each with it its own "attendant evils."[70] First, there was factory labor. New-York was a major industrial center in a leading industrial state.[71] For example, in the city, Mr. Brace estimated that as many as fifteen hundred children under the age of fifteen worked in the paper collar industry alone. CAS agents had found children as young as "*only four years of age*" in the tobacco factories. Mr. Brace argued that "a child put at hard work in this way is ... stunted in growth or enfeebled in health."[72] He added, "The employer is in the habit of getting labor where he can find it, and does not much consider whether he is allowing his little employees the time and leisure sufficient for preparing themselves for life."[73]

A second form of child labor had taken root in the tenements. In Mr. Brace's words, "a considerable amount of factory labor is performed in the city within the rooms and dwellings of the poor, and these private workshops are not sufficiently inspected, and are often crowded with very young children."[74] This diffuse system of child sweatshop labor added another layer of complexity.

Finally, a third variety of child labor included the street traders who worked independently of employers, "selling newspapers, blackening boots, sweeping cross-walks, gathering refuse, peddling, and playing harps and hand-organs." These occupations, Mr. Brace noted, were "necessities in the city, supporting a vast number of people who would otherwise be semi-paupers" and they could not "be utterly broken up without great hardship."[75] Nonetheless, this kind of labor was a different creature and required different kinds of legislative approaches.

With considerable zeal, CAS tackled these complexities by turning to one of its trustees, legal counsel Charles E. Whitehead, directing him to draft a bill. Mr. Whitehead's proposal would be comprehensive, thoughtful, and progressive. For those reasons, it was also doomed to fail.

***

Mr. Whitehead's CAS Factory Bill

In 1871 the Whitehead factory bill was introduced to the New York State legislature and CAS threw its full advocacy weight behind it. In addition to prohibiting employment of the youngest children in factories—a pipe dream that would not come to pass for decades—and regulating the hours of older youth, the bill mandated minimum workplace safety standards, sought to protect families from undue financial hardship while still enforcing compulsory education laws, increased accountability, and imposed sanctions for violations. The bill, as drafted, had thirteen separate sections, each attempting to carefully address various aspects of the complex problem.

Among other things, it prohibited the employment of children under age ten in "any manufactory or mechanical shop" and no child under twelve could be employed unless able to "intelligibly read." Youth under age sixteen were barred from working more than sixty hours a week and after four o'clock on Saturday afternoon and on five protected holidays (New Year's Day, Christmas, Fourth of July, Washington's Birthday, and Thanksgiving).

Second, the bill linked child labor with compulsory education, limiting the employment of children aged ten to sixteen to nine months per year and requiring three months of school. Significantly, this school requirement could also be met through "part-time" attendance, three hours per day for six months. For families with more than one child aged twelve to sixteen and in which "the labor of such children [was] essential to the maintenance of the family," the children were sequentially rotated through the school requirement so that each child was guaranteed an education. The part-time school option allowed children from poor families to continue to work year round. Overall, the bill sought to strike a balance between protecting family income and insisting on minimum education for children. Also significant, boys and girls were treated equally throughout.

Third, the bill mandated independent record keeping by school authorities and employers. Factory inspectors were authorized to enter the premises "at all working-hours." Furthermore, the bill vested oversight in a salaried "Inspector of Factory Children" appointed by the state governor. The inspector was required to "report annually to the Legislature."[76] In theory, at least, this would permit cross-checking the records.

Fourth, Mr. Whitehead's bill took tentative steps to regulate workplace safety. It required any factory employing children to "be thoroughly painted or whitewashed, lighted and cleaned as the character of the business will permit." More significant, it called for "all trap-doors or elevators, and all shafting, belting, wheels, and machinery running by steam, water, or other motive power, in rooms or places in a factory" in which children were "employed, or through which they [had] to pass" to "be protected by iron screens, or by suitable partitions during all the time when such doors are open, and while such machinery is in motion." Given the number of fatalities and serious disabilities caused by dangerous factory conditions, this provision reflected a significant first step.

Finally, the bill recommended penalties for noncompliance. Teachers who gave false reports of school attendance could be charged with a misdemeanor. Financial penalties ranged from five dollars to one hundred dollars, depending on the violation. Fines could be levied against parents, teachers, and employers. The steepest were imposed for failing to keep records and certificates of school attendance, giving false reports of attendance, and refusing to permit an inspector's entrance to a factory. Finally, the act was to be "printed and hung in each factory," enabling workers to familiarize themselves with its provisions and their legal rights.[77]

CAS agents lobbied long and hard for the Whitehouse bill, taking their advocacy to the state capitol and to the public. The bill was introduced in each legislative session between 1871 to 1876 and defeated every time.[78] Mr. Brace was infuriated. He blamed its failure on "the selfish maneuvers of two or three members, who supposed their interests to be endangered by the Law."[79] In reality there were a number of political forces at work against child labor reform. In 1873, the ever-optimistic Mr. Brace insisted to CAS supporters that it was "not possible to believe that a humane and Christian community [would] ultimately permit it to be defeated."[80] In the short term, he was wrong.

In the end, CAS abandoned the Whitehead bill, choosing instead to try to embed various provisions from it in amendments to other legislation. However, Mr. Brace complained bitterly about the short-sighted nature of this failure for years. In 1880, he wrote, "Hundreds of children, often under 12 years of age, are withdrawn from our schools to labor their 10 hours a day in factories and shops." He added, "Our society presented seven or eight years since, a form of an Act, designed to remedy these evils," but it was rejected.[81]

It wasn't until fifteen years after the Whitehead proposal's debut that the state enacted its first major child labor law, and even then it was limited in scope. The 1886 factory bill "prohibited children under thirteen from working in manufacturing establishments (factories engaged in the actual manufacture of goods)."[82] However, it did not extend its protection to other forms of child labor involving employment in offices, stores, or street trades.

***

Enforced Education, Truancy, and School Funding

While it took New York until 1886 to focus on child labor, the state took a tentative step to link the compulsory education of children with industrial labor in 1874. This law "required children between the ages of eight and fourteen to attend school fourteen weeks a year, of which at least eight must be consecutive."[83] Businesses were not supposed to employ children without being shown a certificate establishing that they had met the educational requirement, and employers were required to maintain records to that effect.[84] One big problem was that the law's entire enforcement was placed not in the hands of an independent factory inspector but rather in the hands of unpaid school trustees.[85]

Voicing a common refrain, Mr. Brace declared the law far inferior to Mr. Whitehead's failed factory bill. Nonetheless, he pledged "hearty cooperation" from CAS.[86] At very least, Mr. Brace believed the law secured "to an immense class of industrious and poor children in our shops and factories one of the most essential rights—the right to education."[87]

Yet two years later, CAS faced a threat to its educational programs. The society had long relied on funds allocated from the "State School Fund" to help finance its schools. In 1876, state legislators contemplated two constitutional amendments. The first would prohibit sectarian schools—those that engaged in "dogmatic teaching" and failed to operate under "the rules and regulations of the State or City authorities of education"—from receiving funds.

Variations on this battle had existed for decades. Since the 1830s, Catholic and Protestant reformers had collided over educational institutions. At the heart of the debate was the question of whether or not the King James Bible, favored by Protestant educators, would be used in school classes. Catholics adamantly objected to this intrusion on their faith and religious freedom. As a practical result, parallel networks of Christian parochial schools developed in New-York, operated by either Catholic or Protestant authorities.

Despite the society's Protestant leanings, Mr. Brace was not concerned with this proposed constitutional amendment because CAS schools were fully compliant with it on both counts. First, he insisted that "great care [was] taken to conform to the rules and regulations of the Board of Education." Second, although the Bible was read, it was done "without note or comment," and no "sectarian doctrine" was taught.[88] The school day started with "the Lord's Prayer and a song," but all "hymns of a dogmatic character" were avoided.[89] Finally, Mr. Brace argued that the society's teachers were "of all sects, some few even being Jews and Catholics."[90]

More concerning to Mr. Brace was the alternative constitutional proposal, which would prohibit private charitable schools from receiving public funds altogether. CAS lobbied against this measure based on three arguments. First, the proposal would "shut out from a share" of state funds schools that were "designed for our poorest children." Second, it would effectively deny education to the poor because "thousands of children" were already excluded from public schools "through want of room." Finally, it would divert funds from the city to Upstate New York. Support for poor children in the city would then be redirected to "children well enough off in the country." The net result, concluded Mr. Brace, "would be providing for the rich, while shutting out the poor." [91]

CAS officers had long been concerned with questions of educational access. The battle took two forms. First, CAS argued for universal schooling for young children and was vocal in its support of "the lower schools," fretting that the youngest children were "not properly cared for."[92] Investment was directed at "scholars in the upper Departments." This left "tens of thousands" of younger children "out in the cold."[93] CAS trustees were appalled, saying, "This ought not to be. It is a crying evil."[94] Mr. Williams argued that if "there [was] one principle more essential than another to the establishment and perpetuation of a Republican form of government" it was "that the masses . . . should have education." He added, "To this end, it is indispensable that primary instruction . . . be extended to every member of the community, 'without fear, favor, or hope of reward.'"[95]

Second, CAS schools had always operated according to three interrelated objectives. One was to provide a rudimentary common education. The second was to provide basic skill training to promote responsible behavior and independence. The third was to partially provide for children's basic needs. Based on these objectives, Mr. Brace made five arguments against public schools. First, they could not "feed or clothe" poor children nor did they have "facilities for cleaning them." Second, they could not "readily teach them a branch of industry." Third, they couldn't accommodate the "necessary irregularity of attendance" of poor children. Fourth, they did not "want verminous and ragged children side by side with the children of respectable mechanics." Finally, they had "no agents to pluck them up and their teachers [had] not the time to reform them."[96] Although Mr. Brace essentially advocated for a separate educational system for poor children that could appear to create a caste system, his reasons were based in his fear that lack of tolerance, access, and expertise in the public system would effectively exclude poor children from education altogether. It was the discriminatory impact of this exclusion of the poor that he objected to.

As for this proposed constitutional amendment, Mr. Brace concluded that "we can not but believe that the present Legislature will so word this amendment" as to retain public support from charitable schools.[97] In the end, he was right. The amendment did not deny public funding to charitable schools, thereby protecting the society's claim on an allocation of public money to help support its academic programs.

***

Street Trades: An Education and Labor Problem

In 1877 truant officers delivered 289 children to CAS schools as part their compulsory education enforcement efforts. Unsatisfied, Mr. Brace had this to say: "But these are a bagatelle to the multitude of children who are apparently engaged in street occupations, and never go to school at all."[98] Therein lay another dimension of the child labor problem.

CAS advocated for amending the existing law to require street traders to carry a permit and give police officers "the right . . . to arrest a street wandering boy or girl" who could not produce a certificate of at least part-time school attendance.[99] Once detained the child would make "an appearance before a Police justice who could either sentence the child to a reformatory as a vagrant" or "release him on sufficient guarantee that he will, in the future, attend some Half-time school."[100] While the use of threat to compel compliance was unusual for Mr. Brace, he was hopeful that the police would serve as truant officer and the child promise future good behavior. The result would be to increase attendance in CAS schools, not increased incarceration in the almshouse. He felt certain the proposal would even gain the "co-operation of the Catholic priests," because "attendance at half-time church schools would be sufficient to show that the child was not a vagrant."[101] Only after such reform, Mr. Brace concluded, would there be "universal school-training in New York."[102] Nonetheless, efforts to regulate street trades would fail to garner legislative support and not come to fruition until after the turn of the twentieth century.[103]

***

Housing Reform

Tenement house conditions in New-York remained miserable even in the late 1870s. Mr. Brace acknowledged the need for "radical improvement" but, for the most part, he left this advocacy to other reformers.[104] However, there was one area of housing that did receive CAS attention. It involved the "low, semi-criminal lodging houses" that existed along the Bowery. These facilities sheltered young boys with adult men. It bothered Mr. Brace that the boys "were permitted to come in at any hour of the night, to gamble all night and sleep in the day." The facilities "were poor and verminous." Nonetheless, they were "attractive to the boys because they themselves were left entirely free of restraint." Of course, Mr. Brace was not in favor of restraint, as employed by asylums, but he was concerned about the lack of responsible adult supervision and unstructured hours of the adult lodging houses.

Mr. Whitehead and Mr. Brace journeyed to Albany to lobby. Here they were met with swift dismissal. Their proposals were rejected for being too "sweeping and arbitrary" and because under common law it was difficult "to recognize the lodging houses as distinct from the hotel."[105] Undeterred, the men redirected their efforts. Rather than focus on legislative reform, they began to lobby for more stringent licensing regulations with the Board of Health.

They invited public health officials to the NBLH to listen to the stories of "some of the boys who had been in these miserable resorts."[106] CAS lodging house superintendents testified before the health board. Eventually, the officials were persuaded. In 1888, the Board of Health issued a notice to the proprietors of all "Men's Lodging Houses" in New-York, which read as follows:

> Notice is hereby given to the proprietors of Men's Lodging Houses, conducted under permits of the Board of Health, that it is not intended that the number of lodgers allowed by such permits shall include women under any circumstances, nor boys under sixteen years of age unless accompanied by their fathers or legal male guardians. If these conditions are violated, and women or boys are admitted to Men's Lodging Houses, the Board of Health will promptly revoke the permits thus abused.[107]

Mr. Brace noted the new regulation with satisfaction. "The great evil from the crowding of small boys and older ruffians in cheap lodging-houses has been much lessened," he said, and the action resulted in breaking up "most of those haunts in the neighborhood of the Bowery where men and boys were lodged together."[108]

***

Bridging the Class Divide in a Gilded Age

Mr. Brace considered all this legislative drafting, lobbying, and general advocacy on behalf of the poor part of being "active in the labor of charity."

Although the CAS board of trustees were professionals in their own right—bankers, lawyers, judges, and merchants—there was a long-established expectation of service as well. So, in addition to external advocacy, CAS officers and trustees made regular appearances at the lodging houses and industrial schools, reporting their experiences back to the full board.

Many were tireless in their efforts, such as Mr. Roosevelt. Mr. Brace once recalled urging an ailing Mr. Roosevelt to *share* the burden he had placed upon himself by visiting the boys at the lodging house every single Sunday. Mr. Roosevelt replied resolutely, "I cannot; the fact is, Mr. Brace, I have such a troublesome conscience, I must be there every Sunday evening to really influence the boys."[109] He once sent a check to Mr. Brace for one hundred dollars along with this note: "Will you please send me Monday next a short sketch employing an outline of your views with regard to the best shape our efforts in organizing the charity can be carried out."[110] These actions were characteristic of Mr. Roosevelt. Referring to him, his colleagues would later say: "There is given to some men such a rare combination of thought and actions, that the two processes become almost identical; and when these are associated with high moral purpose, the results are of a character which exceed estimation."[111]

Mr. Brace himself frequently participated in the NBLH Sunday meetings, or "talks," as he called them.[112] Over time, he developed a philosophy about speaking to the newsboys. "The street-boy can not listen to abstract truth: he must have concrete," he said. "Facts and realities are what he needs, and especially the teaching of parables, or dramatic and illustrative modes of instruction."[113] He argued for the need to portray "CHRIST to those boys as a living PERSONALITY, present with them."[114] Lessons could not be doctrinal but rather must be "living Scriptural facts and illustrations of truth."[115]

In keeping with this belief, Mr. Brace shrouded biblical parables in recognizable garb, such as the tale of the rich man and Lazarus. His version featured a selfish rich boy who lived in a handsome house on Fifth Avenue with many servants. The boy had the finest clothes, best food, toys, a pony, and a dog. The poor boy, on the other hand, was the son of ragpicker, a half-orphan with a pious mother. He cared for a lame dog, helped a little street sweeper, and "seemed to love every body and to be always thinking of others and not of himself."[116]

Mr. Brace's "talks" were rarely judgmental. He understood the motivations for boys' vices, such as petty theft, gambling, drinking, and swearing. So his Sunday lessons featured the lure of stealing an apple from an unattended cart, or the temptation of short-changing a gentleman who had accidently overpaid for a newspaper, or using the Lord's name in vain out of habit or in an attempt to imitate older boys. Mr. Brace never minimized the magnitude of the dilemma facing the boys and often sympathized. Nonetheless, he tried to gently nudge his audience to consider the greater rewards of resisting temptations, suggesting small virtuous acts and often using the boys' kindnesses to each other by way of illustration.

In 1866, Mr. Brace published a book, *Short Sermons to the News Boys*. In addition to a collection of sermons, the little tome contained an appendix called "History of the Formation of the Newsboys' Lodging-House." To some extent, it was as much a secular text as a religious one. In addition to the obvious religious content, it also introduced the life of poor vagrant street children to a broad swath of American society unfamiliar with urban poverty. The message was intended for children and adults throughout the country as well as those in wealthy families on Fifth Avenue.

Short Sermons was only a small part of Mr. Brace's efforts to reach across the growing social, economic, and cultural divides. As early as his second annual report, he warned of "the great evil" of separate classes that was creating "two different cities" resulting in the formation of "castes toward one another."[117] By the mid-1870s that prediction was in full bloom. New-York was entering what would become known as the Gilded Age, where extreme wealth was increasingly on display and income inequality was unprecedented.[118] Mr. Brace declared that "the great obstacle to the full success of this charity, and of most charities of this city, is the want of sympathy between different classes."[119] Among other things, he made the following observation: "Wealth is increasing prodigiously on one side" and "the successful have no time, or think they have none, for attending to the poor."[120] He complained that "luxury and position in New York do not sufficiently bring after them responsibility towards those who have not the good things of life."[121] He added, "Surely no one with generous feelings can think of the countless benefactions showered on himself, and then look around on the tens of thousands of human beings deprived of all the best gifts of life, and not feel it his bounden duty to give to others somewhat as Providence has given him."[122]

Mr. Brace's interest in the upper class was not only monetary. He felt certain that one method of enticing New-York's wealthy to feel its "bounden duty" was to visit CAS facilities. Mr. Brace regularly urged them to leave their enclaves and volunteer among poor children. For example, he announced that the society was seeking the "assistance of young gentlemen in our Sunday evening meeting, and other night work in the Lodging-House,"[123] adding that "the presence of Ladies is a great encouragement to the poor lads."[124] He extended the invitation to entire families: "We earnestly invite our citizens to attend with their families, and if possible to aid in the instruction of the lads."[125] In Mr. Brace's view, this volunteer work united rich and poor, making "one link between them."[126] Once exposed to poor children it was impossible to "pass one of them . . . as indifferently as before."[127]

There was no better time of year to appeal to the public than around the holidays, particularly Thanksgiving and Christmas. In fact, in November 1861, the CAS trustees passed a resolution noting that it was "very important that the Society should collect funds at this season, when the sympathies of the public are called out toward poor children sufficient to provide for the wants of the Society during the winter and avoid incurring a debt or interrupting our operations."[128] Mr. Brace was particularly talented at writing fund raising appeals that pulled at the heartstrings and that also contained facts and figures on how contributions could help. In response to one of Mr. Brace's Christmas appeals "on behalf of the Poor Children in New York," one donor wrote, "It will not do to let an appeal like yours pass unheeded. I should feel as though I had turned the Master himself from my door."[129]

Holidays were also an excellent time to request in-kind donations. One November Mr. Macy was invited to pick up "a barrel of apples—for the children's Thanksgiving," while another donor told him to expect "10 Turkeys from R. F. Westcott, on Wednesday by Express."[130] Thanksgiving dinners were bountiful from the start. The first at the NBLH included turkey, potatoes, apples, cakes, peanuts, and—as a special treat—oyster stew carted in by an oysterman from Fulton Market. The boys feasted until they could eat no more, some consuming three or four plates of turkey and potatoes before moving on to dessert. "Look at me, I'm unbuckled," said one at the time. "I'm as big as an Alderman tonight!"[131]

Significantly, holidays also offered the perfect opportunity to invite the public to share a meal with the children or help in its service. In the late 1880s, one notable visitor was the five- or six-year-old granddaughter of Mr. Roosevelt. The little girl, Eleanor, arrived with her father, Elliot Bulloch Roosevelt.[132] This was her first introduction to poor children like the newsboys, and it initiated a third generation of the sprawling Roosevelt family's interest in the lodging house and its residents. Later she reflected that "very early I became conscious of the fact that there were men and women and children around me who suffered in one way or another" and recalled the time "when my father took me for the first time to help serve Thanksgiving Day dinner" at the NBLH. She recalled being "tremendously interested in all these ragged little boys" and learning from her father "that many of them had no homes and lived in little wooden shanties in empty lots, or slept in vestibules of houses" yet they "were independent and earned their own livings."[133] She remembered that after dinner, "the boys themselves put on an entertainment." Then she confessed that "if I hadn't been so sleepy I would have enjoyed it, but I am afraid I disgraced myself by placidly going to sleep."[134]

As an adult, the future first lady turned a critical and reflective eye on her own family's "long-involvement with public good."[135] She described her parents as coming from two different threads. Her mother, she said, "belonged to that New York City Society which thought itself all important." This, she declared was "Society with a capital *S*." However, her father's branch of the family came from society with a lowercase *S*.[136] The family on her paternal side "was not so much concerned with society spelled with a big *S* as with people, and those people included the newsboys from the streets of New York," she wrote.[137] Indeed, this side of the family included her grandfather and his other son, her beloved Uncle Teddy. These were the Roosevelts who rolled up their sleeves and got to work among the poor wherever needed.

Mr. Brace would have agreed with Eleanor Roosevelt's assessment of her family forebears. He once wrote of her grandfather that "fortune" for Mr. Roosevelt was "a gift of God to be used for all. Social position was only one implement to aid him in all kinds of good causes."[138]

In the last quarter of the nineteenth century, Mr. Brace and his colleagues did their best to mend the fraying social fabric and bring together poor vagrant children and New-York high society. In 1890, an extraordinary book of photographs by Jacob Riis documenting how the "other half" lived in New-York's dismal tenements would introduce extreme poverty to wealthy New-Yorkers in the comfort of their own homes.[139] However, decades before that, Mr. Brace was urging a different approach. He called upon the wealthy to visit poor children, not as voyeurs, but in active service.

***

CAS Extended Family and Their Dependents

Charity work for CAS officers and trustees was often a family affair. Like the involvement of the Roosevelts, the Brace family involvement extended beyond the secretary himself. Mr. Brace's brother worked in the CAS Emigration Branch for years. His brother-in-law was the superintendent of CAS schools. Mr. Brace's wife, Letitia, was a volunteer in the industrials schools and for other charitable endeavors. In a playful letter to their daughter, Emma, written on a dreary New-York day of torrential rain and melting snow, Mr. Brace reported returning home from work late one evening. "I got home at 11:30, but no wife!" he wrote. Mrs. Brace was occupied until well past midnight at the Nineteenth Century Club discussing the possibility of establishing a "religious trust (as they do for standard oil or sugar)," he told his daughter. Its purpose would be to "supply villages with a good article at low rates."[140]

Family involvement in charity work was common. Mr. Macy's sisters founded and ran the Cottage Place Industrial School. At the NBLH, both Mr. and Mrs. O'Connor were paid employees (although Mary O'Connor's paycheck was smaller than her husband's). Many had worked shoulder to shoulder with the same unselfish commitment of helping poor children for decades. They were united in their belief that service to the poor should offer support but not unduly interfere. Unrelated by blood, these charity workers were essentially fictive kin by virtue of their shared mission. Not surprisingly, the loss of any one of them sent ripples of sorrow through the entire network.[141] In just five years, CAS suffered two such intimate wounds.

In 1882, Mr. Macy, Mr. Brace's indispensable right-hand man who ran the central office for twenty-nine years, died suddenly. His stunned colleagues mourned his death and paid tribute, calling him a man of "high character and cheerful service" who was "perfectly willing to be without thought of honor or reward" in his work.[142] In addition, the trustees turned their attention to his grieving widow and two children. The appreciative board resolved that Mr. Macy's "salary be continued to his family for the space of one year." In addition, they directed "$150 . . . toward his funeral expenses."[143]

Then in 1887, after thirty years at the helm of the NBLH, Mr. O'Connor died. Saddening matters further for the CAS family and the newsboys, Mrs. O'Connor herself was "suffering from an incurable disease."[144] Given the couple's three decades of service, the loss of Charles and Mary O'Connor signaled an end of a dynasty. Together they had nurtured the NBLH to maturity and tended to thousands of homeless street boys as if they were their own. In addition, the couple had raised their own four children at the NBLH.

Again the trustees took action on behalf of the family. They resolved "that in view of the long continued and faithful services of the late Mr. Charles O'Connor, and of his wife" to appropriate "a sum not exceeding $2000 (Two thousand dollars) . . . for the benefit of the family of Mr. O'Connor, the payment not to exceed eighty dollars ($80) per month." As a practical matter, this covered most of the family income for a one-year period. The trustees appropriated another $250 to help defray Mr. O'Connor's funeral expenses.

This was an era when the death or disability of the primary breadwinner could rapidly plunge a family into destitution. It would take another two decades for the first state widow's pension law to be enacted, and private pensions were not yet common practice. However, the CAS trustees sought to cushion the financial hardship for both the Macy and O'Connor families. While it was only a tentative step in ensuring the welfare of employee dependents, it reflected the society's continuing experimentation with how to best manage a morally responsible charitable agency.

Notes

1. Minutes of the Board of Trustees, October 16, 1867, vol. 4, 1861–1872, in the Victor Remer Historical Archives of the Children's Aid Society (1836–2006). New-York Historical Society Archives. Guide to the Records of the Children's Aid Society 1836–2006, Series I, New-York Historical Society.
2. *Fifteenth Annual Report of the Children's Aid Society* (New York: Wynkoop & Hallenbeck, 1868), 20.
3. *Fifteenth Annual Report*, 48.
4. *Sixteenth Annual Report of the Children's Aid Society* (New York: Wynkoop & Hallenbeck, 1869), 21.
5. *Sixteenth Annual Report*, 19.
6. *Sixteenth Annual Report*, 23, 63.
7. *Sixteenth Annual Report*, 23.
8. *Sixteenth Annual Report*, 23.
9. *Seventeenth Annual Report of the Children's Aid Society* (New York: Wynkoop & Hallenbeck, 1869), 13.
10. *Sixteenth Annual Report*, 21.
11. *Fifteenth Annual Report*, 48.
12. *Fifteenth Annual Report*, 48.
13. Donation Correspondence (1864–1885), in the Victor Remer Historical Archives of the Children's Aid Society (1836–2006). New-York Historical Society Archives. Guide to the Records of the Children's Aid Society 1836–2006, Series VI, box 25, folder 10, March 1868–July 1868, New-York Historical Society.
14. Donation Correspondence, box 25, folder 8, March 1867–January 1, 1868.
15. Donation Correspondence, box 25, folder 8, March 1867–February 25, 1868.
16. Donation Correspondence, box 25, folder 9, January 1868–February 1868.
17. Donation Correspondence, box 25, folder 2, February 28, 1870.
18. Donation Correspondence, box 25, folder 10, June 11, 1868.
19. *Seventeenth Annual Report*, 42.
20. *Seventeenth Annual Report*, 42.
21. *Seventeenth Annual Report*, 35.

22. *Eighteenth Annual Report of the Children's Aid Society* (New York: Wynkoop & Hallenbeck, 1870), 39.
23. *Seventeenth Annual Report*, 42. The society rented the Park Place premises at five thousand dollars per annum for the first two years, with a five-hundred-dollar increase for the last three. Minutes of the Board of Trustees, March 17, 1869, vol. 4.
24. *Twentieth Annual Report of the Children's Aid Society* (New York: Wynkoop & Hallenbeck, 1872), 35; Minutes of the Board of Trustees, February 21, 1872, vol. 4.
25. *Twenty-First Annual Report of the Children's Aid Society* (New York: Wynkoop & Hallenbeck, 1873), 47.
26. The site was at the juncture of Duane, William, and New Chambers streets. Because these streets no longer intersect, modern readers must consult old city maps to understand how the intersection of these streets could produce the wedge of property purchased by CAS.
27. *Twenty-Second Annual Report of the Children's Aid Society* (New York: Wynkoop & Hallenbeck, 1874), 19–20. In New-York, Leopold Eidlitz, a Czech immigrant, was already a well-known architect in the latter half of the nineteenth century, although few of his buildings survive today. Identified as "the first Jewish architect to practice in the United States" (*Encyclopedia Judaica*), he designed churches and synagogues (such as St. George's Church, 1846–1848, and Temple-Emanu-El on Fifth Avenue, 1866–1868); commercial properties (particularly banks, such as Continental Bank, 1856, and American Exchange Bank, 1857); public buildings (such as the assembly chamber of the New York State Capitol and the final work on the "Tweed Courthouse"); civic works (Brooklyn Academy of Music); and private residences (such as the home of the flamboyant showman, P. T. Barnum). Biruta Erdmann, *American National Biography Online*, 2000, https://oxfordindex.oup.com/ (James Stevens Curl and Susan Wilson, eds., "Leopold Eidlitz," *The Oxford Dictionary of Architecture*, 3rd ed. [New York: Oxford University Press, 2015]; Andrew Scott Dolkart, "Eidlitz, Leopold," in Joan Marter, ed. *The Grove Encyclopedia of American Art* [New York: Oxford University Press, 2011]). In addition to his building projects, Eidlitz was "a founder of the American Institute of Architects and an active participant in its affairs," giving lectures and delivering papers (Dolkart). He also authored a significant book on architectural theory, published in 1881, entitled *Nature and the Function of Art, More Especially of Architecture*.
28. *Twentieth Annual Report*, 35.
29. *Twenty-Second Annual Report*, 47.
30. "The Latest Work of the Children's Aid Society. Opening of the New Building for the Newsboys' Lodging-House—Interesting Exercises," *New York Times*, July 22, 1874.
31. *Thirty-First Annual Report of the Children's Aid Society* (New York: Italian School Printing Department, 1883), 21. Interestingly, most CAS annual reports were produced by commercial publishers. However, between 1878 and 1883, the twenty-sixth through the thirty-first annual reports were published by the society's Italian

School Printing Department, located at 156–160 Leonard Street. Although CAS had several Italian programs, the school on Leonard Street had a large number of children from the "southern provinces of Italy." The practice appears to have been abandoned after 1883 when CAS returned to commercial printers.

32. *Twenty-Second Annual Report*, 20; Minutes of the Board of Trustees, April 16, 1873, vol. 4; *Thirty-First Annual Report*, 21. It is not clear from the early records what kind of fire protocol existed in CAS facilities in the late 1800s. However, it is interesting to note that in 1908, CAS trustees decided to add an "iron stairway" to the front of the West Side Italian School, in addition to the one in the "rear which leads into an alley." At the time, CAS was routinely practicing fire drills with the industrial school children and, according to board of trustee minutes from May 20, 1908, the children "now leave the building in one minute in the fire drills." These institutional fire precautions predate the tragic and infamous Triangle Shirtwaist Factory Fire of 1911, which prompted greater attention to fire regulations in New York. Minutes of the Board of Trustees, vol. 9, 1907–1914.

33. This reference comes from a fire log on display at the New York City Fire Museum at 278 Spring Street. The fire log is opened to this page because it also captures the record of a historic and devastating fire that occurred on February 2, 1860, at a tenement house at 142 Elm Street. The Elm Street fire, in which twenty residents lost their lives, was blamed on "shoddy construction" (Glen R. Corbett and Donald J. Cannon, *Historic Fires of New York City* [Charleston, SC: Arcadia Publishing, 2005], 30). It started in a basement bakery and quickly "burned away" the building (*New York Times*, February 3, 1860). The tragedy led New York's city council to enact its first "fire escape law" (Corbett and Cannon, 30). It is possible that my two sources—John Morrow's book and the New York Fire Department fire log—are reporting different fires at the same street intersection that year. Here I treat the two as the same fire.

34. John Morrow, *A Voice from the Newsboys* (San Diego: University of California Press, 1860), 39–40, Digital Archive, www.hathitrust.org, 73–74.

35. Morrow, *Voice from the Newsboys*, 73–74.

36. Morrow, *Voice from the Newsboys*, 73–74.

37. Morrow, *Voice from the Newsboys*, 73–74.

38. *New York Times*, July 22, 1874. Mr. Williams, deposited rents from the "fine store" which moved in the ground floor into a CAS sinking fund "to liquidate the mortgage indebtedness" which had been "incurred in the completion of the new Newsboys' Lodging-House (*Twentieth Annual Report*, 35; *Twenty-Second Annual Report*, 20.)

39. *Twenty-First Annual Report*, 48.

40. *Twenty-Second Annual Report*, 20; *New York Times*, July 22, 1874.

41. "The Latest Work," *New York Times*, July 22, 1874.

42. "The Latest Work," *New York Times*, July 22, 1874.

43. "The Latest Work," *New York Times*, July 22, 1874.

44. *Twenty-Second Annual Report*, 19–20.
45. According to Mr. Brace, the boys at the NBLH were "more of the true *gamin*" than some other children served by CAS. By that he meant, they were "sharp, ready, light-hearted, quick to understand and quick to act, generous and impulsive, and with an air of being well used 'to steer their own canoe' through whatever rapids and whirlpools" (Brace, *The Dangerous Classes*, 343–344). In 1874, CAS conducted a survey of the composition of children in all of its lodging houses. In the NBLH, about half the boys were orphans, another 12 percent had mothers in prison, and 10 percent had been deserted by parents. Other causes of application included parents who were "drunkards," homeless, or in the hospital, and families in which the father had "gone off with other woman" or was at sea. In addition, some boys had been turned out by stepfathers or didn't remember ever seeing their parents. Newsboys' Lodging House: Causes of Application in 100 Boys (circa 1874), in Guide to the Records of the Children's Aid Society 1836–2006, Series IX, box 42, folder 12, New-York Historical Society.)
46. Interestingly, CAS also began actively returning "lost" or "runaway" children back home. Although the society had always done so informally, beginning in the 1860s, CAS kept track of the number of "street boys" it induced "to leave their vagrant life and return to their parents" (*Seventh Annual Report of the Children's Aid Society* [New York: Wynkoop, Hallenbeck & Thomas, 1860]). When parents arrived seeking information at the NBLH or central office, a "description of the missing one" was taken and then when a boy "answering the description appears we send word to the inquirer to come and see the boy" (*Nineteenth Annual Report of the Children's Aid Society* [New York: Wynkoop & Hallenbeck, 1871], 18). By 1871, on average, three children a day were being "restored to friends and relatives" (*Nineteenth Annual Report*, 18). For example, in 1879 the NBLH returned 565 boys. Under similar conditions today, a parent would file a Missing Person's Report with the local police department. In addition, the National Center for Missing and Exploited Children is entirely devoted to this activity.
47. *Thirty-Fifth Annual Report of the Children's Aid Society* (New York: Wynkoop & Hallenbeck, 1887), 25.
48. *Twenty-Third Annual Report of the Children's Aid Society* (New York: Wynkoop & Hallenbeck, 1875), 20.
49. *Eleventh Annual Report of the Children's Aid Society* (New York: Wynkoop & Hallenbeck, 1864),
50. Minutes of the Board of Trustees, vol. 3, 1853–1861, in Records of the Children's Aid Society 1836–2006, New-York Historical Society.
51. *Tenth Annual Report of the Children's Aid Society* (New York: Wynkoop, Hallenbeck & Thomas, 1863), 39.
52. Newsboys' Lodging House: Testimonial Letters from Residents, 1889 and Undated, in Guide to the Records of the Children's Aid Society 1836–2006, Series IX, box 42, folder 13, February 25, 1889, New-York Historical Society; Helen Campbell,

"From Darkness to Daylight" (1892), reprinted in Kenneth T. Jackson and David S. Dunbar, eds., *Empire City: New York through the Centuries* (New York: Columbia University Press, 2002), 377.
53. NBLH, Testimonial Letters, February 25, 1889; Campbell, "From Darkness," 377.
54. *Twenty-Third Annual Report*, 20.
55. *Twenty-Fifth Annual Report of the Children's Aid Society* (New York: Wynkoop & Hallenbeck, 1877), 9–10; *Twenty-Sixth Annual Report of the Children's Aid Society* (New York: Italian School Printing Department, 1878), 9.
56. Robert H. Bremner, *The Public Good: Philanthropy & Welfare in the Civil War Era* (New York: Alfred A. Knopf, 1980), 184; Miriam Z. Langsam, *Children West: A History of the Placing-Out System of the New York Children's Aid Society, 1853–1890* (Madison: State Historical Society of Wisconsin for Department of History, University of Wisconsin, 1964), 37.
57. *Eighth Annual Report of the Children's Aid Society* (New York: Wynkoop, Hallenbeck, & Thomas, 1861).
58. *Twelfth Annual Report of the Children's Aid Society* (New York: Wynkoop & Hallenbeck, 1865), 20.
59. Charles Loring Brace, *The Dangerous Classes of New York and Twenty Years' Work Among Them*, 3rd ed. (New York: Wynkoop & Hallenbeck, 1880), 109; *Twenty-Third Annual Report*, 20.
60. "The Latest Work," *New York Times*, July 22, 1874.
61. NBLH: Testimonial Letters, February 25, 1889.
62. *Thirteenth Annual Report of the Children's Aid Society* (New York: Wynkoop & Hallenbeck, 1866), 47.
63. *Thirteenth Annual Report*, 49–52.
64. In 1860 Charles Darwin's influential and controversial book, *Origin of the Species*, was published in the England. As noted by Hunter A. Dupree, among its earliest U.S. supporters of intellectual note was Asa Gray, Mr. Brace's relative through marriage to Jane Lathrop Loring, his aunt. Gray was both a friend of Darwin's and a close friend and intellectual mentor to Mr. Brace. Gray loaned an early copy of Darwin's book to Mr. Brace, who read it immediately. Randall Fuller credits Mr. Brace with taking the book to a dinner where he was the guest of honor. The dinner was hosted by Franklin Benjamin Sanborn on January 1, 1860. The book was the topic of discussion among the four diners, who also included Amos Bronson Alcott and Henry David Thoreau. All four men, united in their radical abolitionist views, would be influenced by Darwin's work. Mr. Brace spent a good deal of time trying to integrate the great intellectual threads of his day—including progressive religious thought as well as scientific advances—to apply them to his own field of philanthropy. While he can be faulted in hindsight for its flaws, Mr. Brace deserves credit for attempting to incorporate the best scientific evidence of the day into his thinking about charity work.
65. *Thirteenth Annual Report*, 50.

66. *Thirteenth Annual Report*, 50.
67. *Thirteenth Annual Report*, 35.
68. Jeremy P. Felt, *Hostage of Fortune: Child Labor Reform in New York State* (Syracuse, NY: Syracuse University Press, 1965), 3.
69. *Twenty-First Annual Report*, 4.
70. *Thirty-Second Annual Report of the Children's Aid Society* (New York: Wynkoop & Hallenbeck, 1884), 4.
71. Felt, *Hostage of Fortune*, 1.
72. Brace, *The Dangerous Classes*, 353; emphasis in original.
73. Brace, *The Dangerous Classes*, 353–354.
74. *Thirty-Sixth Annual Report of the Children's Aid Society* (New York: Wynkoop & Hallenbeck, 1888), 9–10.
75. *Twenty-First Annual Report*, 4.
76. Jeremy Felt has rightly identified many shortcomings of the Whitehead bill. These include "the loose educational standard implied in the words 'intelligibly read.'; the absence of a valid requirement for proof of age; the acceptance of a teacher's certificate, readily obtained in overcrowded schools; and the request for only one factory inspector to cover the entire state" (p. 4). I argue that despite these shortcomings, the bill was fairly radical in its day. I also take issue with Felt's last point. Arguably, the intent of insisting on a governor-appointed state factory inspector wasn't just to ensure that a single individual would be responsible "to cover the entire state" so much as to create a position of public oversight and accountability with direct reporting responsibility to the state legislature. Certainly, in New York, where the rampant corruption of Tweed's Tammany Hall was fresh in mind, this state oversight would seem warranted. Despite these limitations, Felt acknowledged that "the Children's Aid Society bill of 1872 foreshadowed later legislation such as the factory Act of 1886" (p. 4).
77. Brace, *The Dangerous Classes*, 362–365.
78. Felt, *Hostage of Fortune*, 4.
79. *Twenty-First Annual Report*, 8.
80. *Twenty-First Annual Report*, 8.
81. *Twenty-Eighth Annual Report of the Children's Aid Society* (New York: Italian School Printing Department, 1880), 7.
82. Felt, *Hostage of Fortune*, 20. The factory law of 1886 rested on a "notarized affidavit" from parents attesting to a child's age, and employers were required to have a certificate for all "working children under sixteen, showing the young employee's name, age, date, and place of birth." Boys under the age of eighteen (and women under twenty-one) "were forbidden to work more than sixty hours a week." Anyone "knowingly" violating the law "could be fined up to $100." It also authorized a governor-appointed and salaried chief factory inspector.
83. Felt *Hostage of Fortune*, 7.
84. Felt *Hostage of Fortune*, 7.

85. *Twenty-Second Annual Report*, 7–8; *Twenty-Eighth Annual Report*, 6.
86. *Twenty-Second Annual Report*, 7–8.
87. *Twenty-Second Annual Report*, 7–8.
88. *Twenty-First Annual Report*, 25.
89. *Twenty-First Annual Report*, 25.
90. *Twenty-First Annual Report*, 25.
91. *Twenty-Fourth Annual Report of the Children's Aid Society* (New York: Wynkoop & Hallenbeck, 1876), 6–8.
92. *Sixteenth Annual Report of the Children's Aid Society* (New York: Wynkoop & Hallenbeck, 1869), 69.
93. *Sixteenth Annual Report*, 69.
94. *Sixteenth Annual Report*, 69.
95. *Sixteenth Annual Report*, 69.
96. *Twenty-Fourth Annual Report*, 6–8.
97. *Twenty-Fifth Annual Report*, 9–10.
98. *Twenty-Fifth Annual Report*, 4–5.
99. Minutes of the Board of Trustees, January 16, 1884, vol. 7, 1879–1895, in the Victor Remer Historical Archives of the Children's Aid Society (1836–2006). New-York Historical Society Archives. Records of the Children's Aid Society 1836–2006, New-York Historical Society; *Thirty-Second Annual Report*, 8–9.
100. *Twenty-First Annual Report*, 5.
101. *Twenty-First Annual Report*, 5.
102. *Thirty-Second Annual Report*, 8–9.
103. Felt notes that "in 1903, after long, acrimonious debate, the New York legislature passed the nation's first Street Trades Law. Applying only to newsboys in first-class cities, the law prohibited boys under ten and girls under sixteen from selling newspapers and required newsboys under fourteen to obtain a badge and permit (the standards for a badge were the same as for an employment certificate except that no literacy test was given)" (p. 158).
104. *Twenty-Fifth Annual Report*, 3–4.
105. *Thirty-Sixth Annual Report*, 8–9.
106. Emma Brace, ed., *The Life of Charles Loring Brace* (New York: Charles Scribner's Sons, 1894), 448–449.
107. *Thirty-Sixth Annual Report*, 8–9.
108. *Thirty-Seventh Annual Report of the Children's Aid Society* (New York: Wynkoop, Hallenbeck & Co., 1889), 6.
109. Brace, *The Dangerous Classes*, 457.
110. Donation Correspondence, box 28, folder 1, December 6, 1873.
111. *Twenty-Sixth Annual Report*.
112. Charles Loring Brace, *Short Sermons to the News Boys With a History of the Formation of the Newsboys' Lodging-House* (New York: Charles Scribner, 1866), v.
113. Brace, *Short Sermons*, v.

114. Brace, *Short Sermons*, v.
115. Brace, *Short Sermons*, v.
116. Brace, *Short Sermons*, 71.
117. *Second Annual Report of the Children's Aid Society* (New York: M. B. Wynkoop, 1855), 11.
118. For a superb book examining the wealthy classes during this same period see Sven Beckert, *The Monied Metropolis: New York City and the Consolidation of the American Bourgeoisie, 1850–1896* (Cambridge, UK: Cambridge University Press, 2001).
119. *Thirty-Fourth Annual Report of the Children's Aid Society* (New York: Wynkoop, Hallenbeck, 1886), 3.
120. *Thirty-Fourth Annual Report*, 3.
121. *Thirty-Fourth Annual Report*, 3.
122. *Thirty-Fourth Annual Report*, 3.
123. *Thirty-Sixth Annual Report*, 27.
124. *Thirty-Fifth Annual Report*, 25.
125. *Thirty-First Annual Report*, 15.
126. *Second Annual Report*, 11.
127. *Second Annual Report*, 11.
128. Minutes of the Board of Trustees, November, 1861, vol. 4.
129. Donation Correspondence, box 26, folder 8, December 1870. One astute donor sent his donation in January, writing, "I was intending to send for Christmas, but concluded to wait a while thinking there might be a lull in your receipts after the holidays" (Donation Correspondence, box 25, folder 5, December 1867–January 1868).
130. Donation Correspondence, box 27, folder 9, November 24, 1873.
131. William Colopy Desmond, Incidents and Sketches Among the Newsboys, vol. 48, in The Victor Remer Historical Archives of the Children's Aid Society (1836–2006). New-York Historical Society Archives. Records of the Children's Aid Society 1836–2006, New-York Historical Society.
132. The Roosevelt family tree is complicated. In short, Theodore Roosevelt Sr.'s children included two sons, Theodore "Teddy" Roosevelt (who would become the twenty-sixth president of the United States) and Elliot Bulloch Roosevelt (who was father to Eleanor Roosevelt). Eleanor herself will grow up to become First Lady, after she married her fifth cousin, once removed, Franklin Delano Roosevelt and he was elected the thirty-second president of the United States. James R. Roosevelt—a second CAS trustee who assumed the position on the board immediately after Theodore Roosevelt Sr.'s death in 1878—was a brother of Franklin Delano Roosevelt. James R. Roosevelt was married to Helen Schermerhorn Astor. So his in-laws were William Blackhouse Astor Jr. and Caroline Webster Schermerhorn Astor. All three families, the Roosevelts, Astors, and Schermerhorns were financial supporters of CAS.

133. Eleanor Roosevelt, "This Is My Story," *Ladies' Home Journal*, May 1937, 15.
134. Roosevelt, "This Is My Story," 15.
135. Roosevelt, "This Is My Story," 12.
136. Roosevelt, "This Is My Story," 12.
137. Roosevelt, "This Is My Story," 12.
138. Brace, "The Silent Workers," in *The Dangerous Classes*, 455.
139. Jacob A. Riis, *How the Other Half Lives: Studies among the Tenements of New York* (1890, repr., New York, Dover Books, 1970); Bonnie Yochelson, *Jacob A Riis: Revealing New York's Other Half: A Complete Catalogue of His Photographs* (New Haven, CT: Yale University Press, 2015).
140. Charles Loring Brace to Emma Brace, February 25, 1888, in Emma Brace, *Life of C. L. Brace*, 446.
141. When Mr. Roosevelt died in 1878, Mr. Brace was appalled to read the words of a pundit who dismissingly concluded that his life had "been a shadow, and [had] pursued shadows." Mr. Brace read the account and was indignant. "No," he wrote emphatically. Mr. Roosevelt's life "to me it seems a permanent Force in this city, that will work on generation after generation, through his family, through his friends, and all who have felt it. It is not a shadow, here or elsewhere, but a light going on brighter and brighter until it merge into the perfect day" (Brace, "The Silent Workers," in *The Dangerous Classes*, 457).
142. Jared Macy, Minutes of the Board of Trustees, January 19, 1882, vol. 7.
143. Macy, Minutes of the Board of Trustees, January 19, 1882, vol. 7.
144. *Thirty-Fifth Annual Report*, 25. Mr. O'Connor was replaced by Rudolph Heig, who became the fourth superintendent of the NBLH.

10

The Society Mr. Brace Built

A LIFE'S WORK

*Our Saturday was a little enlivened by one of those incidents somewhat
characteristic of us and which in the hands of a book maker
would be of some value.*

—EDWARD. P. SMITH, *Daily Journal*, 1855

IN 1889, MR. Brace composed his thirty-seventh annual report for CAS. Over the decades the reports had grown in size—this one was 117 pages—but remained relatively stable in format. Mr. Brace solicited reports from employees from every branch of the society's work; each laid out his or her accomplishments, presented statistical tables, offered success stories, and made appeals for unmet needs. From the treasurer and assistant treasurer, Mr. Brace received a financial report, a list of contributions, and a collection of letters received by the central office. Mr. Brace's own opening narrative contained updated statistics but also an introductory essay addressing an issue of the day.

Every year, the board of trustees authorized an initial printing of ten thousand to twelve thousand copies to be distributed not only in New-York but also across the United States and around the globe. Mr. Brace received letters congratulating him on CAS work from Illinois and Iowa as well as Germany, India, and beyond. Many writers described being inspired and some, spurred into action. In recent years, Mr. Brace told a colleague that he had "received news of work like ours started in Australia, England, San Francisco, and in Washington, all seeking to follow our tracks."[1]

***

Neighborhood-Based Programing

The annual report demonstrated the remarkable growth of CAS. Inserted into the thirty-seventh was a fold-out map of Manhattan containing twenty-five large red rectangles designating "Stations of Children's Aid Society." Each signified a neighborhood-based program that served as an anchor for a constellation of services.

One cluster consisted of lodging houses. After successfully piloting the experimental NBLH in 1854, Mr. Brace replicated it as funds became available. Just two years later he added a lodging house for homeless girls. By 1889, there were six lodging houses in total. They included the NBLH, the Girls' Temporary Home,[2] the Tompkins Square Lodging-House,[3] East-Side Lodging-House,[4] Forty-Fourth Street Lodging-House,[5] and West-Side Lodging-House.[6] Each offered food, clothing, shelter, night classes, and Sunday meetings.

In addition, each lodging house was based on the voluntary participation model that infused all CAS work. Children could come and go from the shelters at will. They facilities welcomed children from any religion, ethnicity or racial background; girls and boys alike. The methods of practice employed within the programs involved adult guidance through persuasion, not coercion. These approaches were child-friendly and developmentally appropriate. They often rested on good-natured humor and on an understanding of the individual developmental needs of a particular child. Mistakes were expected and tolerated. They were treated as learning opportunities. Each new educational tool introduced to the programing, be that a savings bank, a Sunday meeting, or evening class, was tailored to appeal uniquely to street savvy youngsters.

All this was a far cry from the rigid and discipline-driven methods employed by the private and public child asylums, such as the House of Refuge, favored by many charity workers of the day. These programs relied on police and court referrals as well as the deprivation of liberty in prison-like institutions. Mr. Brace's lodging house model—although working with poor children who shared virtually all the same characteristics as those committed to asylums—sought to decouple the notion of poverty and crime. By offering children a stable base, the lodging houses reduced the need of children to engage with street-based survival strategies that led to criminal arrests. The educational programs offered at the lodging houses and job referrals made from them provided children a more positive path to successful adulthood. Of course, Mr. Brace's goal was to prevent criminality and delinquency that other charity workers assumed was linked with poverty.

The pull-out map also marked the locations of all CAS's educational programs, a second major branch of service. In 1889, this included twenty-one industrial schools[7] and twelve night schools scattered across the city, including one at the NBLH.[8] Among these schools were two ethnicity-based programs. One was a German school, first opened in 1853, and the second, an Italian school opened in 1856.[9] Both of these programs were still going strong thirty years later, catering to the unique needs of their respective immigrant populations. Supplementing the schools, CAS also supported two free reading rooms for young men.[10]

These educational programs were also unique. They were nonresidential and therefore offered additional support to poor families in their own neighborhoods. They were targeted on poor children who were otherwise excluded from other public and private schools. Although the primary focus was on the children, by providing food, clothing, bathing facilities and other amenities, the industrial schools help supplement poor family needs as well. From the start, unlike European counterparts, Mr. Brace rejected the notion children be trained in the manufacture of particular product, a specific trade, or for a certain position, such as servants for a wealthy home. He favored training children in basic skills, common education, and general good habits, believing this would better serve them in the longer run. Finally, the educational methods employed rejected rigid methods, rote learning, and strict disciplinary approaches favored in other settings and employed object method learning with its comparable flexibility and freedom. It was an approach that was more consistent with Mr. Brace's overall philosophy.

In addition to these core branches of service, by 1889, CAS had a well-established network of health- and disability-related facilities for children and mothers. These included the Crippled Boys' Brush-Shop,[11] the Summer Home,[12] the Health Home,[13] the Sick Children's Mission,[14] and the Cottage for Crippled Girls.[15] Each facility answered to its own historical roots but contributed to the overall breadth of the society's network of New-York-based services.

Of course, all these various branches of service were connected through the multifunctional Central Office. From the start this office filled a variety of needs within the agency and with the public. It was often the first stop for children referred from police officers, immigration officials, or other charity workers. Here, needy children might find food and clothing and be referred to a lodging house, industrial school, placing out, an employment situation or to another charity. Parents seeking help with custodial care, or employment situations for their offspring or aid in locating missing children were helped as well. The emigration branch was managed through this office, including screening, travel arrangements, recording keeping and on-going follow up. Donations—both monetary and material—were received and distributed from the office. In addition, the central office staff actively corresponded with the public and with all children formerly associated with its work. In doing so, the Central Office sought to meet the unique and various needs of each of CAS constituents.

***

Quantification and Amplification of CAS's Work

The facilities were staffed by hundreds of employees and volunteers. That year, twenty-seven men and women were listed in the front matter of the annual report. By generic category, they included eleven visiting agents, ten superintendents and matrons, two western agents, one resident western agent, one southern agent, a superintendent of schools, and an assistant treasurer. But this group merely represented CAS's managing class and the tip of the iceberg. They supervised hundreds of paid employees and volunteers who worked at the programs on a daily basis. In 1889, these included 151 teachers who collectively earned $59,631.38.

CAS worked with staggering numbers of children and by any measure its impact was enormous. In 1889 alone, the total "number under charge of the Society" was 38,853.[16] The lodging houses had sheltered 12,153 unique boys and girls, served 264,391 meals and—using nightly stay as a unit of measure—offered 220,018 shelters. The newsboys' facility by itself had served 7,177 unique boys that year, averaging 163 a night, for a total of 59,522 lodgings and 83,081 meals.[17] As he typically did in the annual reports, Mr. Brace also tallied up the cumulative number of children served since the opening of the facilities. For the NBLH, this amounted to 239,560 unique boys.[18]

Similarly, the Education Branch was doing mighty service. That year, the industrial and night schools had educated, partially fed, and partially clothed 11,331 children. This included supplying 697,080 meals. An additional 4,540 individuals had spent time at the Summer Home (averaging three hundred per week), 5,839 mothers and sick infants were sent to the Health Home, and another 1,439 were given food and medicine through the Sick Children's Mission. The physician in charge of the Health Home treated 1,048 adults and 1,836 children with common ailments such as diarrhea, enteritis, cholera, malaria, anemia, and gastroenteritis and uncommon conditions and diseases such as hydrocephalus, meningitis, spinal disease, trismus, otorrhea, and rachitis.[19]

***

Outside New-York: The Emigration Branch

In addition to its New-York–based services, CAS continued to tout its crowning jewel, the Emigration Branch. In 1889, it placed 2,210 boys, 977 girls, 132 men, and 232 women in homes or set them up with employment outside New-York. As usual, the report contained detailed tables offering statistical portraits and narrative descriptions of the work.

CAS's emigration branch differed from similar placing out practices employed by other charities and missions of the period. Among the most significant was Mr. Brace's refusal to indenture children by legal contract and refusal to involve the court system in the placement of children. If things went badly, CAS stood ready to take the child back and try again; however, neither party, foster parent nor child, should be bound in an unworkable relationship. Although Mr. Brace used the language of adoption in making the placing out system a more sympathetic one in the public eye, in fact, it was a hybrid system of employment placement and family fostering. In that regard Mr. Brace supplemented normative family practices of the day both in terms of delegating child custody responsibilities when under stress but also in easing the transition for young workers from children's street trades to more secure and promising opportunities in the adult labor market.

Emigration parties had left every month of the year, placing from 259 to 366 individuals per month. Their destinations were thirty-one of the then-existing forty-five states in the Union, as well as the District of Columbia, the Washington Territory, and Canada. Nearly half of the children identified as American and hundreds came from one of seven countries: Germany, Ireland, England, Poland, Scotland, Bohemia, and Sweden. Dozens more came from Italy, Hungary, France, and Russia, and a smattering came from Cuba, Japan, Spain, Denmark, Holland, China, and Armenia. About one-third were orphans while the others came from one- or two-parent homes. A little over two hundred were returned to parents or friends. Mr. Brace calculated the cumulative number of children sent out of New-York—adding the 207 boys and girls placed in 1854 to the 3,551 placed in 1889 and all those in between—and arrived at a grand total of 89,441 children.[20]

In addition, this report reflected CAS's ongoing efforts to both supervise and evaluate the Emigration Branch. Now in charge of this task was Mr. L. W. Holste, the assistant treasurer. He insisted CAS's practice was to keep "a close oversight... by the agents of our Society for several years" but acknowledged after ten or fifteen years that contact had diminished.[21] Even so, there was no such thing as a "closed case" for CAS and former children's records were continually updated. That year, Mr. Holste took "special pains" in launching an extensive campaign to write "personal letters of inquiry" to five hundred children placed between 1869 and 1875 (fifteen to twenty-one years earlier). He received hundreds of replies in response. Of course, those replying only reflected a small number of the total children placed out. Nonetheless, they do offer some insights into a variety of placement outcomes.

Many contained the kind of long-term success stories CAS loved to hear and report. Other former charges were more critical or suspicious of CAS motives. While not fully accepting responsibility for the anguish children may have experienced by being separated from parents sometimes without a full understanding of why the separation had occurred, Mr. Holste acknowledged that some children grew up believing that "through the machinations of an enemy while they were young they were 'made away' with." He noted that "most every letter" contained requests for information about family and friends from whom the writer had been separated. By then, CAS was taking great pains to help track down that information, if requested. This included checking CAS's own record books, consulting other charities, and even posting advertisements in newspapers soliciting information. "In many cases," Mr. Holste reported, "we have found friends and reunited families."[22] He offered examples of these successes, although the information obtained was not always what former children hoped for. Such was the case for a boy named Willy, whose entire account, Mr. Holste acknowledged, read "like the super-sensational incidents of a dime novel."[23]

In a letter to Mr. Holste in 1888, Willy expressed frustration that his adoptive family in Lansing, Michigan, had showed "so little interest in his pedigree."[24] He asked for information about his two sisters and his father, whom he believed was a "notable soldier who died for his country during the Civil War." Mr. Holste consulted Mr. Macy's books and learned that CAS had received Willy from the commissioner of charity in 1865 as a five-year-old. There was no additional information, so Mr. Holste contacted New-York's superintendent of the out-door poor. He was informed that Willie and his two sisters had been left, as orphans, at the nursery on Randall's Island after their father was incarcerated at Sing Sing, a state prison. An aunt had retrieved and raised the two girls, but left Willy behind. So after spending two years in the orphanage, he had been turned over to CAS and sent west. Mr. Holste, still on a quest for helpful information, published an advertisement in the evening newspapers. To his surprise, the next morning a man arrived in the office announcing he was Willy's older brother. Willy's father had died after release from prison by either falling or jumping from a window, and one sister had been murdered in a house of ill fame (according to a story featured in the penny presses). The second sister, however, worked in a dry goods store and was doing well. Mr. Holste put the surviving family members in contact with one another and later learned from Willy's sister that "William had written often" and that she planned to "go visit him the following spring."

While it is just a single story, Willie's case hints at some of the complications of placing out histories. As a child, Willie had been deceived into believing a more heroic story about his father than reality supported. Clearly, his case reflects the limitation of kin care in a family facing hard times as well as apparent differential treatment based on the gender of the children. Although it is impossible to know what would have happened had CAS not intervened, in all likelihood he would have spent decades under the restrictive care and supervision of the city's almshouse, isolated and institutionalized on Randall's Island with thousands of poor children. While the answer can never be known, it is reasonable to pose the question which was the better option for him under the circumstances?

Stories like that of Willy must have been the very best part of an annual report for many readers. Every year, dozens of letters, carefully curated by the assistant treasurer from the hundreds received, were published as appendices. Mr. Brace had artfully used these heartfelt portraits—stories, incidents, thank-you notes, and progress reports—to tout CAS's mission to the public since its very first days, when Mr. Colopy jotted down "incidents and sketches" from the NBLH.

***

Financial Health, Real Estate Ownership, and Contributions

An indispensable part of any annual report was its detailed account of the society's financial health. CAS's stewardship of resources was impeccable. This year's report contained a table of total receipts and expenditures, listed by year, since the society's founding. In 1853–1854, receipts totaled $4,732.77

but by 1888–1889, annual receipts had grown to a whopping $410,974.52.[25] That year, expenditures totaled $409,561.69, leaving a balance of $1,413.83.

As usual, distinguished New-Yorkers making particularly large gifts were individually acknowledged. In 1889, one was a gift of $53,612.42 from Mrs. William Douglas Sloane to purchase lots and cover construction costs for a new school on Sixth Street. CAS had cautiously and systematically expanded its real estate portfolio over the years. Mr. Brace had recently written a friend, "We have had a very busy winter—opening or preparing for three or four new buildings, and otherwise extending our work."[26] By 1889, CAS owned no fewer than fifteen "substantial buildings"[27] as well as the land they occupied. Even more remarkably, all were "entirely free from debt or encumbrance."[28] In addition, CAS leased space for others, which caused the treasurer to grumble about having to pay $16,582.89 in rent for schoolrooms that year.

The final pages of the annual report were always reserved for a line-by-line accounting of all of the "subscriptions and donations" received. The thirty-seventh annual report included twenty printed pages, each containing two columns of donor names and contributions. No amount was too small to mention. So, this one included acknowledgment of the four cents received from Charles Cheney, the thirteen cents from his sister, Ruth, and the two dollars from their mother. Mr. Brace had long encouraged the "widow's mite" but he especially loved donations from children, believing it helped forge character and would cultivate a lifelong interest in philanthropy. Scores of donations came as collections from Sunday schools, seminaries, grammar schools, and church congregations, or as proceeds from fairs held on behalf of CAS.

Significantly, CAS's donor base was not restricted to New-York, and contributions flowed in from New England and nearby states such as New Jersey, Connecticut, Massachusetts, Vermont, Rhode Island, Maine, New Hampshire, and Pennsylvania, but also from more distant places such as Illinois, Iowa, Minnesota, Colorado, North Carolina, and Florida. In short, the donor base was national in scope. The society occasionally incurred the wrath of distant charities that accused CAS of encroaching on their own local fund-raising jurisdictions.[29]

The alphabetized listing of donors democratized all contributions. However, sizeable offerings came from New-York's financial royalty. Members of the Astor family made sixteen separate gifts that year, totaling six thousand dollars.[30] They had been contributing to CAS annually, ever since Mrs. Astor's first gift of fifty dollars in 1853. There were also donations from the Roosevelts, Schermerhorns, Rockefellers, Morgans, Livingstons, Hamersleys, Vanderbilts, and Dodges.

Following the lists of cash donations were another ten pages of acknowledgments for in-kind donations earmarked for individual branches of the society's work.[31] This included vast amounts and a great variety of food and clothing; items such as hats, gloves, pants, dresses, and shoes as well as holiday turkeys, candy, cakes, pies, apples, potatoes, and "96 jelly cups, 12 fruit juices." In-kind donations also included bedding, toys, books, magazines, pencils, blackboards, easels, harmonicas, silver thimbles, scissors, soap, furniture—including high chairs, steamer chairs, and wicker chairs—and rugs. Also noted was an offer from a doctor volunteering "30 visits to poor families" to provide in-home medical care.

***

Prevention Claims: Juvenile Crime and Public Health

In addition to compiling reports from others, Mr. Brace wrote his own. In part, it consisted of predictable text and familiar arguments. For decades he had made claims about reducing juvenile crime and lowering the rate of child mortality and had touted the economic efficiency of CAS relative to other charities. The thirty-seventh annual report was no different.

Mr. Brace's argument about juvenile crime took five pages of statistical tables and analysis to develop. He used public data from the board of police justices between 1875 and 1888 "to prove the diminution of children's offences." He made the same assertion dating back to 1855 but then had had to use evidence gathered "from the old reports of the different district prisons" that came from "the former Board of Charities and Corrections."

Mr. Brace's argument consisted of comparing the relative increase in New-York's overall population with its rates of serious crimes and juvenile offenses. He supplied tables for both boys and girls, examining petit larceny and vagrancy as well as arraignments and commitments for more serious offences like grand larceny, burglary, and other felonies. Having established significantly lower relative numbers of violations in recent years when compared with the growth in population, he happily concluded, "This remarkable decrease in all crimes against person and property ... is one of the most striking evidences ever offered of the effects of such labors as those of this Society, and of many similar charities."[32] He insisted that the numbers proved that "such labors are diminishing the supply of thieves, burglars, vagrants, and rogues" in the city.[33] Mr. Brace can be faulted for flaws in his causal arguments but not for his zealousness in attempting to establish the impact of CAS's prevention efforts with existing data.

The sanitary section followed similar reasoning. Mr. Brace documented an increase in the tenement-house population from 1869 to 1888. He then compared it to the relatively lower rate in child mortality than would be predicted, given the population growth. He ended by concluding that "the deaths have by no means increased in the same ratio." Even more notable was Mr. Brace's assertion that in the NBLH's thirty-six year history, "there has been no case of any contagious or foul-air diseases" and "only one death (from pneumonia, in 1858)."[34] Given the sanitary conditions of the day, it was a remarkable achievement. Mr. Brace attributed these outcomes to "scrupulous cleanliness, ventilation, and proper food."[35]

Finally, since the earliest days, Mr. Brace had made arguments about CAS's economic efficiency. The thirty-seventh annual report included this common refrain. Branch by branch, he calculated the unit cost of service and compared it to other interventions. For example, the expense of operating the lodging houses (after deducting for construction costs) was divided by the average number of nightly lodgings for a cost per child of $43.75. By comparison, Mr. Brace reported "the average cost per year for each prisoner in The Tombs is $107.75, and the Roman Catholic Protectory draws from the City Treasury over $100 annually for each of its inmates." Similarly, for the emigration program, after calculating "the total cost for railroad fares, clothing, food, salaries," and dividing by the total number of children placed out, Mr. Brace concluded that each child (and some adults) were sent out at an expense of $8.88 per person. In comparison, he estimated that "any child placed in an asylum or poorhouse for a year undoubtedly cost nearly $140." "Surely this is economical charity," Mr. Brace declared.[36] At its core, Mr. Brace was making an argument that his prevention approach to juvenile delinquency was far more cost effective than the alternative of linking poverty and crime through court-ordered institutionalization of children in poor houses, child asylums or refuges, and prisons.

***

A Bittersweet Report: A Changing of the Guard

Despite all the routine aspects of this annual report, Mr. Brace's introductory essay was markedly different in tone than previous ones. CAS had suffered two significant loses that year. One was the death of Judge Hooper C. Van

Vorst, a trustee for twenty-four years. He was a jurist who had gained "unequaled experience" in "a somewhat new department of law": that of "social clubs and of charities."[37] The judge left what Mr. Brace called an "intellectual bequest" to CAS. In his last year, the judge spent "many hours in studying our Constitution and by-laws, and left behind a careful argument as to the weak and strong points" and "our rights under the laws. This will be a guide to the Society for generations to come," wrote Mr. Brace.[38]

The second loss came with the death of Mr. John Warburton Skinner, CAS's superintendent of schools for twenty-two years. Mr. Skinner had been responsible for running the entire educational wing of the society. He was a man with a "sunny, loving nature" and had a "keen, scientific interest in every new development in the methods of education."[39] Significantly, Mr. Skinner had also been married to Mr. Brace's older sister, Mary, for forty years.[40] So for Mr. Brace, this loss was personal as well as professional.

In rapid succession, the deaths of two men who had spent nearly a quarter of a century working for CAS hit Mr. Brace hard and highlighted the inevitable fact that CAS torch bearers were "waxing in years."[41] "We cannot hope," wrote Mr. Brace "that all our present laborers and guides will continue much longer in the field."[42] He concluded that it was a "fitting time to ask, 'What has given this work its success and endurance, and what is likely to be its future?'"[43]

***

Devoted Workers and a Sound Foundation

Mr. Brace's answer to the first of the questions was twofold. CAS had been successful because of the quality of its staff and the soundness of the principles that guided its labors. His highest praise went to the "workers, both volunteer and employed," who were the sustaining life blood of the society. "No human mind can ever measure the self-denial and devotion," he wrote, acknowledging that they had worked for the poor "with the same zeal with which others strive for money or fame."[44] Their reward was "not in the world's applause" but rather "in the fruits of their efforts."[45]

Second, Mr. Brace attributed CAS's success to the fact "beneath this earnestness" of its labor force, that "certain great principles were clearly and steadily followed out during those thirty-seven years."[46] These were the same underlying principles that had animated the work, without deviation, since its first day. "The great idea of the Children's Aid Society," Mr. Brace wrote, "has been to help the children help themselves."[47] Each branch of the work, he noted, was "carried out with continual reference to the great principle of teaching self-help."[48] Mr. Brace had no doubt that a poor child who was taught "good habits and good morals" would grow up to be "a self-supporting man or woman."[49]

Over the years, Mr. Brace often summarized CAS's underlying beliefs. First, "lessons of industry and self-help" were preferable to handouts. Second, education—elementary, vocational, and moral—was essential for both the individual child and society as a whole. Education was the cornerstone of Mr. Brace's poverty and crime prevention efforts. Third, education must be offered "in union with the supply of bodily want." In other words, without stable housing, food, clothing, and sanitation, children could not thrive. Fourth, "individual influence and home life" was better than institutionalization. Finally, when possible, children should be removed from the toxic, overcrowded, conditions of New-York and placed in the developing western territories where they had greater opportunities.

***

Call to the Future

Having answered the retrospective question, Mr. Brace turned to the future, wondering if a next generation might be induced to "take up the laboring oar in our great struggle with poverty, vice, and wretchedness."[50] He felt certain that women would continue to volunteer their services to the poor but worried about men. "There is, unfortunately, in the city an impression among the young gentlemen that [this] is not a proper field for their efforts," he wrote. "This is a great mistake." He asserted, "We need young men to influence these lads in many different ways." In fact, young men could "promote [the lads'] happiness and welfare in a thousand little ways impossible to specify," he added.[51]

Mr. Brace then turned to CAS leadership. "The success of this Society in the future will depend, of course, mainly on its management. It has been from the beginning remarkably fortunate in its choice of trustees and managers."[52] Like that of Judge Van Vorst, the tenure of most of the trustees had lasted a lifetime. They had been an unfailingly loyal and hardworking lot. Mr. Brace wrote reassuringly, "The younger members who have recently entered the Board are taking a like part in its work with their older predecessors, and we hope thus to continue to secure the humane services of men of like character and devotion."[53] Optimistic as usual, he concluded that there was "every reason to believe that the character of the management will continue as it has been."

Privately, however, Mr. Brace must have had his own position in mind. That fall, Mr. Brace's oldest son, C. Loring, had been sufficiently concerned about his father's taxing work schedule that he offered to return home to serve as an assistant and gradually take "more and more responsibility off his father's shoulders." Mr. Brace was "unwilling ... as yet to view the possibility of needing an assistant" although it was clear that he took comfort in the offer.[54] Despite his reluctance to accept help, his decision to dwell on the past and the future of CAS in the thirty-seventh annual report proved timely. It would be the last one Mr. Brace ever wrote.

***

Mr. Brace's Death

Although publicly forward thinking, privately Mr. Brace was increasingly contemplating his own mortality. That January he had written to a friend, thanking him "for the kind sympathy in my ailments" and going on to say that the future was "very uncertain, but I wait, as you will understand, in perfect calmness." He added, "You can imagine how devoted and untiring a nurse dear Letitia has been."[55]

During their thirty-six-year marriage, Mr. Brace had rarely been separated from his wife, Letitia, so his letters to her were few in number but poignant in content. After Mr. Skinner's passing he wrote, "J.'s sudden death gives me many serious thoughts." As usual, Mr. Brace expressed being at peace with his own demise. The couple's children were grown, and he felt "more easy about death now the children are pretty well cared for."[56] He used the letter as an opportunity to express his gratitude to his wife: "I often think of what a happy life we have had together, and how much good you have done me, and I suppose I have you, intellectually. God bless you, ever! . . . I love you more than ever!"[57] He wrote, "It will be well with us in the unseen, I am persuaded. Life has been very pleasant, and the unseen life must be more and better."[58]

For all his acceptance of death, his daughter Emma reported that "it was rarely possible for him to speak to those closest to him of his weakness and failing health."[59] Nonetheless, by early 1890, it was clear that Mr. Brace's health was declining. On February 6, he wrote another rare letter to his wife: "I am better but tired. I think unceasingly of your devoted love and service of kindness and affection. God bless you!"[60] In May, Mr. Brace's son finally insisted on returning to New-York to help with CAS business.[61] Two months later, hoping it would be good for Mr. Brace's health, the family traveled to Europe, meeting in Munich and continuing on to Switzerland. On this trip, Emma said her father's "patience and sweetness were unfailing" but as the trip by carriage progressed, it "grew hourly more painful to all."[62] By the time they arrived in Campfer on August 2, Mr. Brace was in "an alarmingly feeble state," and it was clear that he was gravely ill.[63]

Mr. Brace had once expressed a wish that his last views on earth be of the Hudson River Valley in the fall. "If one cared for last looks at death," he wrote, "I should pray that mine might be of the glorious Hudson in autumn, and I could scarcely hope that the Unseen could offer anything more lovely."[64] Instead, Mr. Brace slipped into unconsciousness in a room that looked out "over one of the loveliest of the Engadine" views nestled in the bucolic Alps. Three days later, on August 11, 1890, with his wife and two of his children by his side, the sixty-four-year-old Mr. Brace died peacefully. His family buried him in a little cemetery at St. Moritz under a simple stone with an epitaph that read as follows: "After he had served his generation by the will of God, he fell asleep."[65]

***

Tributes: Words and Actions

News of Mr. Brace's death traveled the globe; tributes poured into the central office and condolence letters reached Letitia. Many recognized the enormity of his contributions. Trustee Egisto P. Fabbri said to his colleagues, "Few men can boast of having accomplished in their lifetime so much *real* good for humanity and for society as Mr. Brace." A friend wrote Letitia that "he has lived the life of four thinkers and workers, instead of one."[66] Another trustee, William E. Dodge Jr., said, "No stronger, braver, or more self-sacrificing life has ever been lived in New York." He called Mr. Brace's work "an example of what may be done by large brains, a big heart, and rare common-sense concentrated on one worthy object."

Mr. Dodge noted that Mr. Brace's "management of a great and constantly growing charity has been a marvel of ability and success."[67] From a preacher, Letitia received another letter of condolence: "I think that his work in the Aid Society was the most far-seeing and courageous work of the city's philanthropy."[68] After singing his praises, the *New-York Evening Post* concluded that he "became a master of his vocation" and had a "world-wide reputation."[69] Mr. Dodge asserted that "the memory of his work can never die."[70]

Condolences also came from the society's front lines. One industrial school teacher spoke for all her colleagues:

> I expect to open school on Monday and I shall feel, as I enter the schoolroom, that Mr. Brace has left to us, as a sacred legacy, that we should now, as never before, work with all the energy and the wisdom given us for the causes to which he gave his life. How to go on without reference to Mr. Brace, how to disassociate him from the work, I cannot conceive, and I know all the teachers feel as I do. None but those intimately associated in the work can appreciate, as can we who worked with him, the painstaking care, the attention to minute detail, his knowledge of every teachers' ability, his just and even grateful acknowledgment of her work . . . his unstinted and open praise, and his encouragement of every effort made to advance the educational and moral status of the unfortunate. We knew just where to find Mr. Brace; just where he stood on every question; and his "yes" and "no" meant more than a volume from others.[71]

In the aftermath of Mr. Brace's death, the CAS board of trustees unanimously approved the appointment of his son, C. Loring Brace, as successor and the society's second secretary.[72] In addition, the trustees sponsored a public memorial service for Mr. Brace. It was held at NBLH.

When Mr. Brace first accepted his position in early 1853, CAS existed only as a plan sketched out in a single paragraph on a sheet of blue notepaper. On the second day of his employment, he had ventured out after midnight with the *Tribune* foreman to see the haunts frequented by the newsboys. Within a year, he had rented a loft in the Sun Building and hired Mr. Tracy to wrangle a gaggle of unruly boys to order in the NBLH, thus launching one significant branch of Mr. Brace's visionary plan. So, it could not have been more fitting that the board of trustee decided to rename the facility the Brace Memorial Lodging House. With that final action, a new chapter for the lodging house and the society began.

Notes

1. Letter from Charles Loring Brace to Dr. George Howard, in Emma Brace, ed., *The Life of Charles Loring Brace* (1894; facsimile of the 1st ed., New York: Arno Press, 1976), 426.
2. Girls' Temporary Home was located at 27 St. Mark's Place.

3. Tompkins Square Lodging-House was located 295 East Eighth Street. This building, first built in 1886 and designed by the architects, Vaux & Radford, was designated a historic landmark by the Landmark's Preservation Commission in 2000.
4. The East-Side Lodging House was located at 287 East Broadway.
5. Forty-Fourth Street Lodging House was located at 247 East Forty-Fourth Street.
6. The West-Side Lodging House was located at 400 Seventh Avenue.
7. CAS industrial schools in 1889 included Avenue B School, 607 East Fourteenth Street; Avenue C School, 304 East Fourth Street; Cottage Place School, 208 Bleecker Street; Duane Street School, 9 Duane Street; East River School, 247 East Forty-Fourth Street; East Side School, 287 East Broadway; Eleventh Ward School, 295 Eighth Street; Eighteenth Ward School, 404 East Nineteenth Street; Fourteenth Ward School, 256 Mott Street; Fourth Ward School, 73 Monroe Street; Fifth Ward School, 186 Franklin Street; Fifty-Second Street School, 573 West Fifty-Second Street; Fifty-Third Street School, 340 West Fifty-Third Street; German School, 272 Second Street; Italian School, 156 Leonard Street; Lord School, 135 Greenwich Street; Park School, Sixty-Eighth Street near Broadway; Thirty-Fifth Street School, 314 East Thirty-Fifth Street; Sixteenth Ward School, 211 West Eighteenth Street; West Side Italian School, 24 Sullivan Street; and West Side School, 400 Seventh Avenue.
8. Many of the night schools shared facilities with lodging houses. They included German Night School, 272 Second Street; Italian Night School, 156 Leonard Street; Newsboys' Night School, 9 Duane Street; Eleventh Ward Night School, 295 Eight Street; East Side Night School, 287 East Broadway; Lord Night School, 135 Greenwich Street; Fifty-Second Street Night School, 573 West Fifty-Second Street; Fourteenth Ward Night School, 256 Mott Street; Forty-Fourth Street Night School, 247 East Forty-Fourth Street; West Side Italian Night School, 24 Sullivan Street; Eighteenth Ward Night School, 404 East 19th Street; and West Side Night School, 400 Seventh Avenue.
9. From 1869 to 1872, CAS also operated a "colored school" that closed due to neighborhood gentrification, the scattering of the population, and the opening of other facilities. It was located at 185 Spring Street and catered to neighborhood children as well as older students (over the age of twenty-one) who had not received a grammar school education and traveled from "distant parts of the city." (*Seventeenth Annual Report of the Children's Aid Society* [New York: Wynkoop & Hallenbeck, 1869]). In 1869, the school's rolls included 348 pupils, with an average of eighty-nine attending daily (*Seventeenth Annual Report*, 33). Because the rate of homelessness and poverty was particularly high in this population, CAS sought special funds to provide midday meals. However, by 1871, "the destruction of that part of Sullivan street occupied by colored people, and the opening of new colored schools" had dramatically impacted attendance (*Nineteenth Annual Report of the Children's Aid Society* [New York: Wynkoop & Hallenbeck, 1871], 33). Finally, in 1872, "the opening of Fifth Avenue, and the scattering of our pupils over the

city" resulted in CAS's decision to close the school (*Twentieth Annual Report of the Children's Aid Society* [New York: Wynkoop & Hallenbeck, 1872], 18).
10. CAS's free reading rooms were located at 208 Bleecker Street and 135 Greenwich Street.
11. The Crippled Boys' Brush-Shop was located at 247 East Fourth Street.
12. The Summer Home was located on Bath Beach in Long Island.
13. The Summer Health Home was located on Coney Island.
14. The Sick Children's Mission was located at 287 East Broadway.
15. The Cottage for Crippled Girls shared a facility with the Summer Home on Bath Beach on Long Island.
16. *Thirty-Seventh Annual Report of the Children's Aid Society* (New York: Wynkoop, Hallenbeck, 1889), 19.
17. *Thirty-Seventh Annual Report*, 31.
18. Mr. Brace proudly boasted that the boys themselves had contributed $172,776.38 toward payment of the total operating cost of $433,256.76 of the NBLH since opening. *Thirty-Seventh Annual Report*, 31.
19. *Thirty-Seventh Annual Report*, 48.
20. *Thirty-Seventh Annual Report*, 31.
21. *Thirty-Seventh Annual Report*, 20.
22. *Thirty-Seventh Annual Report*, 27.
23. *Thirty-Seventh Annual Report*, 28.
24. *Thirty-Seventh Annual Report*, 29.
25. *Thirty-Seventh Annual Report*, 60. In 1889, CAS receipts included $39,555.90 in public funds from the board of education's state school fund and another $70,000 from the city and county of New York.
26. Letter from Charles Loring Brace to Rosalie Flower, in Emma Brace. *Life of C. L. Brace*, 459.
27. Buildings and properties owned by CAS included the NBLH on Duane, William, and Chambers streets; Sixteenth Ward Industrial School, 211 West Eighteenth Street; Girls' Lodging-House, 27 St. Mark's Place; Italian School Building, 154–156 Leonard Street; East Side Lodging-House, 287 East Broadway; West Side Lodging-House, Thirty-Second Street and Seventh Avenue; Summer Home, Bath, Long Island; Health Home, West Coney Island; Tompkins Square Lodging-House, 295 Eighth Street at the corner of Avenue B; East Forty-Fourth Street Lodging-House, Forty-Fourth Street and Second Avenue; Memorial School, 256–258 Mott Street; Avenue C School, 630–634 East Sixth Street (under construction); Jones Memorial School, East Seventy-Third Street (under construction); and lots for the proposed Henrietta Industrial School, 215–217 East Twenty-First Street.
28. *Thirty-Seventh Annual Report*, 56.
29. For example, Mr. Brace raised the ire of a pastor in Waltham, Massachusetts, in 1873. The pastor felt CAS was encroaching on the philanthropic base of charities in the vicinity of Boston. In a letter dated December 9, the man wrote, "I feel

impelled to write a word in response to your Christmas Circular just received and in response to previous circulars and report [sic] received by me for quite a series of years. Noble as your work of charity is and well deserving of support. I confess I cannot see why it appeals to churches in Eastern Massachusetts. The Boston organization similar in object to your own appeal to us regularly and strongly and with great propriety. Our responsibility is in that direction. If New York appeals to Conn and Western Mass, I, for one, should think the (sic) did well. But to Eastern Mass I think the appeal is mis-directed. Feeling so I might, as probably most ministers about me do, drop your appeal without notice. But I cannot continue to do so year after year without frankly telling you that I do not think that we, who are near to Boston are properly called upon to aid your work (in N.Y.), good as it is." Box 28 Folder 1 Donation Correspondence In Guide to the Records of the Children's Aid Society, Series VI—Financial and Fund-Raising Records, 1853-1949. Sub-subseries VI.1.C: Donation Correspondence, 1864–1885.
30. *Thirty-Seventh Annual Report*, 84–103.
31. *Thirty-Seventh Annual Report*, 103–112.
32. *Thirty-Seventh Annual Report*, 16.
33. *Thirty-Seventh Annual Report*, 16.
34. *Thirty-Seventh Annual Report*, 17.
35. *Thirty-Seventh Annual Report*, 17.
36. *Thirty-Seventh Annual Report*, 19.
37. *Thirty-Seventh Annual Report*, 7.
38. *Thirty-Seventh Annual Report*, 7.
39. Emma Brace, *Life of C. L. Brace*, 459.
40. John Sherman Brace, *Brace Lineage* (Bloomsburg, PA: G. E. Elwell, 1914), 39.
41. *Thirty-Seventh Annual Report*, 3.
42. *Thirty-Seventh Annual Report*, 3.
43. *Thirty-Seventh Annual Report*, 3.
44. *Thirty-Seventh Annual Report*, 3–4.
45. *Thirty-Seventh Annual Report*, 3–4.
46. *Thirty-Seventh Annual Report*, 3–4.
47. *Thirty-Seventh Annual Report*, 4.
48. *Thirty-Seventh Annual Report*, 6. For example, a year earlier Mr. Brace had written, "Our Lodging Houses for homeless children are not merely shelters, but training-schools in self-help. The boys are induced to save their hard-earned pennies (which they formerly squandered) and deposit them in the savings banks of these homes by an offer of high interest. Those who have nothing receive loans from a fund "to start boys in business," or are supplied with material to blacken boots, or otherwise set to work. The crippled are trained in brush-making. The girls are taught housework, cooking, or laundry-work, hand sewing, dress-making, and machine-sewing, and the more intelligent, type-writing. In the Industrial schools the children of the tenement-house poor (not homeless) are trained in hand-sewing, crocheting,

darning, and machine-work. The more advanced in lacework, carving, modeling, printing and the like; others in "kitchen gardening," or play housework, and a number of classes in such branches of plain cooking as a tenement house family would need.

"It is not thought necessary to give these children a thorough knowledge of a trade, but rather to train hand and eye so that afterwards, they can use their skills in easily acquiring a given branch. They are early schooled into habits of industry, and with this class these habits are the greatest possible safeguards afterwards against vice. (*Thirty-Sixth Annual Report of the Children's Aid Society* [New York: Wynkoop & Hallenbeck,1888], 1).

49. *Thirty-Seventh Annual Report*, 4.
50. *Thirty-Seventh Annual Report*, 3.
51. *Thirty-Seventh Annual Report*, 8–9.
52. *Thirty-Seventh Annual Report*, 7.
53. *Thirty-Seventh Annual Report*, 7.
54. Mr. Brace once confessed to his son, "I think I made a mistake in not educating my boys in Children's Aid Society matters. It arose from my excessive respect for the soul's independence" (Emma Brace, *Life of C. L. Brace,* 435–436). This "excessive respect" was a quality that Emma, his daughter, said pervaded "all his relations with others" (Emma Brace, *Life of C. L. Brace,* 436).
55. Letter from Charles Loring Brace to Dr. George Howard, in Emma Brace, *Life of C. L. Brace*, 470.
56. The Braces had four children: C. Loring; born June 6, 1855; Emma, born October 5, 1859; Robert, born October 3, 1861; and Leta, born October 19, 1864. Brace, John Sherman (1914; J. S. Brace, *Brace Lineage*, 40).
57. Letter from Charles Loring Brace to Letitia Brace, in Emma Brace. *Life of C. L. Brace*, 462. The Braces' daughter, Emma, attributed the lack of surviving letters between the spouses to the fact that they were rarely separated. "Separation [from Letitia] was never endured where it could be avoided, and Mr. Brace was usually accompanied by his wife even when he was obliged to remain in New York to attend the evening meetings or night schools of the Children's Aid Society," she wrote (p. 435).
58. Emma Brace. *Life of C. L. Brace*, 462.
59. Emma Brace. *Life of C. L. Brace*, 475.
60. Emma Brace. *Life of C. L. Brace*, 474–475.
61. Emma Brace. *Life of C. L. Brace*, 475.
62. Emma Brace. *Life of C. L. Brace*, 479.
63. *Thirty-Eighth Annual Report of the Children's Aid Society* (New York: Wynkoop & Hallenbeck, 1890), xx.
64. Letter from Charles Loring Brace to E. B. Redmayne, in Emma Brace, *Life of C. L. Brace*, 430.
65. Emma Brace. *Life of C. L. Brace*, 480.

66. Letter from Dr. George Howard to Letitia Brace, in Emma Brace. *Life of C. L. Brace*, 484.
67. Emma Brace. *Life of C. L. Brace*, 484.
68. Letter from R. Heber Newton to Letitia Brace, in Emma Brace. *Life of C. L. Brace*, 484.
69. Emma Brace. *Life of C. L. Brace*, 481.
70. Emma Brace. *Life of C. L. Brace*, 484.
71. Emma Brace. *Life of C. L. Brace*, 482.
72. Mr. Brace's second son, Robert, was appointed head of the Emigration Department of CAS. J. S. Brace, *Brace Lineage*, 40.

Afterword

Charles Loring Brace's Legacy and Implications

BRIDGING SUPPORT FOR POOR FAMILIES

Those of us who will soon pass away will ask no higher honor than to have moved others in coming years to carry on in like spirit these great enterprises of compassion and mercy.
—CHARLES LORING BRACE, 1889

CHARLES LORING BRACE'S current legacy rests largely in historical accounts that apply social or moral control frameworks to interpreting charity work of the nineteenth century. I have argued that careful empirical investigation of the Children's Aid Society (CAS)—specifically anchored in a case study of the Newsboys' Lodging House (NBLH) and its relationship to the agency's broader mission and philosophy—challenge these social control theses and have implications for Brace's overall legacy as a social work innovator.

Of these social control narratives, two major threads have particular purchase. One explores the roots of our modern juvenile justice system and the early "invention" of juvenile delinquency as a social problem. The second explores the early roots of our modern child protective services, or foster care system. Both systems are now well-established public apparatuses that rely heavily on the legal system for enforcement. On one hand, juvenile justice intervention occurs when minors have committed criminal acts but—by virtue of their age—are not tried as adults or when they habitually engage in problematic "status offense" behavior (such as running away, violating curfew, truancy, or ungovernability). On the other hand, child protective services intervenes when state actors determine children are maltreated (either abused or neglected, both broadly defined) by their caregivers or at risk of maltreatment.

At its most basic level, the former system purports to address bad behavior of children while the latter focuses on the unfitness or misdeeds of parents or guardians. In either case, authority to intervene in the otherwise private affairs of the family rests in the police power of state actors. Since both systems disproportionately impact poor families—particularly families of color—claims are made that bureaucratic mission creep and decades of institutionalization have given rise to large and entrenched systems of public surveillance of low-income families. In this regard, social control-oriented historical accounts have some validity.

Historical accounts of juvenile delinquency often begin with developments in the early to mid-nineteenth century with the evolution of the mixed population poorhouses into specialized establishments for children, including orphanages, refuges, juvenile asylums, and reformatories. Generically, these child asylums quickly assumed characteristics akin to penal institutions. Despite assertions of their benevolent intentions, asylum managers restricted children's liberty, relied on highly regimented daily routines, imposed corporal punishments, and indentured children by binding contract when they were old enough to work. By 1899, these reformers' ideas crystalized with the creation of the first separate court for children, which evolved into our formal juvenile justice system of today. It is a system—essentially patterned on adult criminal practices—that relies primarily on police and probation officers, as well as lawyers and judges, for its operation.

The second historical thread examines the early roots of our modern foster care system, which scholars argue emerged from the "placing out" or emigration parties conducted from the mid-nineteenth into the early twentieth centuries. Like our modern juvenile justice system, today's foster care system is implemented by social workers and case workers who are empowered by state authority and supervised through the legal system, often by the very same family or juvenile courts responsible for delinquency cases.

Bruce Bellingham has referred to the dominant historical accounts associated with placing out—or the so-called orphan train movement—as "philanthropic abduction" narratives. Generically these accounts frame activities of charity workers as practices that intentionally broke up poor (mostly immigrant) families, forcibly removed children, and transported them to distant western territories to reproduce their own class-based sensibilities. In its heyday, dozens of different societies from cities on the East Coast employed these methods, sometimes also indenturing children. By combining indenturing with placing out, charity workers merged involuntary servitude practices long associated with overseeing poor, dependent, and orphaned children. The history of the overall orphan train movement doesn't often distinguish between the efforts of different charities or tease out their unique characteristics or policies. There is good reason to examine single institutions that might yield a more nuanced picture of the development of various practices.

Toward the last quarter of the nineteenth century, many charity workers and reformers associated with both the juvenile justice and placing out movements relied on the increasingly widespread and generally accepted legal doctrine of *parens patriae*. This doctrine vested asylum managers and charity workers with authority to intervene with poor children—who were deemed at-risk of vagrancy, immorality, criminality, or misbehavior—or their parents, who were deemed unfit or unequal to the task of raising children for a variety of reasons. Problematically, these charity workers tended to merge ideas of poverty and criminality into a muddled social problem, which criminalized the poor. Historians have argued that in doing so, such reformers trod on parental authority, curtailed the civil rights of both parents and children, and impinged on children's liberty interests, all under the benevolent guise of "child saving."

***

Brace's Legacy: Challenging the Reductionist "Either–Or" Trope

I have argued that the work of Charles Loring Brace and CAS is often placed at the nexus of these two distinct historical threads. In doing so, scholars have repeatedly resorted to a reductionistic narrative trope: Brace opposed asylums only because he so actively promoted its alternative, placing out. Interestingly, this proposition is somewhat paradoxical. On one hand, Brace is depicted as a minor hero in the juvenile delinquency literature for his unequivocal opposition to child asylums. On the other hand, he is cast as a comparative villain in the philanthropic abduction literature for his pioneering role in the systematic use of placing out poor children. This either–or framing—that he opposed one but supported the other—is correct as far as it goes. In his vocal opposition to asylums, Brace often touted the relative benefits of emigration.

Yet the substance of Brace's objections to asylums is worth consideration in light of the overall efforts of CAS as an institution. First, he objected to child asylums as isolated, congregate care facilities. He opposed restricting children's freedom and removing them from their natural environment. By mid-century—just as he was starting his work with CAS—thousands of poor children were warehoused in public and private asylums for children isolated on Randall's Island stranded in the middle of the East River, removed from the bustling city. Nothing about this isolation and institutionalized approach sat well with Brace. Second, Brace opposed the methods of social work practice employed *within* the asylums themselves. These included their regimented, militaristic nature; the mechanical and rote strategies used in their educational programs; and the harsh corporal punishments doled out for even minor transgressions. He believed these rigid approaches only taught technical adherence to arbitrary rules but wouldn't help children internalize proper behavior. In short, his opposition to asylums rested in the facility structure, the practice methods employed within them, and children's physical and social isolation from their natural environment.

Unlike asylum supporters who tended to comingle notions of poverty with criminality, Brace resisted this association. He often noted that poor children were inclined to good, kind, and generous impulses that needed to be nurtured and that if they drifted into crime, it was because of environmental and situational factors, not because of inherent character flaws. Brace understood that homeless children—unsupervised and left to their own devises on the city streets—were likely to resort to pragmatic survival strategies that included a mixture of street peddling, scavenging, begging, and pilfering. Turning to petty crimes, pick-pocketing, or prostitution to survive were not unreasonable choices for children responding to inhospitable environmental conditions and with limited options. Furthermore, even honest work like hawking newspapers was an occupation best suited to small children but one that was quickly outgrown, leaving teenagers or young adults with little formal education and few marketable skills. In short, life in New-York for vagrant children was difficult and viable pathways out of poverty were limited.

Brace warned the public about the dangers of ignoring hordes of homeless children, both for the children's sake and because of their potential collective threat to society. Nonetheless, he didn't equate poverty with criminal behavior. In fact, his entire programmatic focus was on preventing children from going down this seemingly inevitable future path as a result of the public's neglect.

Although Brace responded to asylum advocates by promoting the relative benefits of CAS's system of placing children "in the country," careful empirical investigation of these practices, particularly as they apply to teenage newsboys, cast doubt on the philanthropic abduction narratives. For example, CAS insisted on parental consent before placement; parents often sought CAS's help, requesting western placements for their children; newsboys living at the lodging house sought employment opportunities in the West themselves; even once placed, many boys returned to their biological families in New-York; depending on the age and status of the boy, placements reflected hybrid fostering and employment situations; and CAS often reunited missing children with their parents or cooperated by supplying families with information. In addition, Brace firmly, repeatedly, and publicly rejected indenturing children, which impinged on their free will and created binding legal contractual obligations that altered the rights and responsibilities of all the parties involved. In short, the evidence suggests there were fluid relationships among CAS agents, the boys, and their families (both biological and foster) and that there was mutual accommodation and no indication of coercion.

In building on Bruce Bellingham's thesis that CAS's emigration branch actually supported normative practices of delegating custodial care during times of family stress, I argue that it also supported normative practices of easing children away from child labor activities, such as peddling newspapers, to more sustainable (and arguably more profitable) adult employment occupations (such as farming, carpentry, and railroad work). Given westward expansion into new states and territories, these trades and professions offered greater lifelong opportunities for poor children than those available to them in New-York. Taken together, CAS aided poor children by supplementing existing family coping and child labor strategies as needed, rather than acting as a destructive force in breaking families apart. While there is no doubt that Brace personally believed children were better off in the country than in New-York and he lobbied for this outcome, there is scant evidence that CAS forced the choice on any child or his parents. In addition, placements were revocable if any party changed their mind.

That said, I argue the reductionist either–or trope used to characterize Brace's work has had more troubling consequences for his legacy for five additional reasons. First, this framing implies a sharp dichotomy between urban and country practices, such that there has been a tendency to shift the historical focus away from the various programs offered by CAS in New-York in favor of exclusive attention on the emigration branch. The vast network of services CAS provided in New-York is essentially invisible in the historical record. In fact—as Brace's final annual report dramatically illustrates—the number of children actually aided in the city far exceeded the numbers sent out to country. Brace deserves recognition for his role in reducing the suffering of hundreds of thousands of poor children in urban New-York, regardless of his work with the emigration branch.

In 1866 Brace summarized CAS's entire effort as "very simple." He wrote that the society consisted of "a Central Office, Agents to find the poor children, Schools to educate them and give them habits of industry, Lodging-Houses to shelter, train, and clothe them, and Western Agents to convey them to homes in the West."[1] Yet, this very simple structure belies the underlying sophistication of the design.

CAS engaged children and families through outreach efforts. It provided evening entertainment in the form of meetings, educational classes, and reading rooms. It conducted neighborhood-based Sunday meetings. These gatherings—in addition to distracting children from saloons, "low theaters," and gambling dens, which CAS agents felt were negative influences—provided warm, sanitary, well-lit spaces and sites for distributing food or clothing. CAS offered flexible, neighborhood-based educational programs for children who would otherwise be excluded from public schools. Similar to other CAS venues, these schools partially fed and clothed children and were equipped with bathing facilities, an amenity not available in their home tenements or shanties. CAS operated a central office as a one-stop social service agency where children might receive a small loan to start in business or an employment referral and where families might seek help on behalf of their children.

It is worth noting that CAS's urban programs benefited three different populations: homeless children without parents, guardians, or caregivers; those with parents who were temporarily or permanently incapacitated; and those living with intact families or single parents. Although Brace's rhetoric was almost exclusively focused on children—and he clearly saw advantages in working with young clients—in reality, CAS services had secondary consequences for their families. The choice of how children (and families) used CAS was up to them, but several options were available.

For example, truly homeless children—or those with parents who were too incapacitated or overwhelmed to care for them—could stay at the lodging houses. These facilities provided stable housing, clean and hygienic living conditions, wash rooms, regular meals, and minor medical care and supervision. The shelters were available for short stays (days, weeks, or months) or longer stays (years). This permitted aid to orphans as well as children with parents with temporary or permanent incapacities.

Alternatively, for children living with intact families, CAS ran industrial schools and a central office that provided supplemental support, such as occasional meals, articles of clothing, and employment referrals in New-York and the vicinity as well as in the country. The evidence points to CAS providing a full range of options depending on the needs of the individual child and, by extension, his family. Acknowledgment of the independent agency of poor children and their parents challenges social control narratives that rely on the passivity of clients and are based on assumptions about unwelcomed, unilateral intrusion by charity workers.

The either–or trope suggests CAS's focus was exclusively on the country and not the city when, in fact, CAS was focusing on both at the same time. So, often overlooked is that for nearly forty years, Brace administered a network of services that provided food, clothing, shelter, education, job training, and employment to children in New-York.[2]

Second, and more significantly, the either–or narrative trope facilitates the near historical invisibility of CAS's lodging houses as an important modality of child welfare intervention. There are good reasons the lodging houses should be seen as a direct and significant counterpoint to the child asylum movement. However, due in part to Brace's intentional rhetorical sleight of hand in referring to his facilities as *lodging houses*—not poor houses, work houses, or asylums—and in calling their residents *lodgers*—not inmates—CAS's lodging houses have escaped comparison.

In reality, CAS lodging houses had similarities with asylums. Both sheltered hundreds of poor children each night in congregate care facilities. Both provided food, clothing, and education. Arguably, both worked with exactly the same population of impoverished, vagrant children, some of whom had committed petty crimes. However, the similarity ends there. The significance of the comparison rests in the stark distinctions between the two. Brace experimented with a dramatically different kind of facility and radically different methods of practices. In the parlance of the day, he characterized his lodging houses as a form of "out door relief"—community-based aid—as opposed to "in door relief"—institutional care—promoted by asylum advocates.

CAS lodging houses did not criminalize poor children or punish them for minor transgressions. In fact, the lodging houses challenged virtually all the underlying assumptions and methods of control that animated asylums and put into action Brace's entire vision for an alternative.

Unlike asylums, the lodging houses were scattered throughout the city in the poorest neighborhoods, not isolated or removed from the urban environment. They weren't restrictive institutions. With the exception of an established evening curfew, boys could come and go as they pleased. Relatedly, the lodging houses did not take court remands. Therefore, they were not coercive and relied entirely on persuading the young lodgers of the value of the service there. Additionally, they did not resort to corporal punishment or require strict obedience. Nor were boys subject to overly moralistic or pietistic sermons. The staff sought to induce good behavior based on incentives and rewards and guide boys to better choices through minor, temporary corrective sanctions and verbal disapproval. There were few rigid rules, but those that did exist were clearly articulated and the boys were held accountable. However, virtually no rule or regulation couldn't be bent if the individual circumstances of a boy warranted exception. There is a good deal of evidence of CAS's willingness to tailor its program to the individual, developmental needs of each child. CAS saw its mission as cultivating the boys' natural goodness (such as their inclination toward generosity, kind acts to each other, and peer support) while curbing behaviors deemed less desirable (e.g., stealing, gambling, and drinking).

In addition, the lodging houses didn't rely on regimented programing. Although daily rhythms included predictable events, a good deal of evidence is supportive of situational flexibility. No scheduled activity couldn't be interrupted to capitalize on a political event making headlines or because of the arrival of a lodger with a unique talent for fiddle playing (temporarily turning classroom into dance hall). CAS staff introduced a variety of educational tools, such as the savings bank, night classes, and Sunday meetings, but they were designed to aid in overall child development and build skills to foster independence. All were rooted in incentive-based reward systems that encouraged but did not require participation. There is abundant evidence of playful and respectful interpersonal exchanges between the boys and the lodging house superintendent, instructors, and other CAS staff.

In short, the lodging houses were based exclusively on the voluntary participation of street youth engaged through persuasion and did not resort to legal coercion, deprivation of liberty, or police power. The facility design and location and the practice methods employed within it made the lodging houses dramatically different from child asylums. Historical accounts that skip over this comparison overlook the significance of lodging houses in the landscape of urban services to poor children in nineteenth-century New-York. This lodging house modality enacted Brace's progressive vision of delinquency prevention.

A third problem with the either–or historical characterization of Brace's work that impacts his legacy consists of undervaluing Brace's innovation in connecting programs into a network of outdoor services under the unified umbrella of a single agency. CAS's various branches and departments facilitated intra-agency referrals, which essentially established a continuum of care that could be triggered from a variety of entry points and deployed based on the needs and desires of its clients. Brace believed this was among CAS's most novel features. Close examination of the NBLH offers a window into these interconnections and the operation of CAS as whole. In particular it exposes CAS's internal logic, the elegance of the integrated design, and the overall ambitious nature of its goals.

CAS entry points for service included initial contact through outreach efforts at evening schools or Sunday meetings or because children or parents sought help at the central office. Children could be referred to the lodging houses, industrial schools, or the central office for further help. Conversely, the central office referred children to schools or lodging houses within CAS's network or to employment situations in both New-York and the country, managed through CAS's emigration branch. This overarching design permitted CAS to support a complex array of family situations, offer flexible support and a variety of options, and supported an active referral flow within the CAS system, which could be tailored to the unique needs of those involved.

Taken together, Brace's CAS system tackled a stunning array of what modern social workers would call "insecurities" and "disparities." He sought to reduce housing, food, and income insecurities. He tackled medical care, hygiene, sanitation, and education disparities. His organizational structure provided both for children's immediate basic needs (food, clothing, and shelter) and their long-term development and growth. He wanted to cultivate independent living skills and self-sufficiency. Brace's goals amounted to nothing short of eradicating poverty, decreasing crime and delinquency, reducing illiteracy, reducing unemployment, and improving child and maternal health outcomes.

Empirical investigation of CAS and the NBLH challenges either–or framing in yet a fourth way: while each branch of service was similar to charity practices employed in Europe and elsewhere in the U.S. in some respects, each was also modified. I have argued that the significance of CAS's similarities to other charities pale in comparison with the importance of the collective adaptations. Each alteration Brace made brought CAS's program branches under a uniform logic that permeated the entire agency.

At the core of these adjustments were Brace's objections, both explicit and implicit, to all forms of coercion, legal or otherwise. Obviously, Brace rejected formal asylums and offered lodging houses in their stead, thereby reinventing the congregate care model, avoiding court remands and law enforcement involvement. He also rejected legal and contractual forms of policing the poor. His industrial schools and evening programs were adapted to accommodate poor children's life and work situations in the community; the teaching methods utilized within the schools involved the participatory engagement of children free from rigid discipline, punishment, and control. He refused to indenture children, not wanting to alter existing rights of any of the parties, including children, parents, employers, or foster parents. He operated a central office, available to poor children and families on a walk-in basis. This common philosophy of working with the poor on a voluntary basis—and respecting the free will of all parties—suffuses the entire interconnected network of CAS programs. This is why empirical investigation of CAS as a specific case is particularly warranted. The internal logic of Brace's agency is often lost or minimized in social control historical accounts that make mid-level claims about the institutional development of juvenile justice or placing out by combining evidence from dozens of different charity organizations with varying policies.

A final aspect of the either–or narrative trope that does disservice to Brace's legacy rests in the tendency of historiographies to focus exclusively on the interactions of charity workers with the poor, based on assumptions that reformers were blinded to issues of social class. Importantly, Brace sought to bridge the class divide that existed in antebellum New-York and grew dramatically during the Gilded Age. His target was not only the poor but also the wealthy. He was troubled by extreme income inequality, a division he described as almost creating "separate castes." He criticized the wealthy for living in a geographic, social, and economic bubble. He warned them of the associated risks, including civil unrest and political upheaval. He appealed to their Christian values but wasn't above stirring their fears by reminding them of the hazards of leaving poor children to fend for themselves on the city streets, certain to develop into the "dangerous class."

At the same time, he solicited donations from them by touting the virtues and good character of poor children, often illustrating these qualities with colorful and compelling stories. He reminded the wealthy that poor children were no different from their own and that their needs were identical. He begged them to visit the society's schools and lodging houses or, better yet, to volunteer their services. He never failed to invite them to join the children for holiday meals, Sunday dinners, or Sabbath meetings. He believed that the economically better off needed to understand what life looked like across the social class divide.

Taken altogether, Brace's overall approaches were remarkably modern. Several aspects are worth noting. His city-based interventions were decentralized and neighborhood based. His philosophy was rooted in youth empowerment and youth development. His programs attempted inclusivity and preached tolerance. There is little evidence that CAS overtly discriminated based on religion, ethnicity, nativity, race, gender, or ability status. CAS experimented with culturally appropriate programs—albeit to a limited degree—operating both a German and an Italian school and hiring visiting agents and teachers based on their fluency in the language and familiarity with the culture. Although Catholic critics leveled complaints against both CAS's Italian school and its placing out programs, CAS's approach was largely nondenominational and arguably primarily secular. This was threatening to Catholic charities, whose primary mission was preserving the religion. In addition, Brace based his actions on the best scientific evidence of the day and sought to systematically evaluate the impact of CAS's work. In doing so, he parted ways with religious missionaries and forged a more professional basis for charity work. He pioneered practices in nonprofit administration, including record-keeping, fund-raising, staffing, and governance. Finally, he advocated for policy reforms—albeit in their earliest forms—at state and municipal levels to address compulsory education, truancy, factory child labor, street-selling child labor, and housing. All told, CAS was experimenting with an extraordinary range of pioneering approaches to social work practice, social welfare administration, institution building, and policy advocacy.

These efforts were initiated nearly a half-century before most social work scholars place the progressive era roots of the social work profession. A good deal of the child saving philanthropic scholarship starts in the third quarter of the nineteenth century or the early twentieth century. For example, in scholarship exploring prominent progressive social workers such as Jane Addams, Ellen Gates Starr, Julia Lathrop, and Louise DeKoven, they have become synonymous with the "child saving movement" and radical legislative reforms enacted during the early twentieth century. Yet it is worth noting that in Chicago, Jane Addams's influential Hull House was just beginning its second year as Brace penned his final annual report for CAS. Brace had already spent a lifetime—nearly four decades—forging his practices and building his institution.

***

Modern Implications: A Nod to the Future

Brace's CAS sat at the crucible of forces that would eventually produce state interventions that arguably continue to police poor families to this day through the juvenile justice and child welfare systems. However, Brace's tenure at CAS existed before these developments were formally institutionalized through policy reform in the late nineteenth and early twentieth centuries. It is impossible to know—had he lived longer or been born later—whether Brace would have joined the movement to police poor families. Nonetheless, his resistance to the key features that animate policing systems—such as institutional asylum care, judicial involvement, legal contracting, diminished civil liberties, and curtailment of free will—should make us hesitant to assume his willingness to fully endorse these directions.

Interestingly, because of CAS's place at the nexus of the early roots of both the juvenile justice and child protective services, the most analogous current comparison with his program of services escapes notice. His lodging houses most closely resemble our current runaway and homeless youth programs. The similarity extends to their historical roots, institutional design, and methods of practice employed within. The first modern runaway and homeless youth shelters were initiated as radical alternatives to mainstream institutions during the 1960s and 1970s. Among other things, the counter-culture founders resisted interactions with "straight" (unhip) establishment institutions, were skeptical of law enforcement, and operated youth-centered, youth-initiated programs. When federal policy was enacted in 1974 in the form of the Runaway Youth Act, it was conceptualized as a juvenile delinquency prevention strategy and embedded within the Juvenile Justice and Delinquency Prevention Act. Modern runaway and homeless youth shelters (or basic centers), transitional living facilities, and outreach efforts were all designed to intervene with street youth at risk of exploitation, criminal involvement, and sex work, based on noncoercive strategies and independent of law enforcement. In short, today's runaway and homeless youth networks look almost identical in origin, philosophy, and operation to those Brace first introduced through his NBLH in 1854.

Like CAS, modern runaway and homeless youth facilities rely on a mixture of public and private funds. Brace advocated for such a funding mix, believing that this option afforded financial stability and security to institutions but didn't hinder the creativity fostered by competition for private donations. Unfortunately, for modern service providers, the limited public investment in this hybrid financial flow isn't always beneficial. Runaway and homeless youth programs must often compete for time-limited, discretionary grants, unlike the financial stability and security afforded systems such as juvenile justice and child welfare, which are legally mandated. In the end, current homeless youth services are second-class citizens in the overall array of child welfare programs.

Re-examining Brace's CAS model takes on extra import by comparison in this regard. Today, the runaway shelter system often serves children who are at risk of dual system involvement when it comes to foster care and juvenile justice and are likely to be estranged from public schools. In short, they are young people who have fallen through the various cracks in our public systems, which function largely as independently operated and closed systems of services rather than integrated, holistic, programs seeking to promote the best outcomes for individual children.

Unlike these modern structures, Brace's design attempted to offer a comprehensive range of voluntary services supporting poor children and, by extension, their families that systematically integrated these various child and family policy domains. Arguably, the breadth of CAS's efforts encompassed our modern runaway and homeless youth network, public education, foster care, adoption, transitional living, and job training and placement. Brace's CAS sought to bridge crisis help with skill building and longitudinal support. It was a system that recognized the value of early intervention and prevention and that tried to avoid juvenile justice and public policing entirely. It embraced families facing a complex range of stressful situations. CAS offered a continuum of care that was flexible enough to support poor children and families based on their unique needs under a variety of circumstances.

Of course, there are modern advocates and organizations that attempt similarly ambitious agendas such as the Harlem Children's Zone (HCZ) in New-York. Among other things, HCZ advertises its comprehensive programing as being of "unprecedented scale," taking a "holistic approach," creating a "pipeline to success," "starting early," "building character," and being "driven by data."[3] It makes longitudinal commitments to children and families and has an established track record of success. It isn't difficult to find similarities in HCZ's overall vision with Brace's set of strategies. Both embody bold and ambitious agendas, prioritize the holistic needs of children and families, make comprehensive and longitudinal investments, and seek to foster long term well-being and success.

Similar to HCZ, there is Brace's very own CAS, still standing and serving families in New-York over 165 years later. In his last report, Brace optimistically wrote that "even in the distant future" he had "every reason to hope" that CAS would continue with "the same economy" and "unselfish enthusiasm for humanity." It would please him to know that the CAS of New-York is still going strong. Furthermore, according to Charity Navigator—an independent evaluator that rates charity performance for overall quality, financial health, accountability, and transparency in order to assess the charity's "commitment to good governance, best practices and openness with information"—the CAS of New-York received four stars—the highest possible rating—in each of the categories assessed in 2016.[4]

Despite the good work of these modern agencies in specific geographic locations, it is difficult to make arguments that our overall public investments as a nation in children and families come anywhere close to employing the practices we know work best based on the pioneering work of various progressive advocates, including Brace. Our social safety net is frayed and fractured beyond comprehension. We often take a regulatory and punitive approach to poor families. Family policy is almost nonexistent and arguably middle- and low-income families are fairly low on the list of funding priorities.

In the U.S. today, nearly one in five children live below the federal poverty line and, in 2016, nearly half of them lived in extreme poverty.[5] Relatedly, nearly one in five children live in food-insecure households.[6] Educational disparities continue to exist, with poor children, children of color, children with disabilities, and those who speak English as a second language faring less well than others.[7] Scholars have documented the school-to-prison pipeline and the U.S. stands almost alone in the world with its high incarceration rates of both adults and children.[8] Gang violence has plagued cities like Chicago and Baltimore. In 2015, sixteen percent of the young people aged twenty to twenty-four years were categorized as "idle teens" or "disconnected youth," defined as young adults who are neither in school nor employed.[9] Homeless street youth can be found in every city. Environmental hazards compound problems and contribute to chronic illnesses such as asthma in Detroit and lead poisoning in Flint. Poor families struggle and children suffer.[10]

Furthermore, in the U.S., income and wealth inequality have "reached levels not seen since the 1800s."[11] Ethnic, religious, and racial tensions have flared. We are in a time of unprecedented mass migration and dislocation.[12] Some of these contemporary challenges are remarkably familiar to those faced by Charles Loring Brace in the latter half of the nineteenth century.

For today's social justice workers, the problems can seem daunting and, at times, almost insurmountable. Yet during the mid-nineteenth century, Brace tackled a remarkably similar list of social ills, including extreme poverty; illiteracy; inequality; criminality; gang violence; and ethnic, racial, and religious intolerance. Undeterred, he devised a grand plan rooted in a deeply held sense of social, moral, and economic justice. Prophetically, he wrote in his last annual report for CAS, "The death of its leaders need make no difference, except that their example might in memory add a fresh stimulus to efforts for humanity and for God."[13] For today's social justice advocates, who may be discouraged by the grand challenges they face, Brace's life and the work of CAS may perhaps offer a fresh stimulus for inspiration, courage, and action.

Notes

1. *Thirteenth Annual Report of the Children's Aid Society* (New York: 1866), 5.
2. At the time of Brace's death, one trustee noted that without Brace, "there would have probably been no such an Institution" and without the institution with "its vast far reaching influence," one "cannot help wondering" what would have happened (Letter from Mr. Fabbri to Mr. Booth, August 26, 1890, in Minutes of the Board of Trustees, vol. 7, 1879–1895, Records of the Children's Aid Society, New-York Historical Society Archives).
3. See Harlem Children's Zone at https://hcz.org/about-us/.
4. Charity Navigator uses a four-star, hundred-point system. In 2016, it awarded the Children's Aid Society of New York four stars in all three categories. The society received 93.43 points in its overall rating, 90.72 points for its financial health, and a perfect 100 points for accountability and transparency. See the Charity Navigator website: https://www.charitynavigator.org/index.cfm?bay=content.view&cpid=628.
5. "Kids Count Data Center," The Annie E. Casey Foundation, http://datacenter.kidscount.org/topics; Children's Defense Fund, *The State of America's Children* (Washington, DC, Children's Defense Fund, 2017), 16. See also Kathryn Edin and Luke H. Shaefer, *$2.00 a Day: Living on Almost Nothing in America* New York, Houghton Mifflin Harcourt, 2015).
6. CDF, *State of America's Children*, 6.
7. CDF, *State of America's Children*, 6; National Center for Education Statistics, *The Nation's Report Card: Trends in Academic Progress 2012* (Washington, DC: Institute of Education Sciences, U.S. Department of Education, 2013), https://nces.ed.gov/nationsreportcard/subject/publications/main2012/pdf/2013456.pdf.
8. Akiva M. Liberman and Jocelyn Fontaine, *Reducing Harms to Boys and Young Men of Color from Criminal Justice System Involvement* (Washington, DC: Urban Institute, 2015), https://www.urban.org/research/publication/reducing-harms-boys-and-young-men-color-criminal-justice-system-involvement/view/full_report; Children's Defense Fund, *America's Cradle to Prison Pipeline* (Washington, DC: Children's Defense Fund, 2007) https://www.childrensdefense.org/wp-content/uploads/2018/08/cradle-prison-pipeline-report-2007-full-lowres.pdf; Roy Walmsley, *World Prison Brief: World Prison Population List*, 11th ed. (London: Institute for Criminal Policy Research, Birkbeck University of London, 2015), http://www.prisonstudies.org/sites/default/files/resources/downloads/world_prison_population_list_11th_edition_0.pdf; Christopher A. Mallett, *The School-to-Prison Pipeline: A Comprehensive Assessment* (New York: Springer, 2015).

9. "Kids Count Data Center" https://datacenter.kidscount.org/.
10. See Kristin S. Seefeldt, *Abandoned Families: Social Isolation in the Twenty-First Century* (New York: Russell Sage Foundation, 2017); See Edin and Shaefer, *$2.00 a Day*.
11. CDF, *State of America's Children*, 6; Testimony of Jared Bernstein before the Senate Budget Committee, U.S. Congress, Hearing on "Assessing Inequality, Mobility and Opportunity" (Washington, DC: Center on Budget and Policy Priorities, February 9, 2012), https://www.cbpp.org/sites/default/files/atoms/files/2-9-12bud-test.pdf.
12. "Figures at a Glance," United Nations High Commissioner for Refugees, http://www.unhcr.org/en-us/figures-at-a-glance.html.
13. *Thirty-Seventh Annual Report of the Children's Aid Society* (New York: Wynkoop, Hallenbeck, 1889), 8.

Index

Tables are indicated by *t* following the page number

For the benefit of digital users, indexed terms that span two pages (e.g., 52–53) may, on occasion, appear on only one of those pages.

abandonment by parents (child abandonment), xlivn67, 84–85, 131–32, 266n1
abolition, abolitionists, 24, 37, 41, 43, 54–55, 197–98, 224, 228–29, 245, 270n64. *See also* slavery
abstinence pledge, 142–43
Addams, Jane, 335
Africa, ship from Liverpool, 71–72, 74, 94n3
Aged and Indigent facility (New York City), 50–51
AIDS (acquired immune deficiency syndrome), xxiii
alcohol intoxication, 141–43
Alger, Horatio, 210
almshouses, 8
American Party, 194, 196–97, 204n47
anti-poverty agenda, 205–30
Appo, George, 192
apprentice-based child labor, xxvi
Astor, John Jacob, 46, 75–76, 78
Astor, William Blackhouse, 46
Astor Place Riots (New York City, 1849), 46–49
asylum advocates. *See also* child asylums; juvenile asylums
   actions against Tracy and Brace, 237–38
   Brace's defense of CAS to, 237–40
   mid-1870s attack on CAS, 264–65
   pessimistic view of the NBLH, 238–39

baby boomers, xvii
Barney (newsboy), 218, 219
bathing requirement, at the NBLH, 130–31
Beecher, Catharine, 38
Beecher, Charles, 37
Beecher, Henry Ward, 37
Beecher, Lyman, 37, 38
begging, xxi–xxii, xxiii
Bellingham, Bruce, xv–xvi, xxxi–xxxiii, xxxiv, 18–19, 326–27
Bender, Thomas, xxxii
Bennett, James Gordon, 88, 98–99n90
The Best Method of Disposing of Disposing of Our Pauper and Vagrant Children (Brace), 275
Bird, George, 101, 118n48
Bloomingdale Lunatic Asylum (New York City), 50–51
Blue Law controversy, 229
board resolution (1863), 253–55

Booch (Little Booch) (newsboy), 25–26, 138–39, 175, 176, 177–78, 179–80, 190, 200, 206
Booth, William A., 228, 247
Boyer, Paul, xxxiii–xxxiv, 15–16
  critique of the NBLH, xxix–xxx, xxxiii–xxxiv
Boys (and Girls) Sunday meetings, 215–16
"boys hotel." *See* Newsboys' Lodging House
Brace, C. Loring (son of Charles), 27, 28, 319
Brace, Charles Loring
  acceptance of invitation to work with children, 92–94, 101
  action plans (1848-1850), 37, 43–45, 50–53
  admiration for New York's street children, 89
  aggressive defense of CAS to asylum advocates, 237–41
  anti-poverty agenda, 205–30
  argument for investing in real estate, 275, 276–78
  arrival in New York, 6, 35–37
  belief in the Emigration Branch, 265–66
  Bellingham's critique of, xv–xvi, xxxi–xxxiii, xxxiv
  Bender's comments on, xxxii
  Boyer's comment on, 15–16
  childhood/family background, 37–43
  civilian Civil War service, 245–46
  clashes with Booth, 247
  concerns for street children, 92
  condolences/tributes after the death of, 318–19
  contribution to "orphan train movement," xiv
  creation of lodging houses for girls, 306
  death of sister/depression of, 53
  description of CAS central office, 154
  disservice of "either-or" reductionist trope of legacy of, 327–35
  Draft Riots and, 250–51
  drafting of "circular" announcing CAS, 105–7
  educational background, 40–41
  effort at bridging the social class divide, 290–94
  embrace of/enthusiasm for placing out, xxvii, 21, 27, 237–38, 239–40, 252, 282, 309, 319
  eternal optimism of, 237
  excerpt of letter to Parker, 101
  failing health/death of, 317–18
  focus on long-term solutions, xxxvii
  formation of Children's Aid Society, 101–15
  hiring of Charles and Mary O'Connor, 26, 226
  impact on child protective services, 7
  impact on juvenile justice system, 7
  implications of Brace's legacy, 335–39
  imprisonment in Hungary, 57
  independent views on Christianity, 42, 52–53
  investigation of Eleventh Ward, 102
  legacy left by, 327–35
  love of debates, 41
  love of hiking (walking), xvii, 24, 38–39, 53, 55, 57, 67n113
  Mason's friendship with, 246–47
  Matsell's alliance with, 60
  Newsboys' Lodging House program, xvi
  onset of public advocacy for social causes, 58
  opinion of uniqueness of newsboys, 104
  opposition to asylum model, 14–15, 327
  opposition to indenturing children, 13, 20–21, 224–25, 237, 328–29, 333–34
  opposition to slavery, 55–57
  optimistic view of social Darwinism, 7
  orphan problem, 265–66
  "orphan train movement" and, xiv, 15
  plan for sending children "into the country," 26, 39, 144–45n1, 159–60, 161, 220, 222–25

presentation to International
Reformatory Exhibition, 282–83
pride in successes of newsboys, 257–58
procuring a permanent residence for
NBLH, 275–96
rejection of inheritance of "bad
traits," 282
request to defend CAS, 237–38
role as Children's Aid Society
secretary, xiv
Short Sermons to the News Boys, 292
strategic language choices of,
xxvii–xxviii
summation of life's work of, 305–19
Sunday "Boys' Meetings" conducted
by, 152
support for compulsory
education, 287
thirty-seventh annual reports
for CAS, 305, 306, 308, 311–12,
313–15, 317
views on Christianity, 42, 52–53
visit to model lodging houses in
London and Liverpool, 114–15
on working with children *vs.* adults,
92, 101
Brace, Emma (daughter of Charles and
Letitia), 294–95, 317–18, 323n57
Brace, Emma (sister of Charles), 38, 40,
41, 53, 63n21, 92
Brace, James (brother of Charles), 38, 63n21
Brace, John Pierce (father of Charles), 38
Brace, Letitia Neill (wife of Charles),
55, 57, 114–15, 245, 294–95, 317,
318, 323n57
Brace Memorial Lodging House, xxxiv–
xxxv, 319
Brentano, Simon, 5
Brooklyn Bridge, 2, 78
Brown, John, 197
Bull Run, Battle of, 244–45

CAS. *See* Children's Aid Society
cash donations, 163–64

castaways, xix
Castle Garden immigration center, 154,
163, 169n19
Catholic Protectory, 251, 252, 253, 314
Central Office, of CAS, 21–22
Brace's description of, 154
cash donations, 163–64
clothing donations, 156–57, 164–67
clothing swap shop at, 166
connection of outlying branches, 307–8
food donations, 166–67
library for poor children location, 111
location, 153–54
Macy's role in running, 151–68
referrals to, 110, 154–56
role as employment clearing
house, 158–60
as transfer point when dropping off
children, 159–60
child abandonment, xlivn67, 84–85,
131–32, 266n1
child asylums. *See also* asylum advocates;
juvenile asylums
benefits of, 108
Brace's opposition to, 11, 13–14, 23, 107,
207, 282, 319, 327–28
discipline-driven methods of, 10–12, 306
NBLH's distinctions from, 121–22,
124–25, 127, 144, 155, 238–39, 240,
289–90, 331
NBLH's similarities with, 331
penal character/discipline within, 10–11
reliance on indenture, contractual
rights in, 12–13, 238–39
child labor, 86. *See also* newsboys
apprentice-based, xxvi
"attendant evils" of, 284
CAS trustees policy advocacy,
26–27, 283–84
consequences of, xxvi–xxvii
income and, 86–87
labor placements by CAS, 20
placing out strategies and, 20
street-based trades, 86, 284, 289

Child Protective Services (CPS), xiv, 7
child saving movement, 335
child welfare system, origins of, 7
Children's Aid Society (CAS).
　　See also central office, of CAS;
　　Emigration branch; industrial
　　schools; Newsboys' Lodging House
　asylum advocates attack on,
　　237–38, 264–65
　board of trustees
　　decision-making, 111–12
　Brace's aggressive defense of, to asylum
　　advocates, 237–41
　Brace's extended family employment
　　with, 294–96, 319
　Brace's founding of, xlv
　Brace's thirty-seventh annual report
　　for, 305, 306, 308, 311–12, 313–15, 317
　cash donations, 163–64
　Catholic Protectory and, 251, 252,
　　253, 314
　"circular" informing the public
　　of, 105–7
　Civil War and, 244–45
　clothing donations, 156–57, 164–67
　creation of, 101–15
　daily routine implementation, 102
　data on impact of, 308
　description, 6
　Education Branch of, 308–9
　education-related issues,
　　concerns, 286–89
　Emigration Branch, xiv, 13–14, 15, 21, 23,
　　202n25, 223, 224, 235, 241, 253–54,
　　265, 266n1, 268n22
　employment of visiting agents, 110–11
　evidence-informed hypotheses on
　　working of, xxxiv
　freedoms offered to children in, 14–15
　Halliday's efforts against, 237, 240
　health- and disability-related
　　facilities, 307

　high tolerance for boys' bad
　　behavior, 261–63
　Holste's supervision/evaluation
　　of, 310–11
　impact of 1863 board resolution, 253–55
　incorporation of, 101, 115–16n9
　industrial schools, 6, 21–22, 25, 109–10,
　　152–53, 159, 265, 282, 295, 307–8,
　　320n7, 321n27
　leadership changes, 246–47
　Macy's central office role, 151–68
　modern social services comparison, xxxvii
　neighborhood-based programming
　　of, 306–8
　Newsboys' Savings Bank, xxviii, 14–15,
　　26, 205, 216–17, 221–22, 227, 279,
　　281–82, 322–23n48, 332
　night schools, 6, 21–22, 23, 205–6,
　　207–9, 320n8, 323n57
　office work/first circular, 1855
　　blueprint, 105–7
　open door policy of, 148n99, 159
　opening of Newsboys'
　　lodging-house, 113–14
　orphan problem, 265–66
　"orphans-only" policy, 133
　O'Sullivan's popularity with, 186
　placing out system, xxvii, 13–22, 26
　plan for sending children "into the
　　country," 26, 39, 144–45n1, 159–60,
　　161, 220, 222–25
　policy advocacy for child labor,
　　education, housing, 283–84
　press-foreman and newsboys, 103–5
　process of obtaining Newsboys'
　　Lodging House, 275–96
　quantification/amplification of work
　　of, 308–9
　referrals to the central office, 110, 154–56
　results of experimentation,
　　exploration, 112–13
　services offered by, xiv

Stansell's comment on, xxxi
support for Whitehead's factory bill, 284–86
threats to educational programs of, 287
Twenty-Fourth Annual Report, 235
Westmore's opposition to, 240–41
Williams and, 101, 116n18, 117n44, 163–64, 276–77, 278, 279, 288, 298n38
workshops for boys, 107–8
cholera epidemic (New York City), xxv, 49–50, 82–83, 308–9
"circular" announcing CAS to the public, 105–7
City of Women: Sex and Class in New York, 1789-1860 (Stansell), xxix
Civil War
  Brace's wartime civilian service, 245–46
  Emancipation Proclamation, 248–51
  Olmsted, Frederick, service, 245–46
  placing out of NBLH and, 243–45
  slavery issues, 248
Clinton, DeWitt, 2–3
clothing donations, 156–57, 164–67
Clyde Times newspaper, 220
Cogan, Michael (newsboy), 186–88
Coleman, Matt. *See* Fatty (Matt Coleman) (newsboy)
Colopy (Mr. Colopy). *See* Desmond, William Colopy ("Mr. Colopy")
"Colored" Home (New York City), 50–51
Colored Orphan Asylum (New York City), 50–51
Comon, Eddie (newsboy), 221
Comon, Pat (newsboy), 142–43, 206, 211, 213, 221
compulsory education, 26–27, 283–85, 286–87, 289, 334–35
Conscription Act, 249–50, 251
correspondence of Jared Macy, 235–66
Cottage for Crippled Girls, 307

Cottage Place Industrial School for Girls, 152–53, 250, 270–71n65, 295, 320n7
couch surfing, xix
criminal behavior, xx
Crippled Boys' Brush-Shop, 307

The Dangerous Classes (Brace), 205
Darwin, Charles, 37–38
Day, Benjamin H., 88. *See also The Sun*, penny press
Deaf and Dumb Asylum (New York City), 50–51
DeKoven, Louise, 335
Desmond, William Colopy ("Mr. Colopy"), 119, 144–45n1
  attendance at Nassau Coffee Saloon, 179, 180
  CAS staff position of, 143, 144–45n1
  comment about the "Professor," (newsboy) 175
  comment on school spelling lessons, 211
  comment on the school library, 210
  interactions with Billy Patterson (newsboy), 189, 190
  interactions with Cogan (newsboy), 186–88
  the "Professor's" (O'Sullivan) mentoring of, 183–85
  regular meals at Nassau Coffee Saloon, 179
  role in assisting Macy at CAS, 163–65
DeWitt, Simeon, 74–75
"diaper squad." *See* Youth Services Unit (YSU)
diarrheal diseases, 82–83, 308–9
Dickens, Charles, 36, 71
discipline, within child asylums, 10–12, 306
The Discovery of the Asylum: Social Order and Disorder in the New Republic (Rothman), 8
dock children, 90
Dodge, William E., 246, 277–78
Dolan, Tom (newsboy), 220

Douglass, Frederick, 54–55
Draft Riots, 250–51
Driscoll, Danny, 192
drug abuse, xxii
Duane Street, New Chambers lodging house, 278, 297n26

Eastside Lodging House (for girls), 306
Eaton, Augustine, 93, 101
education. *See also* industrial schools; industrial schools for girls; night schools
 CAS trustees' policy advocacy for, 285
 compulsory education, 26–27, 283–85, 286–87, 289, 334–35
 fiscal educational plan, 216–20
 library and reading room, 209–11
 moral educational plan, Sunday meetings, 215–16
 NBLH night school, 206–8
 one-room schoolhouse, 208–9
 Public School Society donations, 125–26, 208
 reading lessons, 212–13
 school funding, and, 286–89
 spelling lessons, 208, 211
 truancy issues, xviii, xxxixn16, 283–84, 286–89
 Whitehead's factory bill and, 284–85
 writing class, 213
Eidlitz, Leopold, 278, 297n27
Eleventh Ward, 5, 102, 320n8
Elliot, Charles W., 101
Ellsworth, Elmer Ephraim, 230
Emancipation Proclamation, 248–51
Emigration Branch of CAS, xxxv–xxxvi, 15, 21, 23, 223, 224, 268n22
 Board of Trustees institutionalization of, 253–54
 Brace's belief in, 265, 268n22, 273n112
 Brace's defense/justification for, 13–14
 Brace's family members working for, 294–95

 linking with the NBLH, 254
 Macy's work at, 241
 responsibilities of, 309–11
 role in "placing out" boys and girls, xiv, 25, 235–36, 266n1, 309–11
 Tracy's work at, 202n25, 223
emigration parties, 159–60, 220–22
employment opportunities, 85–86
 child labor, 86–87
 employment plan, 220–22
Enrollment Act (1863), 249

factory bill, 284–86
family violence, xix, xxxix–xln19
Fatty (Matt Coleman) (newsboy), 25–26, 129, 142–43, 174, 175, 180–82, 197–98, 199, 200, 210, 212, 214–15, 218–19, 220
fever nests, in tenant housing, xix
fiscal educational plan, 216–20
Five Points
 employment experiment at, 59
 The Great Metropolis Guide announcement of, 51
 Halliday's supervisory position, 237
 Italian School within, 168–69n6
 limited effectiveness with children, 108
 negative living conditions in, 77–78, 81, 85
 original location description, 95n34
 Pease's creation of, 59
 Pease's missionary work at, 58
 potential merger with NBLH, 155
Forrest, Edwin, 46–47. *See also* Astor Place Riots
Forty-Fourth Street Lodging House (for girls), 306
foster care system, xiv
Free School Society, 207
Fugitive Slave Act (U.S., 1850), 55
fundraising campaign, for purchasing NBLH, 275, 276–77

gangs, xv, 193–98. *See also* Poole, William ("Bill the Butcher")
Garrison, William, 54–55
Gilman, William C., 101, 117n45
girls' lodging houses, 306
Girls' Temporary Home, 306
Glendinning, Mr., 120, 179, 181. *See also* Nassau Coffee Saloon
Good Samaritan, biblical story, 216
Goodrich, Samuel Griswold (aka Peter Parley), 209
Gray, Asa, 37–38
Great Fire of 1835 (New York City), 3
Greeley, Horace, 147n68, 246, 248

half-orphans, xxvi, 49–51, 131–32, 254
Halliday, Samuel B., 237, 240
Harlem Children's Zone (HCZ), 337
health-/disability-related facilities, of CAS, 307
Health Home, 307, 308–9
The Herald, penny press, 88
hiking (walking)
  Brace's love of, xvii, 24, 38–39, 53, 55, 57, 67n113
Holste, L. W., 310–11
homelessness, federal definition, xliii–xlivn47
House of Refuge (New York City), 9
  background/description, 9
  Catholic Protectory and, 252
  description, 9–10
  efforts at keeping newsboys from, 153, 186
  harsh discipline-driven methods of, 10–11, 105, 306
  "hiring out" of children by, 13
  NBLH's comparison with, 128, 306
  New York State Legislature's establishment of, 238
  opening of, 9, 238
  reasons for being sent to, 191, 192
  Tracy's warning to newsboys about, 190

Howland, Benjamin J., 101, 117n44
Hughes, John, 248–49
Hull House, 335

imprisonment in Hungary, 57
indenturing of children, 12–13
  Brace's opposition to, 13, 20–21, 224–25, 237, 328–29
  in child asylums, 12
  in East Coast societies, 326–27
  in public/private institutions, 13
Independent, abolitionist newspaper, 245
industrial schools, 6, 21–22, 25, 152–53, 159, 265, 282, 295, 307–8, 320n7, 321n27. *See also* night schools
industrial schools for girls, xxxii, 24, 109–10, 152–53
industry nuisances, in tenant housing, 83–84
Institution for the Blind (New York City), 50–51
International Reformatory Exhibition (London, 1865), 282–83
into the country (sending children to the country), 26, 39, 144–45n1, 159–60, 161, 220, 222–25
Ireland, potato blight, 44
Ives, Levi Silliman, 251–52

Jack (aka: Broken-Nose, Dutchy, Friday, Sunday) (newsboy), 175–76, 183–85, 211
Jerry-the-Oysterman, 120. *See also* Nassau Coffee Saloon
Juvenile Asylum (New York City, 1851), 9
juvenile asylums, xvi, 8, 9, 25, 105, 207, 240–41. *See also* child asylums

Kansas-Nebraska Act (1854), 196–97
kicked-out, xix
King, Howard, 154–56
King, William L., 93, 101, 117n46, 154–56

Know-Nothing political party, 45–46, 194, 196, 198
Krohn, Philip, 160

Ladies Home Missionary Society, 58–59
Ladies of the House of Industry of the Friendless, 157–58
Lathrop, Julia, 335
Leeds, Hugh, 71–73
Leonard, Moses G., 93, 101
library and reading room, 209–10
Lincoln, Abraham, 229, 242, 248–51
literary gatherings, 43
livestock nuisances, in tenant housing, 83–84
Livingston, Robert J., 281–82, 312
loitering offense, xxi
Loring, Jane Lathrop, 37–38
Lying-In Facility for Destitute Females (New York City), 50–51
Lynch, Anne Charlotte, 43

Macready, William Charles, 46–48. *See also* Astor Place Riots
Macy, Jared, 25, 26, 151–68
  ability to detect fraud, deceit, 160–61
  Brace's nickname for, 151
  correspondence of, 235–66
  data on children placing out, 235
  Desmond's role in assisting, 163–65
  emigration process details, 235–36
  endless errands, odds and ends, 163
  enjoyment of pressing demands, 167–68
  eternal optimism of, 237
  founding of industrial schools for girls, 152–53
  good humor of, 161–62
  hosting of nightly gatherings for boys, 152–53
  love for the recalcitrant, ill-behaved children, 153
  management of donations to CAS, 14–17
  offer of help for Solomon (newsboy), 241
  "out door relief" focus of, 155
  pride in successes of newsboys, 257–58
  public reading rooms opened by, 152–53
  reading to the newsboys from the scriptures, 216
  role as Brace's assistant, 152
  role in dealing with difficult cases, 156–58
  role in making employment placements, 158–59
  role in newsboys lives, 151, 152, 153, 154–56
  running of CAS central office, 151–52
Magdalen Female Benevolent Facility (New York City), 50–51
Malabar, ship, 71–73, 74, 94n4
malaria, 79, 82–83, 308–9
Manassas, Battle of, 245
Mason, John L., 101, 116n18, 117n46, 246–47
Matsell, George Washington
  Astor Place Riots (1849) and, 46–49
  Brace's alliance with, 60
  categories of youthful vagrants, 90–92
  report on child vagrancy, xiii, 35–36, 49, 60, 90–92
  report on "rogue fraternity's" unique language, 191
  role as NYC police chief, 35–36
  Stansell's comment on, xxix
Metropolitan Police Department, 227–28, 229
Michigan, newsboys' problems in, 263–64
Mickety (newsboy), 129
Milwaukee Sentinel newspaper, 220–21
Missouri Compromise (1820), 196–97
moral educational plan, Sunday meetings, 215–16
Morris, Governeur, 74–75

Morrow, Johnnie (newsboy)
  background, 87, 174
  comment about Protestant boys, 175
  death of, 230
  impression of Newsboys' Lodging House, 126, 128
  peddling of matches by, 178, 184
  physical disability of, 174
  return visit to NBLH, 226–27
  A Voice from the Newsboys, 98n85, 173, 183, 226–27
Munford, Battle of, 244
Municipal Police Act (1844, New York State), 45–46

Nassau Coffee Saloon, 120, 175–76, 179–83, 187–88
Native American Party, 204n47
NBLH. *See* Newsboys' Lodging House
neighborhood-based programming, 306–8
Neill, Letitia, 55, 57
Neill, Robert, 54–55, 57
New York City
  Astor Place Riots, 46–49
  Brace's arrival, first years (1848–1850), 43–45
  cholera epidemic (1849), 49–50
  Conscription Act and, 249–50, 251
  description/layers and flavors, 1–2
  Emancipation Proclamation's impact on, 248–51
  European immigration to, 44–45
  expansion planning, 74–76
  historical background, 2–6
  housing reforms, 289–90
  juvenile asylum movement, 8–10
  onset of urban development plans, 74–78
  orphan/half-orphan asylums, 50–51
  pickpocketing criminal activities, 191–93
  Police Riot (1857), 227–28
  problems with gangs, xv, 193–98
  segregated help for poor people, 50–51
  social class "fault line" in, 49
  street gangs, 45
  tenant-housing living, 78–81
New York Herald newspaper, 228–29
New York Juvenile Asylum, 240–41
New York State Legislature, 238
New York Times newspaper, 245
New York Tribune, newspaper, 246
newsboys. *See also* runaways; individual newsboys
  admission process, NBLH, 128
  alcohol intoxication issues, 141–43
  backing out of going to the country, 256–57
  bathing requirement, NBLH, 130–31
  Brace's opinion of uniqueness of, 104
  Civil War service, 242
  costs for admission to NBLH, 135–36
  deaths of Morrow and Ellsworth, 230
  earnings potential of, 71
  employment opportunities, 258–59
  homelessness of, 89–90
  independence/vagrancy of, 89
  initial skepticism of the NBLH, 119
  intake process, NBLH, 128–29
  issues concerning parents, 131–34
  leaving without warning by, 259–61
  lodging houses for, xxxiv–xxxvii
  Macy's dealing with difficult cases, 156–58
  Nassau Coffee Saloon's popularity with, 179–83
  NBLH's loan policy for, 280–81
  nickname issues, NBLH, 129
  obtaining a permanent lodging house for, 275–96
  the O'Connor's guidance, support of, 208, 243, 244, 280–82
  parental abandonment and, xlivn67, 84–85, 131–32, 266n1

newsboys (cont.)
   paying for housing *vs.* theater attendance, 137–41
   penny press and, 88–89
   plundering by dock children, 71–72, 90
   problems in Michigan, 263–64
   returning back home by, 255–56
   Sabbath Committee charges against, 228
   sodgering behavior, 149n105
   successes of, 257–58
   Sunday Blue Laws controversy, 228–29
   terminology origin, xxvii–xxviii
   time spent with Macy, 151
   ubiquitousness of, 24, 89
   voluntary participation at NBLH, xvi, 128
Newsboys' Debating Society, 206
Newsboys' Lodging House (NBLH), xvi, 23. *See also* education
   admission process, 128
   African American children at, 148n99
   asylum advocates pessimistic view of, 238–39
   basic service structure, 127–29
   bathing requirement, 130–31
   Boyer's characterization of, xxix–xxx, xxxiii–xxxiv
   Boys (and Girls) Sunday meetings, 215–16
   Brace's alternative programs at, 23
   Brace's experimentation, explorations, 23
   Brace's replication of, 306
   CAS's data on, 6
   comparison with child asylums, 121–22
   costs paid by children for admission, related issues, 135–36
   creation of, 113–14
   description of, xxvii, 6
   donations for purchase of, 277–78, 281, 293, 303n129
   employment plan, 220–22
   as experiment model, 143–44
   facility, description, 125–27
   fiscal educational plan, 216–20
   fundraising campaign for purchasing, 275, 276–77
   goal to prevent delinquency, 191
   grand opening and moving in, 279–80
   growing pains of, 247–48
   hiring of Charles and Mary O'Connor, 26, 226
   impact of the closing of, xxxv
   instability issues, 225–26
   intake dilemmas/shaping agency policy, 131
   intake process, 128–29
   issues concerning parents, 131–34
   loan policy for newsboys, 280–81
   location decision, 126
   matching funds for purchase of, 277, 278
   Metropolitan Police Department and, 227–28, 229
   minor name variations, 144–45n1
   Morrow's impression of, 126, 128
   Morrow's return visit to, 226–27
   nickname issues, 129
   night school, 206–8
   notice to quit Sun Building, 276
   number of residents, 146n42
   the O'Connor's role in the growth of, 247–48
   one-room schoolhouse, 208–9
   open door policy of, 148n99, 159, 198, 252–53
   orphan problem, 265–66
   Park Place temporary facility, 276, 278, 297n23
   placing out/Civil War service by boys, 243–45
   potential merger with Five Points, 155
   process of obtaining, 275–96
   Public School Society donations, 125–26, 208

referrals to, 154–56
remarkable features of, xxvii–xxviii
renaming as Brace Memorial Lodging House, xxxiv–xxxv, 319
Roosevelt, Sr.'s role in purchase of, 277–78, 291
rules/exceptions to rules, 25, 121, 122, 124, 128, 131–32, 138–39, 141–42, 143–44, 148n95
Stansell's characterization of, xxix–xxx, xxxii
steps in opening of, 119–44
street youths initial skepticism about, 119
successes of, 143–44
Sun Building, 121, 126, 164, 247–48, 276, 279, 319
Sunday dinners, 227, 229, 334
Tracy's role in establishing, 88–142, 143–44, 147n66, 148n84
voluntary *vs.* coercive participation, 128
voluntary youth participation in, xvi
youth-friendly inner workings at, xxxiv
Newsboys' Lodging House (NBLH) night school, 206–8
Newsboys' Savings Bank, xxviii, 14–15, 26, 205, 216–17, 221–22, 227, 279, 281–82, 322–23n48, 332
night schools, 6, 21–22, 205–6, 207–9, 265, 307, 320n8, 323n57
nighttime offenses, xxi

Oberfield, Richard, xx
O'Brien, James (newsboy), 244
O'Connor, Charles and Mary, 276
    Blue Law controversy and, 229
    CAS's promotion of, 226
    death of Charles, 295
    improvements made to NBLH by, 227
    NBLH's hiring of, 26
    positive feelings for Park Place facility, 276
    role in growth of the NBLH, 247–48, 280–82
    support and guidance for newsboys by, 208, 243, 244, 280–82
O'Driscoll, Denis (newsboy), 155–56
Old Ladies Home (New York City), 50–51
Olmsted, Frederick Law, xxxiv, 37, 39, 41, 43, 54–55, 245–46
Olmsted, John Hull, 39, 54–55
Olmsted, OTHER BROTHER, 37
one-room schoolhouse, 208–9
Oppenheimer, Samuel, 241–42
Origin of the Species (Darwin), 37–38
Orphan Asylum (New York City, 1806), 9, 12
orphan/half-orphan asylums, 50–51
orphan train movement, xiv, 7, 15, 19–20, 326–27
orphans. *See also* runaways
    almshouse/nurseries placement of, 8, 10, 73–74
    Brace's use of the term, 19
    cholera's creation of, 49–50
    half-orphans, xxvi
    New York City facilities for, 50–51
    ocean passage and, 73–74
O'Sullivan, Danny (the Professor) (newsboy), 25–26, 129, 142–43, 175
    abstinence pledge taken by, 142–43
    background, 175
    comic routine of, 185
    glorified begging by, 185
    inclination to travel (wander) of, 176–77
    mentoring of "Sunday" and Mr. Colopy, 175–76, 183–85
    popularity with CAS staff, 186
    self-sacrificing generosity of, 175–76, 200

panhandling, xxiii
parens patriae legal doctrine, 12–13, 28, 327

parents
    child abandonment by, xlivn67, 84–85, 131–32, 266n1
    physical abuse by, 132–34
Park Place lodging house, 276, 278, 297n23
Parker, Theodore, 54–55, 101
Patterson, Billy (newsboy), 25–26, 189–91, 213
Pease, Lewis Morris, 58–59, 60, 154–55
penny press. *See also* specific penny presses
    impact on the newspaper industry, 98–99n90, 99n100
    newsboys and, 88–89
    types of, 89
philanthropic abduction, 15–21, 326–27, 328–29
Phillips, Wendell, 41
physical abuse, by parents, 132–34
pickpocketing, 137–38, 186, 191–94, 199, 202n18
placing out (placing out system)
    Bellingham's critique of, xxxi–xxxii, 16–20, 326–27
    Brace's embrace of/enthusiasm for, xxvii, 21, 27, 237–38, 239–40, 252, 282, 309, 319
    Civil War service and, 243–45
    Emigration Branch differences with, 309
    Ive's experimentation with, 251–52
    juvenile delinquency and, 7, 13–15
    Macy's data (1861-1866), 235
    NBLH's link with, 265
    orphan train movement, 15, 19–20
    potential complications of, 311
    role of Emigration Branch, xiv, 25, 235–36, 266n1, 309–11
    Tracy's role in developing, 26
Poggioli, Bernard "Bernie," xiii–xiv, xvi–xvii, xviii, xxxviiin8. *See also* Youth Services Unit (YSU), Port Authority Police Department
Poole, William ("Bill the Butcher"), 193–96, 203n27

Port Authority Bus Terminal (PABT), xiii–xiv
Port Authority Police Department, xiii
    Youth Services Unit (YSU), xvi–xvii, xviii, xxxviiin8
ports (for arrival of ships)
    Africa (ship), 71–72, 74, 94n3
    Malabar (ship), 71–73, 74, 94n4
    newsboys moneymaking and, 71
poverty
    anti-poverty agenda, 205–30
    begging and, xx
    Brace's focus on, xxxvii, 6, 22–23, 24, 28, 50, 59, 107, 121–22
    Five Points area and, 85
    New York City and, 1, 5
    orphans and, xxviii
    Tracy's anti-poverty agenda, 131, 143–44, 205–27
    vagrant children and, xxxv, 17
the Professor. *See* O'Sullivan, Danny (the Professor) (newsboy)
prostitution, xxii
Protestant Half-Orphan Asylum (New York City), 50–51
public health special nuisances, 83t
public nuisance offense, xxi
Public School Society, 125–26, 208
pushouts, xix

Randall's Island, New York, 10, 36
Randolph, A. D. F., 101
Reily, John (newsboy), 243–44
returning home, by newsboys, 255–56
Roger (newsboy), 218
Roman Catholic Half-Orphan Asylum (New York City), 50–51
Roman Catholic Orphan Asylum (New York City), 50–51
Roosevelt, Eleanor, 294
Roosevelt, Elliot Bulloch, 293–94
Roosevelt, Theodore, Sr., 277–78, 291
Ross, Catherine J., 12

Rothman, David J., 8, 9
Runaway and Homeless Youth Act
 (RHYA, 1974), xvii, 336
runaways (runaway youths, homeless
 youth). *See also* newsboys
 causes/reasons, xix
 criminal behavior by, xx
 definitions, labels, xix–xx
 extreme pragmatism of, xxiii
 historical invisibility of, xxix–xxx
 homelessness, federal definition,
  xliii–xlivn47
 initial skepticism about NBLH, 119
 lying/"coloring of truth" by, xviii
 nineteenth century street youth,
  xxiv–xxv
 nineteenth century youth vagrancy,
  xxv–xxvii
 survival strategies, xx–xxii
 terminology variations, xix
Russell, William C., 93, 100n123, 101,
 115n1, 117n44
Rutgers Female Institute, 43
Rutherford, John, 74–75
Ryrie, Alexander, 71–72, 94n3

Sabbath Committee, 228
Sanitary Commission, 245–46
sanitation issues, tenant-housing, 82–83
scarlet fever, 82–83
Seward, William, 229
sex trafficking, xxiii–xxiv
sex work, sexual favors, xxii
sexual abuse, xxii
sexual abuse, sexual exploitation, xxii
sexual bartering, xxiii–xxiv
Shakespeare Hotel, 278
ships for ocean passage
 the Africa, 71–72, 74, 94n3
 dangers and risk factors, 73–74
 disembarking chaos in Manhattan, 74
 the Malabar, 71–73, 74, 94n4
 orphan children passengers, 73–74

vessel options for travelers, 72–73
Short Sermons to the News Boys
 (Brace), 292
shoveouts, xix
Sick Children's Mission, 307
"The Silent Workers" (Brace), 151,
 304n141
The Silent Workers (Brace), 151
Sixpenny Savings Bank, xxvi, 216–17
Sixth Ward, 76–78, 83–84
slavery. *See also* abolition, abolitionists
 Brace's absolute opposition to, 55–57
 Neill's opposition to, 54–55
 New York State abolishment of, 45
small pox, xxv, 82–83, 83*t*
Smith, Edward P., 246, 305
social class divide, Brace's efforts in
 bridging, 290–94
social control scholarship, xv–xvi
social Darwinism, 7, 37–38, 62n20,
 268–69n26
Society for the Reformation of Juvenile
 Delinquents, 238
Society of St. Vincent de Paul
 (New York), 251–52
Solomon (newsboy), 241–42, 243
Stansell, Christine, xxix, 11
Starr Gates, Ellen, 335
Stephen (newsboy), 132, 243
Stowe, Harriet Beecher, 37
street-based subcultures, xv
street outreach and drop-in programs, xvii
Strong, George Templeton, 47–48
Summer Home, 307, 308–9
The Sun, penny press, 88, 89, 228
Sun Building, 121, 126, 164, 247–48, 276,
 279, 319
Sunday Blue Laws, 228–29
Sunday dinners, NBLH, 227, 229, 334
survival sex, xxiii–xxiv

Talmadge, Frederick, 228
Taylor, Alfred, 160

Taylor, Henry, 160
tenant-housing living, 78–81
   description of living conditions, 79–81, 84–85
   livestock and industry issues, 83–84
   public health-related issues, xxvi, 82–83, 83t, 84–85, 290
   reconstructed *vs.* new (modern), 71
   vermin, sanitation, fever nests, 82–83
throwaways (thrownaways), xix
The Tombs, shelter, 51, 77–78, 84, 174, 190, 192, 195–96, 314
Tompkins Square Lodging House (for girls), 306
Tracy, Charles C., 154
   administration of spelling lessons, 212
   anti-poverty agenda, 205–30
   attendance at Nassau Coffee Saloon, 179, 180–81
   commitment in establishing NBLH, 88–142, 143–44, 147n66, 148n84
   comparison to Charles Brace, 120
   cultural heritage of, 175
   employment plan/emigration parties, 220–22
   enjoyment in working with the boys, 162
   fiscal educational plan of, 216–20
   interaction with Billy Patterson, 189–91
   launching of moral educational plan, Sunday meetings, 215–16
   loss of patience with Cogan (newsboy), 188
   morning routine at the NBLH, 173
   NBLH educational initiatives of, 205–6, 207–8
   peace work of, 197–200
   as pickpocketing victim, 192–93, 200
   plan for sending children "into the country," 220–22
   relocation to Michigan, 237–38
   role in CAS's experimental western emigration, 26
   start of the Newsboys' Savings Bank, 205
   successes in working with vagrant youth, 120–21, 122–25, 129, 207
   superintendent role at CAS, 113–14
transitional living facilities, xvii
Tribune, newspaper, 89, 103–4, 138, 197–98, 319
truancy issues, xviii, xxxixn16, 283–84, 286–89
typhus/typhoid fever, xxv, 82–83

U.S. Christian Coalition (USCC), 246

Valise (newsboy), 129, 173–74, 219
Van Buskirk, James, 160
A Voice from the Newsboys (Morrow), 98n85, 173, 183, 226–27

West-Side Lodging House (for girls), 306
Wetmore, Apollos R., 240–41, 269n33
Whitehead, Charles E., 284–86
Williams, J. Earl, 101, 116n18, 117n44, 163–64, 276–77, 278, 279, 288, 298n38
Willy (newsboy), 310–11
workshops for boys (CAS), 107–8
Wright, Henry C., 54–55
Wright, M. P., 197

Yank (George Clark) (newsboy), 213, 221–22
youth homelessness, xiv–xv
youth rights movement (1960s), xvii
Youth Services Unit (YSU), Port Authority Police Department, xiii, xxxviiin8
   comparison with social workers, xvii
   origins/role of, xvi–xvii
   Poggioli's leadership role, xiii
   primary goal of, xvii

Zelizer, Vivian A., 20

www.ingramcontent.com/pod-product-compliance
Ingram Content Group UK Ltd.
Pitfield, Milton Keynes, MK11 3LW, UK
UKHW022152230426
12049UKWH00003BA/56